D0163583

SOVIET JEWRY SINCE THE SECOND WORLD WAR

SOVIET JEWRY SINCE THE SECOND WORLD WAR

POPULATION AND SOCIAL STRUCTURE

Mordechai Altshuler

STUDIES IN POPULATION AND URBAN DEMOGRAPHY, NUMBER 5

GREENWOOD PRESS
NEW YORK • WESTPORT, CONNECTICUT • LONDON

HOUSTON PUBLIC LIBRARY

R0157264257
SSC

Library of Congress Cataloging-in-Publication Data

Altshuler, Mordechai.
   Soviet Jewry since the Second World War.

   (Studies in population and urban demography,
ISSN 0147-1104 ; no. 5)
   Bibliography: p.
   Includes index.
   1. Jews—Soviet Union—History—1917-   .
2. Jews—Soviet Union—Statistics.   3. Soviet Union—
Ethnic relations.   4. Soviet Union—Statistics. .
I. Title.   II. Series.
DS135.R92A729   1987   947'.004924   86-12139
ISBN 0-313-24494-4 (lib. bdg. : alk. paper)

Copyright © 1987 by Mordechai Altshuler

All rights reserved. No portion of this book may be
reproduced, by any process or technique, without the
express written consent of the publisher.

Library of Congress Catalog Card Number: 86-12139
ISBN: 0-313-24494-4
ISSN: 0147-1104

First published in 1987

Greenwood Press, Inc.
88 Post Road West, Westport, Connecticut 06881

Printed in the United States of America

The paper used in this book complies with the
Permanent Paper Standard issued by the National
Information Standards Organization (Z39.48-1984).

10 9 8 7 6 5 4 3 2 1

THE PUBLICATION OF THIS BOOK
WAS MADE POSSIBLE BY A GENER-
OUS GRANT FROM THE ANNA BAILIS
FOUNDATION, MR. LOUIS BAILIS,
CHAIRMAN.

MY DEEPEST GRATITUDE MUST
ALSO BE EXPRESSED TO THE
ALEXANDER SILBERMAN INTER-
NATIONAL SCHOLARSHIP FUND
FOR ITS GENEROUS GRANT,
WHICH MADE POSSIBLE THE
PREPARATION OF THE MANU-
SCRIPT FOR PUBLICATION.

CONTENTS

TABLES AND GRAPHS

TABLES

GRAPHS

PREFACE

In the last decade, the struggle of Soviet Jewry for the rights to emigrate and to practice their religion and culture has been brought to the attention of the world at large. The social and demographic character of this community, however, and the changes that have taken place in it have not for the most part received adequate scrutiny. This book presents for the first time a comprehensive picture of the social and demographic developments within Soviet Jewry since World War II. Through a wide selection of statistical data, it examines such areas as Soviet Jewry's occupational structure, patterns of residence, and membership in the ranks of the Communist party, as well as such fundamental issues as family composition, intermarriage, and fertility. The study bears out the contention that important regional differences exist within the Soviet Jewish population. Throughout the book, the analysis of developments related to Jews has been carried out in the context of the Soviet population as a whole and in comparison with other Soviet nationalities. The results should be of use to those with an interest in Soviet nationality problems, as well as to specialists in Jewish research. Covering the four decades from the mid-1940s to the present, the study offers insight from a new perspective on what has been happening to Soviet Jews in the postwar era.

Only limited and fragmentary data on this population have been published. This book could not have been completed without recourse to the collections of the Israel National and University Library (Jerusalem), the library of the Center for Research and Documentation of East European Jewry at the Hebrew University (Jerusalem), the New York Public Library, the Library of Congress (Washington, D.C.), and, primarily, the library of Columbia University (New York). Many thanks to these institutions and to their staffs for their efforts in making available to me otherwise unattainable documents and tabulations. In addition, I would like to thank Zvi Gitelman (Ann Arbor, Michigan), Theodore Friedgut (Jerusalem), and Murray Feshbach (Washington, D.C.), who provided me with photographic copies of important material.

It is my pleasant duty to thank those who provided helpful and strategic advice at various stages of the research and writing: Uziel Schmelz and Sergio DellaPergola of the Demography Department of the Institute of Contemporary Jewry of the Hebrew University, who read portions of the manuscript and commented on demographic and statistical aspects of the work; Shmuel Ettinger, Khone Shmeruk, and Murray Feshbach, whose comments were especially useful in preparing the final drafts; G. Kenan, N. Greenwood, and E. Lederhendler, who translated the book into English and helped with the final editing.

Special thanks are due to the Memorial Foundation for Jewish Culture (New York), the Institute of Contemporary Jewry, and the Center for Research and Documentation of East European Jewry at the Hebrew University of Jerusalem, which enabled me to complete the research.

SOVIET JEWRY SINCE THE SECOND WORLD WAR

1 HISTORICAL BACKGROUND AND METHODOLOGICAL PROBLEMS

DEMOGRAPHIC AND SOCIAL TRENDS IN SOVIET JEWRY

The basic demographic trends to be observed in the Jewish population of the Soviet Union in the period between the two world wars represent a continuation of patterns that commenced at the beginning of the twentieth century. The first signs of declining rates of Jewish natural increase were already manifest by the turn of the century, and the tendency to emigrate from historical areas of settlement had become a permanent feature by this time as well. Jewish migration from the *shtetlekh* (small towns with a largely Jewish population) to urban areas, with the resulting development of large concentrations of Jews there, was also apparent by the end of the nineteenth century. Shifts in Jewish employment trends and social stratification accompanied these new patterns of mobility, residence, and population growth.

The Soviet regime restricted—and ultimately eliminated—some of the Jews' traditional sources of livelihood while offering possibilities of their integration into other sectors of the economy that previously had been almost completely closed to them. Rapid industrialization directed by centralized planning, along with heightened government control of all areas of life, increased the demand for a more versatile work force, required for an expanding economic and administrative system. During the 1930s, therefore, many Jews found employment in this system. The Jewish white-collar class in the USSR expanded steadily.

The Holocaust did not essentially alter the general demographic and social trends in the Soviet Jewish population of the interwar period; it did, however, accelerate them significantly. In the wake of the Holocaust, the already-urban Jewish community became a metropolitan population. Concentrations of more than 100,000 Jews came into being, accounting for a significant proportion of Soviet Jewry. The white-collar class multiplied, with special growth witnessed in the professional stratum. Along with these new social patterns came a further decline in the rate of Jewish natural increase. This, together with assimilation, caused a decline of the Jewish population beyond that brought about by the Holocaust, in which about half of Soviet Jewry was annihilated.

Immediately prior to World War I, there were about 5.2 million Jews in the Russian Empire[1]—close to 40 percent of world Jewry.[2] Jewish emigration from the empire from the 1880s until World War I amounted to approximately 1.7 million persons.[3] It appears therefore that Russian Jewry in 1914, including those who had emigrated, amounted to 7 million persons, about half of all Jews worldwide at the time. The rapid growth of this community occurred chiefly during the second half of the nineteenth century, when the average rate of natural increase appears to have reached about 2 percent, as opposed to a rate of 1 to 1.3 percent in the first half of that century and about 1.5 to 1.6 percent from the end of the century until the outbreak of World War I.[4] As a consequence of this high rate of natural increase, the percentage of Jews in the total population in their areas of residence rose.[5]

The basic reasons for the Jewish population's rapid growth were improvements in levels of sanitation, hygiene, and health care, resulting in a rise in average life expectancy and reduced infant mortality, principally of infants in their first year of life. In addition, the norms of traditional Jewish society continued to promote high fertility levels. From the end of the nineteenth century and chiefly from the beginning of the twentieth, however, the economic and social modernization of Russia's Jewish population began to affect Jewish birthrates, which no longer reached those of the surrounding population. The percentage of Jews in the total national population therefore began to decline, and mass emigration caused this process to accelerate.

Adjustments in Russia's western border after World War I and the Communist revolution caused a fragmentation of Russian Jewry, with segments of the community situated in Poland, Lithuania, Latvia, and Rumania. Those territories included within the interwar borders of the USSR had in 1897 contained approximately 2,675,000 Jews—some 51 percent of Russian Jewry at the time.[6] Emigration to Western Europe and overseas from these regions, as from Russia as a whole, continued until the outbreak of World War I.

The world war, and the Russian Revolution and civil war that followed, struck grievous blows at Russian Jewry. Front lines passed through regions heavily populated by Jews; consequently many communities were damaged and hundreds of thousands of Jews uprooted from localities close to the front. During the civil war, a particularly cruel and prolonged conflict in the areas of the former Pale of Settlement, many Jews were killed or wounded either during military action or during pogroms carried out by militias and bandit gangs at war with the Soviet regime. Famine and epidemics accompanied these events, further swelling the casualty rolls. Because of the civil war and pogroms on the one hand and the tough, cruel "war communism" regime on the other, tens of thousands of Jews sought sanctuary in Poland, the Baltic states, and Rumania. It is not surprising, then, that between 1897 and 1923, the Jewish population in Soviet territory declined by about 2 percent, not taking into consideration the rate of natural increase, which we do not know, for those twenty-six years.[7]

With the stabilization of Soviet rule and the introduction of the New Economic Policy (NEP), which brought the Jewish population some respite, Jewish population growth resumed, though natural increase no longer attained prewar levels. The average annual rate of increase for the years 1923-1926 was approximately 1.3 percent[8].

The rapid industrialization that began in the Soviet Union at the end of the 1920s led to significant Jewish migration to industrial and administrative centers and to the integration of many Jews into the technical and professional stratum. The same period witnessed a spirited campaign designed to undermine the traditional Jewish way of life. This too probably affected population growth. Indeed, a January 1939 census showed a Jewish population of 3,020,000 in the USSR.[9] During the twelve years from December 1926 to January 1939, therefore, the average annual rate of Jewish increase was about 1.0 percent. This low rate was the result of several factors, including socioeconomic modernization processes, as well as intermarriage, especially frequent in the Jews' new areas of residence. Signs of increased aging in the Jewish population were recognized as early as the 1930s, and it became reasonable to expect that in time Jews would reach negative natural increase.[10] In 1939 and 1940, however, Soviet annexation of new territories resulted in a rise of more than 60 percent in the Jewish population of the USSR.

The Soviet Union annexed the eastern sections of Poland, Bessarabia (Moldavia), and North Bukovina, along with the three Baltic states (Lithuania, Latvia, and Estonia) in their entirety. The number of Jews in these areas was estimated at close to 1.88 million, believed to have been grouped as follows: eastern Poland, 1.3 million; Bessarabia and North Bukovina, 330,000; Lithuania (excluding Vilna and surroundings), 150,000; and Latvia and Estonia, 100,000.[11] These Jewish communities differed from those of the preannexation Soviet territory in both the socionational and the demographic senses. Intermarriage was but a marginal phenomenon in these "new" Soviet Jewish communities, and their natural increase was apparently higher than that of the "old" Soviet Jews. In addition to the permanent Jewish residents of these newly annexed areas, there were between 200,000 and 300,000 Jewish refugees from parts of Poland occupied by the Germans in 1939.[12] We may therefore estimate that the Jewish population of the Soviet Union numbered between 5 million and 5.2 million—about a third of world Jewry—on the eve of the Soviet-German war.[13]

Nazi Germany's surprise attack on the Soviet Union in June 1941, caused the Soviet military framework to collapse. Orderly evacuation of the civilian population was not effected on a significant scale in most of the newly annexed areas, or beyond, in some parts of the prewar Soviet Union. When evacuation was arranged, it concentrated on members of the party and state apparatus. A number of Jews, too, were rescued in this way. Sometimes individual Jews attempting to escape from the Nazi invaders were forced to double back because the Wehrmacht advanced more swiftly than they could flee. When the Soviets were able to evacuate industrial plants and their workers to the interior, Jews associated with them were rescued as well. Some Jews, especially men and young people, survived as a result of induction into the Red Army. Only a very few Jews were rescued from the Holocaust by the partisan movements or found shelter among the Gentile population. The great majority of Soviet Jews who remained in Nazi-controlled areas was killed—for the most part murdered in the vicinity of their homes. Since no records were kept of the number of killings, only estimates are available. Estimates of the number of Jewish Holocaust victims in the Soviet Union fluctuate between 2.5 million and 3.3 million.[14] It seems reasonable to assert that half or more of Soviet Jewry was annihilated. From the demographic point of view, therefore, the Holocaust resulted in a tragic acceleration of trends launched many years before.

Jewish emigration from traditional areas of residence, one of the characteristic demographic features of Soviet Jewry, has been a permanent factor of major significance since the 1880s. Until the outbreak of World War I, tens of thousands of Jews had left Russia each year to escape pogroms and to relieve their economic distress; most went to the Americas. The war, the revolution, and the resulting difficulties of leaving the Soviet Union on the one hand and restrictions on entry of Jews into other countries on the other either reduced emigration or brought it nearly to a halt. At the same time, however, the possibilities of migration to the central and eastern regions of the USSR increased. From 1915 onward, Jewish migration from the Pale of Settlement toward the interior became significant and developed momentum in the late 1920s with the onset of rapid industrialization. By the beginning of 1939, some 37 percent of Soviet Jewry resided outside the former Pale,[15] as compared with 26 percent at the end of 1926 and 6 percent in 1897.[16] The onetime Jewish heartland was conquered by the Nazis; a large majority of its Jewish inhabitants was killed, and only a portion of those evacuated returned after the war. Consequently the proportion of Soviet Jewry dwelling outside the historical areas of Jewish residence was even greater after 1945 than it had been before the war.

Even those who returned to the former Pale (the Ukraine, Belorussia, Latvia, Lithuania, and Moldavia) did not return to their former places of residence because of the continuing anti-Semitism they encountered there and also because many could not bring themselves to live on the site of their families' slaughter. As a result of the Holocaust, therefore, two demographic trends first evinced in the nineteenth century quickly became the definitive sociodemographic pattern of the Jewish population: concentration in cities and the growth of large agglomerations in major centers.

It was by no means the Holocaust alone, however, that brought this change about. Jewish migration away from small towns is one of the general modern characteristics of East European Jewry, and pronounced indications of this were well evident as early as the beginning of the present century. The pogroms and "war communism," however, destroyed the economic base of the *shtetl* almost completely. Even during the NEP period, when private commerce and craftwork were permitted, the *shtetl* was not reconstituted. Many of its residents were classified as "rightless" (*lishentsyi*)—that is, not entitled to many of the social services provided by the state.

It is therefore natural that many of the younger and more enterprising *shtetl* residents, able to adapt to the new conditions, left home. Accelerated Soviet industrialization and urbanization provided more attractive alternatives. Indeed, the proportion of *shtetl* dwellers in the total Jewish population steadily declined. As early as 1897, the *shtetl* population in fifteen provinces (*guberniia*) of the Pale of Settlement (excluding Poland) amounted to 36 percent of all Russian Jews, with 44 percent situated in the cities.[17] In 1926, only 26 percent of the Jewish population of the Ukrainian SSR, Belorussian SSR, and the RSFSR (Russian Republic) was found in *shtetlekh*,[18] as compared with 64 percent in cities.[19] During the latter half of the 1920s and in the 1930s as well, migration from the *shtetlekh* accelerated, though its exact extent and dimensions are unknown. With the outbreak of World War II, therefore, Soviet Jewry had become urbanized, with large concentrations in the major cities.

Indeed the development of large Jewish agglomerations was discernible as early as the nineteenth century. Although at the beginning of the century, the entire Russian Empire (itself largely rural) did not contain a single Jewish community of 10,000 persons, there were thirty-seven such communities by the end of the century.[20] This pattern intensified after 1900 (table 1.1).

TABLE 1.1

JEWISH COMMUNITIES BY SIZE AND YEAR, FOR SELECTED AREAS

| | FIFTEEN PROVINCES OF THE PALE | | | | TOTAL USSR | |
| | 1897 | | 1910 | | 1926 | |
SIZE OF JEWISH COMMUNITY	NO. OF SETTLE-MENTS	% OF JEWISH POPULATION	NO. OF SETTLE-MENTS	% OF JEWISH POPULATION	NO. OF SETTLE-MENTS	% OF JEWISH POPULATION
Total	37	25.2	56	39.8	30	43.7
50,000	3	7.1	7	13.5	7	26.4
25,000–50,000	11	10.8	14	12.5	6	7.1
10,000–25,000	23	7.3	35	13.8	17	10.2

Sources: Y. Lestschinsky, *Dos idishe folk in tsifern* (Berlin, 1922), pp.48–51; L. Zinger, "Chislennost' i geo-graficheskoe razmeshchenie evreiskogo naseleniia SSSR," *Evrei v SSSR* (Moscow, 1929), pp. 38–51.

By the mid-1920s, close to half of Soviet Jewry lived in concentrations of more than 10,000 persons. The most rapid growth occurred in cities in which the number of Jews exceeded 50,000. Although precise data are not available for the period between 1926 and 1939, it is reasonable to assume that the process of cumulative concentration of Jews in a limited number of metropolises continued in the wake of urbanization and industrialization. Some even claim that by the beginning of 1939, close to 40 percent of Soviet Jewry was concentrated in only six major cities.[21] The consequences of the Holocaust and the effect it had on the residential mobility of those who survived the war significantly accelerated the process.

The metropolis, in which most of the larger Jewish concentrations came into being, generally serves as a locus for acculturation and assimilation but also provides possibilities for the expression of Jewish identity. A large agglomeration of Jews in a free society is capable of developing a variety of differing social contexts sufficient for the satisfaction of the individual's cultural and spiritual needs without forgoing the possibility of advancement in the modern world. This, however, did not hold true under Soviet rule, where legitimate Jewish activity was bound to a uniform standard dictated by the authorities in terms of substance, medium, and language (Yiddish). Acculturation, even if only linguistic in nature, was considered—by many Jews and by the authorities—the expression of integration into surrounding society that could come about only at the expense of restrictive national tendencies. An a priori contradiction, then, was posited between the individual Jew's social and professional advancement and the expression of his or her national aspirations. A relation of reciprocity came into being in the USSR between the integration of Jews into economic, social, and academic life on the one hand and deepening assimilation on the other. Examination of the transformations that occurred in the occupational structure of Soviet Jewry between the world wars may also be used therefore as an indicator of changes in the extent of involvement in Jewish national life.

The transformations in the occupational distribution and social stratification of Soviet Jewry in the period preceding World War II were further reaching than those in any other East European Jewish community. These shifts, too, are rooted in the nineteenth century. The 1897 census reveals that 39 percent of the Jews in the Russian Empire earned their living in the productive sectors of the economy[22] (Manufacturing and crafts and agriculture):

Commerce and trade	38.7 percent
Manufacturing and crafts	35.4 percent
Private household and other services	6.6 percent
Undefined employment	5.5 percent
Public service and free professions	5.2 percent
Transport and shipping	4.0 percent
Agriculture	3.6 percent
Military service	1.0 percent[23]

Jewish entrepreneurs contributed to the development of the banking and insurance sectors, the railway system, and other industries as well. Almost 32 percent of employed citizens engaging in commerce and trade in the Russian Empire were Jews.[24] Although much of Jewish commerce was small in scale, one-fourth of the value of all Russian commercial turnover appears to have been in Jewish hands.[25] The data on how Jews earned their living therefore indicate the extent to which Jews were involved in the various sectors of the economy. We should, however, compare these 1897 data with the results of the 1926 census. For this purpose, we shall use the social standard of measurement according to which economically active persons were grouped in the latter census.[26]

At the time of the 1897 census, 54.4 percent of economically active Jews were "merchants, owners of enterprises or persons without a defined occupation." This heterogeneous group apparently included artisans who engaged in commerce on a part-time basis, recipients of remittances from abroad, and hundreds of thousands of peddlars as well. It may be assumed that this stratum constricted somewhat between 1897 and the outbreak of World War I, though it still accounted for a large proportion of the Jewish population.

As of 1897, 25 percent of economically active Jews were salaried employees, distributed as follows: 11 percent laborers in workshops or small enterprises, 4 percent industrial workers, and 10 percent white-collar workers. The proportion of salaried workers steadily increased as a consequence of accelerated capitalist development that drove many of those previously engaged in small business and crafts into wage labor. Artisans accounted for 18.4 percent of economically active Jews, most of them working independently or together with family members. Many, however, found it difficult to cope with the harsh competition in the developing economy and were forced either to emigrate or to join the salaried class. The activities of the Jewish Colonization Association (founded in 1891) and other philanthropic organizations made their lot somewhat easier by providing credit for turnover, purchase of raw materials, or building up of inventory. Until 1914, hundreds of credit unions developed, also functioning as producers' and consumers' cooperatives. They facilitated purchase of raw materials, helped finance seasonal labor, and offered support in the event of illness, accident, or other calamity. These mutual-assistance associations filled more than an economic role; they also served as social cells.

In view of the restrictions placed on Jews who sought to reside in villages, their relative numbers in agriculture, small in any case, declined at the end of the nineteenth century. The 1897 census reveals that 2.2 percent of self-supporting Jews were farmers. This small stratum was almost completely destroyed during the years of civil war and pogroms. The danger of injury at the hands of rioting gangs was greater in the villages than in towns and cities, and many Jewish farmers fled their holdings. The NEP crisis of 1923-1924, however, led many Jews to turn to agriculture, which they viewed as the only way out of economic distress. This trend received added impetus with the beginnings of planned agricultural settlement, encouraged and directed by the Soviet authorities, on the basis of rural communities that offered programs for economic development and even cultural bases for the development of Jewish national existence in the Soviet Union. Indeed the stratum of Jewish farmers grew, comprising 8.3 percent of all economically active Jews in the country in 1926. This trend continued during the remainder of the decade. By 1930, farmers accounted for about

10 percent of all self-supporting Jews.[27] In the 1930s, however, a tendency to abandon agriculture appeared, although a fairly large tract in the Soviet Far East known as Birobidzhan was set aside for Jewish settlement and was declared a Jewish autonomous *oblast'* (region) within the RSFSR.

The stratum of "merchants, owners of enterprises or persons without a defined occupation" was economically destroyed in the earliest days of the Soviet regime. The property of the wealthy was damaged or confiscated; commerce collapsed in the period of war communism. When trade was allowed to resume during the NEP, it no longer resembled that of prerevolution days; it was more reminiscent of peddling. It is no wonder, therefore, that merchants comprised only 8.8 percent of self-supporting Jews at the end of 1926. If, however, we add the unemployed (10 percent)—since they apparently often engaged in commerce on a part-time basis—as well as those whose occupation was classified as "other" (3.2 percent), the aggregate category of "merchants or persons without a defined occupation" accounts for 22 percent of the total. Moreover, Jewish commerce played an important role in the national economy even during this period. In 1926, close to 20 percent of all business licenses were granted to Jews.[28] Jews comprised about 55 percent of those engaged in commerce in the Ukraine, Belorussia, Moscow, and Leningrad.[29]

In contrast to the decline of the Jewish merchant stratum, the proportion of craftsmen rose from 18.4 percent in 1897 to 23 percent in 1926.[30] It appears that some of the Jews driven out of business were absorbed into this group, to the extent that Jews comprised 39 percent of all urban craftsmen in the Soviet Union by 1926.[31] The proportion of Jewish laborers remained almost unchanged (15 percent in 1897, 15.1 percent in 1926), though there was a movement away from labor in crafts in favor of industrial labor.[32]

The furthest-reaching changes occurred with regard to the white-collar class. This group accounted for 10 percent of all self-supporting Jews in 1897, most of them employed in private business, industry, or Jewish public and religious institutions. The census of late 1926 reveals that this group now accounted for 24.7 percent of all economically active Jews.[33] Now, however, all were employed by the Soviet state and party apparatus with its various economic, cultural, and propaganda arms. Many Jews had therefore filled the void left by the aftermath of the revolution, when the traditional clerical, administrative, and intellectual classes boycotted the Soviet regime or were kept out of these positions. The growth of the Jewish white-collar class is indicative of the social trends that were to bring about significant changes in Soviet Jewry.

At the end of the 1920s, the Soviet Union embarked on the path of rapid industrialization. At the same time, control of all aspects of life was increased. Both processes created great demand for manpower. Once again broad opportunities opened for Jews, an urban public with higher levels of mobility and education than those of the surrounding society. Many Jews were recruited into administration, science, and technical professions. A comparison of data from the 1926 census with those of 1939 may hint at the changes that took place in Soviet Jewry during the 1930s, despite the considerable differences that exist between the two sets of data with regard to categorization, classification, and terminology used. While in 1926 the economically active population was grouped into eleven categories, the 1939 census grouped the entire population into only six social strata. Both self-supporting persons and their dependents were classified as belonging to a given social stratum. Moreover, some of the strata were heterogeneous, grouping clerks with scientists, engineers, physicians, and other professionals vastly different from one another with regard to social prestige and income. Nonetheless, it seems useful to examine these 1939 data in detail (table 1.2).

If we assume that the numerical ratio of dependents of economically active persons was more or less identical in each of the social strata, it becomes clear that the proportion of Jews working in agriculture declined from the beginning to the end of the 1930s.[34] It is also noteworthy that on the eve of World War II, Jewish craftsmen (employed in cooperatives and self-employed alike) amount to one-fifth of all economically active Jews and comprised over 12 percent of all such craftsmen in the USSR.

The furthest-reaching changes between 1926 and 1939 took place in the

TABLE 1.2

PERCENTAGE DISTRIBUTIONS OF THE JEWISH AND TOTAL SOVIET POPULATION
BY SOCIAL (OCCUPATIONAL) CLASS, 1939

SOCIAL CLASS	POPULATION		PERCENTAGE OF JEWS IN THE TOTAL
	SOVIET JEWS	TOTAL SOVIET UNION	
White Collar Workers [a] (*Sluzhashchie*)	40.7	17.2	4.2
Laborers	30.5	32.6	1.7
Craftsman in Cooperatives	16.1	2.3	12.4
Kolkhoz Members	5.8	46.4	0.2
Private Craftsmen	4.0 ⎫	1.5	8.1
Other	2.9 ⎭		

Sources: Zinger, 1941, p. 49; *Itogi vsesoiuznoi perepisi naseleniia 1959 goda* (Moscow, 1962), general volume, Tables 1, 28.

(a) Zinger (1941, p. 50) groups white collar workers and laborers together, but states that "the ratio of white collar workers to laborers in the Jewish population at the present time is 4:3." This statement has been used as the basis for our own distribution of the two strata.

proportions of laborers and white-collar workers who were Jewish. The relative size of these two groups within the Jewish population almost doubled. The proportion of laborers among Jews was the same as that of the general population, while the proportion of Jews who were white-collar workers was about two and one-half times greater than their demographic weight.[35] The differential in the higher reaches of the heterogeneous white-collar category, however, was apparently even greater. This stratum took in ever-growing numbers of Jews with higher or secondary vocational education. During the 1935-1936 year about 62,000 Jews were enrolled in institutions of higher education (13.5 percent of total enrollment), with an additional 32,000 enrolled in the secondary vocational schools. Jews were integrated at an accelerated pace into scientific institutions, with the number of those employed in such institutes constantly rising; moreover, about 1,000 Jews studied for the degree of *Kandidat,* the Soviet equivalent of a Ph.D.[36] During the 1930s, therefore, hundreds of thousands of Jews were integrated into Soviet cultural, economic, scientific, and administrative life, with many taking up positions of importance (although in politics, as newer elements replaced veteran cadres, the relative involvement of Jews was reduced). Such wide-ranging integration of Jews in key positions undoubtedly aroused feelings of envy and fed anti-Semitic leanings in Soviet society, but in the light of the repressive regime of the 1930s—particularly in the latter half of the decade—popular resentments arising out of the forced pace of industrial and technical development could not be clearly expressed. The fact that anti-Semitism did not rise to the surface openly tended to strengthen the feeling of some Jews, who had become integrated into the surrounding society and had even taken up positions of influence, that their national origin was no longer an issue of any importance—a conviction that had the effect of furthering their conscious or unconscious separation from what remained of their Jewishness. It may not be incorrect to surmise that the white-collar stratum—particularly its elite—was involved in an assimilation process more advanced than that of the craftsmen, the *kolkhoz* workers, and perhaps even some of the laborers. Hence the distribution of the social strata within the Jewish community is also of importance in determining the nature of Jewish identification.

We have no data on the distribution of the social strata in the USSR's various regions on the eve of World War II; it appears, however, that we may make the following highly reasonable assertions:

1. The proportion of white-collar workers was greater in regions that served as destinations of Jewish immigration.

2. Even in areas of the former Pale of Settlement, the proportion of this stratum was greater in large cities than in small and intermediate-sized ones.

3. Jewish national-cultural life—what there was of it—was stronger in the former Pale of Settlement, where there was some historical continuity, than it was in regions to which Jews had recently migrated.

We may therefore infer that the share of the white-collar stratum, especially its elite, was greater after World War II than it has been on the eve of the Holocaust. In any event, Soviet Jewry was better integrated (at first glance) into surrounding society and more exposed to more advanced assimilation processes than it had been on the eve of the Holocaust. It was, however, precisely for this reason that the Holocaust, especially the role Soviet citizens played in it, was a profound shock for Soviet Jews. In its aftermath, some Soviet Jews began to wonder about the extent of their integration into surrounding society—second thoughts that seemed to find confirmation in the anti-Semitic policy that the regime pursued during Stalin's last days. Under that policy, Yiddish culture—the sole legitimate framework for Jewish national activity—was virtually obliterated, and Jews who had viewed themselves as integral parts of their surroundings were driven out of their positions in a campaign against cosmopolitans. The individual Jew, in the absence of any collective Jewish framework, therefore faced a cruel dilemma. On the one hand, he felt he was not part of surrounding society and that his affiliation with the Jewish people was formally determined by virtue of its being so recorded in his internal passport; on the other hand, he viewed himself as an inseparable part of the society, culture, and manner of life in which he lived and to whose shaping and development he had given of his spirit and capabilities. The Jew as an individual was forced to cope with the tremendous inner tension that stemmed from this diametric contradiction. His conscious or unconscious reactions to this contradiction also had an indirect impact on demographic and social developments within the Jewish community in the most recent generations.

METHODOLOGICAL PROBLEMS

Definition of Nationality in Soviet Statistics

Nationality in Soviet statistical publications is defined according to differing principles. Current publications and many of the demographic surveys and research studies have determined it by an ethnic-biological standard: one is born of parents of a certain nationality and is therefore registered as belonging to that group, with no legal possibility of changing this registration.[37] When parents are of different nationalities, the newborn is registered according to the mother's affiliation.[38] Upon reaching the age of 16 and receiving his or her first internal passport—which most Soviet citizens must carry—the teenager may choose either parent's nationality though not any third choice.[39] Once having received their first internal passport bearing this national designation, Soviet citizens may not repudiate their declared nationality even if born of parents of differing nationalities.[40] It is therefore probable that sociopolitical occurrences influence the process of defining nationality by ethnic-biological standards only in the cases of offspring of mixed families, and even this only when the first internal passport is issued.

The definition of nationality employed in censuses, however, is meant to determine not the population's ethnic-biological makeup but rather its national affiliation as determined by individuals' subjective principles.[41] This definition of nationality presupposes that in the life of a person, and all the more his or her descendants, changes in national definition may take place by force of shifts in his or her national or even religious perception.[42] It is clear that the strength of one's national identity may influence one's declaration at census time on the one hand, while social and political pressures that either strengthen or weaken this identity are at work on the other. It is therefore possible that certain discrepancies may develop between one's nationality defined according to official documents and that declared to a census taker. Thus, for example, most children under 16 who are born of Jewish mothers and non-Jewish fathers will, as a rule, be registered in official documents as Jews and will appear as such in current statistics. At the same time, it is reasonable to suppose that some of them will be registered in a census as of different nationalities.

Soviet Sources

Up to the mid-1930s, Jewish research institutes in the USSR conducted a number of demographic studies pertaining to the Jews. The government not only allowed them to carry out their surveys but even placed statistical data that had accumulated in government bureaus at their disposal. These studies constitute some of the most important sources for study of social and economic developments within the Soviet Jewish community between the world wars.[43] When the activity of the Jewish research institutes was restricted, a number of Jewish demographers continued pursuing the topic. The last serious study conducted in the USSR of Jewish demography appeared in the latter half of 1941.[44] Although a doctoral dissertation on economic and social developments in the Soviet Jewish community was completed at the University of Moscow in 1947, it was not published, and independent researchers have no access to it.[45] Soviet Jews interested in demographic phenomena continued to deal in the topic; on the whole, however, they had access to no sources of information apart from official Soviet publications, and recourse even to these is at times more easily achieved outside the Soviet Union than inside.[46] One who wishes to study the sociodemographic situation of Soviet Jewry in the most recent generation will therefore be most likely compelled to base research essentially on general sources of Soviet statistics.

The few statistical publications that appeared in the Soviet Union in the decade following World War II were weak in data pertaining to the population's national makeup.[47] The few details they did offer on this topic related to nationalities that had their own union republics. It is therefore clear that these publications tell nothing of the Jews. In the past thirty years, however, an extensive statistical, demographic,[48] and sociological[49] literature has been published in the Soviet Union, and here we find data on the influence the national factor exerts on demographic phenomena. Here, details are not restricted to nationalities with their own union republics; in certain cases they relate also to those that have no such republics, the Jews among them. Soviet publications of the last thirty years that include statistical data about Jews may be divided into two categories: (1) publications based on current statistics and on conclusions of surveys and research studies and (2) publications based on general population censuses.

In published data drawn from current statistics and research deriving from the Offices for Registration of Personal Status (*ZAGS*), nationality is defined as that recorded in official documents.[50] These internal passports serve Soviet citizens when they deal with the authorities in family matters (births, marriage, divorce, death), residence (*propiska*), education, and work, and it is these documents that citizens must use when they fill out forms, of which several have a special copy that is transferred to the Bureaus of Statistics.[51] It appears, however, that only some of the data transferred to these bureaus undergo full analysis, including nationality information.[52] This is borne out by the fact that Soviet scholars seeking information on questions such as intranational or mixed marriages, national definition of offspring of mixed marriages, and the like generally collect the material in the offices of *ZAGS* and police stations (from which internal passports are issued) rather than seeking conclusive statistical material in the Bureaus of Statistics. The material on these and similar topics is fragmentary and relates to miniscule samples and/or limited geographical areas—a city or, at most, a republic. The Bureaus of Statistics appear to restrict processing of data on a national distribution basis to a number of spheres they consider to be of prime importance, such as scientific workers, students, and doctors.

This material can therefore be used to complement other data but cannot provide an overall picture of fundamental demographic phenomena, which are reported in the summaries of the censuses.

Censuses

The fourth Soviet census, the first after World War II, was taken on January 15, 1959.[53] In this census, like those before it, citizens were asked to state their national affiliation and native tongue.[54] The summaries of the census were published in sixteen volumes, and here we find data on the breakdown of the Soviet Jewish population according to sex, native tongue, and distribution by republic, *oblast'*, and capital cities of the republics. The data also contain information on the percentage of marriages and level of education in the Soviet Jewish community.[55] The fifth census was taken on January 15, 1970.[56] Its seven volumes of summaries contain data pertaining to the same topics discussed in the findings of the previous census. In addition, the 1970 census data offer information on second language spoken, family size, and age breakdown.[57] The data from the most recent Soviet census, taken on January 17, 1979, have not yet been released in summary form; only a fraction of the new material is available for scrutiny in the journal of the Central Bureau of Statistics and several other publications. Although the data published from these censuses are highly deficient, they do contain basic and valuable statistical material pertaining to the Jewish community in the USSR.

Each census was preceded with trial censuses and nationwide advisory conferences of Soviet statisticians and demographers. (I shall relate here only those aspects of the precensus stage that may assist in clarifying issues pertinent to my topic.) In a proposed questionnaire sent to the participants in the precensus consultation, article 7 was phrased thus: "Nationality, and, for foreigners, citizenship as well." The enumerators' instruction booklet included the following:

Record the nationality stated by the respondent. Children's nationality is determined by parents. Only in families in which father and mother belong to different nationalities and in which parents find it difficult to determine their children's nationality themselves should preference be given to the mother's nationality. For foreign citizens, indicate the name of the country of which the subject is a citizen after his/her nationality.

Shortly before the statisticians' advisory conference, two Soviet demographers, S. Bruk and V. Kozlov, published an article entitled "Questions of Nationality and Native tongue in the Upcoming Population Census."[58] The authors stressed that although the question of nationality (*natsional'nost'*) had indeed appeared in all previous censuses, it was associatively linked with the broader term *nation* (*natsiia*); therefore respondents belonging to certain ethnic groups declared themselves as affiliated with different national groups. The authors proposed that these distortions be corrected by replacing the question of nationality with one exploring the ethnic groups or peoples (*narod*) to which citizens belong. To emphasize the subjective aspect of the definition of nationality in the census, Bruk and Kozlov suggested phrasing the question thus: "To what nationality (people) do you affiliate yourself?" They also hinted at a lack of clarity in the term *native tongue* (*rodnoi iazyk*) and demanded that it be replaced with a more precise term. Thus the pertinent question would inquire into "the main spoken language and other tongues which you command and often use in day-to-day life." The article aroused great interest and transformed the questions on the definition of nationality and native tongue into one of the foci of deliberations in the statisticians' advisory conference.

In his opening address, P. Pod''iachikh devoted much attention to Bruk and Kozlov's proposals and objected to rephrasing the "nationality" and "native tongue" questions. Of the reasons he offered for his opposition, one was practical—for the change would prevent comparison of the results of the 1970 census with those of previous censuses—and the other doctrinal—for the census, he claimed, was meant to portray not the population's ethnic makeup but rather its national composition.[59] In the debate that followed Pod''iachikh's address, a majority objected to Bruk and Kozlov's proposals. The delegates of the Uzbek and Georgian SSRs, defending the interests of the major peoples in their respective republics, were especially fierce in their opposition.

It is therefore likely that the vague phrasing of the nationality question in Soviet censuses serves the Russians' interests on the one hand and the large border nationalities' interest in submerging small ethnic groups on the other. Indeed, the nationality question retained the phrasing used in previous censuses both on the census questionnaire and in the census takers' instruction manual.[60] The major changes in the questionnaire used in the 1970 census compared with its precursor were essentially expressed in the sampling method used. The entire population was surveyed according to an eleven-item questionnaire, while the occupants of every fourth dwelling unit (20 to 25 percent of the population) were given an eighteen-point questionnaire. People of working age (16-59 for men, 16-54 for women) employed in households or working on small private farm plots were asked to fill out an additional ten-point questionnaire meant to provide the authorities with data on manpower not properly utilized in the national economy.[61]

It was noted at the top of the questionnaires that "answers to the questions are meant only for the processing of statistical conclusions concerning population size and composition according to a predetermined program; census takers are forbidden to disclose the content of the answers to anyone."[62] The mass media, too, stressed that the census figures would be put to statistical use only. It is doubtful, however, that these declarations sufficed to remove all citizens' reservations, and some citizens almost certainly took into account the possibility that their answers might serve purposes other than statistical.

The instructions required enumerators to record the answers as told to them by the respondents. If, however, the census taker believed the subject capable of filling out the questionnaire, he or she could leave the questionnaire in the citizen's home and return for it at a later opportunity (though this option does not appear to have been commonly used). Answers were to be recorded precisely as given; census takers were not allowed to request documents as proof, though they did not always honor this injunction strictly.

Support for this hypothesis can be found in "Patterns of Integration among Soviet Immigrants," a study on Soviet Jews in Israel.[63] A sample of 1,566 individuals (including 420 who had arrived in Israel between January 1, 1960, and March 31, 1971) at least 14 years old upon arrival in Israel and at least 18 when the study was conducted (in the latter half of 1971) was selected out of 7,893 Soviet immigrants who reached Israel between January 1, 1960, and March 31, 1971.[64] The subjects were asked "Did you show the census taker your internal passport during your conversation with him?" Three possible responses were provided: "1) Yes, by his request; 2) Yes, by my own initiative; 3) No." Half of the subjects who had reached Israel between January 1, 1970, and March 31, 1971—210—answered this question. Of those who did not, some were evidently no longer in the Soviet Union at the time of the census (January 15, 1970); others stated that they did not recall this detail. Of the 210 who did respond, 86 (41 percent) had presented their internal passports to the census taker—62—(29.5 percent) upon demand and 24 (11.5 percent) by their own initiative. Although these figures may not accurately reflect the percentage of those who produced documents during the 1970 census in the Soviet Union, they give some inkling of how common the showing of documents during the census was. The implication is that Jewish subjects would not have found it comfortable to declare as their nationality something different from the entry in their documents.

In the event that the census taker had not demanded documents, each subject was asked to what extent he or she exerted some other manner of influence on the subject's declaration of nationality. Bruk and Kozlov had hinted at "assistance" of this sort in their article.[65] In the statisticians' advisory conference, Bruk proposed that the census takers' instructions explicitly forbid "altering answers [concerning nationality] given by the subjects or influencing them by 'whispering' (*podskazyvanie*)."[66] Pod"iachikh, addressing himself to this matter in his talk before the same forum, rejected Bruk's proposal, strengthening his position by citing an example from the 1959 census. On the eve of that census, Pod"iachikh related, Cardinal Wyszinski of Poland had instructed the Catholic priests in western Belorussia to influence their followers to declare themselves Polish nationals in the census; otherwise the Catholic churches would be shut down. "If Bruk's proposal is accepted," Pod"iachikh contended, "we will have to sit by helplessly and watch how the national makeup of the population becomes distorted in the census due to incorrect recording of

nationality . . . the result of Cardinal Wyszinski's provocative action."
Pod''iachikh stressed that "should census takers see that a clearly incorrect
response has been given to a certain question, they must make it clear that
the subject is duty-bound to provide accurate data."[67] It is therefore likely
that the census director had not totally rejected the possibility of census
takers' intervention in recording subjects' answers. I have attempted to
clarify this by meeting with people who had participated actively in the
census and by conducting a survey. Despite the commonly held view among
Israeli immigrants from the USSR that the results of the Soviet censuses
were falsified, I have found only two such immigrants, both mountain Jews
(one an enumerator, the other a supervisor) who testified to having been
instructed not to record "mountain Jews" as Jews. (The mountain Jews are
an ancient Jewish community which lives in the eastern part of the North-
Caucasus and Trans-Caucasus, near the Caspian Sea. They speak a Judeo-
Tat language. Their number was about 50,000 in the beginning of the
1970s.) I have reason, however, to assume that this was exceptional, for
these reports relate to a single Jewish ethnic group and a limited geographic
area and because I have found no additional direct testimony to corroborate
them.

The study "Patterns of Integration among Soviet Immigrants" included
two questions meant to clarify the possibility that the very presentation of
the question constituted a sort of guidance and that the subject felt some
pressure even when not consciously applied by the enumerator. One of these
questions was phrased thus: "How did the enumerator present the question
pertaining to nationality? 1) 'Are you a Russian, a Lithuanian, a Ukrainian
or the like?' 2) 'What is your nationality?' 3) some other manner." The
other question was: "Did you sense any sort of pressure when the
'nationality' question was presented?" The possible answers: "1) I felt no
pressure; 2) Yes, I felt pressured to declare myself not a Jew; 3) Yes, I felt
pressured to declare myself a Jew; 4) another kind of pressure."

Two hundred and seven members of the sample group—49 percent of the
subjects who had reached Israel between January 1, 1970, and March 31,
1971—responded to the first question. Of them, 91 percent (188 individuals)
answered that the nationality question had been posed neutrally: "What is
your nationality?" Three percent (6 subjects) said it had been presented by a
listing of nationalities—in a manner that may be viewed as a form of
guidance—and 6 percent (13 respondents) answered that the nationality
question had been presented differently. We may therefore say that
according to the sample group, the nationality question had been posed
neutrally, as per the phrasing of the census questionnaire, in the large
majority of cases.

Of the 210 sample group members who responded to the question of
having felt pressure during the census, 91.9 percent (193 subjects) reported
having felt no pressure; 3.3 percent (7 subjects) had felt under pressure to

declare themselves as Jews; and only 1.5 (3 subjects) reported having felt pressure to declare an affiliation with nationalities other than their own. This sample, of course, was small, and no certain conclusions can be drawn from it. It may, however, suggest that guidance on the part of census takers was insignificant and, when applied, was actually meant to induce Jews to declare themselves as such. It therefore seems that the widespread assumption that a significant number of Jews concealed their Jewishness as a result of explicit or implicit pressure on census takers' part is unfounded and that reasons for the changes in the number of Jews in the Soviet Union must be sought in demographic phenomena within the Jewish community.

2 FUNDAMENTAL ISSUES IN DETERMINING THE SIZE OF THE JEWISH POPULATION IN THE SOVIET UNION

In 1959, when the first census following World War II was held, 2,267,814 Jews were enumerated in the Soviet Union, accounting for 1.1 percent of the population[1]. Twenty years later (January 1979), the most recent census found 1,810,876 Jews, or 0.7 percent of all Soviet Union residents.[2] These twenty years therefore witnessed a decline of 456,938 persons in the Jewish community. Two main factors—internal processes and emigration—account for this phenomenon.

INTERNAL PROCESSES

By "internal processes" I mean the demographic and sociopolitical factors that have influenced the decline in the number of Jews. The most important of these are individuals who may have concealed their Jewish identity in the censuses; the balance of endogamous and exogamous marriages; family structure and size; and rates of birth and natural increase.

Concealment of Jewish Identity in Censuses

If we define any individual with at least one parent of Jewish origin as Jewish, we shall by all accounts find a considerable though inestimable number of Jews of this type unaccounted for in the census. These Jews—whom, for the purposes of this discussion, we shall call marginal

Jews—should be divided into two categories. The first comprises individuals officially registered as non-Jews and, as we may reasonably assume in most cases, have declared themselves members of some other Soviet nationality in population censuses. Because a Soviet resident may not officially change the nationality recorded in his or her documents—though such changes are certainly made de facto in various ways—it is hard to believe that between the censuses, a significant number of Jews adopted a non-Jewish nationality in their internal passports and for that reason declared themselves as something other than Jewish in the most recent census.[3] The second category consists of individuals registered in official documents as Jews but who declared non-Jewish national affiliation in the censuses. With this category of marginal Jews, we should distinguish between two groups: adults (or, more precisely, internal passport holders) and minors, the latter consisting chiefly of offspring of nationally mixed families.

With regard to social and political pressure to conceal one's Jewish identity, it is hard to see any essential difference between the years preceding the 1959 census and those preceding the censuses of 1970 and 1979. The years preceding the first census witnessed a fierce campaign against the Jewish religion, one displaying clear overtones of anti-Semitism (as distinct from general antireligious propaganda). At the same time, in the wake of Israel's 1956 Sinai campaign, the Soviet mass media waged an extensive propaganda campaign against the State of Israel, with which Jews as such were often equated. With regard to an additional factor as well—the hostility of surrounding society or its unwillingness to assimilate the Jews (persisting, instead, in viewing them as members of a different nationality)—it is hard to see any substantial change between the atmosphere that reigned immediately before the 1959 census and the prevailing social climate as the 1979 census approached. If we add to these factors the findings of the survey that imply that census takers often requested subjects' internal passports, it would appear highly reasonable to say that neither the surrounding society nor census takers encouraged Jews to conceal their national identity; in any event, they did not encourage them to do so any more in recent years than in 1959.

The Jews' expectations with regard to integration into surrounding society, to the extent of a desire to adopt a different nationality—chiefly the Russian—appear to have weakened greatly during the intercensus period. Expectations for liberalization and its concurrent opportunities for integration into surrounding society were far greater in the years preceding the 1959 census than they were in the 1960s and 1970s. Furthermore, Israel's victory in the Six-Day War of 1967 served quite a number of Jews as a source of pride; in its wake they no longer considered their Jewish affiliation a cause for embarrassment. In the late 1960s and the 1970s, some Jews who had hoped for integration into Russian society and who might have declared themselves Russian nationals in the 1959 census were attracted to the Jewish national movement. We therefore find no basis for an assumption that a higher percentage of Jews concealed their identity in the census of 1970 or of 1979 than in that of 1959. Most of the intercensus decline in the Jewish population, accordingly, can hardly be explained as originating in a larger number of Jews who had begun to conceal their Jewish nationality.

Support for this hypothesis may be found in the study "Patterns of Integration among Soviet Immigrants." Participants in the study were asked about the nationality they had declared in the censuses of 1959 and 1970. The replies are categorized in table 2.1.

TABLE 2.1

THE NATIONALITY OF SOVIET JEWISH IMMIGRANTS IN ISRAEL,
AS DECLARED TO SOVIET CENSUS TAKERS

NATIONALITY	CENSUS OF 1959		CENSUS OF 1970	
	FREQUENCY	PERCENTAGE	FREQUENCY	PERCENTAGE
Total	1,286	100.0	215	100.0
Jewish	1,275	99.2	212	98.6
Russian	8	0.6	1	0.5
Other	3	0.2	2	0.9

Inasmuch as most of the sample population in the study had already left the Soviet Union by January 15, 1970, when the census was held, and inasmuch as few members of the sample had been counted in that census, the findings are not a firm basis for unequivocal conclusions. They nevertheless appear to support the contention that the percentage of Soviet Jews who concealed their national identity in the 1959 census was probably not significantly different from the percentage in the 1970 census.

The assumption that there is no significant discrepancy between internal passport data and census declarations is supported by a study entitled "The National Reawakening of Soviet Jews."[4] For the purposes of this study, 447 Zionist activists were asked about the nationalities registered in their own internal passports and those of their spouses, in addition to the nationalities they had declared in the 1970 census. A total of 754 (including spouses) answered with regard to internal passport data and 683 with regard to census declarations (the difference being due to the fact that some interviewees had not participated in the census, either having reached Israel previously or not having been counted for other reasons). The respective distribution of nationalities by passports and census declaration appears in table 2.2.

TABLE 2.2

DISTRIBUTION BY NATIONALITY OF ZIONIST ACTIVISTS
AND THEIR SPOUSES IN INTERNAL PASSPORTS AND
IN THE 1970 CENSUS

	INTERNAL PASSPORTS		CENSUS OF 1970	
NATIONALITY	FREQUENCY	PERCENTAGE	FREQUENCY	PERCENTAGE
Total	754	100.0	683	100.0
Jewish	717	95.1	647	94.7
Russian	29	3.9	26	3.8
Other	8	1.0	10	1.5

The sample, though not representative, indicates that Zionist activists and their spouses display a rather high correlation with regard to registration of nationality in identity documents and in census declarations.[5]

Another group with potential for a discrepancy between data recorded on official documents and population census declarations is that of minor offspring of mixed nationality families. Although children are generally registered by mother's nationality until the age of 16, census takers are instructed to help parents in such families to define children's nationality when the parents find it difficult to do so themselves.[6] There is reason to assume that minors, even those born to Jewish mothers, were registered in a considerable proportion of the mixed families according to the nationality of the non-Jewish parent at census time. The result is a discrepancy between official document registration and census results. However, most offspring of mixed marriages declare themselves non-Jewish nationals in any case upon receiving their first passports.[7] Therefore, in terms of the Soviet Jewish community's future demographic development, these minors' declarations of national affiliation are more significant than their nationality as recorded in personal documents. Moreover, the practice of registering the offspring of exogamous marriages as non-Jews was as well accepted in the 1959 census as it was in that of 1979. Accordingly, if the proportion of such minors was indeed greater in the 1970 and 1979 censuses than it was in the 1959 census, we should view this as an outcome of the proliferation of mixed marriages and of various assimilatory processes affecting the second generation of these families.

Endogamous and Exogamous Marriages

One of the important factors that shape the demographic profile and consequently influence the size of the Soviet Jewish community is intermarriage. We shall examine three aspects of this phenomenon: mixed marriages; nationality as a factor in the selection of spouse; and the national definition of mixed marriage offspring.

Mixed Marriages

Intermarriage (marriage involving one non-Jewish spouse) has become a phenomenon of great scope and significance in Jewish communities the world over in recent generations.[8] In the Soviet Union, the Jewish spouse in such a marriage commonly distances himself or herself from the Jewish community in favor of greater identification with the non-Jewish spouse's group, a process pursued by the offspring. The percentage of non-Jews in the Soviet Union who approach Judaism as a consequence of marriage with a Jew is negligible. Intermarriage accordingly has significant impact on the size, structure, and rate of natural increase of the Jewish community in the Soviet Union.

Marriages between Jews and non-Jews—rare among Russian Jews in the beginning of the twentieth century—became rather common as early as the 1920s, as seen in table 2.3.

Between 1924 and 1927, the percentage of intermarriages involving Jews was nearly 5.2 times greater in the European part of the RSFSR than it was in Belorussia and 3.4 times greater than it was in the Ukraine. Of 3,727 Jewish men and women who married non-Jews in 1926, 85.5 percent married Russians (2,729) or Ukrainians (998).[9]

Recently published data concerning intermarriage in 1936 may indicate a trend in this regard in the second half of the 1920s and the first half of the

TABLE 2.3

PERCENTAGE OF MIXED MARRIAGES AMONG ALL MARRIAGES
WHICH INCLUDED AT LEAST ONE JEWISH PARTNER,
FOR SELECTED UNION REPUBLICS, BY YEAR, 1923–1927

| | YEAR OF MARRIAGE | | | | | MEAN |
REPUBLIC	1923	1924	1925	1926	1927	1924–1927
RSFSR (European)	*	23.6	26.3	34.4	38.1	30.6
Ukraine	*	7.9	8.6	9.7	10.0	9.1
Belorussia	3.7	5.0	5.4	6.1	6.9	5.9

Sources: Computed by *Natsional 'naia politika VKP(b) v tsifrakh* (Moscow, 1930), p. 41; *Statisticheskie materialy po evreiskoi demografii i ekonomike*, No. 4 (1929), pp. 21–22; U. Engelman, "Intermarriage Among Jews in Germany, USSR and Switzerland," *Jewish Social Studies*, No. 2 (1940), pp. 168–174.

* Data not available.

1930s. While 2,729 Jews married Russians in European RSFSR, the Ukraine, and Belorussia in 1926, 9,454 did so in 1936. Because intermarriage in the mid-1920s was rare outside these three republics, we may reasonably state that the number of marriages between Jews and Russians nationwide grew by approximately 3.5 times during the 1926-1936 decade. The number of marriages between Jews and Ukrainians also grew in the decade under discussion, from 998 to 3,610 (362 percent). In the case of Belorussian Jews, too, the 1936 intermarriage rate exceeded that of 1926 by 200 percent.[10] For the Soviet Union as a whole, therefore, it appears that the percentage of Jewish intermarriage was at least 2.5 times greater in the mid-1930s than it was in the mid-1920s. There may be grounds, however, to take the view that the percentage of intermarriage among Soviet Jews fell somewhat in the 1940s and the early 1950s as a result of an awakened national identification among Soviet Jews engendered by the Holocaust and the anti-Semitism displayed by surrounding society and the regime, both of which would tend to increase social distance between Jews and non-Jews.[11] Other factors, however, caused the rise in the proportion of Jews entering into intermarriage to resume: the postwar concentration of Jews in big cities where marriages involving different national groups are more frequent; the admission of progressively greater numbers of Jews to institutions of higher education, where unmarried Jews and non-Jews encounter one another socially; and the lack of any organized framework, even a Soviet one, in which Jewish youth might spend time.[12] Although a number of tourists in the Soviet Union during the 1960s indeed reported a high percentage of Jewish intermarriage there, their testimony went no furter than impression and cannot serve as a basis for even a cautious estimate. Only in the 1960s did isolated data capable of supporting a rough estimate of the impact of intermarriage on shaping the demographic profile of the Soviet Jewish community begin to appear in print.

The data at our disposal with regard to intermarriage of Soviet Jews relate to eight places and dates, as indicated in table 2.4. Items 5, 6, and 7 of the table relate to areas that had not been under Nazi occupation and whose Jewish populations consist of several ethnic communities. Ashkenazi (European) and Bukharian Jews live side by side in Tashkent; mountain Jews dwell alongside European ones in Dagestan and its capital, Makhachkala.

In all the republics and cities, apart from Khar'kov and the Oktiabr' *raion* in Tashkent, the percentage of intermarriage involving Jewish women was lower than that involving Jewish men. Let us assume that the intermarriage ratios of Jewish women and men, respectively, were identical throughout the Ukraine to the average proportions in all the republics and cities (apart from Khar'kov) for which we have figures. Calculating on that basis, we can estimate that of every 100 marriages involving a Jewish woman in 1969

TABLE 2.4

PERCENTAGES OF JEWISH AND MIXED MARRIAGES
BY SEX, PERIOD, AND AREA *

AREA	PERIOD	MARRIAGES OF JEWISH MALES			MARRIAGES OF JEWISH FEMALES			PERCENTAGE OF SOVIET JEWRY [a]
		TOTAL	TO JEWS	TO NON-JEWS	TOTAL	TO JEWS	TO NON-JEWS	
1) Estonia	1965	100 (35)	37.1 (13)	62.9 (22)	100 (28)	46.4 (13)	53.6 (15)	–
Estonia	1968	100 (56)	26.8 (15)	73.2 (41)	100 (29)	51.7 (15)	48.3 (14)	0.2
2) Latvia	1960–64 [b]	100	64.0	36.0	100	65.2	34.8	1.6
3) Ukraine	1969	100	63.0	37.0	– Not available –			36.1
4) Khar'kov	1960	100 (662)	73.3 (485)	26.7 (177)	100 (720)	67.4 (485)	32.6 (235)	3.6
5) Dagestan ASSR	1967 [c]	100 (137)	78.8 (108)	21.2 (29)	100 (137)	78.8 (108)	21.2 (29)	1.0
6) Makhachkala	1959–68	100 (907)	82.1 (745)	17.9 (162)	100 (869)	85.7 (745)	14.3 (124)	–
7) Tashkent Oktiabr' raion	1962 [d]	100	93.2	6.8	100	91.4	8.6	2.2 [e]
Kuibyshev raion		100	63.9	36.1	100	68.9	31.1	
8) Belorussia (ten cities)	1975	100 (824)	65.7 (541)	34.3 (283)	100 (705)	76.7 (541)	23.3 (164)	–

Sources: *Narodnoe khoziaistvo Estonskoi SSR v 1969 g.* (Tallin, 1970), p. 26; A. Kholmogorov, *Internatsional'nye cherty sovetskikh natsii* (Moscow, 1970), p. 89; A. Boiarskii, "Stranitsy bol'shoi biografii," *Izvestiia*, May 9, 1971; M.Kurman, I. Lebedinskii, *Naselenie bol'shogo sotsialisticheskogo goroda* (Moscow, 1968), p. 126; *Sovremennaia kul'tura i byt narodov Dagestana* (Moscow, 1971), pp. 184–185; Iu. Evtsigneev, "Natsional'no-smeshannye braki v Makhachkale," *Sovetskaia etnografiia*, No. 4 (1971), p. 82; K.Khanazarov, "Mezhnatsional'nye braki," *Obshchestvennye nauki v Uzbekistane*, No. 10 (1964), pp. 26–31; *Etnicheskie protsessy i obraz zhizni* (Minsk, 1980), p. 260.

* Frequencies shown in parenthesis, where available.

(a) Data relating to marriages during the first half of the decade were calculated according to the figures for Jewish population in each area or city given in the previous census; for the latter part of the decade, we have used the figures from the census at the end of the decade.

(b) The data are based on a sociological study which in turn was based on a sample, including employees in 120 factories, administrative offices, cultural institutions and the like. The sample totalled 13,707 individuals, of whom 1.2% were Jews.

(c) For Dagestan and its capital city, Makhachkala, marriages between Jews and Tats — in Soviet usage, synonymous with Mountain Jews — were considered as "Jewish" (i.e., endogamous) marriages.

(d) For the purposes of the study, 1,000 ZAGS forms were examined from the Oktiabr' raion, in the city's oldest part, and another 1,000 from the Kuibyshev raion, in the city's newest section. The forms were chosen according to the order of their registration on January 1, 1962. Wherever the first set of 1,000 presented difficulties, another 1,000 were checked. Over 5,000 forms were examined in all.

(e) Jews of the entire city.

in the Ukraine, 33.5 percent were exogamous unions. Table 2.5 shows the percentages of mixed marriages.

TABLE 2.5

PERCENTAGES OF MIXED MARRIAGES AMONG ALL MARRIAGES
INVOLVING AT LEAST ONE JEWISH PARTNER

AREA	PERCENTAGE
Estonia (1965,1968)	76.7
Belorussia (1975)	54.8
Latvia (1960–64)	52.3
Ukraine (1969)	51.5
Khar'kov (1960)	45.9
Dagestan ASSR (1967)	34.9
Makhachkala (1959–68)	27.7
Tashkent (1962)	34.2

The data indicate discrepancies in the proportion of intermarriage among Jews dwelling in the various regions of the Soviet Union, a fact that has to be taken into account in any estimate of intermarriage within the Soviet Jewish community as a whole. In order to reach such an estimate, we shall divide the Soviet Jewish community into three geographic (administrative) areas:

Area 1: The Latvian, Lithuanian, Moldavian, Belorussian, and Ukrainian SSRs together with the RSFSR, excluding the autonomous republics (because of the population of mountain Jews in the autonomous republics of the RSFSR, all Jews living there will be included in area 2).[13] There is reason to assume that the percentage of intermarriage involving Jews is lower in the Lithuanian SSR and especially in Moldavia than it is in the Ukraine and in Belorussia, This, however, is offset by the higher intermarriage rate in the RSFSR. Accordingly, we shall apply the average percentage of intermarriage occurring in Belorussia, Latvia, the Ukraine, and Khar'kov to all the Jews resident in this area.

Area 2: Eight Union Republics (Uzbekistan, Georgia, Azerbaidzhan, Kazakhstan, Tadzhikistan, Kirghizia, Turkmenia, and Armenia) and the autonomous republics of the RSFSR. For this area we shall apply the average percentage of intermarriage occurring in Tashkent, Dagestan, and the city of Makhachkala.

Area 3: The Estonian SSR, where the Jewish community is very small, but its especially high intermarriage rate should be considered separately.

Weighting the computation of the national average of Jewish intermarriage according to the percentage share of each area in the Soviet Jewish population, we arrive at a figure of 48.6 mixed marriages for every

TABLE 2.6

PERCENTAGE OF MIXED MARRIAGES AMONG ALL MARRIAGES INVOLVING AT LEAST ONE
JEWISH PARTNER, FOR SPECIFIED CATEGORIES OF SOVIET REPUBLICS

AREA [a]	PERCENTAGE OF SOVIET JEWRY		PERCENTAGE OF MIXED MARRIAGES
	1959	1970	
1	86.8	85.5	51.1
2	12.9	14.3	32.3
3	0.3	0.2	76.7

(a) See text.

100 involving at least one Jewish spouse (table 2.6). Because this is only a
calculated estimate, however, we should say that for every 100 marriages in
the Soviet Union involving at least one Jewish partner through the
mid-1970s, between 40 and 50 were mixed. It therefore appears that the
percentage of mixed marriages in the Soviet Jewish community during this
period approximated the percentages prevailing in some Western Jewish
communities.[14]

Nationality as a Factor in Choice of Spouse

Among the many interrelated factors influencing choice of mate
(including sexual compatibility, social status, and level of education) in
multiethnic societies, the nationality of the mate also plays a role. An
attempt to measure the effect of nationality on mate selection was made by
the Soviet ethnographers O. Gantskaia and G. Debets, who examined
marriage forms in *ZAGS* submitted between 1945 and 1964 in the Novaia
Vil'nia *raion* of the city of Vil'nius. They compared the actual and the
expected frequencies of endogamous marriages. Their hypothesis was that
theoretically, with the influence of nationality factor out, the frequency of
marriage between Jewish males and Jewish females should be equal to the
percentage of Jewish grooms among all grooms multiplied by the
percentage of Jewish brides among all brides. The data presented by
Gantskaia and Debets are for the most part graphs of percentage distributions; only for 1948 are frequencies also presented. In that year, 0.318
percent of all bridegrooms were Jewish, as were 0.254 percent of all brides.
The expected percentage of marriages between Jewish brides and grooms
was 0.08 percent. The actual frequency of endogamous marriages among
the Jews in the Novaia Vil'nia *raion* that year, however, was 2.54 percent.
Gantskaia and Debets suggest that the influence of nationality on mate
selection can be measured by calculating the ratio of the expected and the
observed frequencies of endogamous marriages. The larger is the difference
between the expected and the observed frequencies, the stronger is the effect

of nationality on mate selection.[15] I have used this method to examine the influence of nationality on the selection of a Jewish mate in the areas for which we have data (table 2.7).

TABLE 2.7

OBSERVED AND EXPECTED PERCENTAGES OF ENDOGAMOUS JEWISH MARRIAGES
IN SELECTED AREAS

AREA AND PERIOD	EXPECTED	OBSERVED	RATIO $\frac{\text{OBSERVED}}{\text{EXPECTED}}$
Estonia (1965)	0.01	0.12	12:1
Estonia (1968)	0.01	0.13	13:1
Khar'kov (1960)	0.34	4.07	12:1
Makhachkala (1959–68)	0.32	4.76	15:1
Belorussia (1975)	0.19	3.07	16:1
Vil'nius:			
Novaia Vil'nia raion (1945–64)	0.03	1.30	43:1
Dagestan ASSR (1967)	0.02	1.00	50:1

Sources: As for Table 2.4 and O. Ganskaia, G Debets, 1966.

The observed proportion of endogamous marriages is greater than the expected in all areas examined. It would seem that on balance, Soviet Jewry is endogamous rather than exogamous, though the strength of this tendency varies by area and is everywhere quite low. Overall, rates of intermarriage are high though considerably less than what they would be under conditions of random mate selection. There appear to be two characteristic groups of ratios. The first, seen in Vil'nius and Dagestan ASSR, show a ratio of more than 40:1 between observed and expected percentages of endogamous marriage. Relative to other areas, there appears to be a tendency to avoid intermarriage. The other areas show much lower ratios—16:1 or less. It is presumed on the basis of the data presented here that Makhachkala has a higher proportion of European Jews than the rest of Dagestan ASSR, which accounts for its higher rate of intermarriage.

A related method of measuring the influence of any factor on the selection of a mate—nationality in our case—may be examined by means of marriage index as well.[16] If the observed rate of endogamous marriages exceeds its theoretical probability, an attraction among members of a single national group is said to exist; if the observed rate is smaller than the theoretical (smaller than zero), we may speak of rejection. Such a "marriage index" may therefore allow us to measure quantitatively the strength of nationality as a factor of influence in selection of mate.

Soviet statistician and demographer Mikhail Ptukha proposed his own marriage index formula in a methodological article published in 1922.[17] Soviet demographers, reconsidering the subject of marriage in the 1960s, put Ptukha's formula to use for measuring the impact of nationality upon selection of mate.[18] Data on the influence of nationality on selection of mates, compiled by the Ptukha method, appeared in print concerning the entire Ukraine (1969), the Ukrainian capital of Kiev (1970), and Kishinev, capital of Moldavia (1950, 1971, 1980). Because the Ukraine and Moldavia were home to more than one-third of all Jews in the Soviet Union, we might study other data by the same method and further explore the variations in impact of the nationality factor upon selection of mate among Jews in the various republics (table 2.8).

TABLE 2.8

MARRIAGE INDICES OF JEWS BY SELECTED AREA AND PERIOD

AREA	PERIOD	MARRIAGE INDEX
Kishinev	1950, 1971, 1980	+88.3
Makhachkala	1959–1968	+83.0
Dagestan ASSR	1967	+79.1
Belorussia	1975	+69.9
Khar'kov	1960	+68.5
Ukraine	1969	+66.3
Kiev	1970	+56.1

Sources: As for Table 2.4, and: *Vliianie sotsial'no-ekonomicheskikh faktorov na demograficheskie protsessy* (Kiev, 1972), pp. 65–66; L. Chuiko, "Opyt analiza mezhnatsional'nykh brakov v SSSR," *Razvitie naseleniia* (Moscow, 1974), pp. 47–54; V. Naulko, *Razvitie mezhetnicheskikh sviazei na Ukraine* (Kiev, 1975), p. 151; A. Susokolov, A. Novitskaia, "Etnicheskaia i sotsial'no-professional'naia gomogennost' brakov," *Sovetskaia etnografia*, No. 6 (1981), pp. 14–26.

The figures indicate that the Jews of Kishinev were attracted to spouses within their own group by a factor of 1.5 times greater than were the Jews of Kiev and 1.3 times greater than the Jews of the Ukraine as a whole. Moreover, despite variations in the influence of nationality as a factor in selection of mates among Jews in the different republics, we should note that the tendency of Jews to pursue endogamous marriage is greater than that of some of the major nationality groups in their union republics.[19] The Jews' rejection of marriage with members of other national groups is substantial as well, as the indexes on marriages of Jewish men and women with Russians and Ukrainians illustrate (table 2.9).

Table 2.9 illustrates that the rejection factor with regard to marriage of Jewish men and women with members of other national groups is rather strong in most republics and cities for which we have data (with the

TABLE 2.9

MARRIAGE INDICES BY SELECTED NATIONALITY, AREA, PERIOD, AND SEX

AREA	PERIOD	JEWISH MALES WITH ...		JEWISH FEMALES WITH ...	
		RUSSIAN	UKRAINIAN	RUSSIAN	UKRAINIAN
Kishinev	1950, 1971, 1980	−77.7	−87.7	−86.7	−91.7
Makhachkala	1959–1968	−71.6	−64.6	−87.2	−76.9
Dagestan ASSR	1967	−8.7	−48.5	−52.7	−47.8
Belorussia	1975	−47.1	−58.8	−62.3	−69.6
Khar'kov	1970	−67.6	−78.4	−58.7	−71.9
Ukraine	1969	−18.9	−77.1	−38.0	−79.5
Kiev	1970	−26.3	−73.8	−57.3	−85.7
Estonia	1965, 1968	+78.7	+40.8	+10.7	−15.1

Sources: See Table 2.8.

exception of Estonia). Ukrainians in most cases are more rejected than
Russians as marriage partners. Jewish women reject marriage with non-
Jews, whether Russian or Ukrainian, more strongly than Jewish men reject
Russian and Ukrainian women (in all localities apart from Khar'kov).
Furthermore, the index confirms a phenomenon that we have previously
noted (and is evident in Jewish communities in other countries): that
marriages involving Jewish men and non-Jewish women are more commonplace than marriages between Jewish women and men of another
nationality. As a practical consequence, most offspring of families in which
one parent is Jewish are registered as non-Jews, a fact that almost certainly
affects official registrations and census data.

National Definition of Offspring of Mixed Marriages

The matter of the ethnic identification of children in families where there
is only one Jewish parent is of prime concern to our study. In the Soviet
Union, this becomes a matter of official record, and the national identity of
members of mixed families is finally determined when young people are
issued their first internal passports at the age of 16.[20] The sources of
information on the topic are the police stations where each passport
applicant fills out a form (Form 1) that requires the listing of parents'
respective nationalities together with the applicant's choice.[21]

Data concerning the choice of nationality among 16 year olds of mixed
Russian-Jewish parentage relate to the following cities: (1) a sample
consisting of about 40 percent of Form 1 (filled out by first-time passport
applicants) in two police stations (of a total of four or five) in the cities of
Vil'nius, Riga, and Tallin between 1960 and 1968;[22] (2) figures based on
examination of 30 percent of Form 1 filled out at the Ordzhonikidze

municipal police stations and the forms of all recipients of first internal passports in the city of Cherkessk between 1960 and 1968;[23] and (3) two sources for the city of Makhachkala, one based on examination of 90 percent of Form 1 submitted at the police station of that city between 1960 and 1968 and the other consisting of complete absolute numbers concerning the national definition of the offspring of mixed marriages between 1965 and 1969. With regard to Makhachkala, table 2.10 provides average data based on the two sources.[24]

TABLE 2.10

DECLARATION OF NATIONALITY BY THE OFFSPRING
OF MIXED RUSSIAN-JEWISH COUPLES (PERCENTAGES)

CITY	PERIOD	DECLARING JEWISH NATIONALITY	DECLARING RUSSIAN NATIONALITY
Makhachkala	1960–1969	28.4	71.6
Vil'nius	1960–1968	14.0	86.0
Tallin	"	10.0	90.0
Riga	"	6.7	93.3
Ordzhonikidze	"	–	100.0
Cherkessk	"	–	100.0

Sources: G. Sergeeva and Ia. Smirnova, "K voprosa o natsional'nom samosoznanii gorodskoi molodezhi" *Sovetskaia etnografiia*, No.4 (1971), pp. 86–92; *Sovremennaia Kul'tura i byt naradov dagestana* (Moscow, 1971), p. 188.

Although the data are not sufficient to estimate the percentage of mixed marriage offspring registered in internal passports as Jews, we may reasonably assert that a large majority of these youth (most with Jewish fathers and Russian mothers, the most common combination) are registered as Russians. The percentage of youth in the Jewish community of the Soviet Union is therefore declining as indicated in current Soviet statistics and in population census results.

Family Composition and Size

The tabulations on endogamous and mixed marriages within the Soviet Jewish community pertain to marriages registered over a limited time frame. Information on the percentage of uninational or multinational families, by contrast, is derived by the cumulative recording of marriages over a long period of time. Furthermore, the data cited concerning the marriages of Jews are derived from *ZAGS* statistics (information recorded in official documents), whereas data concerning families are based on population censuses (declarations).

The term *family* may be defined differently in various Soviet publications, with its meaning determined in each case according to the nature and purpose of the study in question. In population censuses, the family unit is conventionally defined by a measure of economics that is, a joint budget or regular, permanent economic relations.[25] Although the Soviets use the term *family* for this social unit, because of the economic definition, the term may refer to couples, nuclear families, and extended-family arrangements. We therefore shall use the term *household* as an all-inclusive equivalent to the Soviet terminology, retaining its economic connotation as well. With regard to nationality, Soviet households are classified as uninational and multinational. Each one, according to census questionnaires, must have a head of household, either a man or a woman as determined by the family itself. When a family has difficulty determining its head, the person who provides the greatest input to the household budget is chosen; thus, an economic criterion is used.

Mean Household (Family) Size

The average size of the Soviet household was found to be 3.7 individuals in the censuses of 1959 and 1970 and 3.5 in the 1979 census (corresponding figures for the urban population: 3.5 in 1959 and 1970, 3.3 in 1979; for the rural population: 3.9 in 1959, 4.0 in 1970 and 3.8 in 1979). Average household size, however, varies in different parts of the Soviet Union and among different national groups. Table 2.11 charts average household size by nationality of the head of household (1959 census findings).

TABLE 2.11

**MEAN HOUSEHOLD SIZE,
BY NATIONALITY OF THE HEAD OF HOUSEHOLD, 1959**

NATIONALITY	PERSONS	NATIONALITY	PERSONS
Estonian, Latvian	3.1	Tatar	4.1
Jewish	3.2	Kazakh, Kirgiz, Armenian	4.6
Lithuanian, Russian Ukrainian	3.6	Azerbaidzhani	4.8
Belorussian	3.7	Turkmen, Uzbek	4.9
Moldavian	3.9	Tadzhik	5.0
Georgian	4.0		

Source: V. Urlanis, *Rozhdaemost' i prodolzhitel'nost' zhizni v SSSR* (Moscow, 1963), p. 72.

Households headed by Jews were, on the average, smaller than most of those of other ethnic groups as early as the 1959 census, though this figure is only an average and does not reflect the situation in all republics. The

Jewish household in Georgia almost certainly exceeded the national average, and there was no uniformity of size in the European republics either (for example, a figure of 3.3 individuals in Latvia).[26]

TABLE 2.12

MEAN SIZE OF UNI-NATIONAL JEWISH HOUSEHOLDS,
BY REPUBLIC, 1970, 1979

REPUBLIC	MEAN HOUSEHOLD SIZE		REPUBLIC	MEAN HOUSEHOLD SIZE	
	1970	1979		1970	1979
RSFSR	3.1	2.9	Moldavia	3.2	–
Ukraine	3.1	2.9	Belorussia	3.3	3.0

Calculated from Table 2C.

The 1970 census data pertaining to households are based on the sampling questionnaire, which was distributed to about one-quarter of the population. The Bureau of Statistics in each SSR determined the main national groups dwelling in the respective republics and each national group's areas of residence. The sample data, though applying to these national groups and these alone and pertaining only to those principal areas of residence (which were never identified), were projected onto the general population of each respective national group. The Bureau of Statistics of four SSRs (RSFSR, the Ukraine, Belorussia, and Moldavia) listed the Jews as one of the major peoples residing in those republics. In only two SSRs (Belorussia and Moldavia) and the Jewish autonomous *oblast'* (Birobidzhan), however, were the samples broadened to cover all Jews dwelling in the respective republics; in the other republics (RSFSR and the Ukraine), the data relate to certain areas that were not identified.

The size of the uninational Jewish household, too, varies to a certain extent among the republics, as the 1970 and 1979 census data illustrate (table 2.12; see also tables 2C and 2D).

The scattered findings from the 1970 and 1979 censuses on household size among Jews indicate that Jewish households decreased in average size over the course of that decade in the three SSRs (RSFSR, the Ukraine, and Belorussia). In 1970, two-member households constituted 36.6 percent of all uninational Jewish households in these republics, whereas the corresponding figure for 1979 was 43.7 percent (a relative increase of 19.4 percent). At the same time, households of four or more persons decreased from 32.9 percent of the total to only 25.6 percent—a relative decline of 22.2 percent (see table 2D).

The Soviet findings concerning the size of uninational Jewish households

Appendix tables 2A-2E appear at the end of this chapter.

(from the 1970 and 1979 censuses) and households headed by Jews (from the 1959 census) are consistent with data on the size of households among Soviet immigrants to Israel. The size of these immigrant households was determined by criteria similar to those used in the Soviet Union. Available data relate to all of 1971 and from August 1972 until the end of December 1975, a period during which close to 86,000 immigrants reached Israel from the Soviet Union. The 1971 arrivals were divided into two groups— Ashkenazi and Georgian Jews—and those arriving between August 1972 and December 1975 were sorted into three groups—Ashkenazi, Georgian, and Bukharian Jews (table 2.13).[27]

TABLE 2.13

MEAN SIZE OF SOVIET JEWISH IMMIGRANT HOUSEHOLDS IN ISRAEL,
BY CULTURAL BACKGROUND, 1971, 1972–1975

PERIOD	CULTURAL BACKGROUND		
	ASHKENAZI	GEORGIAN	BUKHARIAN
1971	3.2	4.0	–
August 1972–December 1975	3.1	3.7	4.4

The 1970 census data on average Jewish household size, corroborated by data on the immigrants, indicate correlation in many cases between household size and changes in the size of the Jewish community in several SSRs.

By citing an average household size of 3.1 or 3.2 individuals, I do not mean to assert that each household had an average of 1.1 or 1.2 children. In certain households one or both parents of one or both spouses were residing together and running a joint household; in others, divorced, widowed, or unmarried women together with their children constitute household units. This notwithstanding, it is fair to say that Jewish fertility is greater and the age structure consequently younger in those republics in which the average Jewish household is larger.

Uninational and Multinational Jewish Households

Since data on Jewish and mixed-Jewish households are sketchy, we must resort to indirect calculation techniques to arrive at even rough estimates. First, however, I should clarify the terms I shall use. A *uninational Jewish household* (as this term is defined in the Soviet Union) is one in which every member has declared himself or herself Jewish in the census. A *multinational Jewish household* is one in which declarations of nationality in the census are not all the same and at least one of whose members is identified as Jewish. *Household members living separately* are individuals who live apart but maintain regular economic relations with their households. *Individuals* are people with no household ties.

The few data on the Jewish household consist of the following (table 2.14): the uninational Jewish household in the Ukraine, based on a 5 percent sample from the 1959 census;[28] the number of uninational Jewish households in Belorussia, Moldavia, and Birobidzhan in 1970 and the number of individuals living in these households (see table 2C).

In the light of the paucity of data, I shall try to estimate the number of mixed households by the elimination method. I shall make two assumptions to this end: (1) that the percentages of household members living separately and of individuals among the Jews are equivalent to the corresponding values for the total population of the republic in question, and (2) that the mean size of the multinational Jewish household is identical to the mean size of the uninational Jewish household or of households headed by Jews.

TABLE 2.14

DIVISION OF THE JEWISH POPULATION AMONG PERSONS LIVING WITH THEIR HOUSEHOLDS AND THOSE LIVING APART, FOR SELECTED AREAS

CENSUS	AREA	JEWISH POPULATION TOTAL	NOT LIVING IN HOUSEHOLD [a]	LIVING IN A HOUSEHOLD
1959	Ukraine	840,314	85,292	755,022
1970	Belorussia	148,011	16,237	131,774
"	Moldavia	98,072	8,532	89,540
"	Jewish Autonomous oblast'	11,452	1,318	10,134

(a) Includes "persons living apart from their households" and "individuals." The percentages of those two groups in the total population were calculated from *Itogi, 1959,* Ukraine volume, Table 59 and *Itogi, 1970,* vol. 7, Table 22.

On the basis of these figures, then, we shall examine the distribution of those Jews who live either in uninational or in multinational Jewish households (table 2.15).

Every multinational Jewish household has at least one Jew or one non-Jew. We may therefore divide the number of Jews who dwell in multinational households by the average size of the uninational Jewish household less 1 (one non-Jew), the result being the minimum number of mixed-Jewish households (or, in Soviet terminology, mixed families). If, however, we assume that every mixed-Jewish household has only one Jew, the number of Jews living in multinational household is equal to the number of multinational households (table 2.16).

If these assumptions are correct, for every 100 households in which at least one resident member declared himself or herself a Jew for census

TABLE 2.15

JEWISH POPULATION LIVING IN HOUSEHOLDS, BY TYPE OF HOUSEHOLD,
FOR SELECTED AREAS

		UNI-NATIONAL		MULTI-NATIONAL	
CENSUS	AREA	NUMBER OF PERSONS	PERCENTAGE	NUMBER OF PERSONS	PERCENTAGE
1959	Ukraine [a]	636,477	84.3	118,545	15.7
1970	Belorussia [b]	114,705	87.0	17,069	13.0
"	Moldavia [b]	85,728	95.7	3,812	4.3
"	Jewish Autonomous oblast' [b]	7,786	76.8	2,348	23.2

(a) The 1959 census indicates, for the Ukrainian SSR, 4,842,664 urban and 5,784,535 rural households (*Itogi, 1959,* Ukraine volume, Table 59). Of these, 3,569,043 urban households were uni-national (73.7%), as were 5,449,032 rural households (94.2%). There were 199,866 urban Jewish uni-national households (5.6% of the total), and 5,449 rural households of this type (0.1%). From the sample data discussed here it appears that in 1959 there were 205,315 uni-national Jewish households, with 3.1 persons per household, on the average (Naulko, 1965, pp. 110, 111).

(b) The data on Belorussia, Moldavia, and the Jewish Autonomous oblast' were computed from Table 2C.

TABLE 2.16

JEWISH UNI-NATIONAL AND MULTI-NATIONAL HOUSEHOLDS

CENSUS	REPUBLIC	NUMBER OF UNI-NATIONAL HOUSEHOLDS	NUMBER OF MULTI-NATIONAL HOUSEHOLDS	MULTI-NATIONAL HOUSEHOLDS PER 100 UNI-NATIONAL HOUSEHOLDS
1959	Ukraine	205,315	56,450–118,545	28–58
1970	Belorussia	34,759	7,421–17,069	21–49
"	Moldavia	26,790	1,733–3,812	7–14
"	Jewish Autonomous oblast'	2,290	939–2,348	41–103

purposes, there were 21.6 to 36.6 multinational Jewish households in the Ukraine (1959), 6.1 to 12.5 in Moldavia (1970), 17.6 to 32.9 in Belorussia (1970), and 29.0 to 50.6 in the Jewish autonomous *oblast'* (Birobidzhan).

The figures also indicate that the percentage of multinational Jewish households among all households in which at least one member was recorded as a Jew was approximately three times greater in the Ukraine in 1959 than it was in Moldavia in 1970. In 1970, the percentage of mixed households among all households in which at least one member declared himself or herself Jewish for census purposes was in Belorussia more than 2.5 times greater—and in the Jewish autonomous *oblast'* (Birobidzhan) roughly 4.5 times greater—than the percentage of mixed households in Moldavia.

The differences among the republics with respect to the distribution of uninational and multinational Jewish households also expresses itself in data on the offspring of Jewish mothers and non-Jewish fathers. A study undertaken in the Ukraine on the basis of *ZAGS* birth records has revealed that about 20.6 of every 100 births by Jewish women between 1958 and 1961 involved non-Jewish fathers. An identical study conducted in Moldavia between 1959 and 1965 showed that 8.3 of every 100 births by Jewish women involved non-Jewish fathers.[29] It is therefore apparent that the birth of children involving Jewish mothers and non-Jewish fathers was 2.5 times more frequent in the Ukraine than in Moldavia. Because most children of multinational parentage are registered as non-Jews, development in this regard will influence the growth or decline of the Jewish population in these republics.

Since the frequency of intermarriages appears to have increased—at least through the mid-1970s—the percentage of mixed couples is higher in the younger age brackets—those at the peak of their fertility—than in the older age brackets.

A survey conducted in one of the cities of the RSFSR under semiunderground conditions by Zionist activists in the Soviet Union during the mid-1970s corroborates this assumption. In this survey, the sex, age, and family situation (uninational and multinational couples) of 803 Jews were studied (table 2.17). Although this study, conducted under irregular conditions in one city in the RSFSR, cannot serve as a basis for estimating the number of binational couples among Jewish households, it does hint

TABLE 2.17

MARITAL STATUS AND TYPE OF MARRIAGE BY SEX AND AGE:
GROUP OF URBAN JEWS, RSFSR (PERCENTAGES)

AGE	SEX, MARITAL STATUS AND TYPE OF MARRIAGE					
	MALE			FEMALE		
	SINGLE	JEWISH SPOUSE	NON-JEWISH SPOUSE	SINGLE	JEWISH SPOUSE	NON-JEWISH SPOUSE
20–29	53.5	20.7	25.8	55.7	27.3	17.0
30–39	6.5	52.0	41.5	22.1	58.3	19.6
40–49	4.8	58.2	37.0	10.6	76.7	12.7
50–59	–	62.7	37.3	5.7	71.6	22.7
60+	–	82.0	18.0	1.8	94.4	3.8

Source: I. Akharon (Izidor Liast), "Issledovaniia demograficheskikh osobennostei evreiskogo naseleniia SSSR," *Evreiskii samizdat* (1978) vol. 15, p. 166.

that the percentage of such couples in the younger age brackets is consistently rising. We may therefore say that the influence of intermarriage on the diminishing numbers of Jews in the Soviet Union has progressively grown, at least through the mid-1970s.

Fertility and Natural Increase

The post-World War II period witnessed a considerable increase in fertility in most European countries, known as the baby boom. As a consequence of the heavy losses that the male population in the Soviet Union absorbed during the war, the harsh economic situation, and the mass expulsions undertaken in the latter half of the 1940s, fertility in the Soviet Union not only failed to rise after the war but actually seems to have fallen relative to the war years.[30] Although fertility registered an increase in the 1950s, the rate resumed its downward trend in the 1960s.[31] The general trends probably affected the Jewish population as well. I shall therefore mention a number of general demographic phenomena relevant to the subject.

First, there is considerable interregional variation in the crude birthrate (table 2.18). The range for 1960 was a low of 16.6 births per 1,000 persons in Estonia to a high of 42.6 in Azerbaidzhan. These discrepancies persisted into the 1960s as well. In 1970, crude birthrates varied from 14.5 in Latvia to 34.8 in Tadzhikistan.[32] The prominent Soviet demographer V. Urlanis notes that a birthrate of 16-20 per 1,000 is very low, hardly enough to maintain current population size.[33] A decisive majority of Jews in the Soviet Union therefore appears to dwell in areas of low birthrates.

Second, the general fertility rate (births per 1,000 women in the 15-49 age bracket) is lower in the urban than in the rural population.[34] Furthermore,

TABLE 2.18

CRUDE·BIRTHRATE IN THE USSR BY REPUBLIC
1959–1960, 1965–1969

BIRTHRATE	REPUBLIC	PERCENTAGE OF SOVIET JEWRY, 1959
11–15	Latvia, Estonia	1.85
16–20	RSFSR, Ukraine, Belorussia, Lithuania	83.35
21–25	Georgia, Moldavia	6.47
26–30	Kazakhstan, Armenia	1.29
31–40	Uzbekistan, Azerbaidzhan, Kirgizia, Tadzhikistan, Turkmenia	7.04

Source: *Vestnik statistiki,* No 2 (1975), p. 87.

the fertility rate appears to fluctuate in inverse ratio to the size of the city in question; it is lower in larger cities than in medium or small ones.[35] The lowest fertility rates in the Soviet Union are those of Moscow and Leningrad.[36] Because a majority of Jews dwell in large cities, we have reason to surmise that the fertility of Jewish women is similarly affected.

A third factor that exerts great influence on fertility rates is spouses' and particularly wives' education levels.[37] Peter Mazur, who examined fertility rates in the Soviet Union in 1959 with regard to four variables (percentage of women in the 16-54 age bracket with low educational attainment; male-female education discrepancies; percentage of nonworking women, and percentage of marriages among women aged 16 or over) reached the conclusion that "for the urban sector of this region [the European USSR, where family planning is practiced] the most substantial proportion of the total variation in fertility is explained by education of women."[38] In other words, as the percentage of women with higher education among all women in a community rises, the fertility rate in that community drops.[39] Because discrepancies exist among the various republics with regard to the percentage of Jews with higher education, we have reason to assume that the fertility rates of Jewish women in those republics are similarly affected.

Fourth, the number of children per family is a function of mothers' social stratum, as data in table 2.19 (from the 1970 census) demonstrate. Inasmuch as most Jewish women are white-collar workers (*sluzhashchie*), the birthrates of Jewish mothers are almost certainly among the USSR's lowest.

TABLE 2.19

NUMBER OF CHILDREN PER 1,000 MOTHERS, BY SOCIAL STRATA OF MOTHER

OCCUPATION	URBAN POPULATION	RURAL POPULATION
Total	1,684	2,344
Laborers	1,774	2,377
Members of kolkhozes	–	2,437
White collar workers	1,537	1,918

Source: V. Boldyrev, *Itogi perepisi naseleniia SSSR* (Moscow, 1974), p. 38.

Fifth, surveys taken in certain parts of the Soviet Union have shown that the number of children desired is inversely related to family income.[40] Because a large proportion of the Soviet Jewish population falls into above-average income strata, we have reason to suppose that this factor too affects the fertility of Jewish women.

Finally, although the practice of family planning has lessened in importance as a major factor in fertility, women's age upon marriage still exerts an influence.[41] Jewish women, on the average, are older upon marriage than non-Jewish women in the overall urban population, as the data in table 2.20 (1970 census) indicate.

TABLE 2.20

PROPORTION OF MARRIED WOMEN IN THE JEWISH AND TOTAL URBAN POPULATION, BY AGE AND REPUBLIC, 1970
(Per 1,000 women in the relevant population)

| REPUBLIC | AGE | | | | | |
| | 16–19 | | 20–29 | | 30–39 | |
	JEWISH	TOTAL	JEWISH	TOTAL	JEWISH	TOTAL
Mean	48	76	556	650	834	834
Ukraine	57	89	569	679	825	848
Belorussia	34	58	510	646	819	849
Moldavia	63	91	606	667	873	848
Latvia	37	66	538	609	820	791

Calculated from Table 2B and *Itogi, 1970*, vol. 2, Table 6.

In those republics for which we have information, the percentage of Jewish women who are married at age 16-29 is lower than the percentage of all urban women who are married in this age bracket, though Jewish and non-Jewish women in the 30-39 age bracket prove equal in this regard. If we assume identical rates of widowhood and divorce for Jewish and non-Jewish urban women, about 184 women per every 1,000 who reached the age of 39 by the 1970 census had married while in the 30-39 age bracket, as opposed to 278 Jewish women who had done so, yielding a ratio of 1.5:1. If a woman's age upon marriage influences the number of children she bears, the fertility of Jewish women in Soviet cities is lower than that of the general urban female population in the areas under study.

Before examining the few figures at hand concerning the Jews' natural increase and age structure, we should reemphasize that these data reflect not only purely biological changes but the results of acculturation and the consequences of intermarriage as well.

Although no comprehensive data have been made public concerning crude birthrates within the Soviet Jewish community, the fragments of information at hand may enable us to reach a rough estimate.

U. Schmelz, relying on data concerning the age structure of the Jewish population in the RSFSR (according to the 1970 census) and the application of a life table representing a plausible mortality level, derived a mean crude birthrate of 6.0 per 1,000 for the Jews in the RSFSR in the 1959-1970 intercensus period.[42]

Khar'kov oblast', according to the 1959 census, was home to 84,192 Jews

(10 percent of the Jews in the Ukraine all told). Eight hundred children born in Khar'kov *oblast'* during 1960 were registered as Jews, yielding an average crude birthrate of 9.5 per 1,000 for that year, a figure that may be applied to the Ukraine as a whole.[43]

A total of 41.0 children were born per 1,000 Jewish females in Uzbekistan in 1959.[44] Since the 1959 census reported 50,650 Jewish females in Uzbekistan, 2,127 Jewish children were born in Uzbekistan that year. Because the census of that year reported 94,344 Jews in Uzbekistan, the Jewish community in that republic registered a crudé birthrates of 22.6 per 1,000.

The crude birthrate for the Jews of Moldavia may be derived from statistics pertaining to the crude birthrate of five other national groups (table 2.21).

TABLE 2.21

CRUDE BIRTHRATE IN MOLDAVIA, BY NATIONALITY, 1970

NATIONALITY	CRUDE BIRTHRATE	POPULATION	NUMBER OF BIRTHS [a]
Total	19.4	3,568,873	69,236
Gagauzian	21.1	124,902	2,635
Moldavian	20.6	2,303,916	47,461
Bulgarian	17.9	73,776	1,321
Ukrainian	17.5	506,560	8,865
Russian	15.4	414,444	6,382
Jewish	*	98,072	*
Other	*	47,203	*

Source: V. Zelenchuk, *Naselenie Moldavii*, (Kishinev, 1975), p. 44.

*   Not available.

(a) Calculated by the author.

Since the number of births in the five national groups for which crude birthrate figures are supplied is 66,664, the number of birth among the Jews and the other national groups is 2,572. By assuming that the crude birthrate for the other national groups was equivalent to the average for Moldavia (19.4 per 1,000), we arrive at a figure of 916 children of "other" nationalities. The remaining births in Moldavia in 1970—1,656—were therefore Jewish children—a crude birthrate of 16.9 per 1,000.

The data on crude birthrates are not uniform. Schmelz's calculation with regard to the RSFSR is an annual average for an eleven-year period; the data pertaining to Khar'kov apply to 1960, those for Uzbekistan to 1959, and those for Moldavia to 1970. In order to arrive at a common denominator we must take the changes in crude birthrate during the 1960s into account. We have therefore assumed that the crude birthrates of the Jewish population have changed in measures identical to those in the general population of each republic, as the data in table 2.22 illustrate.

TABLE 2.22

CRUDE BIRTHRATES IN THE JEWISH AND TOTAL POPULATION,
FOR SELECTED REPUBLICS AND DATES

	CRUDE BIRTHRATE	
REPUBLIC AND DATE	TOTAL POPULATION [a]	JEWISH POPULATION
Ukraine		
1960	20.5	9.5
1969	14.7	6.7 [b]
Uzbekistan		
1959	37.2	22.6
1969	32.7	19.9 [b]
Moldavia		
1970	19.4	16.9

(a) On the changes in the crude birth rates by republic, see *Vestnik statistiki,* No 2 (1971), p. 87.

(b) Reconstructed estimate.

The annual mean crude birthrate for the Jewish population during the intercensus period (1959-1970) was 8.1 per 1,000 in the Ukraine and 21.3 in Uzbekistan. With regard to Moldavia, we shall project the 1970 rate over the entire period.

To arrive at an estimated crude birthrate for the Jews of the entire Soviet Union, we should divide the country into at least four regions:

a) RSFSR

b) Uzbekistan, Georgia, and Azerbaidzhan

c) Moldavia

d) The remaining ten republics of the USSR

We arrive therefore at an estimated mean crude birthrate for Soviet Jewry as a whole during the intercensus period (1959-1970) of 8.9 per 1,000 (table 2.23). If the mortality rate Schmelz calculated for the Jews of the RSFSR (15.5 per 1,000) is roughly applied to the Soviet Jewish population as a whole and assuming that the mean crude birthrate of 8.9 per 1,000 is correct as well, then the Jewish population declined during the eleven-year period by an annual average of 6.6 per 1,000. However, given the fluctuations of the birthrate across the various republics, we may also posit variations in

TABLE 2.23

ESTIMATE OF CRUDE BIRTHRATES OF JEWS BY REGION, 1959–1970

REGION	PERCENTAGE OF SOVIET JEWRY	CRUDE BIRTH–RATE
Mean	–	8.9
a	38.1	6.0
b	8.8	21.3
c	4.4	16.9
d	48.7	8.1

the age structure of the different Jewish populations, leading to differences in mortality rates too. The stated average of 15.5 per 1,000 is almost certainly too high. Moreover, my calculations of the mean crude birthrate was based on an assumed equivalency between the decline of this rate among Jews and the general population in each of the respective republics during the 1960s. Yet since the crude birthrate among Jews was already very low at the beginning of that decade, it is unlikely that the relative decrease in the Jewish birthrate was equivalent to that which occurred in the Soviet population in general. The estimate of 8.9 per 1,000 is therefore very conservative; a somewhat higher birthrate among Soviet Jews during the 1960s is consequently a fair assumption.

For our discussion of natural increase, a more detailed look at age distribution is essential in order to assess mortality rates and the potential for population growth. The reports of the 1959 census findings did not include data in this area. In the reports of the 1970 census, we find data only on the Jewish population of the RSFSR. By approaching the data through indirect methods, however, we can still arrive at an estimate of the Soviet Jewish community's age distribution in early 1959. Schmelz used a retroactive calculation based on the 1970 RSFSR figures.[45] In order to discover the age distribution for other republics in 1959, we can use data on education among Soviet Jews, which were published in both 1959 and 1970. The 1959 census reports made available statistics on the proportion of Jews (per 1,000 Jews in the population) in eight republics who had had seven or more years of schooling. From these figures it is simple to derive the absolute numbers of Jews with that educational level in those republics at that time.[46] In the summary reports of the 1970 census, comparative data from 1959 were also cited for five of the republics: the percentage of Jews over the age of 10 who had seven or more years of schooling.[47] Clearly, it is only in the over-10 age bracket that seven years of schooling may be attained, and therefore the 1959 figures cited in 1970 must have been based on the absolute number of those with seven or more years of schooling.

Thus, we can calculate that figure on the basis of the 1959 census reports. Following this procedure, we may classify the Soviet Jewish community as of 1959 into two age brackets: 0-9 and 10 or over (table 2.24).[48]

TABLE 2.24

JEWISH AND TOTAL URBAN POPULATION BY BROAD AGE GROUPS,
FOR SELECTED REPUBLICS, 1959

	FREQUENCY		PERCENTAGES			
	JEWISH 0-9	POPULATION 10+	JEWS 0-9	10+	URBAN POPULATION 0-9	10+
Mean	217,882	1,779,579	10.9	89.1	19.0	81.0
RSFSR	84,781	790,526	9.7	90.3	19.4	80.6
Ukraine	90,217	750,094	10.7	89.3	17.7	82.3
Belorussia	23,033	127,051	15.3	84.7	20.5	79.5
Moldavia	14,997	80,110	15.8	84.2	20.5	79.5
Latvia	4,794	31,798	13.1	86.9	14.6	85.4

According to Schmelz's estimates (which are based on the age structure in the RSFSR in 1970) the Jewish population of this republic displayed the distribution in 1959, shown in table 2.25. Schmelz's estimate as to the percentage of those aged 0-9 among all Jews in the RSFSR in 1959 approximates my own calculation very closely. However, his assertion that this age distribution is applicable to all the Jews of the Soviet Union and his conclusion that "the aging [process] among the Jews in the Ukraine and Belorussia was even more severe than that in the RSFSR" are not precise. The Jewish population of the RSFSR was older than that of any other republic for which we have direct or indirect statistics as early as 1959.

TABLE 2.25

ESTIMATE OF JEWISH POPULATION IN THE RSFSR BY AGE, 1959

AGE	PERCENTAGE	AGE	PERCENTAGE
0-4	3.9	29-38	14.9
5-8	3.5	39-48	15.6
9-18	9.9	49+	38.4
19-28	13.8		

Source: U. Schmelz, "Al baayot yesod ba-demografia shel yehudei brit– ha-moatsot", *Behinot*, No. 5 (1974), p. 47.

With regard to the age distribution of the Jewish population by sex, the data prove that boys and girls in the 0-9 bracket were almost equal in number. Because women outnumber men in the general population, however, the percentage of girls aged 0-9 among all Jewish females (9.85 percent) is lower than that of boys of the same age group among all Jewish males (12.35 percent).

The 1959 data concerning distribution of the Jewish population in five republics into two age groups relate to 88.1 percent of all Jews in the Soviet Union. Of the remainder, most dwelled in Asian republics (Uzbekistan, Georgia, Azerbaidzhan, and Kazakhstan) where the Jewish population is younger and crude birthrates higher. We may therefore say that children aged 0-9 accounted for at least 11 percent of all Jews in the Soviet Union in the 1959 census. The percentage of children in this age bracket was lower in the Jewish community than in the general urban Soviet population and lower than their weight in the general population of these republics. It is clear that the Jewish population is aging, a process especially acute in the RSFSR as the age distribution in this republic, according to the 1970 census, indicates (table 2.26).

TABLE 2.26

AGE DISTRIBUTION OF THE JEWS IN THE RSFSR, 1970

AGE	FREQUENCY	PERCENTAGE
Total	807,915	100.0
0-10	56,002	6.9
11-15	34,335	4.3
16-19	31,375	3.9
20-29	88,006	10.9
30-39	121,675	15.1
40-49	129,563	16.1
50-59	131,592	16.3
60+	213,379	26.5
Unknown	1,988	–

Source: *Itogi, 1970*, vol. 4, Table 33.

This age distribution explains both the severe aging of the Jewish population and consequently a high mortality rate. The resulting age structure, together with use of the Soviet life table, enabled Schmelz to conclude that average Jewish mortality in the RSFSR during the intercensus period reached 15.5 per 1,000 in the population.

The only empirical, nonreconstructed crude death rate available for the Jews relates to the Khar'kov *oblast'* for 1960, with 977 deaths of Jews recorded that year.[49] Since 1959 census data indicate a Jewish population of 84,192 in the *oblast'*, the crude death rate for 1960 was 11.6 per 1,000, as compared with a crude birthrate of 9.5 for that year. The negative balance of natural increase was thus 2.1 per 1,000 in the Khar'kov *oblast'*—lower than Schmelz's estimate for the Jews of the RSFSR but still negative.

If we assume that the mortality rate for the Jews of the Soviet Union between 1959 and 1970 approximated the average of Schmelz's estimates for the RSFSR and the empirical data gathered in the Khar'kov *oblast'* (13.5 per 1,000 with a crude birthrate of 8.9 per 1,000), the Jewish population once again may be said to be in a state of decline, at an average annual rate of 4.6 per 1,000.

In addition to the erosion caused by internal demographic processes, the Soviet Jewish community has dwindled as a consequence of emigration.

EMIGRATION

Although emigration figures are not made public in the Soviet Union, we can examine the dimensions of emigration according to sources published in the West, particularly in Israel. The first post-World War II population census (1959) was held when the process of repatriation to Poland had ended and when almost all Jews who left the Soviet Union did so on Israeli visas.[50] Although these data include some non-Jews (who, moreover, had declared themselves as such for census purposes), their exact number, certainly small, is unknown and is offset in part by Jews who emigrated on visas of other countries. Accordingly, our inquiry will treat all those who had exited the Soviet Union on Israeli visas as declared Jews for census purposes.

The 1960s (1959-1970) and the 1970s (1970-1979) evince markedly different pictures of Jewish emigration in terms of volume. A total of 9,052 Jews (an annual average of 823 individuals), or 0.4 percent of the Jewish population, left the Soviet Union between the 1959 census and early 1970.[51] The proportion of the elderly among the emigrants was especially high, resulting in a minimal demographic impact on the Soviet Jewish population. By contrast, 174,174 Jews (an annual average of 19,353), or 8.8 percent of all Jews in the Soviet Union, left the country between the census of 1970 and that of 1979 (see table 2E).[52] Another 88,280 Jews left the Soviet Union between the most recent census and the end of 1985 (an annual average of 12,611 individuals): 4.8 percent of the Jews enumerated in the census. This emigration has had a twofold effect: direct influence on the dwindling of the Soviet Jewish community and acceleration of demographic processes within that community.

These emigrants, like most other emigrant populations, are younger on the whole than the general Soviet Jewish population. This assumption may be corroborated by comparing the age structure of immigrants to Israel from the Soviet Union with that of the Jews of the RSFSR as found in the 1970 census. A total of 96,200 individuals born before the 1970 census immigrated to Israel from the Soviet Union between 1971 and 1975. Graph 2A below plots their age distribtuion.

GRAPH 2A

AGE PYRAMID OF JEWS IN RSFSR IN 1970, AND IMMIGRANTS IN ISRAEL
FROM USSR FROM 1971–1975 BORN BEFORE 1970 (PERCENTAGES)

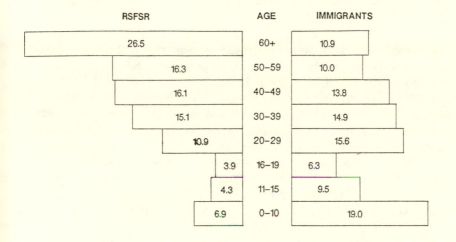

RSFSR	AGE	IMMIGRANTS
26.5	60+	10.9
16.3	50–59	10.0
16.1	40–49	13.8
15.1	30–39	14.9
10.9	20–29	15.6
3.9	16–19	6.3
4.3	11–15	9.5
6.9	0–10	19.0

Sources: *Itogi, 1970,* vol. 4, Table 33; Y. Florsheim, "Le-dmuto ha-demografit shel ha-kibuts ha-yehudi be-vrit-ha-moatsot", *Behinot,* No. 7 (1976), p. 62.

Although the processes of aging that affect the Jewish population are more advanced in the RSFSR than in other republics, we should not consider the large age discripancies between the emigrants and the Jews of the RSFSR a consequence of regional differences alone. The fact that the emigrant population consists of higher percentages of children and youth and a lower proportion of the aged (60 and over) obviously tends to accelerate the aging process afflicting Soviety Jewry.

An additional factor of influence, albeit indirect, on the acceleration of this process is the emigrants' ethnic structure. Non-Ashkenazi Jews (those of Georgia and Bukhara and the mountain Jews) display a higher fertility than that of Ashkenazi Jews. Although the non-Ashkenazi ethnic groups comprised no more than 6.5 percent of all Soviet Jews in the early 1970s, they accounted for approximately 27 percent of the Jewish emigrants in the intercensus period (1970-1979). The departure of more than one-third of Soviet Jewry's demographically most fertile group has also tended to accelerate the processes of population decline.

Furthermore, the proportion of multinational households in the remaining Soviet Jewish community is rising as the percentage of such households among the emigrants falls. The percentage of multinational households has been estimated at 1 percent for the Soviet emigres reaching Israel and at 12 to 14 percent among those immigrating to the United States. It therefore appears that mixed-nationality households account for 4 to 5 percent of all emigrants from the Soviet Union in the 1970s (during the 1970-1979 intercensus period); their proportional weight was between 4.4 and 9.2 times smaller than the rate prevailing for the Jews of the Ukraine in 1959, 3.6 to 8.2 times smaller than the rate for Belorussian Jews in 1970, and 1.2 to 2.5 times smaller than among the Jews of Moldavia that year.

The combined cumulative influence of emigration has therefore contributed indirectly to the acceleration of processes whereby the Jewish community of the Soviet Union is dwindling.

The Soviet Jewish population decreased by approximately 457,000 individuals between the censuses of 1959 and 1979. Since roughly 183,000 Jews emigrated during that period, the loss of 274,000 Jewish individuals in a twenty-year span (1959-1979) may be attributed to the results of intracommunity processes yielding an average annual decline of 0.66 percent.

The 1960s and the 1970s evinced substantial differences in the rate of Jewish population decrease explained by factors other than the direct consequence of emigration. The annual average rate of decrease during the 1960s (1959-1970), 0.45 percent, nearly doubled in the 1970s (1970-1979) to 0.87 percent. This accleleration was influenced both by indirect factors linked to emigration and by the cumulative results of years of low fertility and high levels of intermarriage, which have engendered an increasingly pervasive process of aging.

If we assume that the Soviet Jewish population has continued to shrink between the most recent census and the middle of 1985 at a rate equivalent to that of the 1970s, the Jewish population may be said to have dwindled during this period, for reasons other than emigration, by approximately 102,000 individuals. Accordingly, Soviet Jewry numbers 1,621,000 individuals in mid-1985 (1,811,000 as of the 1979 census, minus 88,000 emigrants between the census and the end of 1985 and a natural decrease of 102,000).

In the wake of internal demographic processes, excluding emigration as a factor, we may therefore predict that the Jewish population of the Soviet Union will stand at 1.2 million to 1.4 million individuals in the year 2001. Should an average annual emigration of approximately 20,000 individuals take place, this figure will fall to 800,000 to 900,000. These developments, however, depend considerably on Soviet government policy. A policy of discrimination and restrictions with regard to the second- and third-generation offspring of mixed-nationality families, if adopted, will have its impact too on the overall number of Jews in the Soviet Union.

In conclusion, I have found no reason to assume the existence of a substantial discrepancy between the number of adult Soviet Jews as recorded on official documents and as declared in population censuses. The percentage of individuals who concealed their Jewish identities did not grow between the 1959 cencus and the polls of 1970 and 1979. We therefore have little cause to question the census data as accurately reflecting the number of individuals registered as Jews in official documents.

The Jewish community, as judged by both official documents and other data, shows clear indications of an aging process that, together with the indirect influence of emigration, is causing its numbers to dwindle at an accelerating rate. Inasmuch as most offspring of mixed-nationality marriages are registered—in official documents and in census data—as non-Jewish nationals, intermarriage too is contributing to the acceleration of the aging process. Concurrent low fertility rates exacerbate the aging of Soviet Jewry all the more. The Jewish community of the Soviet Union, like many other Jewish groups in the developed countries, is therefore in the midst of a process of population decrease, hastened directly and indirectly by emigration.

PROPORTION MARRIED AMONG JEWISH MALES AGE SIXTEEN AND OLDER, BY AGE AND REPUBLIC
(CENSUSES OF 1959 AND 1970)

REPUBLIC AND DATE	TOTAL	16-19	20-24	25-29	30-34	35-39	40-44	45-49	50-54	55-59	60+
RSFSR, 1959	.758	.013	.177	.662	.859	.924	.944	.943	.935	.918	.846
Ukraine, 1959	.781	.011	.183	.717	.895	.954	.963	.963	.957	.950	.877
Ukraine, 1970	.788	.014	.409	.427	.882	.922	.946	.963	.949	.954	.865
Belorussia, 1959	.764	.010	.181	.711	.910	.962	.974	.974	.966	.957	.883
Belorussia, 1970	.767	.010	.394	.440	.898	.933	.960	.974	.959	.962	.873
Moldavia, 1959	.818	.010	.201	.752	.929	.964	.975	.975	.962	.961	.861
Moldavia, 1970	.781	.021	.448	.514	.922	.947	.965	.975	.962	.961	.786
Azerbaidzhan, 1959	.745	.034	.244	.764	.904	.942	.947	.956	.951	.916	.867
Latvia, 1959	.773	.021	.178	.656	.866	.924	.936	.929	.935	.881	.829
Latvia, 1970	.742	.013	.394	.416	.862	.895	.924	.932	.920	.915	.834
Lithuania, 1959	.812	.030	.226	.735	.900	.962	.973	.973	.955	.914	.833
Estonia, 1959	.750	.020	.199	.676	.884	.908	.916	.942	.928	.892	.782

AGE

Sources: *Itogi, 1959*, Table 56 of the appropriate volumes; *Itogi, 1970*, vol. 4, Table 35.

TABLE 2B

PROPORTION MARRIED AMONG JEWISH FEMALES AGE SIXTEEN AND OLDER, BY AGE AND REPUBLIC
(CENSUSES OF 1959 AND 1970)

REPUBLIC AND DATE		TOTAL	AGE									
			16-19	20-24	25-29	30-34	35-39	40-44	45-49	50-54	55-59	60+
RSFSR,	1959	.511	.033	.293	.673	.758	.748	.671	.608	.529	.478	.298
Ukraine,	1959	.556	.042	.380	.760	.815	.776	.677	.605	.547	.524	.366
"	1970	.571	.057	.553	.569	.796	.825	.635	.791	.537	.604	.369
Belorussia,	1959	.569	.036	.358	.736	.800	.777	.675	.608	.555	.534	.402
"	1970	.575	.034	.543	.510	.790	.819	.638	.785	.545	.602	.384
Moldavia,	1959	.636	.064	.523	.821	.859	.845	.765	.703	.630	.548	.347
"	1970	.632	.063	.679	.606	.852	.873	.732	.853	.592	.697	.417
Azerbaidzhan,	1959	.546	.156	.452	.782	.797	.785	.676	.643	.563	.517	.290
Latvia,	1959	.612	.038	.404	.789	.840	.820	.762	.689	.592	.517	.317
"	1970	.587	.037	.601	.538	.829	.820	.724	.806	.557	.666	.360
Lithuania,	1959	.634	.063	.433	.819	.844	.839	.750	.670	.585	.469	.325
Estonia,	1959	.600	.013	.433	.784	.835	.771	.768	.731	.614	.525	.261

Sources: *Itogi, 1959*, Table 56 of the appropriate volumes; *Itogi, 1970*, vol. 4, Table 35.

TABLE 2C

FREQUENCIES OF JEWISH HOUSEHOLDS BY SIZE, FOR SELECTED REPUBLICS, 1970, 1979

| NUMBER OF PERSONS IN HOUSEHOLD | RSFSR [a] | | BIROBIDZHAN | REPUBLIC | | | | |
| | 1970 [b] | 1979 | 1970 | UKRAINE [a] | | BELORUSSIA | | MOLDAVIA |
				1970	1979	1970	1979	1970
Total	14,495	127,281	2,290	185,866	146,290	34,759	32,199	26,790
2	5,812	56,544	663	69,837	64,714	10,674	12,334	9,054
3	4,204	39,327	573	58,000	44,352	9,729	10,046	8,271
4	3,150	22,239	619	39,890	26,319	9,613	7,198	6,472
5	1,065	6,904	292	14,058	8,586	3,574	2,027	2,341
6	224	1,615	102	3,308	1,920	949	468	526
7	20		28	559		156		114
8	12	652	10	150	399	44	126	8
9	4		2	44		4		4
10+	4		1	20		16		–

Sources: *Itogi, 1970,* vol. 7, Tables 30, 31; *Vestnik statistiki,* No. 6 (1983), pp. 73, 76, 77.

(a) These data refer to the "chief areas of [Jewish] settlement," which have never been specifically identified.

(b) Without the Jewish Autonomous oblast' = Birobidzhan.

TABLE 2D

PERCENTAGE DISTRIBUTION OF JEWISH HOUSEHOLDS BY SIZE, FOR SELECTED REPUBLICS, 1970, 1979

NUMBER OF PERSONS IN HOUSEHOLD	REPUBLIC								
	RSFSR (a)		BIROBIDZHAN	UKRAINE (a)		BELORUSSIA		MOLDAVIA
	1970 (a)	1979	1970	1970	1979	1970	1979	1970
Total	100.0	100.0	100.0	100.0	100.0	100.0	100.0	100.0
2	40.1	44.4	29.0	37.6	44.2	30.7	38.3	33.8
3	29.0	30.9	25.0	31.2	30.3	28.0	31.2	30.9
4	21.7	17.5	27.0	21.4	18.0	27.7	22.3	24.2
5	7.4	5.4	12.8	7.6	5.9	10.3	6.3	8.7
6	1.6	1.3	4.5	1.8	1.3	2.7	1.5	2.0
7	0.1		1.2	0.3		0.4		0.4
8	0.1	0.5	0.4	0.1	0.3	0.1	0.4	0.0
9	0.0		0.1	0.0		0.0		0.0
10+	0.0		0.0	0.0		0.1		0.0

Computed from Table 2C

(a) See notes to Table 2C.

TABLE 2E

JEWISH EMIGRANTS FROM USSR BY YEAR AND COUNTRY OF DESTINATION, 1959-1985

| | | COUNTRY OF DESTINATION | | | |
| | | ISRAEL | | OTHER | |
	FREQUENCY	FREQUENCY	PERCENTAGE	FREQUENCY	PERCENTAGE
Total	271,506	168,541	62.1	102,965	37.9
1959	7	7	100.0	–	–
1960	102	102	100.0	–	–
1961	128	128	100.0	–	–
1962	182	182	100.0	–	–
1963	388	388	100.0	–	–
1964	539	539	100.0	–	–
1965	1,444	1,444	100.0	–	–
1966	1,892	1,892	100.0	–	–
1967	1,162	1,162	100.0	–	–
1968	229	229	100.0	–	–
1969	2,979	2,979	100.0	–	–
1970	1,027	1,027	100.0	–	–
1971	13,022	12,964	99.6	58	0.4
1972	31,681	31,430	99.2	251	0.8
1973	34,733	33,277	95.8	1,456	4.2
1974	20,628	16,749	81.2	3,879	18.8
1975	13,221	8,293	62.7	4,928	37.3
1976	14,261	7,257	50.9	7,004	49.1
1977	16,736	8,253	49.3	8,483	50.7
1978	28,865	11,998	41.6	16,867	58.4
1979	51,333	17,277	33.7	34,056	66.3
1980	21,472	7,394	34.4	14,078	65.6
1981	9,448	1,762	18.6	7,686	81.4
1982	2,683	731	27.2	1,952	72.8
1983	1,320	391	29.6	929	70.4
1984	883	332	37.6	551	62.4
1985	1,141	354	31.0	787	69.0

Sources: Z. Alexander, "Immigration to Israel from the USSR," *Israel Yearbook on Human Rights* (Tel-Aviv, 1977) vol. 7, pp. 319, 321; Z. Alexander, "Mediniyut ha-aliya shel brit-ha-moatsot (1968–1978)," *Behinot*, No. 8–9 (1977–78); *Ha-inteligentsia ha-yehudit bivrit ha-moatsot* (Tel-Aviv, 1982) vol. 6, p. 86; Zvi Netser, "Ha–'aliya mibrit ha-moatsot bishnat 1981," *Shvut*, vol. 9,(1982), p. 14; The Jewish Agency – Immigration Department, Reports for 1982, 1983 , 1984. Table 4; monthly reports, 1985.

3 THE GEOGRAPHIC DISTRIBUTION OF SOVIET JEWRY

Certain changes in the geographic distribution of Soviet Jewry took place in the twenty-year intercensus period (1959-1979) as a consequence of differences in birthrates, natural increase and intermarriage, emigration, (see graph 3A) and, in part, internal migration. Since few data from the most recent census have been made public, however, analysis of these factors must rely chiefly on the 1959 and 1970 census summaries, addressing the 1979 poll in only a partial manner.

DISTRIBUTION OF THE JEWS BETWEEN EUROPE AND ASIA

The Soviet Union is divided for administrative-political purposes into fifteen union republics. Of these, eight are in Asia and six in Europe, with the fifteenth, the RSFSR, spanning both continents. The RSFSR, geographically the largest and the most populous of the republics, is divided into fifty-five *oblast's* (districts) and *krais* (a large territorial-administrative unit) in addition to sixteen autonomous republics. Of these, thirty-five *oblast's* and *krais*, as well as nine autonomous republics, are in Europe.[1]

The summaries of two censuses (1959, 1970) provided data on the Jewish population in fourteen *oblast's, krais*, and autonomous republics of the European parts of the RSFSR. The 1959 census reported 607,151 Jews in this area and the 1970 census 572,551. Accordingly, the Jewish population

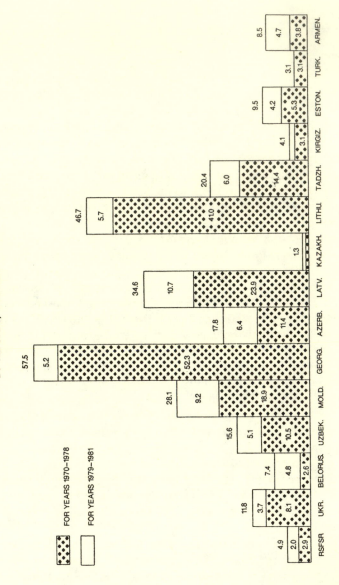

GRAPH 3A

PERCENTAGE OF EMIGRANTS OF THE JEWISH POPULATION
BY REPUBLIC, 1970–1981

FOR YEARS 1970–1978

FOR YEARS 1979–1981

of the European area of the RSFSR (for which data on Jews from both censuses have appeared) decreased by 5.7 percent, a rate lower than that for the RSFSR as a whole, in the intercensus period.

As for the Asiatic part of the RSFSR, summaries of the two censuses (1959, 1970) provided data on the Jews in twelve *oblast's, krais,* and autonomous republics. The 1959 census reported 134,880 Jews dwelling in this area and the 1970 census 120,739. The census data, then, indicate a 10.5 percent decrease of the Jewish population in the Asiatic RSFSR areas, a rate that exceeds the average for the RSFSR as a whole.

Turning to the *oblast's, krais,* and autonomous republics of the RSFSR for which 1959 census summaries fail to provide a breakdown of the Jewish population, this census reports 133,726 Jews, and the 1970 poll indicates 114,625. In this area, therefore, the Jewish community diminished by 14 percent between the censuses, a rate almost twice the average for the Jews of the RSFSR all told. These facts cast doubt on the opinion, based chiefly on impressions, that significant numbers of Jews were migrating from the European to the Asiatic parts of the RSFSR.[2]

By means of these figures on the distribution of the RSFSR's Jews between the European and the Asiatic sections of that republic, we may examine changes in the distribution of Soviet Jewry between the two continents.

Table 3.1 shows that no substantial changes took place during the 1960s with regard to the distribution of Soviet Jewry by continent. The Jewish community in the European USSR (excluding that part of the RSFSR for which the pertinent data were not given in detail) decreased by 5.6 percent between the censuses, as opposed to a decline of only 0.1 percent in the

TABLE 3.1

DISTRIBUTION OF THE SOVIET JEWISH POPULATION
BY CONTINENT, 1959, 1970

CONTINENT	1959		1970	
	FREQUENCY	PERCENTAGE	FREQUENCY	PERCENTAGE
European USSR	1,759,353	77.6	1,661,292	77.3
RSFSR	607,151	26.8	572,551	26.6
Other union republics	1,152,202	50.8	1,088,741	50.7
Asian USSR	375,185	16.5	374,790	17.4
RSFSR	134,880	5.9	120,739	5.6
Other union republics	240,305	10.6	254,051	11.8
Not detailed in 1959 (RSFSR)	133,276	5.9	114,625 [a]	5.3

Calculated from Table 3B.

[a] This number includes oblast's, krais and autonomous republics for which data on Jewish residents was not published from the 1959 census.

Asiatic sector. The decrease in the Jewish population in the Asiatic part of
the Soviet Union stems chiefly from diminishing numbers of Jews in the
Asiatic area of the RSFSR. In the union republics situated in Asia, by
contrast, the Jewish population grew by 5.7 percent during the intercensus
period. We may therefore say that the factors behind the decrease in the
Jewish population of the RSFSR generally also influence Jewish
demography in the Asiatic sector of this republic as well, though not the
Jewish communities in the Asiatic union republics.

Because summaries of the 1970 census provide details about the Jews in
twenty *oblast's, krais*, and autonomous republics of the RSFSR in addition
to the 1959 data, we can determine the distribution of Soviet Jewry between
Europe and Asia in 1970 with greater precision. Our findings indicate that
almost four-fifths of all Soviet Jews resided in the European sector of the
country in the beginning of the 1970s (table 3.2).

TABLE 3.2

DISTRIBUTION OF THE SOVIET JEWISH POPULATION BY CONTINENT, 1970

CONTINENT	FREQUENCY	PERCENTAGE
European USSR	1,706,603	79.3
RSFSR	617,862	28.7
Other union republics	1,088,741	50.6
Asian USSR	408,617	19.0
RSFSR	154,566	7.2
Other union republics	254,051	11.8
Not detailed in 1970 (RSFSR)	35,487	1.7

Calculated from Table 3B.

JEWISH POPULATION IN THE UNION REPUBLICS

With regard to changes in the Jewish population during the 1960s
(1959-1970), we may categorize the union republics of the USSR as follows,
as shown in table 3.3: republics in which the Jewish population decreased at
a rate exceeding the national average (category a); republics in which the
rate of decrease failed to reach the national average (category b); and
republics in which the Jewish population grew in that period (category c).

Republics in which the Jewish population decreased at a rate exceeding
the national average by 2.4 percent (category a) were home to 75.8 percent
of all Soviet Jews in 1959. Republics in which the Jewish population
decreased by a percentage smaller than the national average (category b)
served as residence for 9.6 percent of all Soviet Jews in 1959. Finally, the

TABLE 3.3

REPUBLICS, BY TYPE OF INTERCENSAL CHANGE IN THE JEWISH POPULATION, 1959, 1970

| GROUPING (a) | REPUBLIC | CENSUS YEAR | | RATIO: |
		1959	1970	1970 / 1959
a	RSFSR, Ukraine, Turkmenia	1,719,696	1,588,535	.924
b	Belorussia, Kazakhstan, Lithuania, Kirgizia, Estonia	216,850	212,232	.979
c	Uzbekistan, Moldavia, Georgia, Azerbaidzhan, Latvia, Tadzhikistan, Armenia	331,268	349,940	1.056

(a) See text

union republics in which the Jewish population grew were home to 14.6 percent of the Jews in the Soviet Union when the 1959 census was held.

A breakdown of this type for the 1970s must take into account the additional factor of emigration, which occurred at varying rates in the different republics. Table 3.4 indicates that the demographic differences that surfaced among the Jewish populations of the republics during the 1960s persisted into the 1970s, with the factor of emigrants added to the data of the most recent census. The two republics (the RSFSR and the Ukraine) in which close to three-fourths of all Soviet Jews lived (72.6 percent, to be precise) displayed a rate of decrease exceeding the national average. In Belorussia, by constrast, the Jewish community, including emigrants, declined at a lower rate than that of the entire country. The Jewish population in six republics, emigrants included, increased in relation to 1970. In most of these republics, this development, the continuation of a process that had become evident in the 1960s, is the result of a more favorable age structure, a relatively low incidence of intermarriage, and, in the Baltic republics, a positive balance of internal migration as well.

The differences in emigration rates among Jews of the various republics in the 1970s led to some changes in the distribution of the Jewish population between republics that served Soviet Jews as major areas of residence in the period between the two world wars (the RSFSR, the Ukraine, and Belorussia); republics that in greater part were annexed to the Soviet Union during World War II (Moldavia, Lithuania, Latvia, and Estonia), and the southern republics.

Table 3.5 illustrates a slight shift of the Jewish population to the south and northwest during the 1960s. These areas, however, are the ones where subsequent emigration rates exceeded the national average.

TABLE 3.4

DISTRIBUTION OF SOVIET JEWS AND EMIGRANTS BY REPUBLIC, 1970–1979

	FREQUENCIES			RATIO	
	1970	1979	EMIGRANTS 1970–1979	$\frac{1970}{1959}$	$\frac{1979}{1970}$ (Inc. Emigrants)
Total	2,150,707	1,810,876	174,174 [a]	.948	.923
RSFSR	807,915	700,651	23,006	.923	.896
Ukraine	777,126	634,154	62,807	.925	.897
Belorussia	148,011	135,450	3,848	.986	.941
Uzbekistan	102,855	99,908	10,844	1.090	1.077
Moldavia	98,072	80,127	18,579	1.031	1.006
Georgia	55,382	28,298	28,937	1.074	1.033
Azerbaidzhan	41,288	35,497	4,716	1.027	.974
Latvia	36,680	28,331	8,749	1.002	1.011
Lithuania	23,564	14,697	9,672	.955	1.034
Tadzhikistan	14,615	14,667	2,098	1.177	1.147
Estonia	5,288	4,966	279	.973	.992
Kazakhstan Kirgizia Turkmenia Armenia	39,911	34,130	639	.956	.871

Sources: Table 3A and Z. Alexander, "Immigration to Israel from the USSR," *Israel Yearbook on Human Rights* (Tel Aviv, 1977) vol 7, p. 324; Z. Alexander, "Medinyut ha-aliya shel brit-ha-moatsot (1968–1978)," *Behinot, No. 8–9*, (1977–78), p. 44.

(a) The data on distribution of emigrants by republic relate to recipients of Israeli visas and not to those who actually left. The number in the latter category is smaller by 2,866 individuals and apparently consists of people who decided to postpone or cancel their emigration in addition to individuals who received visas in 1978 but who departed in 1979. We have therefore assumed that this discrepancy is divided proportionately among all the emigrants in accordance with their distribution by republic. The data made public were cited together for 1968–1971. In 1968 and 1969 (until the census of January, 1970) 3,208 persons were issued Israeli visas. We have therefore assumed that their distribution by republics was proportional to the entire emigrant population in the years under analysis; we have subtracted from their number accordingly.

THE RURAL POPULATION

According to the 1959 census, 4.7 percent of the Jewish population—106,112 Jews—lived in rural areas. The rural Jewish population fell by 56.6 percent between 1959 and 1970 to a figure of 46,056, or 2.1percent of the entire Soviet Jewish community, in the latter year. The trend has persisted since. About 27,200 Jews (1.5 percent of the entire Soviet Jewish community) were reported as dwelling in rural areas in the 1979 census.[3] It may be said, therefore, that the process of relocation of Jews from rural to urban areas is nearly completed in the USSR.

TABLE 3.5

PERCENTAGE DISTRIBUTION OF JEWISH POPULATION, BY REPUBLIC GROUPS,
1959, 1970, 1979

	1959	1970	1979
(A) RSFSR, Ukraine, Belorussia	82.3	80.6	81.2
(B) Moldavia, Lithuania, Latvia, Estonia	7.1	7.6	7.1
(C) Southern republics	10.6	11.8	11.7

See text.

It is worth noting that close to 80 percent of the decrease in the rural Jewish population—47,908 individuals, of a total of 60,056—took place during the 1960s (1959-1970) in three republics (the RSFSR, the Ukraine, and Georgia).

Three main factors underlie the conspicuous diminution of the rural Jewish population: migration from rural to urban areas, change in localities' administrative status, and biological decrease and assimilation.

The 1950s witnessed a campaign for the expansion of agriculture in the Soviet Union. The Communist party Central Committee decided on September 7, 1953, upon the "reassignment of mechanical engineers from industry and other sectors of the national economy to Machine and Tractor Stations [MTS]" to serve rural districts.[4] The Ministry of Culture was directed to assign 6,500 graduating mechanical engineers from the classes of 1954 and 1955 to rural areas.[5] The authorities resolved in 1954 to grant substantial material benefits to students in secondary vocational schools who would commit themselves to at least three years' work in a rural area.[6] On March 25, 1955, the Central Committee and the Soviet Union Council of Ministers resolved to transfer by July 1 of that year at least 30,000 persons from "party cadres, local soviet administration and economic management" to "permanent work assignments in collective farms."[7] The project of transferring professional, technical, and party personnel to rural areas almost certainly involved quite a few Jews, as the distribution of the rural Jewish population by sex implies. Some of the newly assigned workers considered their stay in a rural area temporary; once their term of commitment had ended, they returned to urban areas.

The second factor that influenced the decrease in the rural Jewish population was change in localities' administrative status. Such change occurred in two forms: redefinition of rural areas as urban and expansion of municipal boundaries.[8]

Once a community previously defined as a village is granted urban status, its population similarly becomes an urban one, though no change has occurred in its way of life. This situation was especially conspicuous in

Georgia, where the 1959 census reported 71 cities and urban settlements (thirty-four cities, thirty-seven urban settlements) while the 1970 census indicated 108 cities and urban settlements (51 cities, 57 urban settlements).[9] The 37 communities defined as rural in 1959 and as urban in 1970 almost certainly contained a great majority of the approximately 7,000 Jews registered as rural residents in 1959 census and as urban in the 1970 poll. The same process was apparently at work in Moldavia, where the 1970 census reported 53 cities and urban communities against only 38 in the 1959 census.[10] Examination of figures for the Ukraine, too, demonstrates the influence of administrative redefinition on the decreasing numbers of rural Jews. According to the 1959 census, 28 percent of all rural Jews in this republic dwelled in Vinnitsa *oblast'*. Between the censuses, the rural Jewish population there decreased by 5,045 persons.[11] The *oblast'* was found to contain 32 cities and urban communities in 1959 and 36 in 1970. [12] We may reasonably assume that a majority of Jews defined as rural in the 1959 census and as urban in 1970 dwelled in the additional four settlements. Although the rural Jewish population of Zhitomir *oblast'* decreased by 1,668 persons in the intercensus period, 8 communities in this *oblast'*, classified in 1959 as rural, were administratively redefined as urban during those years (39 cities and urban settlements in 1959, 47 in 1970).[13] It is therefore reasonable to assume that the Jews who were recorded as rural in the 1959 census and as urban in 1970 indeed resided in these communities.

In Moscow *oblast'*, by contrast, the rural Jewish population dwindled mainly because of expansion of city limits. As early as 1959, summaries of the census gave clear indication that a large majority of the approximately 20,000 (19,682) Jews in Moscow *oblast'* recorded as rural were in fact urbanites in every respect; they had settled in suburban communities on the city periphery due to difficulties in obtaining official residence permits in the city proper.[14] When Moscow's city limits were extended in 1961, 220,000 persons who resided in surrounding areas were incorporated into the city's population. The near-absolute certainty that the annexed population included Jews accounts for most of the decrease of 12,000 in the number of rural Jews in Moscow *oblast'* (8,057 according to the 1970 census).

The third factor that almost certainly had a role in the approximately 57 percent decline of the rural Jewish population in the 1959-1970 period is assimilation and biological decrease. There is reason to assume that the rural Jewish population resembles the urban population more closely than the general rural population with regard to natural increase. By implication, rural Jews are affected by processes of aging and biological decrease. It is also reasonable to assume that the rural Jews' intermarriage rate is no lower than that of the urban Jews.

We may therefore assert that the same factors that caused the Soviet Jewish community in general to decline during the 1960s and 1970s affected the rural Jewish population similarly, aggravated by factors peculiar to the rural areas (a negative migration balance and administrative changes). Some of the Jews defined as rural in the 1959 census resided in communities of wholly urban character; the formal redefinition of these communities' status was more an adjustment to fact than a change in social structure. Additional factors influencing this decrease were the general processes of migration from village to city, in which Jews, too, participated to a certain extent.

The combined impact of the three factors caused the rural Jewish population to shrink by 78,900 persons between 1959 and 1979. The few Jews who remained in rural areas at the end of the 1970s were administrative and service professionals—engineers, physicians, teachers, and the like—who actually constituted an urban element and considered their rural residence a passing phase.

URBAN POPULATION

A total 2,162,702 Jews (95.3 percent of all Soviet Jews) were urban dwellers according to the 1959 census. Corresponding figures for 1970 were 2,104,650 Jews (97.9 percent of the total) and for 1979 1,783,676 Jews (98.5 percent of all Soviet Jews). The percentage of Jews in the general urban population fell concurrently from 2.2 percent in 1959 to 1.5 percent in early 1970 and 1.1 percent according to the 1979 census.

To study the changes in the urban Jewish population, we shall divide the union republics of the Soviet Union into those where the urban Jewish population either decreased (category A) or increased (category B) during the 1960s (see table 3D).

The six republics of category A were home to 77.8 percent of all urban Jews according to the 1959 census and only 75.6 percent in the 1970 poll (table 3.6). Discrepancies in rates of decrease or increase of the urban Jewish population occur not only among the republics but within them as well.

TABLE 3.6

DISTRIBUTION OF JEWISH URBAN POPULATION BY TWO CATEGORIES OF UNION REPUBLICS, 1959, 1970

CATEGORY	1959	1970	RATIO 1970:1959
(A)	1,681,856	1,590,050	.945
(B)	479,846	514,601	1.072

See text.

Appendix tables 3A-3G appear at the end of this chapter.

In the parts of the RSFSR (eighteen *oblast*'s and *krais*, six autonomous republics) for which data from two censuses (1959, 1970) with regard to the Jewish population are available, the urban Jewish population decreased at a rate greater than the republic-wide mean in thirteen *oblast's* and *krais* and in two autonomous republics. In five *oblast's* and *krais* and in four autonomous republics of the RSFSR, by contrast, the decrease was smaller than the average for the RSFSR as a whole, and in some cases the urban Jewish population actually increased. The urban Jewish population of the RSFSR decreased by 5.3 percent between the censuses of 1959 and 1970 but only by 1.8 percent in the *oblast's* of Moscow (including the city), Leningrad (including the city), Kaliningrad, Voronezh, and Novosibirsk (cities that accounted for close to 58 percent of all urban Jews in the RSFSR according to the 1959 census) and increased by 10.1 percent in the four autonomous republics of the Caucasus.

The relatively small drop in the urban Jewish population of Moscow *oblast'* is an outgrowth of administrative changes. We shall therefore examine the changes that occurred in the *oblast's* of Kaliningrad, Voronezh, and Novosibirsk and the autonomous republics of the Caucasus (Dagestan, Kabardino-Balkar, Severo-Osetin, and Checheno-Ingush).

In the three *oblast's*—Kaliningrad, Voronezh, and Novosibirsk—22,062 Jews dwelled in cities as of the 1959 census and 21,962 according to the 1970 census, an intercensus decrease of 0.4 percent. During the same period, the general population of Kaliningrad *oblast'* (formerly Koenigsberg) rose at a rate exceeding the mean for the RSFSR (36 percent in Kaliningrad *oblast'*, 20 percent in the RSFSR as a whole), as did the urban population (36 percent in Kaliningrad *oblast'*, 31 percent in the RSFSR). This indicates substantial migration to Kaliningrad *oblast'* from other areas of the Soviet Union during the 1960s, which almost certainly included Jews. This would account for the intercensus growth in the Jewish population of Kaliningrad *oblast'*. While the urban Jewish population of Voronezh *oblast'* also increased, that of Novosibirsk *oblast'* decreased, though at a rate lower than the mean for Jews in the RSFSR. These developments are apparently attributable to in-migration of Jews. Voronezh and Novosibirsk both have institutions of higher education; Novosibirsk is an important research center. We may be almost sure that these factors lay behind the positive migration balance of Jews to these *oblast's*.

A total of 30,859 Jews dwelled in the urban communities of the four autonomous republics in the Caucasus according to the 1959 census; this figure rose to 33,980 in the 1970 census. The resulting 10.1 percent increase in the urban Jewish population of these autonomous republics exceeded the 8 percent figure registered for the general Jewish population in those areas. By implication, Jews had migrated from villages and/or other parts of the Soviet Union to the cities of the Caucasian autonomous republics. The Jews in these republics also registered positive natural increase, a factor that also contributed to the growth of the urban Jewish population there.

We may therefore say that in most of the *oblast's* and *krais* of the RSFSR, as in several of the autonomous republics, the urban Jewish population declined during the 1960s at a rate faster than the mean for the RSFSR. This decrease should apparently be attributed to two major factors: processes of assimilation of Jews in the *oblast's* of the RSFSR where the urban Jewish population is relatively small (there, apparently, these processes proceed at a pace faster than the mean for the RSFSR as a whole) and the migration balance of the Jews in these *oblast's* was almost certainly negative. Although almost no 1979 census data about the distribution of the Jewish community in the RSFSR are available, the trends that surfaced in the 1960s have apparently persisted.[15]

Turning to the Ukraine, we find published 1959 and 1970 census data pertaining to the urban Jewish population of twenty-one *oblast's*. In the 1960s, the numbers of urban-dwelling Jews declined more slowly than the mean for the Ukraine in six *oblast's* (Dnepropetrovsk, Zaporozh'e, Zakarpat'e, Kiev—including the metropolis—Odessa, and Kherson). The urban Jewish population of these *oblast's* came to 397,639 according to the 1959 census and 387,966 in the 1970 census. The rate of intercensus decrease in the urban Jewish population of these *oblast's*, 2.4 percent, contrasts with the 8.8 percent figure recorded between the censuses in the remaining *oblast's*. Since it is hard to assume any significant differences in natural increase of the Jews between these *oblast's* and others in the Ukraine and inasmuch as we have no reason to hypothesize a lower intermarriage rate in these *oblast's* than the mean for the Ukraine as a whole, we may infer the existence of a positive migration balance to the cities of the six *oblast's* under discussion during the 1960s.

No data have been made public about the distribution of the Jewish population between urban and rural areas by republics—and by *oblast's*—from the most recent census (1979). Because almost all Jews are urban dwellers, however, it will be proper to examine the 1979 data here. Data from the 1979 census have been published with regard to the Jews in nine *oblast's* in which 60 percent of the Ukraine's Jewish population dwelled.

Table 3.7 shows that in the Odessa *oblast'* and in other unspecified *oblast's*, the Jewish population declined during the 1970s to a greater extent than in the Ukraine as a whole. Odessa, however, was a main center of Jewish emigration. Between 1970 and 1979, some 17,400 Jews emigrated from the city. Adding this number to those reported in the census, the Jewish population decrease in the 1970s was in fact only 6.8 percent. Three other cities in the unspecified *oblast's* (Kiev, Chernovtsy, and L'vov) accounted for about 32,100 emigrants in the same period.[16] If we add the emigrating Jews from these cities only to the total of those polled in 1979, the Jewish demographic decline in these unspecified *oblast's* was 11.2 percent.

The 1959 and 1970 summaries of the censuses address the national group

TABLE 3.7

DISTRIBUTION OF THE JEWISH POPULATION (URBAN AND RURAL) OF THE UKRAINE,
BY OBLAST', 1959, 1970, 1979

OBLAST'	FREQUENCIES			RATIO		
	1959	1970	1979	1970/1959	1979/1970	1979/1959
Total	840,311	777,126	634,154	.925	.816	.755
Dnepropetrovsk	73,256	69,287	60,970	.946	.880	.832
Donetsk	42,501	39,988	35,533	.941	.889	.836
Zaporozh'e	20,811	20,242	17,708	.973	.875	.851
Khar'kov	84,192	76,487	64,092	.909	.838	.761
Vinnitsa	50,157	42,251	33,929	.842	.803	.676
Zhitomir	42,048	35,706	28,973	.849	.811	.689
Crimea	26,374	25,614	22,597	.971	.882	.857
Nikolaev	20,277	17,978	15,262	.887	.849	.753
Odessa	121,377	117,233	92,183	.966	.786	.759
Other (a)	359,318	332,340	262,907	.925	.791	.732

Sources: *Vestnik statistiki,* No. 8, (1980), pp. 64–68, and, Tables 3A, 3B.

(a) Not specified in data published from the 1979 census.

distribution of the urban population by *oblast's*, not by cities; we must estimate the size of the various cities' Jewish communities by indirect methods. With this objective in mind, demographer J. Newth has used an ethnic-structure map of the population in the Ukraine and summaries of the 1959 census, which provide accurate data about population size with regard to cities larger than 10,000, to draw up a precise list of the Jewish population of the cities of the Ukraine.[17] Although these calculations may contain inaccuracies of up to 5 percent, they nevertheless allow us to examine the distribution of the Ukrainian Jewish population as reported in the 1959 census. From these data (table 3F), it appears that about 127,000 Jews dwelled in Ukrainian urban communities with overall populations of under 10,000 when the 1959 census was held. The rest of the Ukrainian urban Jewish population, in terms of size of city of residence, was distributed as demonstrated in table 3.8.

The data indicate that 58 percent of all urban Jews in the Ukraine in 1959 dwelled in eight cities with general populations exceeding 300,000 and approximately 26 percent resided in forty-six urban communities with populations between 10,000 and 300,000. Jews accounted for a high percentage in many of these cities (table 3.9).

In six cities that, according to the 1959 census, were home to roughly 22

TABLE 3.8

JEWISH URBAN POPULATION OF THE UKRAINE, BY SIZE OF LOCALITY, 1959

SIZE OF LOCALITY (1,000'S)	NUMBER OF LOCALITIES	JEWISH POPULATION (1,000'S)	PERCENTAGE OF URBAN JEWISH POPULATION
Total		810	100.0
Less than 10	–	127	15.7
10–30	12	19	2.4
30–100	23	66	8.2
100–300	11	128	15.7
300–1,000	7	316	39.0
1,000+	1	154	19.0

TABLE 3.9

PERCENTAGES OF JEWS IN URBAN LOCALITIES OF THE UKRAINE, 1959

PERCENTAGE OF THE POPULATION	NUMBER OF CITIES	JEWISH POPULATION (1,000'S)
Less than 5	27	92
5–10	17	236
11–15	4	178
16–20	3	133
21+	3	44

percent of the urban Jewish population of the Ukraine, the Jews accounted for more than 15 percent of the population. In twenty-one cities where 51 percent of all urban Ukrainian Jews lived, their presence ranged from 5 percent to 15 percent of the total population. The fact that Jews constituted a considerable portion of the population in several cities almost certainly gave them a sense of community, although these cities had almost no Jewish institutions in which this feeling might be expressed. The size of the Jewish population in many of these cities also contributed to this sense of community.

Data from 1959 on the Jewish population of Ukrainian cities indicate four large Jewish concentrations (more than 50,000 apiece), four intermediate-sized concentrations (between 10,000 and 50,000 Jews in each) and forty-one small concentrations (fewer than 10,000 Jews in each). The large and intermediate concentrations, as defined on the basis of 1959 census data, accounted for approximately 70 percent of all urban-dwelling Jews, while about 30 percent of all urban Jews in the Ukraine resided in concentrations of fewer than 10,000. We can therefore say that as of the

1959 census, most Jews in the Ukraine lived in large and intermediate concentrations, a phenomenon that became even more pronounced in the 1960s and 1970s.

In the neighboring Belorussian SSR, close to one-third (31.8 percent) of the Jews were concentrated in 1970 in Minsk, the only Belorussian city with a population of close to 1 million. During the 1970s, by all appearances, the Jews concentrated in this city to an even greater extent, as the partial 1979 census data available allow us to infer. Data concerning the Jews were published on three of Belorussia's six *oblast's* (table 3.10).

TABLE 3.10

DISTRIBUTION OF THE JEWISH POPULATION (URBAN AND RURAL) OF BELORUSSIA
BY OBLAST', 1959, 1970, 1979

	FREQUENCIES			RATIO		
OBLAST'	1959	1970	1979	1970/1959	1979/1970	1979/1959
Total	150,084	148,011	135,450	.986	.915	.902
Vitebsk	18,986	17,343	15,080	.914	.870	.794
Gomel'	45,007	42,312	38,433	.940	.908	.854
Mogilev	28,438	25,807	23,135	.908	.897	.814
Other (a)	57,653	62,549	58,802	1.084	.940	1.020

Sources: *Vestnik statistiki,* No. 8 (1980), pp. 69–70, and Tables 3A, 3B.

(a) Not specified in data published from the 1979 census.

If the percentage of Jews in Minsk in 1979 was identical to that reported for the three unspecified Belorussian *oblast's* in 1970, then about 44,300 Jews (32.7 percent of all Jews in Belorussia) dwelled in Minsk as of the 1979 census. We may therefore say that the Jewish population in Minsk decreased during the 1970s by a percentage lower than that of the Jews of Belorussia, despite an emigration of close to 2,500 Jews from the city. This would appear to hint at a positive migration balance of Jews to Minsk during the 1970s.

Moldavia presents a similar picture with regard to the distribution of the Jewish population. By means of a map of the ethnic structure of this republic's cities based on the 1970 census and with the help of the summaries of that census, I have determined the approximate distribution of the urban Jewish population (table 3.11). The Jews appear to have accounted for more than 10 percent of the population of only two Moldavian cities. Furthermore, only one city, Kishinev, had a large concentration of Jews, while all other Moldavian Jewish communities were small (fewer than 10,000 persons).

TABLE 3.11

THE JEWISH POPULATION OF MOLDAVIAN CITIES, 1970

| CITY | FREQUENCIES (1,000'S) | | PERCENTAGE | |
	TOTAL	JEWISH	OF JEWS IN POPULATION	OF URBAN JEWISH POPULATION
Total	1130	96	8.5	100.0
Kishinev	356	50	14.0	52.0
Bel'tsy	102	8	7.8	8.3
Bendery	72	6	8.3	6.3
Tiraspol'	105	5	4.8	5.2
Rybnitsa	32	4	12.5	4.2
Soroki	22	2	9.1	2.1
Unknown	441	21	4.8	21.9

Calculated from V. Zelenchuk, *Naselenie Moldavii* (Kishinev, 1973) and *Itogi, 1970,* vol. 1, Table 3.

Kishinev is the only Moldavian city for which we have data on the number of Jews at the end of the 1970s. Its Jewish population as of 1979 was 42,800—8.5 percent of the population of that city and 53.4 percent of all Jews in Moldavia.[18] About 10,000 Jews emigrated from Kishinev between the two most recent censuses (1970-1979).[19] If we add the emigrants to the census data, the number of Jews in Kishinev, emigrants included, will prove to have grown between 1970 and 1979 by 5 percent more than the Moldavian mean, indicating that the migration of Jews to capitals of the various republics, noted during the 1960s, continued during the 1970s as well.

Approximately 37.7 percent of the urban Jewish population as of the 1959 census and 40.2 percent in the 1970 census dwelled in the capitals of the union republics and the city of Leningrad. Since it is hard to suppose that the assimilation rate in the large cities was significantly slower than the average for all Soviet Jews, we may infer a positive migration balance for the Jews in these cities during the 1960s. Since Jews migrated to the republic capitals at a pace slower than the general population's, however, the percentage of Jews in these cities decreased. Of sixteen cities, three had Jewish communities of more than 100,000 in 1970 (Moscow, Leningrad, and Kiev); four were home to between 30,000 and 100,000 Jews (Minsk, Tashkent, Kishinev, and Riga); and nine republic capitals had Jewish communities smaller than 30,000 in each case.[20] Indeed, the concentration of Jews in large cities (chiefly in administrative centers and foci of science and culture), a phenomenon typical of Jewish communities the world over, is evident in the Soviet Union as well.

In numerous European and, more particularly, U.S. cities, many Jews congregate in certain neighborhoods, where they account for a high percentage of the population though their proportion in the population of the entire city remains small. This situation imparts a sense of community and allows for extensive cultural activity. The data at hand do not allow us to determine if this phenomenon exists in the Soviet Union, where the selection of residence in a city depends on many factors beyond the citizen's free choice. However, data on the distribution of the Jewish population in Kiev, based on the 1959 census, may hint that Jews in a number of Soviet cities tend to concentrate in certain quarters. Kiev, however, may be an exceptional case in this sense, for its Jewish population congregates in historically Jewish areas of residence, a factor that does not exist in cities where Jews have resided for only three or four generations. In areas where Jews have settled only recently, however, they appear to dwell chiefly in neighborhoods of white-collar workers, while their presence in workers' neighborhoods is smaller.

TABLE 3.12

JEWISH POPULATION OF KIEV BY DISTRICT, 1959

DISTRICT (CITY RAION)	FREQUENCIES (1,000'S)		PERCENTAGE	
	TOTAL	JEWISH	OF JEWS IN POPULATION	OF JEWISH POPULATION OF KIEV
Total	1,104.3	153.5	13.9	100.0
Darnitskii	94.1	2.0	2.1	1.3
Zaliznichnyi	106.5	10.6	10.0	6.9
Zhovtnevyi	148.3	11.0	7.4	7.2
Leninskii	93.4	23.5	25.2	15.3
Moskovskii	151.1	20.8	13.8	13.6
Pecherskii	123.2	14.2	11.5	9.3
Podol'skii	173.2	33.2	19.2	21.6
Radianskii	81.9	18.8	23.0	12.2
Shevchenkovskii	132.6	19.4	14.6	12.6

Source: *Narodne gospodarstvo mista Kyeva* (Kiev, 1963), p. 168.

The city of Kiev was divided into nine *raions* (administrative districts) in the census year 1959 (table 3.12). Jews dwelled in each of these, though not in equal proportion. The two city center *raions* of Leninskii and Radianskii, where most of the institutions of government and science are situated, were home to 27.5 percent of the city's Jews and 24 percent of the total population there. In other words, roughly every fourth person in central

Kiev was Jewish. In the southern (the Moskovskii and Zaliznichnyi *raions*) and western (Zhovtnevyi and Shevchenkovskii) areas of Kiev, where heavy industry is located, only 11.5 percent of all residents were Jews. The Podol'skii *raion,* the most populous in Kiev and site of a prewar concentration of Jews, was home to about 22 percent of all Jews in Kiev in 1959; one Podol'skii resident out of five was Jewish. By contrast, a mere 1.3 percent of Kiev's Jews in early 1959 dwelled in the Darnitskii *raion*, situated across the Dnepr River, a district almost totally rebuilt after World War II.[21] We may therefore say that the Jews of Kiev concentrate in the central section of the city, where many Jews have always resided. These neighborhoods were home to almost half (49 percent) the Jews of Kiev, who accounted for more than one-fifth (22 percent) of all residents. This situation almost certainly contributes to overestimates of Kiev's Jewish population; in addition, it imparts to the Jews there a sense of community. If a similar phenomenon prevails in other Soviet cities, it provides some measure of understanding the source of the feeling of community, or nationhood, among Soviet Jewry, despite the lack of cultural and religious institutions to foster such feelings.

In the 1960s, and almost certainly during the 1970s as well, the Jews of the Soviet Union continued concentrating in cities, as they have in most other industrialized countries. Jews are attracted to the cities to no small extent by their education, which far exceeds the average for the surrounding population. The range of educational opportunities for children, an important and weighty matter in the considerations of the Jewish family, is broader in a metropolis. The social and economic roles Jews fill in most industrialized countries are also primarily urban, again attracting Jews to metropolises. The large city offers a spectrum of leisure-time entertainment possibilities, a matter of considerable importance to Jews. The combined strength of these factors has therefore turned the Jews of the Soviet Union, like those in most Western countries, into a metropolitan community. Given this trend, Jews have almost vanished from rural areas; even the few who remain there fill positions of a conspicuously urban nature and consider their rural domicile temporary.

The Soviet Jewish community has not gravitated to metropolitan areas at a uniform pace throughout the entire Soviet Union; certain republics, such as Moldavia and, in part, the Ukraine and Belorussia, still host a Jewish population, though a dwindling one, in medium-sized and small cities and towns as well. The Soviet urban Jewish population, like that of most Western countries, may well concentrate in certain neighborhoods. Although this phenomenon is probably related to the desire to live in proximity to their own kind, it is primarily a consequence of the Jews' high representation in certain social strata. In terms of urban ecology, then, a great similarity may be inferred between the Jews of the Soviet Union and Jewish communities in most industrial countries.

TABLE 3A

THE SOVIET JEWISH POPULATION BY REPUBLIC, 1959, 1970

REPUBLIC	1959 % OF TOTAL POPULATION	1959 FREQUENCY	1970 % OF TOTAL POPULATION	1970 FREQUENCY	CHANGE % OF TOTAL POPULATION	CHANGE FREQUENCY	RATIO 1970/1959
Total	1.1	2,267,814	0.9	2,150,707	-0.2	-117,107	.948
RSFSR	0.7	875,307	0.6	807,915	-0.1	-67,392	.923
Ukraine	2.0	840,311	1.6	777,126	-0.4	-63,185	.925
Belorussia	1.9	150,084	1.6	148,011	-0.3	-2,073	.986
Uzbekistan	1.2	94,344	0.9	102,855	-0.3	8,511	1.090
Moldavia	3.3	95,107	2.7	98,072	-0.6	2,965	1.031
Georgia	1.3	51,582	1.2	55,382	-0.1	3,800	1.074
Azerbaidzhan	1.1	40,204	1.1	41,288	—	1,084	1.027
Latvia	1.7	36,592	1.6	36,680	-0.1	88	1.002
Kazakhstan	0.3	28,048	0.3	27,689	—	-359	.987
Lithuania	0.9	24,672	0.8	23,564	-0.1	-1,108	.955
Tadzhikistan	0.6	12,415	0.5	14,615	-0.1	2,200	1.177
Kirgizia	0.4	8,610	0.4	7,680	—	-930	.892
Estonia	0.5	5,436	0.4	5,288	-0.1	-148	.973
Turkmenia	0.3	4,078	0.2	3,494	-0.1	-584	.857
Armenia	0.1	1,024	0.1	1,048	—	24	1.023

Sources: *Itogi, 1959,* Table 54, general volume; *Itogi, 1970,* vol. 4, Table 2.

THE SOVIET JEWISH POPULATION BY OBLAST', KRAI, AND AUTONOMOUS REPUBLIC, 1959, 1970

AREA	1959 % OF TOTAL POPULATION	1959 FREQUENCY	1970 % OF TOTAL POPULATION	1970 FREQUENCY	CHANGE % OF TOTAL POPULATION	CHANGE FREQUENCY	RATIO 1970 1959
R S F S R							
Northwest region							
Oblast' (or ASSR)							
Kaliningrad	0.74	4,520	0.62	4,525	−0.12	5	1.001
Leningrad [a]	3.83	174,694	3.13	168,466	−0.70	−6,228	.964
Murmansk	0.54	3,040	0.33	2,684	−0.21	−356	.883
Pskov	0.32	3,025	0.27	2,335	−0.05	−690	.772
Karelian ASSR	—	—	0.22	1,580	—	—	—
Komi ASSR	—	—	0.19	1,839	—	—	—
Central region							
Oblast'							
Briansk	0.88	13,707	0.73	11,476	−0.15	−2,231	.837
Ivanovo	—	—	0.13	1,764	—	—	—
Kalinin	—	—	0.20	3,456	—	—	—
Kaluga	—	—	0.23	2,278	—	—	—
Moscow [a]	2.76	302,283	2.24	287,839	−0.52	−14,444	.952
Smolensk	—	—	0.48	5,316	—	—	—
Tula	—	—	0.25	4,857	—	—	—
Iaroslavl'	—	—	0.21	2,970	—	—	—
Volga-Viatka region							
Gor'ki oblast'	0.51	18,274	0.46	16,845	−0.05	−1,429	.922
Central Black Earth region							
Voronezh oblast'	0.26	6,197	0.25	6,434	−0.01	237	1.038
Kursk oblast'	—	—	0.31	4,651	—	—	—
Volga region							
Oblast'(or ASSR)							
Astrakhan'	—	—	0.40	3,462	—	—	—
Volgograd	—	—	0.22	5,042	—	—	—
Kuibyshev	0.89	20,185	0.68	18,678	−0.21	−1,507	.925
Saratov	0.64	13,819	0.49	11,992	−0.15	−1,827	.868
Tatar ASSR	0.36	10,360	0.30	9,521	−0.06	−839	.919
North Caucasus region							
Krasnodar krai	—	—	0.17	7,726	—	—	—
Stavropol' krai	—	—	0.27	6,140	—	—	—
Rostov oblast'	0.63	20,864	0.47	18,190	−0.16	−2,674	.872
Dagestan ASSR	2.02	21,427	1.55	22,149	−0.47	722	1.034
Kabardino-Balkar ASSR	0.84	3,529	0.95	5,578	0.11	2,049	1.581
Severo-Osetin ASSR	0.46	2,082	0.37	2,044	−0.09	−38	.982
Checheno-Ingush ASSR	0.74	5,223	0.47	5,045	−0.27	−178	.966

AREA	1959		1970		CHANGE		RATIO
	% OF TOTAL POPULATION	FREQUENCY	% OF TOTAL POPULATION	FREQUENCY	% OF TOTAL POPULATION	FREQUENCY	1970 1959
Ural region **Oblast' (or ASSR)**							
Orenburg	0.48	8,716	0.33	6,885	−0.15	−1,831	.790
Perm'	—	—	0.27	8,096	—	—	—
Sverdlovsk	0.64	26,016	0.49	21,269	−0.15	−4,747	.818
Cheliabinsk	0.64	18,948	0.48	15,677	−0.16	−3,271	.827
Bashkir ASSR	0.22	7,467	0.17	6,681	−0.05	−786	.895
West Siberian region **Oblast'**							
Kemerovo	—	—	0.17	5,012	—	—	—
Novosibirsk	0.54	12,429	0.47	11,864	−0.07	−565	.955
Omsk	0.57	9,459	0.44	8,081	−0.13	−1,378	.854
Tomsk	—	—	0.30	2,381	—	—	—
East Siberian region							
Krasnoiarsk krai	—	—	0.18	5,349	—	—	—
Irkutsk oblast'	0.52	10,313	0.35	8,029	−0.17	−2,284	.779
Chita oblast'	—	—	0.15	1,741	—	—	—
Buriat ASSR	0.40	2,691	0.26	2,090	−0.14	−601	.777
Far East region							
Primorskii krai	—	—	0.22	3,832	—	—	—
Khabarovsk krai	0.87	8,494	0.64	7,461	−0.23	−1,033	.878
Jewish Autonomous oblast'	8.76	14,269	6.64	11,452	−2.12	−2,817	.803
Magadan oblast'	—	—	0.47	1,646	—	—	—
Not specified	—	133,276	—	35,487	—	—	—
UKRAINE **Donets-Dnepr region** **Oblast'**							
Dnepropetrovsk	2.71	73,256	2.07	69,287	−0.64	−3,969	.946
Donetsk	1.00	42,501	0.82	39,988	−0.18	−2,513	.941
Zaporozh'e	1.42	20,811	1.14	20,242	−0.28	−569	.973
Voroshilovgrad (b)	0.57	13,939	0.46	12,539	−0.11	−1,400	.900
Poltava	0.75	12,287	0.63	10,768	−0.12	−1,519	.876
Sumy	0.41	6,259	0.31	4,725	−0.10	−1,534	.755
Khar'kov	3.34	84,192	2.71	76,487	−0.63	−7,705	.909
Southwest region **Oblast'**							
Vinnitsa	2.34	50,157	1.98	42,251	−0.36	−7.906	.842
Zhitomir	2.62	42,048	2.19	35,706	−0.43	−6,342	.849
Zakarpat'e	1.32	12,169	1.03	10,862	−0.29	−1,307	.893
Ivano-Frankovsk	—	—	0.23	3,584	—	—	—

AREA	1959		1970		CHANGE		RATIO
	% OF TOTAL POPULATION	FREQUENCY	. % OF TOTAL POPULATION	FREQUENCY	% OF TOTAL POPULATION	FREQUENCY	1970 1959
Kiev [a]	5.96	168,249	4.75	164,634	−1.21	−3,615	.979
Kirovograd	0.78	9,505	0.61	7,729	−0.17	−1,776	.813
L'vov	1.42	30,030	1.14	27,721	−0.28	−2,309	.923
Rovno	—	—	0.24	2,527	—	—	—
Khmel'nitskii	1.18	19,050	1.00	16,089	−0.18	−2,961	.845
Cherkassy	0.87	13,110	0.69	10,643	−0.18	−2,467	.812
Chernigov	0.81	12,562	0.66	10,335	−0.15	−2,227	.823
Chernovtsy	5.44	42,140	4.43	37,459	−1.01	−4,681	.889
Southern region Oblast'							
Crimea	2.20	26,374	1.41	25,614	−0.79	−760	.971
Nikolaev	2.00	20.277	1.56	17,978	−0.44	−2,299	.887
Odessa	5.99	121,377	4.91	117,233	−1.08	−4,144	.966
Kherson	1.27	10,437	0.98	10,061	−0.29	−376	.964
Not specified	—	9,581	—	2,664	—	—	—
BELORUSSIA Oblast'							
Brest	0.51	6,012	0.39	5,015	−0.12	−997	.834
Vitebsk	1.49	18,986	1.27	17,343	−0.22	−1,643	.914
Gomel'	3.30	45,007	2.76	42,312	−0.54	−2,695	.940
Grodno	0.35	3,745	0.28	3,199	−0.07	−546	.854
Minsk [a]	2.42	47,896	2.21	54,335	−0.21	6,439	1.134
Mogilev	2.44	28,438	2.10	25,807	−0.34	−2,631	.908
UZBEKISTAN Oblast'							
Andizhan	0.48	5,599	0.41	4,404	−0.07	−1,195	.787
Bukhara	1.10	6,424	0.90	8,421	−0.20	1,997	1.311
Kashkadar'ia	—	—	0.30	2,452	—	—	—
Samarkand	1.26	14,496	1.09	15,964	−0.17	1,468	1.101
Surkhandar'ia	0.33	3,076	—	—	—	—	—
Tashkent [a]	2.46	55,657	2.07	59,369	−0.39	3,712	1.067
Fergana	0.76	8,688	0.69	9,200	−0.07	512	1.059
Not specified	—	404	—	3,045	—	—	—
GEORGIA Tbilisi (city)	2.25	17,430	2.20	19,579	−0.05	2,149	1.123
Raions attached to Republic administration	1.09	27,480	0.98	28,400	−0.11	920	1.034
Abkhaz ASSR	0.82	3,332	0.90	4,372	0.08	1,040	1.312
Adzhar ASSR	0.66	1,617	0.50	1,546	−0.16	−71	.956
Iugo-Ostin Autonomous oblast'	1.78	1,723	1.49	1,485	−0.29	−238	.862

	1959		1970		CHANGE		RATIO
AREA	% OF TOTAL POPULATION	FREQUENCY	% OF TOTAL POPULATION	FREQUENCY	% OF TOTAL POPULATION	FREQUENCY	1970 1959
AZERBAIDZHAN							
Baku city and attached localities	2.96	29,204	2.35	29,716	−0.61	512	1.018
Raions attached to Republic administration	0.45	10,904	0.33	11,521	−0.12	617	1.057
Not specified	—	96	—	51	—	—	—
KAZAKHSTAN							
Oblast' (or city)							
Dzhambul	0.18	1,015	—	—	—	—	—
Kzyl-Orda	0.34	1,101	0.22	1,090	−0.12	−11	.990
Chimkent	0.36	3,273	0.26	3,310	−0.10	37	1.011
Alma-Ata (city)	1.85	8,425	1.26	9,180	−0.59	755	1.090
Karaganda	0.49	4,999	0.32	5,040	−0.17	41	1.008
Not specified	—	9,235	—	9,069	—	—	—
TADZHIKISTAN							
Dushanbe (city)	3.84	8,720	3.06	11,424	−0.78	2,704	1.310
Raions attached to Republic administration	0.22	3,673	—	—	—	—	—
Leninabad oblast'	—	—	0.24	2,251	—	—	—
Not specified	—	22	—	940	—	—	—
KIRGIZIA							
Frunze (city)	2.65	5,840	1.38	5,962	−1.27	122	1.021
Raions attached to Republic administration	0.13	1,082	—	—	—	—	—
Not specified	—	1,688	—	1,718	—	—	—
TURKMENIA							
Ashkhabad (city)	0.75	1,276	0.49	1,246	−0.26	−30	.977
Chardzhou oblast'	—	—	0.17	799	—	—	—
Not specified	—	2,802	—	1,449	—	—	—

Sources: *Itogi, 1959,* Table 54 of the relevant volumes; *Itogi, 1970,* vol. 4, Tables 6, 8, 10, 12, 14, 16, 18, 23, 25, 28.

(a) Including the metropolitan region.

(b) 1935–1958: Voroshilovgrad; 1959–1969: Lugansk; since 1970: Voroshilovgrad.

TABLE 3C

THE SOVIET JEWISH RURAL POPULATION, BY REPUBLIC, 1959, 1970

REPUBLIC	1959		1970		CHANGE		RATIO
	% OF TOTAL POPULATION	FREQUENCY	% OF TOTAL POPULATION	FREQUENCY	% OF TOTAL POPULATION	FREQUENCY	1970 1959
Total	**0.10**	**106,112**	**0.04**	**46,056**	**−0.06**	**−60,056**	**.434**
RSFSR	0.08	45,079	0.04	21,401	−0.04	−23,678	.475
Ukraine	0.13	30,280	0.06	12,888	−0.07	−17,392	.426
Belorussia	0.10	5,593	0.05	2,546	−0.05	−3,047	.455
Uzbekistan	0.08	4,421	0.05	3,076	−0.03	−1,345	.696
Moldavia	0.30	6,791	0.09	2,182	−0.21	−4,609	.321
Georgia	0.33	7,752	0.04	914	−0.29	−6,838	.118
Azerbaidzhan	0.07	1,287	0.02	476	−0.05	−811	.370
Latvia	0.05	464	0.04	316	−0.01	−148	.681
Kazakhstan	0.05	2,748	0.02	1,307	−0.03	−1,441	.476
Lithuania	0.02	261	0.01	213	−0.01	−48	.816
Tadzhikistan	0.03	448	0.01	192	−0.02	−256	.429
Kirgizia	0.05	669	0.02	339	−0.03	−330	.507
Estonia	0.03	136	0.03	124	−	−12	.912
Turkmenia	0.02	133	−	52	−0.02	−81	.391
Armenia	0.01	50	−	30	−0.01	−20	.600

Sources: *Itogi, 1959,* Table 53 of the relevant volumes; *Itogi, 1970,* vol. 4, Tables 5, 7, 9, 11, 13, 15, 17, 19, 20–22, 24, 26, 27, 29.

THE SOVIET JEWISH URBAN POPULATION, BY REPUBLIC, 1959, 1970

	1959		1970		CHANGE		RATIO
REPUBLIC	% OF TOTAL POPULATION	FREQUENCY	% OF TOTAL POPULATION	FREQUENCY	% OF TOTAL POPULATION	FREQUENCY	1970 1959
Total	2.2	2,161,702	1.5	2,104,651	-0.7	-57,051	.974
RSFSR	1.4	830,228	1.0	786,514	-0.4	-43,714	.947
Ukraine	4.2	810,031	2.1	764,238	-2.1	-45,793	.944
Belorussia	5.8	144,491	3.7	145,465	-2.1	974	1.007
Uzbekistan	3.3	89,923	2.3	99,779	-1.0	9,856	1.110
Moldavia	13.8	88,316	8.5	95,890	-5.3	7,574	1.086
Georgia	2.6	43,830	2.4	54,468	-0.2	10,638	1.243
Azerbaidzhan	2.2	38,917	1.6	40,812	-0.6	1,895	1.049
Latvia	3.1	36,128	2.5	36,364	-0.6	236	1.007
Kazakhstan	0.6	25,300	0.4	26,382	-0.2	1,082	1.043
Lithuania	2.6	24,411	1.5	23,351	-1.1	-1,060	.957
Tadzhikistan	1.9	11,967	1.3	14,423	-0.6	2,456	1.205
Kirgizia	1.1	7,941	0.7	7,341	-0.4	-600	.924
Estonia	0.8	5,300	0.6	5,164	-0.2	-136	.974
Turkmenia	0.6	3,945	0.3	3,442	-0.3	-503	.873
Armenia	0.1	974	0.1	1,018	—	44	1.045

Sources: *Itogi, 1959,* Table 53 of the relevant volumes; *Itogi, 1970,* vol. 4, Tables 5, 7, 9, 11, 13, 15, 17, 19, 20–22, 24, 26, 27, 29.

THE SOVIET JEWISH *URBAN* POPULATION, BY OBLAST', KRAI, AND AUTONOMOUS REPUBLIC, 1959, 1970

AREA	1959		1970		CHANGE		RATIO
	% OF TOTAL POPULATION	FREQUENCY	% OF TOTAL POPULATION	FREQUENCY	% OF TOTAL POPULATION	FREQUENCY	1970 1959
R S F S R							
Northwest region							
Oblast' (or ASSR)							
Kaliningrad	1.08	4,268	0.82	4,386	−0.26	118	1.028
Leningrad [a]	4.39	173,259	3.47	167,418	−0.92	−5,841	.966
Murmansk	0.55	2,884	0.33	2,318	−0.22	−566	.804
Pskov	1.07	2,750	0.60	2,223	−0.47	−527	.808
Karelian ASSR	—	—	0.30	1,470	—	—	—
Komi ASSR	—	—	0.27	1,594	—	—	—
Central region							
Oblast'							
Briansk	2.47	13,326	1.51	11,348	−0.96	−1,978	.852
Ivanovo	—	—	0.17	1,730	—	—	—
Kalinin	—	—	0.34	3,317	—	—	—
Kaluga	—	—	0.41	2,129	—	—	—
Moscow [a]	3.29	282,601	2.54	279,782	−0.75	−2,819	.990
Smolensk	—	—	0.97	5,122	—	—	—
Tula	—	—	0.33	4,660	—	—	—
Iaroslavl'	—	—	0.30	2,931	—	—	—
Volga-Viatka region							
Gor'ki oblast'	0.95	17,827	0.70	16,695	−0.25	−1,132	.937
Central Black Earth region							
Voronezh oblast'	0.68	5,610	0.51	5,824	−0.17	214	1.038
Kursk oblast'	—	—	0.94	4,581	—	—	—
Volga region							
Oblast'(or ASSR)							
Astrakhan'	—	—	0.64	3,369	—	—	—
Volgograd	—	—	0.32	4,903	—	—	—
Kuibyshev	1.41	19,690	0.94	18,468	−0.47	−1,222	.938
Saratov	1.11	13,004	0.73	11,651	−0.38	−1,353	.896
Tatar ASSR	0.85	10,112	0.58	9,434	−0.27	−678	.933
North Caucasus region							
Krasnodar krai	—	—	0.34	7,173	—	—	—
Stavropol' krai	—	—	0.59	5,789	—	—	—
Rostov oblast'	1.08	20,516	0.74	17,944	−0.34	−2,572	.875
Dagestan ASSR	6.50	20,501	4.29	21,652	−2.21	1,151	1.056
Kabardino-Balkar ASSR	2.02	3,365	1.95	5,458	−0.07	2,093	1,622
Severo-Osetin ASSR	0.84	2,012	0.27	2,015	−0.57	3	1.002
Checheno-Ingush ASSR	1.70	4,981	1.09	4,855	−0.61	−126	.975

AREA	1959		1970		CHANGE		RATIO
	% OF TOTAL POPULATION	FREQUENCY	% OF TOTAL POPULATION	FREQUENCY	% OF TOTAL POPULATION	FREQUENCY	1970 1959
Ural region							
Oblast' (or ASSR)							
Orenburg	0.99	8,248	0.61	6,681	−0.38	−1,567	.810
Perm'	—	—	0.39	7,852	—	—	—
Sverdlovsk	0.82	25,291	0.60	20,942	−0.22	−4,349	.828
Cheliabinsk	0.82	18,611	0.60	15,485	−0.22	−3,126	.832
Bashkir ASSR	0.56	7,167	0.36	6,589	−0.20	−578	.919
West Siberian region							
Oblast'							
Kemerovo	—	—	0.21	4,938	—	—	—
Novosibirsk	0.96	12,184	0.72	11,752	−0.24	−432	.965
Omsk	1.29	9,175	0.79	7,970	−0.50	−1,205	.869
Tomsk	—	—	0.49	2,303	—	—	—
East Siberian region							
Krasnoiarsk krai	—	—	0.28	5,112	—	—	—
Irkutsk oblast'	0.79	9,727	0.47	7,823	−0.32	−1,904	.804
Chita oblast'	—	—	0.22	1,477	—	—	—
Buriat ASSR	0.81	2,244	0.50	1,807	−0.31	−437	.805
Far East region							
Primorskii krai	—	—	0.26	3,264	—	—	—
Khabarovsk krai	0.95	7,959	0.68	7,048	−0.27	−911	.886
Jewish Autonomous oblast'	10.21	11,977	8.67	10,275	−1.54	−1,702	.858
Magadan oblast'	—	—	0.56	1,466	—	—	—
Not specified	—	120,939	—	33,491	—	—	—
UKRAINE							
Donets-Dnepr region							
Oblast'							
Dnepropetrovsk	3.81	72,430	2.70	68,776	−1.11	−3,654	.950
Donetsk	1.16	42,256	0.93	39,834	−0.23	−2,422	.943
Zaporozh'e	2.43	20,113	1.70	19,843	−0.73	−270	.987
Voroshilovgrad [b]	0.71	13,795	0.55	12,460	−0.16	−1,335	.903
Poltava	2.48	12,007	1.56	10,600	−0.92	−1,407	.883
Sumy	1.24	6,025	0.71	4,624	−0.53	−1,401	.768
Khar'kov	5.32	83,740	3.89	76,211	−1.43	−7,529	.910
Southwest region							
Oblast'							
Vinnitsa	11.46	41,648	7.15	38,787	−4.31	−2,861	.931
Zhitomir	9.54	39,805	6.18	35,131	−3.36	−4,674	.883
Zakarpat'e	3.48	9,226	2.88	9,042	−0.60	−184	.980
Ivano-Frankovsk	—	—	0.92	3,529	—	—	—

AREA	1959		1970		CHANGE		RATIO
	% OF TOTAL POPULATION	FREQUENCY	% OF TOTAL POPULATION	FREQUENCY	% OF TOTAL POPULATION	FREQUENCY	1970 1959
Kiev [a]	10.81	167,352	7.18	164,257	−3.63	−3,095	.982
Kirovograd	2.30	8,640	1.33	7,358	−0.97	−1,282	.852
L'vov	3.62	29,701	2.40	27,584	−1.22	−2,117	.929
Rovno	—	—	0.85	2,459	—	—	—
Khmel'nitskii	5.82	17,733	3.63	15,685	−2.19	−2,048	.885
Cherkassy	3.55	12,281	1.86	10,463	−1.69	−1,818	.852
Chernigov	3.49	12,220	1.90	10,229	−1.59	−1,991	.837
Chernovtsy	20.05	40,717	12.73	37,221	−7.32	−3,496	.914
Southern region							
Oblast'							
Crimea	2.90	26,815	2.10	24,089	−0.80	−2,726	.898
Nikolaev	4.74	19,028	2.88	17,417	−1.86	−1,611	.915
Odessa	12.43	118,962	8.71	116,280	−3.72	−2,682	.978
Kherson	2.87	9,556	1.76	9,768	−1.11	212	1.022
Not specified	—	5,981	—	2,591	—	—	—
BELORUSSIA							
Oblast'							
Brest	2.01	5,715	1.08	4,879	−0.93	−836	.854
Vitebsk	4.41	18,092	2.71	16,926	−1.70	−1,166	.936
Gomel'	11.04	42,913	6.76	41,619	−4.28	−1,294	.970
Grodno	1.40	3,513	0.83	3,068	−0.57	−445	.873
Minsk [a]	5.94	46,480	4.03	53,509	−1.91	7,029	1.151
Mogilev	7.61	27,778	4.88	25,464	−2.73	−2,314	.917
UZBEKISTAN							
Oblast'							
Andizhan	1.68	5,011	1.68	4,274	—	−737	.853
Bukhara	4.69	6,122	2.82	8,244	−1.87	2,122	1.347
Kashkadar'ia	—	—	1.65	2,184	—	—	—
Samarkand	4.08	12,835	3.66	14,360	−0.42	1,525	1.119
Surkhandar'ia	1.95	2,583	—	—	—	—	—
Tashkent [a]	4.15	54,709	2.98	58,904	−1.17	4,195	1.077
Fergana	2.49	8,301	2.08	9,149	−0.41	848	1.102
Not specified	—	362	—	2,664	—	—	—
GEORGIA							
Tbilisi (city)	2.47	17,333	2.20	19,579	−0.27	2,246	1.130
Raions attached to Republic administration	2.77	20,106	2.88	27,645	0.11	7,539	1.375
Abkhaz ASSR	2.09	3,124	1.98	4,253	−0.11	1,129	1.361
Adzhar ASSR	1.43	1,585	1.10	1,511	−0.33	−74	.953
Iugo-Ostin Autonomous oblast'	7.02	1,682	4.06	1,480	−2.96	−202	.880

| AREA | 1959 | | 1970 | | CHANGE | | RATIO |
	% OF TOTAL POPULATION	FREQUENCY	% OF TOTAL POPULATION	FREQUENCY	% OF TOTAL POPULATION	FREQUENCY	1970 1959
AZERBAIDZHAN							
Baku city and attached localities	3.01	29,197	2.35	29,716	−0.66	519	1.018
Raions attached to Republic administration	1.32	9,634	0.93	11,052	−0.39	1,418	1.147
Not specified	—	86	—	44	—	—	—
KAZAKHSTAN							
Oblast' (or city)							
Dzhambul	0.37	754	—	—	—	—	—
Kzyl-Orda	0.69	1,045	0.40	1,070	−0.29	25	1.024
Chimkent	0.89	2,965	0.63	3,143	−0.26	178	1.060
Alma-Ata (city)	1.85	8,425	1.26	9,180	−0.59	755	1.090
Karaganda	0.60	4,792	0.39	4,936	−0.21	144	1.030
Not specified	—	7,319	—	8,053	—	—	—
TADZHIKISTAN							
Dushanbe (city)	3.84	8,720	3.06	11,424	−0.78	2,704	1.310
Raions attached to Republic administration	0.79	3,239	—	—	—	—	—
Leninabad oblast'	—	—	0.63	2,215	—	—	—
Not specified	—	8	—	784	—	—	—
KIRGIZIA							
Frunze (city)	2.65	5,840	1.38	5,962	−1.27	122	1.021
Raions attached to Republic administration	0.36	610	—	—	—	—	—
not specified	—	1,491	—	1,379	—	—	—
TURKMENIA							
Ashkhabad (city)	0.75	1,276	0.49	1,246	−0.26	−30	.977
Chardzhou oblast'	—	—	0.39	788	—	—	—
Not specified	—	2,669	—	1,408	—	—	—

Sources: *Itogi, 1959,* Table 54 of the relevant volumes; *Itogi, 1970,* vol. 4, Tables 6, 8, 10, 12, 14, 16, 18, 23, 25, 28.

(a) Including the metropolitan region.

(b) 1935–1958: Voroshilovgrad; 1959–1969: Lugansk; since 1970: Voroshilovgrad.

TABLE 3F

THE URBAN JEWISH POPULATION OF THE UKRAINE BY CITY, 1959
(1,000'S OF PERSONS)

CITY	TOTAL	JEWS	
		FREQUENCY	PERCENTAGE OF TOTAL
Dnepropetrovsk oblast'	**1,899**	**72.4**	**3.8**
Dnepropetrovsk	660	52.8	8.0
Krivoi-Rog	388	11.6	3.0
Other cities	851	8.0	0.9
Donetsk oblast'	**3,656**	**42.3**	**1.2**
Donetsk	699	21.0	3.0
Artemovsk	61	1.8	3.0
Zhdanov	284	2.8	1.0
Other cities	2,612	16.7	0.6
Zaporozh'e oblast'	**829**	**20.1**	**2.4**
Zaporozh'e	435	17.3	4.0
Melitopol'	95	2.8	3.0
Lugansk oblast'	**1,945**	**13.8**	**0.7**
Lugansk	275	5.5	2.0
Other cities	1,670	8.3	0.5
Poltava oblast'	**484**	**12.0**	**2.5**
Poltava	143	4.3	3.0
Kremenchug	87	5.2	6.0
Lubny	29	0.6	2.1
Other cities	225	1.9	0.8
Sumy oblast'	**485**	**6.0**	**1.2**
Romny	36	1.1	3.1
Other cities	449	4.9	1.1
Khar'kov oblast'	**1,574**	**83.7**	**5.3**
Khar'kov	934	81.5	8.7
Other cities	640	2.2	0.3
Vinnitsa oblast'	**363**	**41.7**	**11.5**
Vinnitsa	122	19.5	16.0
Mogilev-Podol'skii	21	4.7	22.4
Tul'chin	12	2.5	20.8
Gaisin	18	1.4	7.8
Khmel'nik	13	1.1	8.5
Other cities	177	12.5	7.1
Volyn' oblast'	**–**	**–**	**–**
Lutsk	56	0.6	1.1
Kovel'	25	1.0	4.0

(Table 3F continued)

CITY	TOTAL	JEWS	
		FREQUENCY	PERCENTAGE OF TOTAL
Zhitomir oblast'	417	39.8	9.5
Zhitomir	106	14.8	14.0
Korosten'	38	6.8	17.9
Berdichev	53	6.4	12.1
Novograd-Volynskii	28	3.3	11.8
Other cities	192	8.5	4.4
Ivano-Frankovsk oblast'	–	–	–
Ivano-Frankovsk	66	1.3	2.0
Kolomyia	31	0.6	1.9
Kiev oblast'	1,548	167.4	10.8
Kiev	1,104	153.5	13.9
Belaia Tserkov'	71	5.6	7.9
Other cities	373	8.3	2.2
Kirovograd oblast'	376	8.6	2.3
Kirovograd	128	5.1	4.0
Other cities	248	3.5	1.4
L'vov oblast'	821	29.7	3.6
L'vov	411	24.7	6.0
Drogobych	42	0.8	1.9
Stryi	36	0.7	1.9
Other cities	332	3.5	1.1
Rovno oblast'	–	–	–
Rovno	56	1.1	2.0
Khmel'nitskii oblast'	305	17.7	5.8
Khmel'nitskii	62	6.2	10.0
Kamenets-Podol'skii	40	2.4	6.0
Starokonstantinov	20	0.8	4.0
Other cities	183	8.3	4.5
Cherkassy oblast'	346	12.3	3.6
Cherkassy	85	5.1	6.0
Uman'	45	2.2	4.9
Smela	45	1.8	4.0
Zolotonosha	25	1.0	4.0
Zvenigorodka	17	0.7	4.1
Shpola	16	0.6	3.8
Other cities	113	0.9	0.8

(Table 3F continued)

		JEWS	
CITY	TOTAL	FREQUENCY	PERCENTAGE OF TOTAL
Chernigov oblast'	350	12.2	3.5
Chernigov	90	7.2	8.0
Priluki	44	2.2	5.0
Nezhin	46	1.4	3.0
Other cities	170	1.4	0.8
Chernovtsy oblast'	203	40.7	20.1
Chernovtsy	146	36.5	25.0
Other cities	57	4.2	7.4
Crimea oblast'	924	26.8	2.9
Simferopol'	186	11.2	6.0
Sevastopol'	148	3.1	2.1
Other cities	590	12.5	2.1
Nikolaev oblast'	400	19.0	4.7
Nikolaev	226	15.8	7.0
Pervomaisk	44	2.2	5.0
Voznesensk	31	0.9	2.9
Other cities	99	0.1	0.1
Odessa oblast'	957	119.0	12.4
Odessa	667	106.7	16.0
Balta	18	1.4	7.8
Other cities	272	10.9	4.0
Kherson oblast'	333	9.6	2.9
Kherson	158	9.5	6.0
Other cities	175	0.1	0.1

Sources: J. Newth, "Jews in the Ukraine", *Bulletin on Soviet and East European Jewish Affairs*, No. 3 (1969), pp. 16–19, and *Itogi, 1959,* Table 54, Ukraine volume.

TABLE 3G

THE SOVIET JEWISH POPULATION IN LARGE CITIES, 1959, 1970

REPUBLIC	1959 % OF TOTAL POPULATION	1959 FREQUENCY	1970 % OF TOTAL POPULATION	1970 FREQUENCY	CHANGE % OF TOTAL POPULATION	CHANGE FREQUENCY	RATIO 1970/1959
RSFSR							
Moscow	4.70	239,246	3.56	251,523	−1.14	12,277	1.051
Leningrad	5.08	168,641	4.12	162,587	−0.96	−6,054	.964
Ukraine							
Kiev	13.89	153,466	9.32	152,006	−4.57	−1,460	.991
Belorussia							
Minsk	7.62	38,842	5.13	47,057	−2.49	8,215	1.212
Uzbekistan							
Tashkent	5.53	50,445	4.03	55,758	−1.50	5,313	1.105
Moldavia							
Kishinev	19.88	42,934	14.00	49,905	−5.88	6,971	1.162
Georgia							
Tbilisi	2.50	17,311	2.20	19,579	−0.30	2,268	1.131
Azerbaidzhan							
Baku	3.01	29,197	2.35	29,716	−0.66	519	1.018
Latvia							
Riga	5.01	30,267	4.18	30,581	−0.83	314	1.010
Kazakhstan							
Alma-Ata	1.85	8,425	1.26	9,180	−0.59	755	1.090
Lithuania							
Vilnius	6.92	16,354	4.43	16,491	−2.49	137	1.008
Kaunas	2.24	4,792	1.40	4,272	−0.84	−520	.892
Klaipeda	0.80	719	0.60	840	−0.20	121	1.168
Tadzhikistan							
Dushanbe	3.84	8,720	3.06	11,424	−0.78	2,704	1.310
Kirgizia							
Frunze	2.65	5,840	1.38	5,962	−1.27	122	1.021
Estonia							
Tallin	1.32	3,714	1.04	3,754	−0.28	40	1.011
Turkmenia							
Ashkhabad	0.75	1,276	0.49	1,246	−0.26	−30	.977

Sources: *Itogi, 1959,* Table 54 of the relevant volumes; *Itogi, 1970,* vol. 4, Tables 6, 8, 10, 12, 14, 16, 18, 23, 25, 28; *Sovetskaia Litva,* May 6, 1971.

4 DISTRIBUTION OF SOVIET JEWRY BY SEX AND INTERNAL MIGRATION

DIVISION BY SEX

The division of Soviet Jewry by sex differs from that of the population as a whole. The census of 1926 indicated 1,115 female Jews per 1,000 males against a ratio of 1,069 in the general population. This high proportion of females resulted from especially high casualties among Jewish males during World War I and the civil war (pogroms) as well as the emigration movement before World War I and after the revolution, in which there was a high proportion of males. The Jewish sex ratio improved in the twelve years between the censuses of 1926 and 1939, which also meant a reduction in the difference between this ratio and that of the population as a whole.

The 1939 census, taken before Soviet annexation of Polish, Rumanian, and Baltic territories, found 1,086 females per 1,000 males in the general population and 1,102 females per 1,000 Jewish males.[1] The differential in the ratio of females to males, a gap that existed in the general population as well as in the Jewish community, had narrowed from 46 females per 1,000 males in 1926 to 16 in 1939. The increase in the proportion of females in the Soviet population between 1926 and 1939 is primarily a consequence of collectivization and mass expulsions, during the course of which more men than women died or were put to death. These factors did less harm to the Jewish community than they did to the general population, and the gap in this sphere between the Jews and the overall population narrowed.

The heavy losses the male population suffered in World War II and the widespread terror of the 1945-1953 period caused the sex ratio in the Soviet Union to worsen. The 1959 census found 1,220 females per 1,000 males.[2] It therefore appears that during those twenty years (1939-1959), the imbalance between the sexes of the general Soviet population grew by 134 females per 1,000 males. In the Jewish community, the imbalance between the sexes grew during that period by only 98 females per 1,000 males. The sex ratio of the Jewish population, according to the 1959 census, was more balanced than that of the overall Soviet population, with 1,200 Jewish females per 1,000 males. According to that census, then, there was an excess in the USSR of 206,556 Jewish females (see table 4B and 4C).

In the 1939-1959 period, the sex ratio was upset less among the Jews than in the general population for two main reasons. First, Jewish men outnumbered Jewish women in the partisan movement, which resulted in a relatively high level of survival of males. More Jewish men than women were inducted into the Red Army in areas captured afterward by the Germans; some of these men, too, survived. Moreover, among those who were evacuated or escaped to the interior, the proportion of males was greater than that of females. It therefore appears that more men than women survived from the Nazi-occupied areas, where most of the Jewish population was annihilated.[3]

Second, the Soviet interior, not conquered by the Nazis, served the Jews as areas of immigration from their historic places of residence. In these areas the percentage of males was higher than that of females. The 1939 census found 957 Jewish females per 1,000 Jewish males in eight SSRs (apart from the RSFSR, the Ukraine, and Belorussia). In the RSFSR, another destination of Jewish internal migration, that census found 1,025 females for every 1,000 males, and in the Ukraine and Belorussia, there were 1,156 Jewish females per 1,000 males.[4]

During the 1960s there was an improvement in the sex ratio of the Soviet population as a whole. According to the 1970 census, there were 1,170 females per 1,000 males. In the intercensus period (1959-1970), then, the gap between the sexes closed by 50 females per 1,000 males. Concerning the Jews, that census found 1,177 females per 1,000 males. It therefore appears that the gap between the sexes in the Jewish community narrowed between the censuses by 23 females per 1,000 males; the excess of Jewish females came to 174,689. Unlike the 1950s, therefore, when the Jewish sex ratio was more balanced than that of the general Soviet population, imbalance in the 1960s was greater for the Jews. Because improvement in the balance between the sexes took place mainly as a result of births, in which the balance between the sexes is generally preserved, the fact that the Jews displayed no improvement alongside that of the general Soviet population

Appendix tables 4A-4C appear at the end of this chapter.

hints that the fertility of the Jews was lower than that of the general population.

Between the censuses (1959-1970), the number of males in the USSR grew by 18.5 percent and of females by 13.5 percent. In the same period, the population of Jewish males declined by 4.1 percent and of Jewish females by 6.0 percent (see tables 4B, 4C). The lower rate of natural increase for Soviet females and the larger decline evinced by Jewish females are consequences of the high incidence of women in the older age brackets; we therefore find a higher proportion of women among deaths.

Differences between the sex ratios exist between urban and rural areas. The 1959 census found 1,229 females per 1,000 males in rural areas and 1,212 in the urban areas—or a rural-urban difference of 17 females per 1,000 males. The 1970 census indicates that in rural areas, there were 1,186 females per 1,000 males and in urban areas 1,158, or a rural-urban difference of 28 females per 1,000 males. In the 1960s, then, the sex differential between the urban and the rural population grew as a consequence of increased migration to the cities.[5] Unlike the overall population, in which the proportion of females in rural areas exceeded their proportion in urban areas, the percentage of females among the Jews was higher in urban than in rural areas. The 1959 census found 1,213 females per 1,000 males in the urban populace and only 980 among nonurban Jews. An additional drop in the percentage of Jewish females in rural areas took place in the 1960s. According to the 1970 census, there were only 891 females per 1,000 Jewish males in rural areas, against 1,184 in the urban areas (see table 4A). We therefore see that in the Jewish community too the difference between the urban and the rural sex ratios widened in the intercensus period (the 1959 census found 233 more females per 1,000 males in the urban than in the rural areas, and 293 in 1970). It is reasonable to assume that these discrepencies between the Jewish rural and urban communities are the result of the channeling of educated and occupationally trained Jews—categories in which, by all appearances, males outnumber females—to work in rural areas. The fact that the percentage of Jewish males is higher than that of females in the rural areas, in the face of a significant excess of females in the overall rural population, almost certainly has an effect on intermarriage, a phenomenon more widespread in the rural than in the urban areas. Because the percentage of Jews dwelling in rural areas is negligible, however, the sex ratio of rural-dwelling Jews does not substantially influence the overall Soviet Jewish community.

The distribution by sex of the Jewish population is not equal in every SSR, a fact that may hint at demographic phenomena in the various Jewish communities. We must first compare the two large Jewish concentrations, the RSFSR and the Ukraine—in each case, home to more than one-third of Soviet Jewry during the 1960s.

Although the Jewish populations in the RSFSR and the Ukraine decreased at almost equal rates in the intercensus period (7.7 percent in the RSFSR and 7.5 in the Ukraine), the decline varied significantly in terms of sex. During this period (1959-1970), the number of Jewish females in the RSFSR dropped by 9.0 percent and that of the males by 6.1 percent. In the Ukraine, by contrast, the drop was almost identical for both sexes (males, 7.4 percent; females, 7.6 percent). The 1970 census found 50,111 excess Jewish females in the RSFSR and 87,030 in the Ukraine. Had the age structure of the Jewish population during the 1960s been identical in the two SSRs and had their birthrates been equal and no out-migration taken place, then in the light of identical average life spans in the RSFSR and the Ukraine, the sex ratios in the two SSRs should have been equal in each census. The findings of the 1970 census, however, do not bear out this assumption.

The 1959 census found 1,169 females per 1,000 males in the RSFSR and 1,255 in the Ukraine. During the 1960s, the differential between the sexes in the Jewish population of the RSFSR was reduced by 37 (1,169 females per 1,000 males in the 1959 census and 1,132 in 1970) and in the Ukraine by only 3 (1,255 females per 1,000 males in the 1959 census and 1,252 in 1970). According to the age composition of the Jewish population in the RSFSR and according to data on natural increase collected in Khar'kov, we may deduce that the rate of natural increase was higher, or the natural decrease lower, for the Jews of the Ukraine than that of the Jewish population of the RSFSR. The gap between the sexes should therefore have narrowed more in the Ukraine than in the RSFSR. If the data indicate the opposite, however, we have grounds to suppose that there was out-migration from the Ukraine to other SSRs, the RSFSR among them, in the 1960s. Since migration streams generally include a disproportionate number of males, the effect of these movements was felt both with regard to the decline in the RSFSR in the difference in the proportions of either sex and in the preservation of this difference in the Ukraine.

In two southern SSRs (Uzbekistan and Azerbaidzhan) where the Jewish population rose between the two censuses (by 9 percent in Uzbekistan and 2.7 percent in Azerbaidzhan), the sex ratio improved significantly as well. There were 1,159 Jewish females per 1,000 males in Uzbekistan in 1959 and only 1,124 in 1970—a narrowing of 35 females per 1,000 males in that SSR. For Azerbaidzhan, there were 1,251 females per 1,000 males in 1959 and 1,200 in 1970; the gap closed there by 51 females per 1,000 males (see table 4A). It is curious, however, that in Georgia, where the Jewish population also grew in the intercensus period (by 7.4 percent), the improvement in the sex ratio was only 10 females per 1,000 males. Here, too, as in the Ukraine, Jewish emigration to other parts of the USSR may explain the phenomenon.

It appears that the considerable improvement in the sex ratio of the Jewish population in two Baltic SSRs—Latvia and Lithuania—is also traceable to migration. The 1959 census recorded 1,140 Jewish females per 1,000 males in Latvia and 1,150 in Lithuania. Between the censuses, this measure declined by 63 females per 1,000 males in Latvia and 81 in Lithuania, meaning that the sex ratio narrowed at nearly 3 times the average for Soviet Jews (23 females per 1,000 males) in Latvia, and more than 3.5 times in Lithuania. Because fertility for the Jews of Latvia and Lithuania is not high, these differences should be attributed in the main to the positive migration balance of the Jews of these SSRs.

INTERNAL MIGRATION

An extensive wave of internal migration swamped the USSR during World War II and the early postwar period. Its general directions are known, but its dimensions are not clear; Soviet publications shed no light on it. Many Jews, whose number we cannot estimate, fled territories about to fall to the Germans during World War II, through organized evacuation or by their own initiative. It appears that a large majority of these Jews returned to their previous areas of residence after the war, but quite a few settled permanently in places where they had spent the war. This hypothesis finds support through a comparison of the few figures published from the 1939 census with data from that of 1959.

The Jewish community in Uzbekistan grew by close to 86 percent between 1939 and 1959 (from 50,809 Jews according to the 1939 census to 94,344 according to that of 1959).[6] In the Bashkir and Tatar autonomous republics and in the Perm' *oblast'* (called Molotov *oblast'* between 1940 and 1957), situated on the border of the Asiatic sector of the RSFSR, the Jewish communities also grew in the intercensus period. In the Bashkir ASSR, 3,800 Jews were reported in 1939 (0.1 percent of the population) as opposed to 6,500 in 1959 (0.2 percent of the population)—a 71 percent increase in Jewish population in that republic.[7] As for the Tatar ASSR, the 1939 census found 6,000 Jews (0.2 percent of the population) and that of 1959 10,400 (0.4 percent of the population)—a 73 percent increase in the Jewish population of that republic.[8] The data from Perm' *oblast'* indicate a similar phenomenon: 4,172 Jews polled in 1939 and 8,096 in 1970.[9] It would appear that in the thirty-one years between the censuses of 1939 and 1970, the Jewish community in that *oblast'* grew by 94 percent. Most of the increase should apparently be attributed to World War II-period migration.

The Soviet statistical institutes have a great deal of raw material pertaining to migratory movements in the forty years since World War II because all citizens who change their permanent place of residence must fill out a detailed form, both in the communities they are leaving and in their new homes. Although they must also note nationality as recorded on their internal passports, it is doubtful that the forms are processed according to nationality group distribution. In any event, no current data have been released concerning the nationality group distribution of internal migrants; in the 1959 census, too, no effort was made to collect data on internal migration. In the 1960s, however, this question became one of the most important problems in the national economy. Certain areas, sometimes those less industrialized, displayed rapid population growth, while others were afflicted with manpower shortages. Certain peoples displayed great mobility, while others remained in their traditional places of residence. These factors led Soviet research and statistical institutions to devote greater attention to studying internal migration and the factors motivating it.[10] Indeed the 1970 census questionnaire included a question meant to examine internal migration.

Census subjects to whom the expanded questionnaire was submitted (tenants in every fourth apartment, or 25 percent of the population) were asked how long they had lived in the city or village in which they dwelled at the time of the census. Those who had lived there two years or less were asked to specify their previous place of residence. The responses to this question, projected into the entire population, supply data on internal migration in the Soviet Union for 1968-1969. The summaries of the census presented findings on this internal migration and its nationality group distribution on the basis of the fifteen nationalities with their own union republics. At the same time, an article on the subject, published in *Vestnik statistiki*, provides details on the internal migration of forty-five peoples, Jews among them.

The census findings revealed that 5.7 percent of all Soviet citizens exchanged their place of residence during 1968-1969 (this figure does not include children up to 2 years of age, who had been born in their parents' new place of residence). If these percentages were similar throughout the eleven-year intercensus period, close to one-third of the Soviet Union's population migrated in that period (31 percent). This migration took place within SSRs (from city to city, village to village, city to village, and vice-versa) and between them, and the data on the migration balance for 1968-1969 inform us of the main directions (table 4.1).

In those two years, the migration balance was positive in the RSFSR and the western SSRs and negative in the Asian SSRs and the Caucasus. In addition to the regional differences, this internal migration is influenced by nationality group habits. From the article on 1968-1969 migration percentages for forty-five Soviet peoples, it appears that there are significant differences among them.[11] Migration rates for twenty peoples—including the Russians, Ukrainians, Belorussians, and Latvians—exceeded 5 percent in those two years. Eleven peoples displayed migration rates between 3.1 percent and 4.9 percent; for seven, it ranged from 2.1 percent to 2.9 percent; and migration percentages for seven other peoples varied from 1.4 percent to 1.9 percent.

TABLE 4.1

INTER-REPUBLIC MIGRATION BALANCES, 1968–1969

REPUBLIC	NET MIGRATION (1,000'S)	NET MIGRANTS 100 TOTAL POPULATION	REPUBLIC	NET MIGRATION (1,000'S)	NET MIGRANTS 100 TOTAL POPULATION
RSFSR	+176	+0.1	Kazakhstan	−22	−0.2
Ukraine	+37	+0.1	Lithuania	+3	+0.1
Belorussia	+2	0.0	Tadzhikistan	−19	−0.6
Uzbekistan	−83	−0.7	Kirgizia	−15	−0.5
Moldavia	−10	−0.3	Estonia	+16	+1.2
Georgia	−36	−0.8	Turkmenia	−11	−0.5
Azerbaidzhan	−29	−0.6	Armenia	+6	+0.2
Latvia	+14	+0.6			

Source: B. Korovaeva, "Migratsiia naseleniia SSSR", *Vsesoiuznaia perepis' naseleniia 1970 goda* (Moscow, 1976), p. 250.

The question therefore arises, What was the extent and direction of Jewish internal migration? Although only partial answers can be provided since only fragmentary data have been released, we may at least point to certain trends.

In 1968-1969, Jewish internal migration in their major areas of residence (which were not specified) amounted to 2.1 percent of all Jews dwelling in those areas.[12] The Jews therefore appear to have belonged to the group of peoples of low geographic mobility. If we assume that the percentages of Jewish migration in their main areas of residence were equivalent to those of all Jews in the USSR, and if we assume that the dimensions of migration throughout the entire intercensus period were equal to those for the two years preceding the 1970 census, we shall see that about 11.5 percent of the Jews of the Soviet Union—close to 250,000 in number—changed their places of residence between 1959 and 1970.

A great majority of the Jewish migrants relocated from one urban community to another, with only a small percentage moving from village to city or vice-versa. In 1968-1969 in the Jews' main areas of residence, 1.8 percent of the Jews dwelling in those areas moved from city to city, 0.2 percent from village to city, and 0.1 percent from city to village. If we project these data onto the entire Soviet Jewish community, it would appear that close to 38,000 Jews moved from one city to another, 4,000 from a rural area to an urban area, and about 2,000 Jews from urban to rural areas in those two years. If these migration percentages were similar throughout the intercensus period, we may conclude that close to 219,000 Jews moved from city to city, close to 24,000 from village to city, and approximately

7,000 from city to village. We may therefore say that part of the intercensus drop in rural Jewish population (about 17,000 individuals) is accounted for in the negative migration balance of rural Jews.

Data on the routes of Jewish internal migration are even scantier than those pertaining to internal migration in general. Even these, however, appear capable of adding more sociodemographic information on the Jews of the Soviet Union.

Subjects in a sociological survey in Latvia between 1964 and 1969 were asked how long they had resided in that republic. The data in table 4.2 relate to the Jews. Most Jews who had reached Latvia by the end of the 1940s had apparently resided in that area before the war. There are grounds, however, to assume that of the Jews who had settled in Latvia in the 1950s and 1960s, a number were of non-Latvian extraction. An age discrepancy appears to exist between the veteran Jewish residents of Latvia and those who had relocated there from elsewhere in the Soviet Union. The survey's director notes that "among non-Latvians [who had migrated to Latvia], 78 percent were in the 20-35 age bracket."[13] It is reasonable to assume that Jews continued to migrate to Latvia in the second half of the 1960s and in the 1970s as well and that the migration balance of Jews in that SSR remained positive. This positive migration balance may likely be one of the factors that contributed to maintaining Jewish population in Latvia between 1959 and 1970 despite the low rate of natural increase prevailing there. It is also likely that in Lithuania, too—similar to its neighbor in many respects—Jewish migration balance was also positive.

Internal migration also exerted a certain influence on differences among various *oblast's* as to the drop of the Jewish population. Thus, for example,

TABLE 4.2

SAMPLE OF JEWS IN LATVIA BY DURATION OF RESIDENCE

PERIOD ENTERED THE REPUBLIC [a]	DURATION OF RESIDENCE (YEARS)	PERCENTAGE OF SAMPLE
Before 1940	26+	14.1
1940–1944	21–25	17.2
1945–1949	16–20	32.8
1950–1954	11–15	10.9
1955–1959	6–10	10.9
1960–1964	1–5	14.1

Source: A. Kholmogorov, *Internatsional'nye cherty sovetskikh natsii* (Moscow, 1970), p. 48.

(a) The five-year intervals listed here are based on our assumption that the data relate to residents in Latvia in 1964, the year when the survey was first carried out.

2,830 Jews relocated to Donetsk *oblast'* in 1968 while only 2,380 Jews left—a positive migration balance of 450 individuals, which explains in part the fact that the Jewish population in Donetsk *oblast'* dropped by only 5.9 percent in the intercensus period while it fell by 7.5 percent in the entire Ukraine.[14] Internal migration also bolstered the Jewish community in Kiev, where Jewish population fell by only 0.9 percent in the intercensus period (1959-1970). A survey in which all forms filled out by in-migrants and out-migrants were examined indicates that 2,150 Jews settled in Kiev and 1,900 left in 1967. In that year, therefore, the Jewish population grew by 250 individuals (about 0.2 percent) as a consequence of internal migration.[15]

Although these scanty data are not sufficient to indicate the full extent of internal migration among Jews in the Soviet Union, they do hint that the influence of this factor on population shifts in the intercensus period was only moderate.

TABLE 4A

NUMBER OF JEWISH FEMALES PER THOUSAND MALES
BY REPUBLIC AND RURAL/URBAN STATUS, 1959, 1970

	TOTAL		URBAN		RURAL	
REPUBLIC	1959	1970	1959	1970	1959	1970
Total	1,200	1,177	1,213	1,184	980	891
RSFSR	1,169	1,132	1,182	1,142	955	841
Ukraine	1,255	1,252	1,264	1,257	1,041	993
Belorussia	1,211	1,193	1,220	1,298	993	950
Uzbekistan	1,159	1,124	1,172	1,133	930	885
Moldavia	1,185	1,174	1,196	1,180	1,046	941
Georgia	1,132	1,122	1,157	1,131	1,005	708
Azerbaidzhan	1,251	1,200	1,258	1,202	1,073	1,097
Latvia	1,140	1,077	1,148	1,082	669	672
Kazakhstan	1,036	1,029	1,076	1,040	734	825
Lithuania	1,150	1,069	1,156	1,070	695	792
Tadzhikistan	1,068	1,074	1,090	1,078	617	811
Kirgizia	1,094	1,130	1,117	1,152	858	757
Estonia	1,130	990	1,127	1,009	1,267	442
Turkmenia	1,149	1,042	1,159	1,045	873	857
Armenia	1,790	1,193	1,775	1,218	2,125	579

Sources: *Itogi, 1959*, Table 53 of the appropriate volumes; *Itogi, 1970*, vol. 4, Tables 4, 5, 7, 9, 11, 13, 15, 17, 19–22, 24, 26, 27, 29.

TABLE 4B

THE JEWISH MALE POPULATION, BY REPUBLIC, 1959, 1970

REPUBLIC	FREQUENCIES		CHANGES	RATIO
	1959	1970	FREQUENCY	1970 / 1959
Total	1,030,629	988,009	−42,620	0.959
RSFSR	403,586	378,902	−24,684	0.939
Ukraine	372,592	345,048	−27,544	0.926
Belorussia	67,896	67,483	−413	0.994
Uzbekistan	43,694	48,417	4,723	1.108
Moldavia	43,533	45,110	1,577	1.036
Georgia	24,192	26,094	1,902	1.079
Azerbaidzhan	17,857	18,761	904	1.051
Latvia	17,096	17,659	563	1.033
Kazakhstan	13,775	13,649	−126	0.991
Lithuania	11,478	11,389	−89	0.992
Tadzhikistan	6,002	7,046	1,044	1.174
Kirgizia	4,111	3,605	−506	0.877
Estonia	2,552	2,657	105	1.041
Turkmenia	1,898	1,711	−187	0.902
Armenia	367	478	111	1.303

See sources cited in Table 4A.

TABLE 4C

THE JEWISH FEMALE POPULATION, BY REPUBLIC, 1959, 1970

REPUBLIC	FREQUENCIES		CHANGES	RATIO
	1959	1970	FREQUENCY	1970 1959
Total	1,237,185	1,162,698	−74,487	0.940
RSFSR	471,721	429,013	−42,708	0.910
Ukraine	467,719	432,078	−35,641	0.924
Belorussia	82,188	80,528	−1,660	0.980
Uzbekistan	50,650	54,438	3,788	1.075
Moldavia	51,574	52,962	1,388	1.027
Georgia	27,390	29,288	1,898	1.069
Azerbaidzhan	22,347	22,527	180	1.008
Latvia	19,496	19,021	−475	0.976
Kazakhstan	14,273	14,040	−233	0.984
Lithuania	13,194	12,175	−1,019	0.923
Tadzhikistan	6,413	7,569	1,156	1.180
Kirgizia	4,499	4,075	−424	0.906
Estonia	2,884	2,631	−253	0.912
Turkmenia	2,180	1,783	−397	0.818
Armenia	657	570	−87	0.868

See sources cited in Table 4A.

5 EDUCATION

Education is one of the important components that determine the sociodemographic profile of the Soviet Union's Jewish community. Statistical data revealing the extent of schooling among Jews are available in two forms: census figures showing the distribution of Jews across education-level categories and current data concerning Jewish students enrolled in VUZ (higher education) and secondary vocational institutions. The first set of data provides the cumulative result of past years' schooling and the second indicates the pattern of Jewish entrance into the youngest strata of the academically and professionally trained (those entering higher or secondary vocational education during the 1960s and 1970s). These data may hint at future developments.

The structure of Soviet education departs from the pattern conventional in many Western countries; before we analyze the statistical data, a preface is therefore in order.

STRUCTURE OF SOVIET EDUCATION

Primary education in the Soviet Union is of four years' duration (grades 1 through 4). Until the 1944/45 year, children began studies at the age of 8; in that year 7 became the standard age for starting school. Compulsory primary education in the USSR was introduced in the early 1930s.[1]

Until 1959, "incomplete" secondary school (*nepolnoe srednee obrazovanie*) involved three years of study (grades 5 through 7). The Eighteenth Communist party Congress (1939) resolved to introduce seven years of compulsory education, but World War II prevented its implementation. With the educational reform of 1959, incomplete secondary schooling was expanded to four years of study (grades 5 through 8) and was made mandatory for the entire population; the Soviet constitution was amended accordingly.[2]

The comprehensive secondary curriculum entailed the completion of ten grades until 1959; from 1959 to 1966 an eleventh year was required; and thereafter the program was shortened once again, grades 9 and 10 now constituting the final course of study.[3]

Secondary vocational education (*srednee spetsial'noe obrazovanie*) includes institutions called *tekhnikum* and other secondary vocational schools (for the reader's convenience, I shall henceforth use the term *tekhnikum* for all institutions of secondary vocational education). A *tekhnikum* provides a secondary education along with occupational training and is one of the major institutions that train the subacademic professional stratum. This sector also recruits personnel from other types of technical schools (two years of study beyond high school) and technical-vocational schools (one additional year). *Tekhnikum* candidates are graduates of incomplete or complete secondary schools in accordance with vocation and institution. *Tekhnikum* studies run from two to five years, meaning that graduates are given two to three years of postsecondary education.[4] Graduates are technicians and veterinarians as well as dental technicians, agricultural technicians and agronomists, statisticians and computer programmers, elementary school teachers, librarians, and the like.[5]

Higher education is offered in a variety of institutions that fall into a number of categories differentiated by structure. There were 739 institutions of higher education in the Soviet Union in 1960 and 756 in 1966.[6] These, however, are not divided proportionally among the various Soviet Republics (SSRs).[7] With regard to structure, institutions of higher education include universities, specialized institutes, and polytechnic institutes (when referring to all institutions of higher education, I shall henceforth use the Russian abbreviation VUZ—*vysshye uchebnye zavedeniia*). Most universities are large institutions in terms of number of students and variety of programs of study. There were forty universities in the USSR in 1960 and forty-three in 1967. Although universities accounted for 5.7 percent of all VUZs in 1967, their enrollment accounted for more than 10 percent of the total student population. Nevertheless, there are significant differences among the universities as well. The University of Moscow had a student body of more than 22,000 in 1960; Tashkent State University in Uzbekistan boasted only 6,500.[8] Specialized institutes are generally dedicated to one field or a number of closely related fields. In the mid-1960s there were 28 institutes of economics, 17 of music (conservatories), 206 of education, and 10 of arts and theater. There were also special institutes for training physicians, agronomists, and engineers for various branches of industry. Several institutes formally considered specialized have in fact exceeded the bounds of one branch; there is no significant difference between them and the polytechnic institutes. The latter train engineers for a wide range of professions and are the important centers for training the country's technical intelligentsia. VUZ studies, depending on professional goal, last from four to six years. All higher education, even in the sciences, includes compulsory courses consisting essentially of political and ideological indoctrination.[9]

Soviet institutions of higher education grant only two degrees. Those having completed their courses of study in a VUZ receive a certificate entitling them to work in their chosen occupation and/or continue studying for a graduate degree (*nauchnaia stepen'*) which confers the title *Kandidat*.

The major route to the degree of *Kandidat* is a special postgraduate program called *Aspirantura*. This, according to official definition, is meant to prepare VUZ and *tekhnikum* teachers and researchers. *Aspirantura* candidates must be under 35 years of age and have displayed research and/or teaching capabilities. *Aspirantura* entrance examinations test candidates in three fields: ideology (Marxism-Leninism, dialectical and historical materialism, and the like), the field in which the candidate wishes to specialize, and a foreign language. In the 1960s preference was given to candidates with practical experience in the respective fields they wished to pursue further. Acceptance committees for *aspirants* are made up of teachers and scholars from the VUZ in question, along with representatives of public organizations (such as the Communist party and Komsomol). Curricula are drawn up individually, suited to each *aspirant* according to his or her sphere of specialization and implemented following consultations with his or her adviser. Full-time study in the *Aspirantura* program, at least three years in duration, entails interrupting one's work career and requires one to pass a number of tests and submit a research study which must be publicly defended. Upon its approval, the *aspirant* is awarded the title *Kandidat*.

Tekhnikum or VUZ students may be divided into full-time (day) students and others who continue working as they study. The latter study in the evenings or by correspondence, and the duration of their studies is longer than that of day students.[10] Benefits offered to *tekhnikum* or VUZ students in evening or correspondence programs (special vacation time for study, payments for travel to school) were increased in the 1960s.[11] Consequently, the proportion of these students in the *tekhnikum* and higher education student body rose. Working students are taught in both VUZs and *tekhnikums* where day studies are offered, as well as in specially designated night schools.

Care in planning and strictness of supervision in each educational institution depends on its rank: the higher is the academic level, the more exacting is the scrutiny. The number of VUZ and *tekhnikum* students and their distribution among the various fields of study are determined each year by the Ministry of Higher and Secondary Vocational Education in accordance with general economic development programs and Communist party policy. The number of *aspirants* in each institution is determined and the spheres of their research are set in a similar way. It therefore appears that the Ministry of Higher and Secondary Vocational Education maintains a precise and detailed registration of the enrollment of the institutions under its direct or indirect control. It is not clear if similar registration takes place for those enrolled in other educational frameworks. Census tabulations, by contrast, provide only partial breakdowns of educational attainment for the population of each national group.

DISTRIBUTION OF THE JEWISH POPULATION BY EDUCATION

A number of tabulations concerning the distribution of the Jewish population on an educational attainment basis have appeared in the summary reports of the 1959 and 1970 census findings. Those relating to 1959 include data on the percentage of Jews who had finished incomplete secondary education—that is, those with more than seven years of schooling—according to the 1939 and 1959 censuses. These data, relating to eight SSRs, include distribution according to sex and residence (urban or rural). The 1970 findings offer data on distribution of the Jews in five SSRs by educational level. In a departure from the 1959 data, which relate to the entire Jewish population, the 1970 findings are calculated on the basis of those aged 10 and over. Moreover, while the 1959 findings relate to only two categories—those who have finished incomplete secondary level and those who have not—the 1970 findings relate to six categories: the proportion with VUZ education, those who have attended at least half of a higher course of study (incomplete higher education), those who have finished a secondary vocational curriculum, those who have finished a secondary school, those with incomplete secondary education, and those with a primary education.[12]

The data concerning the Jews' education as of January 1939 relate to four SSRs (the RSFSR, the Ukraine, Belorussia, and Azerbaidzhan), which, prior to the annexation of the western territories into the Soviet Union, were home to 95.3 percent of Soviet Jewry.[13] These figures shed light on Soviet Jews' educational attainments immediately preceding World War II (table 5.1).

The 1939 data show that the percentage of Jews whose education exceeded seven years was higher in areas to which Jews tended to immigrate

TABLE 5.1

PERSONS WITH SEVEN OR MORE YEARS OF SCHOOLING, 1939

REPUBLIC	JEWS (1,000'S)		PERSONS WITH 7+ YEARS OF SCHOOLING PER 1,000 PERSONS		
	TOTAL	7+ YEARS OF SCHOOLING	JEWS	TOTAL URBAN POPULATION	RATIO (3) TO (4)
	(1)	(2)	(3)	(4)	(5)
Total (4 Republics)	2,897	956	330	181	1.82
RFSFR	948	438	462	174	2.66
Ukraine	1,533	429	280	183	1.53
Belorussia	375	77	205	204	1.00
Azerbaidzhan	41	12	293	164	1.79

Source: Calculated according to Zinger 1941, Appendix 2 and *Itogi, 1959*, Table 57 in the relevant volumes.

(the RSFSR, Azerbaidzhan) than it was in their historical areas of residence. Among Jews of the RSFSR, the percentage of those with seven or more years of schooling was 1.7 times higher than among Jews of the Ukraine and 2.3 times greater than among those in Belorussia. Even in Azerbaidzhan, where a small community of mountain Jews dwelled (a factor tending to depress educational attainment averages), the percentage was higher than among the Jews of the Ukraine and Belorussia. The proportion of Jews at this level of education was 1.5 times higher among urban Jews than among village dwellers.

Between the 1939 and the 1959 censuses, far-reaching changes took place in the extent of education in the Soviet Union and in the demographic structure of the Jewish population that survived the Holocaust. During those two decades, the proportion of those with seven years of schooling or more rose by a factor of approximately 3.5 in the USSR.[14] The regions in which Jews with lower average educational levels lived fell to the Nazis, and the Holocaust's worst devastation occurred there. It may be assumed that the proportion of those with low educational levels (children and the elderly) was higher among Holocaust victims than in the total Jewish population. It is therefore natural that the proportion of Soviet Jews with seven or more years of education rose significantly in the intercensus period. Indeed, in the four SSRs for which both 1939 and 1959 data are available, the proportion of educated Jews (by this definition) grew by a factor of 1.7 (330 per 1,000 people in 1939; 566 in 1959). This increase, however, was not uniform in each SSR (see table 5A). In SSRs where the percentage of those with seven or more years of schooling was high in 1939, the percentage of those so educated rose by a factor of approximately 1.5 (the RSFSR, 1.5; Azerbaidzhan, 1.6). By contrast, in SSRs where the proportion of Jews with this extent of schooling was lower in 1939, the intervening twenty years witnessed a rise by a factor of 2 or even 2.5 (the Ukraine, 2.1; Belorussia, 2.5). Because the proportion of Jews with seven years of schooling or more was already high in 1939, however, the increase in each SSR was lower among the Jews than the SSR-wide average increase in any case.

In the eight SSRs where 91.2 percent of Soviet Jewry resided according to the 1959 census, there were 613 Jews with seven years of schooling or more per 1,000 (see table 5B), with a higher percentage among urban than rural Jews.[15] In the urban Jewish population, the proportion was higher among women than men, while the opposite held true for Jews who dwelled in villages.[16] But since the great majority of the Jewish community is urban, the percentage of Jews with seven or more years of schooling among all Jews in these SSRs was higher among females than among males (612:1000 for men; 614:1000 for women). In 1959, the percentage of Jews at this educational level exceeded that pertaining to the urban population of other Soviet national groups. It exceeded that of Georgians by 13 percent, that of Latvians by 27 percent, and that of Russians by 66 percent.[17] Compared with each other, however, the Jewish populations of the eight SSRs surveyed exhibited substantial differences in educational attainment.

In SSRs where the percentage of Jews at the educational level under discussion exceeded the overall Soviet Jewish average as early as the 1930s, the percentage was higher at the end of the 1950s as well. The proportion of the educated among the Jews of the RSFSR was 19 percent higher than that of the Ukraine, 35 percent higher than that of Belorussia, and 58 percent higher than that of Moldavia (see table 5B). In the five SSRs for which data from both the 1959 and 1970 censuses have been published and in which an average of 87.5 percent of Soviet Jews resided in the two census years (88.1 percent in 1959, 86.8 percent in 1970), the percentage of educated Jews rose between the censuses but not at a uniform pace in each SSR. The intercensus period (1959-1970) witnessed a growth of 8 percent in the RSFSR, 13 percent in Latvia, 15 percent in the Ukraine, 17 percent in Belorussia and 27 percent in Moldavia (see table 5C). Between 1959 and 1970 the rate of increase was faster among the urban Jewish population and among males (see table 5D).

The rise in the proportion of the educated (seven or more years) in the

Appendix tables 5A-5N appear at the end of this chapter.

eleven-year period (1959-1970) led to a fall in the proportion of those with primary education or less, as the data in table 5.2 show. Taking into account the fact that this table includes children from the last grade of primary school (the 7-11 age bracket), it becomes clear that the proportion of adult Jews with less than primary-level education is miniscule and that an overwhelming majority has incomplete secondary or higher levels of education (at least seven years of schooling). The incomplete secondary education launched in the late 1950s and incorporated into the Compulsory Education Law, however, does not bestow social and economic status in the Soviet Union. We should therefore take special interest in examining the distribution of the Jews in this category according to educational levels.

TABLE 5.2

PROPORTIONAL DISTRIBUTION OF THE JEWISH POPULATION BY YEARS OF SCHOOLING,
FOR SELECTED REPUBLICS, 1959, 1970
(PER 1,000 PERSONS AGE 10+)

SCHOOLING AND YEAR	REPUBLIC				
	RSFSR	UKRAINE	BELORUSSIA	MOLDAVIA	LATVIA
Seven and Over Years of Schooling					
1959	764	657	606	520	687
1970	824	750	710	660	773
Four Years of Schooling (primary education)					
1959	152	205	235	293	214
1970	116	158	190	227	163
Less Than Four Years of Schooling					
1959	84	138	159	187	99
1970	60	92	100	113	64

Source: *Itogi, 1970,* vol. 4, Tables 39–41, 47–48.

The 1959 census findings reveal the percentage of Jews in certain SSRs with seven or more years of education; moreover, published findings of the 1970 census included 1959 data for comparison purposes concerning the distribution of Jews aged 10 or over according to educational levels. Because no one under ten years of age could have accumulated seven years of schooling, we may calculate the distribution of the Jewish population by educational levels in the 1959 census in rather accurate and absolute figures (see tables 5E, 5F).

The five SSRs for which 1959 educational data were published, along with figures comparable to that year in summary reports of the 1970 census findings, were home to about 88 percent of Soviet Jews in 1959. Twenty-one percent of the general Jewish population of those SSRs had either completed or fulfilled half of a VUZ program in 1959; 10.2 percent had secondary vocational education; 14.8 percent had secondary education; and 15.8 percent had incomplete secondary education. The data from the five SSRs enable us to estimate the distribution of the Jewish population by educational levels in the Soviet Union as a whole (table 5.3). (For the purposes of this estimate, we shall apply the data pertaining to Latvia's Jews to the other two Baltic SSRs—Lithuania and Estonia—and apply data from Moldavia to the southern union republics—the Uzbek, Georgian, Azerbaidzhan, Kazakh, Tadzhik, Turkmen, and Armenian SSRs.)

TABLE 5.3

JEWISH AND TOTAL URBAN POPULATIONS BY LEVEL OF SCHOOLING, 1959
(PER 1,000 PERSONS)

POPULATION	VUZ	VUZ INCOMPLETE	SECONDARY VOCATIONAL	SECONDARY	INCOMPLETE SECONDARY	LESS THAN 7 YEARS
(1) Jews (est.)	160	37	97	144	161	401
(2) Total [a]	32	13	55	74	203	623
Ratio (1) to (2)	5.0	2.9	1.8	2.0	0.8	0.6

(a) Calculated from *Itogi, 1959*, general volume, Table 22.

It thus appears that approximately one-fifth of Soviet Jews (19.7 percent) in 1959 had completed half or more of a VUZ program and that about one-fourth (24.1 percent) had either secondary or secondary vocational education. Although this percentage is influenced to a certain extent by the relatively small share of children in the Jewish population, it stems essentially from the great appeal of education for the Jews as virtually the only avenue to social prestige and status. The result was a large differential between the educated stratum of Jews and that of the general urban Soviet population. In 1959 the proportion of those who had completed at least half of a VUZ program was 4.4 times greater among Jews than in the general urban population, and the incidence of secondary or secondary vocational education was almost twice as high (a factor of 1.9). Because higher education confers relatively high social rewards and an improved living standard, the factor under discussion is generally related to expressions of envy and hatred of Jews in Soviet society.

My estimate indicates that only about 56 percent of Soviet Jews had less than secondary education in 1959 as opposed to about 83 percent of the general urban population. If we recall, however, that this percentage includes children and youth who could not have attained this level of education because of age, it appears that fewer than half the adult Jews in the Soviet Union had education below the secondary level in 1959.

In order to understand the particular circumstances of each Jewish community in the Soviet Union, general data are not enough; we should also examine the Jews' educational attainments on a regional basis. The 1959 census data indeed reveal large disparities in Jewish educational levels among the various SSRs. In the RSFSR, the percentage of Jews who had completed at least half of a VUZ program was 3.3 times higher than that of Moldavian Jewry, 2.4 times higher than that of the Jews of Belorussia, and 1.9 times higher than that of the Jews of the Ukraine. This disparity narrows when one considers secondary vocational[18] or secondary[19] education and almost totally disappears at the level of incomplete secondary education. Because a large majority of young adults who have completed secondary schooling aspire to VUZ studies, it is natural that the possibility of attaining higher education greatly concerns not only the Jews in the several SSRs where the incidence of secondary education was especially high; it becomes a problem of growing importance for Jews everywhere in the USSR.

Distribution of educated Jews on the basis of sex varies with the level of schooling. In the five SSRs in which 87.8 percent of Jewish males and 88.3 percent of Jewish females dwelled according to the 1959 census, 10.2 percent of Jewish men and 11.6 percent of Jewish women had completed either secondary school or a secondary vocational program. When considering those who had completed either a secondary vocational program or at least half of a VUZ program in the five SSRs under discussion, we find that the proportions shifted slightly: 21.2 percent of the males and 20.3 percent of the females.[20] It therefore appears that in terms of professional education, the percentage differential between women and men was very small in 1959, widening somewhat in the following eleven years. The 1970 census found 363 professionally educated male Jews and 319 female Jews per 1,000 Jews (aged 10 or over) in the five SSRs under discussion.[21]

Data from the 1970 census contained a more detailed breakdown of educational attainment in the five SSRs where 86.8 percent of all Soviet Jews lived (see table 5G). By weighting these data, using the same procedure described for table 5.3, we can estimate Jewish population distribution by educational level in the USSR as a whole.

The data in table 5.4 reveal that although the percentage of Jews with higher education grew significantly, the increase was smaller among them (34 percent) than it was in the total Soviet population (83 percent) and even the general urban population (55 percent).[22] Three major factors were almost certainly at work in accounting for this situation:

TABLE 5.4

THE JEWISH POPULATION BY LEVEL OF SCHOOLING, 1959, 1970
(PER 1,000 PERSONS AGE 10+)

			LEVEL OF SCHOOLING				
YEAR	VUZ	VUZ INCOMPLETE	SECONDARY VOCATIONAL	SECONDARY	INCOMPLETE SECONDARY	PRIMARY	0–3 YEARS
(1) 1959	179	42	108	162	180	197	132
(2) 1970	239	45	137	193	148	156	82
Ratio (2) to (1)	1.34	1.07	1.27	1.19	0.82	0.79	0.62

1. The small incidence of VUZ education in the general Soviet population and even the urban population in 1959.

2. The aging of the Jewish population and consequently a dwindling of the stock of candidates for higher education.

3. Difficulties encountered by Jews seeking to advance to higher studies.

Data on the percentage of those who had completed at least half of a VUZ program reveal an insignificant increase in the intercensus period. While the percentage of Jews at that level rose by 7 percent between the two censuses, the general and urban Soviet population showed a growth of 18 percent during the same interval.[23]

The first two of the three explanatory factors cited with regard to VUZ education have almost certainly also affected the proportion of Jews with secondary vocational education. Indeed, the intercensus period displayed a 27 percent rise in the number of Jews with such education, while the respective corresponding figures for the urban and general Soviet populations were 34 percent and 42 percent (table 5.5).[24] The gap between the Jews' level of education in 1970 and the percentage of similarly educated members of the general urban population of the USSR is explained by the Jews' already high educational levels.

TABLE 5.5

JEWISH AND TOTAL URBAN POPULATIONS BY LEVEL OF SCHOOLING, 1970
(PER 1,000 PERSONS AGE 10+)

			LEVEL OF SCHOOLING				
YEAR	VUZ	VUZ INCOMPLETE	SECONDARY VOCATIONAL	SECONDARY	INCOMPLETE SECONDARY	PRIMARY	0–3 YEARS
(1) Jews (est.)	239	45	137	193	148	156	82
(2) Total [a]	62	20	91	156	263	250	158
Ratio (1) to (2)	3.9	2.3	1.5	1.2	0.6	0.6	0.5

(a) Source: *Itogi, 1970*, vol. 3, Table 3.

Comparison of the 1959 and 1970 census data pertaining to Jewish and general urban educational levels demonstrates that the previous "overrepresentation" in secondary schooling, with respect to the Jews' share in the urban population, virtually disappeared during the 1960s. Similarly, the gap between the percentage of VUZ-educated Jews and the proportion of Jews in the urban population also decreased during that decade. We may expect this trend to continue in the future, a projection borne out by data concerning student enrollment. The rapid growth of the VUZ-educated stratum has led to fierce job competition, a struggle in which the Jews have not fared well—in part because they are a weak link in the Soviet nationalities system and in part because the percentage of VUZ-educated Jews is still far higher than that of any other nationality group in the Soviet Union, making it relatively more difficult for them to maintain their past share of the job market.

TABLE 5.6

DISTRIBUTION OF URBAN POPULATION OF SELECTED NATIONALITIES
BY LEVEL OF SCHOOLING, 1970
(PER 1,000 PERSONS AGE 10+)

	LEVEL OF SCHOOLING				
NATIONALITY	VUZ	VUZ INCOMPLETE	SECONDARY VOCATIONAL	SECONDARY	INCOMPLETE SECONDARY
Jewish (est.) [a]	239	45	137	193	148
Georgian [b]	155	38	97	301	143
Armenian	76	27	59	224	205
Estonian	66	24	92	156	244
Russian	60	18	96	145	271
Ukrainian	58	17	94	183	263

(a) Total Population.

(b) For the tabulations on the Georgians, Armenians, Estonians, Russians and Ukrainians, see *Itogi, 1970*, vol. 4, Table 36.

The percentage of Jews who had completed VUZ training was about four times higher than that achieved by urban Russians and Ukrainians (table 5.6). The social perception of this situation frequently finds its reflection in tension and competition. In the field of secondary education, where many aspire to attend VUZs, the gap between the Jews and the Ukrainians and Russians has greatly diminished.

Differentials among educational levels of the Jews in the various SSRs also narrowed to a certain extent in the intercensus period (1959-1970). If in 1959 the percentage of Jews who had completed at least half of a VUZ program was 3.3 times higher in the RSFSR than in Moldavia, this ratio narrowed to 2.5 in the 1970 census. The proportion of Jews at that educational level was 2.4 times higher in the RSFSR than in Belorussia in 1959 and only twice as high in 1970; corresponding figures for the Ukraine were 1.9 in 1959 and 1.7 in 1970. Nevertheless, in 1970 the percentage of Jews in the RSFSR who had completed at least half a VUZ program was 41 percent higher than the figure for Jews in the Soviet Union as a whole (according to my estimate).

Since 1970 census data pertaining to the Jews of the RSFSR deal with their distribution by age brackets as well, we may calculate absolute numbers of the Jews at each educational level and compare them to 1959 data (table 5.7). It therefore appears that the proportion of the VUZ educated among those who had declared themselves Jews grew in the RSFSR during the intercensus period. Current enrollment figures for the VUZs and vocational training schools also suggest that the major increase during the 1960s in VUZ education among the Jews is what tended to depress the Jews' proportional share in the secondary vocational sector.

TABLE 5.7

THE JEWISH POPULATION OF THE RSFSR BY LEVEL OF SCHOOLING, 1959, 1970
(FREQUENCIES)

			LEVEL OF SCHOOLING			
YEAR	TOTAL	VUZ	VUZ INCOMPLETE	SECONDARY VOCATIONAL	SECONDARY	INCOMPLETE SECONDARY
1970 [a]	510,531	213,134	34,077	83,643	106,567	73,110
1959	603,961	211,084	45,056	94,882	136,737	116,202
Difference	−93,430	+2,050	−10,979	−11,239	−30,170	−43,092
Ratio:						
1970 to 1959	0.85	1.01	0.76	0.88	0.78	0.63

(a) Calculated from *Itogi, 1970*, vol. 4, Tables 33, 39.

SECONDARY VOCATIONAL EDUCATION *(TEKHNIKUM)*

A sixteen-year period (1961/62-1976/77) witnessed a 95 percent increase in the number of students in *tekhnikums*. The number of Jewish students, by contrast, dropped by close to 25 percent during the same period (see table 5H). As a consequence, the percentage of Jewish students in total *tekhnikum* enrollment dropped from 1.9 percent to 0.7 percent—a 63.2 percent decline. In the 1961/62 academic year, there were 19.5 *tekhnikum* students per 1,000 individuals recorded in the 1959 census as Jews, while in 1970/71 there were 18.6 *tekhnikum* students for every 1,000 individuals counted as Jews in 1970. The intercensus decline in the number of Jewish students in *tekhnikums* exceeded the drop in percentage of general decline in the size of the Jewish population. With regard to the proportion of *tekhnikum* students in the general population, the Jews ranked first among Soviet national groups in 1961/62, but their role was smaller in comparison with that of *tekhnikum* students in the urban populations of most of these nationalities (apart from the Armenians at 16.3 per 1,000) (table 5.8).

TABLE 5.8

NUMBER OF *TEKHNIKUM* STUDENTS PER THOUSAND POPULATION BY NATIONALITY, FOR THE TOTAL AND URBAN POPULATIONS, 1961/62 AND 1970/71

| NATIONALITY | YEAR AND TYPE OF POPULATION | | | |
| | 1961/62 | | 1970/71 | |
	TOTAL	URBAN	TOTAL	URBAN
Jewish	19.5	20.4	18.6	19.0
Lithuanian	14.4	40.9	21.2	45.3
Estonian	14.4	30.6	15.4	27.9
Russian	13.2	22.8	21.0	30.8
Latvian	13.0	27.4	13.8	26.1
Ukrainian	10.3	26.2	16.5	34.1
Belorussian	9.6	29.6	16.5	37.8
Georgian	9.2	25.5	14.5	32.9
Armenian	9.2	16.3	17.2	26.5
Kazakh	8.6	35.8	13.5	50.4
Azerbaidzhani	8.5	24.3	13.1	34.3
Turkemenian	7.2	28.2	9.6	30.9
Kirgiz	6.9	63.8	10.7	73.5
Uzbek	5.7	25.9	10.5	42.2
Moldavian	5.2	40.1	11.5	56.5
Tadzhik	5.2	24.4	8.3	31.9

The calculations are from the censuses of 1959 and 1970. The tabulations on the tekhnikum students are from *Srednee spetsial'noe obrazovanie*, pp. 72–73 and *Narodnoe obrazovanie, nauka i kul'tura v SSSR*, (Moscow, 1971), p. 196.

Between the two censuses the percentage of Jewish *tekhnikum* students dropped, with the Russians and Lithuanians taking precedence—meaning that the latter groups' presence in the subacademic professional intelligentsia will be greater than the Jews' in proportion to their populations.

In terms of absolute numbers of Jewish *tekhnikum* students, the sixteen-year period (1961/62-1976/77) may be divided into two intervals: five years (1961/62-1965/66) of constant growth and a discernible decline not only in relative but also in absolute figures beginning in 1966/67.

Planning in the field of secondary vocational education in the Soviet Union takes place along with consideration of the ratio of those receiving this education to VUZ students. This being so, we should examine this ratio as it applies to Jewish students as well.

For every 1,000 VUZ students, there were 898 in *tekhnikums* in 1961/62, 958 in 1970/71, and 959 in 1972/73. We can thus infer that until the early 1970s, the number of *tekhnikum* students grew on a country-wide average more rapidly than the number of VUZ students. In the following years, this trend began to change: there were 943 *tekhnikum* students per 1,000 VUZ students in the 1974/75 academic year and only 933 in 1976/77.

During the 1960s, the increase in the number of *tekhnikum* students did not exceed that of the number of VUZ students in the cases of all nationalities. Of the fifteen nationalities with their own union republics, five (Russians, Lithuanians, Estonians, Latvians, and Azerbaidzhanis) exhibited the opposite phenomenon: a more rapid growth in the number of VUZ students than that of *tekhnikum* students.[25] A similar trend occurred among the Jews. There were 561 *tekhnikum* students per 1,000 Jewish VUZ students in 1961/62, 550 in 1965/66, and 370 in 1970/71. In 1972/73, however, the pattern was reversed, with the relative number of Jewish *tekhnikum* students growing steadily. In 1976/77, for every 1,000 Jewish VUZ students, there were 498 *tekhnikum* students. It therefore appears that the more recent direction of change in the ratio between *tekhnikum* students and those in higher education has been the reverse among Jews of the overall Soviet trend. Moreover, the changed ratio among Jews stemmed not from an increase in Jewish *tekhnikum* enrollment but rather from a decline in the number of Jewish VUZ students in relation to the number of *tekhnikum* students. This trend should be attributed to three major factors:

1. Heightened restrictions against Jews in the VUZs.
2. Encouragement of secondary school graduates to continue postsecondary studies in *tekhnikums*.
3. The proportion of VUZ students among Jewish emigrants, which was apparently greater than that of *tekhnikum* students.

Tekhnikum studies take place in three frameworks: day, evening, and correspondence courses, with the percentage of students in the latter two programs constantly rising (from 38 percent of those admitted into *tekhnikums* in 1958 to 48 percent in 1961). In the 1961/62 academic year, 55.9 percent of the Jewish *tekhnikum* students studied in evening or correspondence frameworks as against a nationwide average of 49.3 percent. It would seem that the percentage of Jews among *tekhnikum* day students (1.62 percent) was smaller than their proportion in evening (2.12 percent) and correspondence studies (2.10 percent).[26]

Differences also exist between women and men as to the distribution of

Jewish *tekhnikum* students in the various study frameworks. Of all male Jewish students in *tekhnikums* in 1961/62, 60.4 percent were enrolled in evening or correspondence frameworks, while only 58.8 percent of the female students entered those frameworks that year. Since the evening and correspondence studies take longer than day studies, the proportion of women among Jewish *tekhnikum* graduates appears higher than that of all women enrolled in these educational institutions. However, the percentage of Jewish women among *tekhnikum* students is actually lower than the national average. In 1961/62 women comprised 48 percent of all *tekhnikum* students; in 1970/71 this figure climbed to 54 percent. Among Jewish students, by contrast, women accounted for 44 percent of all *tekhnikum* enrollment in 1961/62 and 51 percent in 1970/71. While the absolute number of Jewish *tekhnikum* students diminished during the 1960s (44,116 in 1961/62; 40,000 in 1970/71), the number of women students increased slightly (19,380 in 1961/62; 20,200 in 1970/71).

For each 1,000 males counted as Jews in the 1959 census, 24 were enrolled in *tekhnikums* in 1961/62; the corresponding figure for Jewish women was 15.7 per 1,000. Between the two censuses, the proportion of men in *tekhnikums* fell as that of women rose. For every 1,000 men counted as Jews in 1970, 20 were *tekhnikum* students, as opposed to 17.4 per 1,000 Jewish women. If we take into account the fact that the percentage of Jewish women enrolled in day studies was higher than that of men during the 1960s and if we consider the fact that the percentage of female *tekhnikum* students among all Jewish women was on the upswing, during the 1960s the proportion of women among all Jews with secondary vocational education rose.

Highly significant differences existed among the various SSRs as to the ratio of Jewish students in the Jewish population. In three SSRs (RSFSR, Belorussia, and Kirgizia), 20 or more students per 1,000 individuals registered as Jews in 1959 were enrolled in *tekhnikums* in 1961/62; in seven SSRs (the Ukraine, Moldavia, Latvia, Kazakhstan, Lithuania, Azerbaidzhan, and Turkmenia), there were between 15 and 20; the lowest percentage—5.3 students per 1,000—was in Georgia (see table 5I).

The scanty data pertaining to Jewish students in the *tekhnikums* of the RSFSR, which accounted for about 40 to 44 percent of all Soviet students between 1961 and 1976, hint at the changes that took place in this sphere in the latter half of the 1950s (see table 5J). The absolute number of Jewish students in RSFSR *tekhnikums* dropped by 2,990 between 1956 and 1960, and their share in the overall student body fell by 11.8 percent. We have reason to assume that a parallel phenomenon had taken place throughout the Soviet Union in the 1950s. The year 1961 marked the start of an increase in the number of Jewish students in RSFSR *tekhnikums*, though their proportion in the total enrollment of these institutions continued to decline. Moreover, the proportion of Jewish *tekhnikum* students in the RSFSR among all Jewish students in these institutions nationwide displayed a downward trend in 1963 (43.6 percent in 1961/62; 39.2 percent in 1963/64). But in the fourteen years between 1963 and 1976, the number of Jewish *tekhnikum* students dropped by 35 percent in the Soviet Union and by 33.3 percent in the RSFSR. The proportion of Jews in the total *tekhnikum* student body dropped during this period by 57.6 percent in the Soviet Union overall and by 54.5 percent in the RSFSR (see tables 5H and 5J). These changes during the 1960s did not occur at a uniform pace throughout the USSR. While on a nationwide level the number of Jewish *tekhnikum* students continued to rise in absolute terms until 1965/66, with the downward trend setting in that year, the upward trend lasted until 1966/67 in Kazakhstan and until 1970/71 in Moldavia.[27] If on the national level a consistent decline in the percentage of Jewish *tekhnikum* students is discernible throughout the 1960s, their relative numbers, too, continued to rise in Azerbaidzhan until 1962/63 and in Uzbekistan until 1963/64.[28]

In the 1960s in the Soviet Union as a whole, the number of Jewish *tekhnikum* students declined in comparison with Jewish VUZ students, but such was not the case in Moldavia, Uzbekistan, and Azerbaidzhan. In Moldavia, the number of Jewish *tekhnikum* students per 1,000 Jewish VUZ students grew from 976 in 1965/66 to 1,138 in 1972/73.[29] A similar trend may be discerned in Uzbekistan, where the number of Jewish *tekhnikum* students per 1,000 Jewish VUZ students grew from 380 in 1960/61 to 719 in 1965/66. After that year, however, the trends typical of Soviet Jewry in general began to operate here too: a diminishing number of Jewish *tekhnikum* students in comparison with the number of VUZ students.[30]

The available data concerning Jewish *tekhnikum* students in various SSRs indicate that the pace of the changes is affected by both local conditions of the Jewish community in each SSR and the broader Soviet situation. In almost every SSR, however, we can see a trend toward more rapid growth in the number of Jewish VUZ students with respect to those in institutions of secondary vocational education. This points to a shrinking proportion of Soviet Jews in the subacademic professional intelligentsia stratum in the 1960s, brought about by the concomitant growth of the Jewish VUZ-educated sector. This trend was reversed in the 1970s, apparently due in large measure to government policy on accepting Jews into institutions of higher learning.

HIGHER EDUCATION (VUZ)

Since higher education is one of the paths to social mobility and economic advancement in the Soviet Union, many young people aspire to advance to this level of study. The significant increase in the number of secondary school pupils during the 1960s tended to magnify the demand for higher education as well.[31] In surveys taken among high school graduates, between

70 and 80 percent expressed a desire to go on to higher education; the percentage among their parents was even higher.[32] The number of VUZs and their capacity, however, has not kept pace with the growing numbers of high school graduates who desire to enter them, although VUZ enrollment increased 2.5 times between 1956 and 1978, resulting in a total figure of 5,109,200.[33]

Most VUZ candidates aim for acceptance into a day program because this takes less time to complete than evening or correspondence studies and, in most cases offers scholarships. The ability of the VUZ system to absorb new students, however, is limited. In 1950, the ratio of secondary school graduates to those accepted into VUZ day studies was 1:1; that is, every high school graduate was able to be accepted into VUZ day studies. In 1971, by contrast, the ratio was 1:4; only one of every four high school graduates could be accepted into VUZ day studies. The numerical gap between those finishing secondary school and VUZ students widened progressively during the 1970s.[34] It is therefore natural that admittance to such institutions, especially their day programs, became a focus of competition and social and nationality group tension during the 1960s and 1970s. This tension even found expression in Soviet publications. A sociologist from Dagestan complained that the percentage of students belonging to the native peoples of the Dagestan autonomous republic, (the Jews were not perceived as a native people in any of the Soviet republics despite centuries of Jewish presence there) was far lower than the proportion of those peoples in the population.[35] Another author, M. Mishin, in a book published by the University of Gor'ki and the RSFSR Ministry of Higher and Secondary Vocational Education, discussed at greater length the balance of the various peoples' representation in the intelligentsia. In this context he wrote:

It appears from the table . . . [of the percentage of scientific workers and students among various peoples] that a number of peoples (Ukrainians, Belorussians, Moldavians, Tatars, Uzbeks, Azerbaidzhanis and others) are still far behind in the development of higher education and the training of scientific cadres relative to the average nationwide level, while certain other peoples (Armenians, Georgians, Jews) have greatly exceeded that level. In other words, the table indicates that not only do traces of the old national inequalities [from the prerevolutionary period] still exist but so do elements of a new inequality, created in the Soviet period. . . . I believe the creation of this new inequality does not lend itself to strengthening and consolidating the Soviet peoples' unity. . . . [Hence] the leadership, aware of relations among the [Soviet] peoples, must not only [move] to equalize [conditions] but also support their equal development.[36]

Mishin aptly expressed the social pressure being exerted on the authorities to increase the proportion of certain peoples—apparently referring in this case mainly to the Russians and Ukrainians—in VUZ enrollment and, as a consequence, in the professional stratum. Because such institutions are government run, the regime plays an important role in shaping the student body's social and national makeup. In this sphere the government was called upon to overcome many contradictions. On the one hand, VUZs must accept the best qualified students irrespective of social origin or nationality for the sake of advancing Soviet science; on the other hand, the government requires that preference be extended to students of backward national groups. Against this background we may also understand the changes that took place in the relative and absolute proportion of Jewish students in the Soviet Union, though conditions peculiar to them were also at work in each respective SSR.

The twenty-three years for which we have almost yearly data on Jewish students (see table 5K) saw a constant decline in the relative share of Jewish VUZ students.[37] Jews accounted for 4.2 percent of total VUZ enrollment in 1956/57 but only 1.2 percent in 1978/9—a fall of 71.4 percent. Since it is hard to discern a uniform trend during the period under discussion when absolute numbers of Jewish students are considered, the period should be divided into three intervals: 1956-1960, 1961-1968, and 1969-1978.

In the 1960/61 academic year, the number of Jewish students was very low (77,177), having dropped by about 7,400 individuals (8.8 percent) since 1956/57. So steep a decline in the number of Jewish students in a five-year period must be understood against the background of Khrushchev's policy of granting preference in higher education to those with work experience, as well as a consequence of policies discriminating against Jews.

In 1960/1961, the only year for which data on students' national group distribution by study framework (day, evening, and correspondence) were published, 44.5 percent of the Jewish students were enrolled in day programs, against an average of 48.2 percent for the entire student body. While Jews in 1960/61 constituted 3.2 percent of overall VUZ enrollment, they accounted for only 3.0 percent of the day students.[38] It therefore appears that in the day VUZ programs, where pressure is stronger, Jews were less represented than the general VUZ enrollment.

In the years 1960/61 through 1968/69, there was a clear upward trend in the number of Jewish VUZ students—an increase of 34,700 individuals (45 percent). During the same interval, however, overall VUZ enrollment grew by 87 percent, meaning that in relative terms, the proportion of Jewish students fell by 21.9 percent.

In the ten years from 1969 through 1978, the number of Jewish students dropped by 52,300 (46.7 percent) as a consequence of toughened restrictions on admitting Jews and emigration of Jews from the Soviet Union. The relatively large-scale emigration of Jews from the Soviet Union began in March 1971, but the toughened stance on accepting Jewish students into VUZs apparently began earlier—as early as the start of the 1969/70 academic year. Attestations of Soviet immigrants to Israel confirm that students who had requested exit permits were not admitted into VUZs or were even expelled, and others who intended to leave the country refrained from applying to such institutions, lest their studies be used as the pretext for denying them an exit permit.[39] As a result of these factors, a moderate fall (1,800 individuals) in the number of Jewish VUZ students took place at the outset of the 1969/70 academic year. This decline became significant as the stream of Jews leaving the USSR accelerated and as distrust of the Jews increased. The decline in the number of Jewish students in the 1970s, even as total VUZ enrollment was rising, brought the percentage of Jewish students in total VUZ enrollment almost to the percentage of Jews in the Soviet urban population: Jews accounted for 1.2 percent of all VUZ students in 1978/79 and 1.1 percent of the urban population according to the 1979 census.

According to the 1970 census, there were 320 VUZ students for every 10,000 in the urban population; among Jews, the figure was 512 per 10,000. By 1979, however, the latter figure had declined to 329, and the general urban figure stood at 312. This pronounced proportional decrease is ample testimony to the heightened discrimination against Jews during the 1970s.

In the 1960s, however, the percentage of Jewish students in the general and the urban populations was still higher than that of any other nationality group in the Soviet Union. Between the two censuses (1959, 1970), however, the percentage of Jewish students relative to the size of the population grew more slowly than did that of other national groups. This situation should be seen as a consequence of three major factors:

1. In the light of the progressive aging of the Jewish population, the percentage of young people was dwindling.

2. Because the percentage of Jewish VUZ students was very high in 1959, the Jewish growth rate would be lower than that of national groups whose student percentage was low.

3. The Jews held a weak position in the struggle for places in VUZs. Therefore their development neither equaled nor resembled that of other national groups with strong positions in the Soviet system.

It is also useful to indicate the changes that took place in the sex ratio of Jewish VUZ students. In 1960/61, women accounted for 40.9 percent of all Jewish VUZ enrollment (31,564 women, 45,613 men) and 3.0 percent of all female VUZ students; the latter figure dropped to 2.1 percent in 1970/71. The percentage of Jewish women among all female VUZ students dropped (−0.92 percent) more than the corresponding proportion of men (−0.86 percent). This situation stemmed from a general increase in the percentage of women among higher education students (43 percent in 1960/61, 49 percent in 1970/71) that was not equaled by the increase in the proportion of Jewish women students. For every 1,000 females registered as Jews in the

1959 census, there were 26 women studying at VUZs in 1960/61, as opposed to 44 men per 1,000.[40] Inasmuch as women's life expectancy is higher than men's, the percentage of elderly women in the Jewish population is higher than that of men, and it is therefore reasonable to assume that no significant differences exist in the lower age brackets between the respective percentages of Jewish male and female VUZ students. The necessary conclusion is that the future VUZ-educated stratum of Soviet Jews will be divided more or less equally between the sexes.

With regard to the distribution of the Jewish students according to professions studied, I have uncovered only two sets of data, both relating to Belorussia: their proportion in the body of medical students (table 5.9) and their share of those admitted to engineering studies.

The figures in table 5.9 indicate that until 1967, a trend of stability or even of a slight increase could be discerned in the proportion of Jewish medical students, along with a similar trend among the Russians and Ukrainians (who accounted for 31.2 percent of the total in 1964 and 32.8 percent in 1966). From 1967 onward, the percentage of Jewish, Russian, and Ukrainian medical students in Belorussia dropped, as the Belorussians' share rose. The Jews also accounted for 7 percent of all students admitted in 1965 into day study programs in the six Belorussian VUZs that trained engineers.[41] At the most, these figures hint that the percentage of Jews studying engineering and medicine in Belorussia may have exceeded their share in total VUZ enrollment. In the absence of additional data, however, we have no way of applying these partial statistics to the entire Jewish VUZ population in the Soviet Union. Any attempt to apply data concerning professional distribution to all VUZ students in the USSR to the Jewish students is speculation. Until additional data appear, we cannot even estimate the professional distribution of the Jews enrolled in VUZs.

TABLE 5.9

DISTRIBUTION OF MEDICAL STUDENTS IN BELORUSSIA BY NATIONALITY, 1964–1969
(PERCENTAGES)

NATIONALITY	YEAR					
	1964	1965	1966	1967	1968	1969
Belorussian	58.4	58.1	58.0	63.8	62.8	65.1
Russian	27.2	29.8	27.3	23.6	24.8	23.2
Jewish	4.8	4.6	5.9	3.8	3.0	3.5
Ukrainian	4.0	3.9	5.5	4.9	4.5	4.2
Polish	3.9	3.0	2.5	2.6	3.6	2.6
Not specified	1.7	0.6	0.8	1.3	1.3	1.4

Source: *Struktura sovetskoi intelligentsii* (Minsk, 1970), p. 90.

Available data concerning national group distribution of *aspirants* as of late 1970 enable us to estimate their number in the early 1960s.[42] In 1970 there were 99,427 *aspirants* in the USSR, of whom 89,344 (89.9 percent) belonged to national groups with their own union republics and 10,083 (10.1 percent) belonged to other national groups. Of the latter, 49.04 percent were Jews.[43] Because of the general policy of encouraging small minorities that had been in effect during the 1960s, we may assume that the percentage of Jewish *aspirants* in 1960 was at least as large as the 1970 figure.[44] At the end of 1960, there were 36,754 *aspirants* nationwide, of whom 32,778 (89.2 percent) were of national groups with their own SSRs and 3,976 (10.8 percent) belonged to other national groups. If the percentage of Jews among the *aspirants* of the latter category was equal to the 1970 figure in 1960, there were at least 1,950 Jewish *aspirants* at the end of 1960 (table 5.10).

TABLE 5.10

TOTAL AND JEWISH ASPIRANTURA STUDENTS FOR SELECTED YEARS

		JEWS				
			PERCENTAGE	CHANGES		CHANGE FROM
	TOTAL	FREQUENCY	OF TOTAL	NUMBER	PERCENTAGE	PRIOR FREQUENCY
1960	36,754	1,950 (a)	5.31	–	–	–
1970	99,424	4,945	4.97	+2.995	–0.34	2.54
1973	98,860	3,456	3.50	–1,489	–1.47	0.70
1975	95,675	2,841	2.97	–615	–0.53	0.82

Sources: *Narodnoe obrazovanie, nauka i kul'tura v SSSR,* (Moscow, 1971), p. 278; *ibid.,* 1977, p. 313; *Vestnik statistiki,* No. 4 (1974), p. 95.

(a) Estimate.

During the 1960s the number of Jewish *aspirants* grew by a factor of 2.5 but dropped in relative terms by close to 6.4 percent. Between 1970 and 1975, by contrast, not only did the relative number of Jewish *aspirants* drop, but their absolute numbers did also—by 42.5 percent. We have reason to assume that this decrease stemmed primarily from restrictions placed on the Jews and was also partly due to emigration.

Inasmuch as VUZ graduates are accepted into *aspirantura* programs, examination of the ratio of VUZ students to *aspirants* is in order. There were 15 *aspirants* per 1,000 students in 1960, 22 in 1970, and 20 in 1975. The highest student:*aspirant* ratio in 1960 appeared among the Azerbaidzhanis: 36 *aspirants* per 1,000 students (1,029 and 28,493). Following them were the Jews (25 *aspirants* per 1,000 VUZ students) and only then the Russians (15), the Ukrainians (11), and so on. In 1970, by contrast, the Jews had the highest *aspirant*: student ratio: 47 per 1,000. After them came the Armenians (28), Azerbaidzhanis (24), Russians (22), Ukrainians (20), and so on. We may therefore say that the academically educated stratum of the Soviet Jewish community grew during the 1960s, as did the stratum of *Kandidats* for which *aspirants* trained. In the first half of the 1970s however, the Jewish academic stratum diminished significantly, and even more so the share of those pursuing their *Kandidat* degree. There were 42 Jewish *aspirants* per 1,000 Jewish students in 1973 and only 40 in 1975 as opposed to 47 in 1970.

The data concerning changes in the 1960s in the number of Jewish VUZ students are not equally valid for all SSRs. We must therefore examine data from the various SSRs as well, insofar as this is possible.[45]

A majority of Jewish students were concentrated in the RSFSR, home of 38.6 percent of Soviet Jews according to the 1959 census and 38.7 percent according to the 1979 census. Sixty-one percent of all Jewish VUZ students in the USSR were found here in 1956/57 and 53 percent in 1976/77. Between 1956 and 1976, the numerical decrease in the Jewish student population was greater in the RSFSR (32 percent) than in the USSR as a whole (21 percent), but the relative drop in the proportion of Jewish students in the total student enrollment was almost identical in the RSFSR to that in the entire nation (see table 5M). Nevertheless, the percentage of VUZ students among the Jews remained higher in the RSFSR than in any other SSR. For every 1,000 individuals registered as Jews in the 1959 census, 53 in the RSFSR were VUZ students in 1960/61 against a national average of 34. In this vast SSR as well, however, various regions yield significantly different findings. For example, there were 78 students in the city of Moscow in 1970/71 for every 1,000 individuals registered as Jews in the 1970 census.[46] In the Omsk *oblast'* there were 51 students in 1965/66 per 1,000 Jews,[47] as opposed to only 23 students per 1,000 reported Jews in the Checheno-Ingush ASSR in 1959.[48] Since the largest concentration of Jewish students was in Moscow, the data concerning national group distribution of students in this city are of great value (table 5.11).

The number of Jewish students in Moscow fell by 40.9 percent between 1970 and 1978. It is hard to attribute so noticeable a drop to demographic factors; undoubtedly it stems rather from severe restrictions on Jewish entry to Moscow's institutions of higher learning. The proportion of Jewish students in Moscow consequently dropped by 42.4 percent, while the Russians' share rose by 2.8 percent. As early as the 1970/71 academic year, the percentage of Jews in Moscow's VUZ student population was lower than the Jews' share of the city's population (3.6 percent), a gap that apparently widened in the latter half of the 1970s. The main reason for this is that the VUZs in Moscow, high-level institutions commanding great

TABLE 5.11

STUDENTS IN INSTITUTIONS OF HIGHER LEARNING BY NATIONALITY IN MOSCOW

YEAR	TOTAL NUMBER	NUMBER OF JEWS	NATIONALITY (%)			
			JEWISH	RUSSIAN	UKRAINIAN	OTHER
1970/71	617,141	19,508	3.16	84.69	4.46	7.69
1974/75	627,285	14,985	2.39	86.20	4.18	7.23
1976/77	641,311	12.049	1.88	86.97	3.97	7.18
1978/79	632,037	11,531	1.82	87.05	3.60	7.53

Sources: *Moskva v tsifrakh, 1966–1970gg.* (1972), p. 132; *ibid.,* 1976, p. 160; *ibid.,* 1980, p. 172.

prestige, serve as a powerful attraction for students from around the entire nation.[49] Here places are set aside for students from other SSRs, who are admitted without entry examinations and at times even with low grades.[50] The restrictions on Jewish admissions are stricter in Moscow than elsewhere. Journalist M. Hindus, who visited the USSR in 1958 and 1960, attests: "Leningrad University is more liberal in admitting Jews than is Moscow University."[51] We should note, however, that the distribution of Jewish students in the RSFSR by study framework (day, evening, correspondence) in 1960/61 was not significantly different for Jews than for other national groups (table 5.12).

TABLE 5.12

DISTRIBUTION OF STUDENTS IN INSTITUTIONS OF HIGHER LEARNING OF THE RSFSR
BY NATIONALITY AND TYPE OF PROGRAM, 1960/61
(PERCENTAGES)

TYPE OF PROGRAM	NATIONALITY			
	JEWISH	RUSSIAN	UKRAINIAN	OTHER
Total	100.0	100.0	100.0	100.0
Day	46.1	46.8	39.8	49.3
Evening	13.5	11.9	7.8	5.7
Correspondence	40.4	41.3	52.4	45.0

Source: *Srednee spetsial'noe obrazovanie v SSSR* (Moscow, 1962), pp. 128–129.

A totally different situation existed in the Ukrainian SSR, home to 37.1 percent of all Soviet Jews according to the 1959 census and 35.0 percent according to that of 1979 (table 5.13). Here the proportion of Jews enrolled in day studies was about 10 percent lower than corresponding percentages for Russians and Ukrainians.[52]

TABLE 5.13

DISTRIBUTION OF STUDENTS IN INSTITUTIONS OF HIGHER LEARNING OF THE UKRAINE
BY NATIONALITY AND TYPE OF PROGRAM, 1960/61
(PERCENTAGES)

TYPE OF PROGRAM	NATIONALITY			
	JEWISH	RUSSIAN	UKRAINIAN	OTHER
Total	100.0	100.0	100.0	100.0
Day	37.5	47.5	48.5	56.3
Evening	19.0	8.7	13.2	10.1
Correspondence	43.5	43.8	38.3	33.6

Source: *Srednee spetsial'noe obrazovanie v SSSR*, pp. 130–131.

In 1960/61 the Jews accounted for 4.5 percent of all VUZ students in the Ukraine but only 3.5 percent of those pursuing day studies.[53] Moreover, while the number of Jewish students in the USSR rose between the 1960/61 and 1961/62 academic years (see table 5K), it did not rise in the Ukraine. About 18,000 Jews studied in Ukrainian VUZs in 1961/1962 as opposed to some 19,000 the previous year (see table 5N). Between the two academic years, the proportion of Jewish students fell by 6.3 percent in the Soviet Union as a whole but by 12.5 percent in the Ukraine (Jews accounted for 4.5 percent of all VUZ students in the Ukraine in 1960/61 and only 3.9 percent in 1961/62). In those years, too, the percentage of Jewish students in the Ukraine within the total of Jewish students in the USSR fell by 5.4 percent (standing at 22.9 percent in 1961/62, as opposed to 24.2 percent in 1960/61). Even before this decline, however, the proportion of students among Ukrainian Jews was one of the lowest in any Soviet Republic. In 1960/61 there were in the Ukrainian SSR 22 students per 1,000 individuals registered as Jews in the 1959 census; a lower proportion was found only in four SSRs: Belorussia (20), Georgia (18), Lithuania (17), and Moldavia (13) (see table 5L). Although data concerning national group distribution of VUZ students in the Ukraine have not been published in the intervening years, the few figures collected do hint that the pressures applied—by either the Ukrainians or the Russians—to lower the proportion of Jewish VUZ students are stronger in the Ukraine than in other SSRs.[54] Indeed, Roy Medvedev also notes that the restrictions on admitting Jews to such institutions are more severe in Kiev than in other Soviet cities.[55]

The changes, however, did not take place at a uniform pace in the other SSRs. In Belorussia and Kazakhstan, there was an increase in the percentage of Russians and Ukrainians in VUZ enrollment, while a decrease occurred among Belorussians, Kazakhs, and Jews.[56] The fluctuations that occurred in the number of Jewish VUZ students in the USSR as a whole were not reflected in Belorussia, where Jewish numerical enrollment in

VUZs remained stable between 1959 and 1962; proportionally, therefore, Jewish VUZ enrollment in Belorussia fell.[57]

The number of Jewish VUZ students grew faster in Kazakhstan than in the USSR in general between 1960 and 1968, raising their proportion among all Jewish VUZ students in the USSR from 1.1. percent in 1960/61 to 1.4 percent in 1967/68 (an increase of 27 percent). But this rise did not keep pace with the rapid increase in the overall number of students in Kazakhstan.[58] The proportion of Jews in the VUZ enrollment of that SSR therefore dropped by 29.4 percent between 1960/61 and 1967/68.[59]

The proportionate representation of Uzbeks in VUZ enrollment in Uzbekistan displayed a clear upward trend over a twenty-one-year period (1950/51-1970/71), whereas the relative weight of Russians, Ukrainians, Tatars, and Jews progressively declined. We may therefore say that here the number of Uzbek students rose as the weight of other nationalities fell. A similar phenomenon was clearly apparent in Azerbaidzhan in the 1940s and 1950s, as data on VUZ students in the city of Baku attest. In the first half of the 1960s, by contrast, an upward trend appeared in the percentage of Russians opposite a prolonged decline in that of Armenians and Jews.[60] We may therefore deduce that the rise in percentages of both Azerbaidzhanis and Russians had come at the expense of the Jews and the Armenians—those national groups less capable than the main regional national group and the Russians of applying pressure.

Throughout most of the 1960s, the rise in the number of Jewish VUZ students in Uzbekistan kept pace with its increase in the Soviet Union as a whole. At the end of that decade and in the early 1970s, however, Jews in Uzbekistan did not experience the same falling enrollment figures observed thoughout the rest of the USSR. The result, then, was an upward trend in the weight of Jewish VUZ students in Uzbekistan in overall Jewish VUZ enrollment in the USSR.

The number of Jewish students rose more rapidly in Moldavia and Lithuania than it did in the nation as a whole. The proportion of Jewish VUZ students in these SSRs in the Jewish VUZ stratum therefore rose from 2.1 percent in 1960/61 to 4.0 percent in 1970/71—an 88 percent increase. Not only did absolute numbers of Jewish VUZ students grow in the two SSRs during the 1960s; even their relative weight in total VUZ enrollment of those SSRs rose discernibly.[61] The background for these increases in student percentages, however, varied from SSR to SSR. In Moldavia, the percentage of Moldavians—and of Jews to a certain extent—in local VUZ enrollment grew at the expense of the Russians and Ukrainians. In Lithuania, by contrast, the percentage of Russian VUZ students—and to a certain extent that of Jews as well—grew as that of Lithuanians fell. In the early 1970s, with growth of emigration, the absolute number and relative proportion of Jewish students began to fall in these two republics, as is indicated by figures from Moldavia.

Table 5.14 shows that over fifteen years (1970-1984), the absolute number of Jewish students fell by more than 57 percent, while their percentage share of the total declined by about 64 percent. The percentage of Jews among VUZ students in Moldavia is likely to decrease even further, judging by the figures on admissions in the last few years. In 1983/84 Jews accounted for about 1.4 percent (142 Jewish students among a total number of over 10,000) of all students admitted, and in 1984/85 their percentage was 1.9 (140 out of 7,334) of all admitted day students in VUZ in Moldavia.

TABLE 5.14

JEWISH STUDENTS IN VUZ OF MOLDAVIA

YEAR	TOTAL	JEWS	% OF TOTAL
1960/61	19,217	1,225	6.4
1965/66	36,318	2,354	6.5
1970/71	44,752	2,723	6.1
1972/73	42,833	2,267	5.3
1980/81	51,300	1,124	2.2
1984/85	53,559	1,166	2.2

Sources: *Vysshee obrazovanie v SSSR*, p. 144; *Narodnoe khoziaistvo Moldavskoi SSR* (Kishinev, 1971), p. 259; ibid., 1974, p. 186; *Sovetskaia Moldavia*, December 17, 1985.

Due to the absence of current data on national group distribution of *tekhnikum* and VUZ students in the RSFSR and the Ukraine, unequivocal conclusions are hard to reach; even the fragmentary data I have been able to accumulate, however, indicate that development was not identical in every SSR. In five SSRs (Moldavia, Uzbekistan, Lithuania, Kazakhstan, and Armenia) for which figures from 1960/61 and 1965/66 are available, the proportionate weight of Jewish VUZ students fell by 11 percent, against a rate double that (22 percent) in the USSR as a whole. In three SSRs (Moldavia, Lithuania, and Uzbekistan), the percentage of Jewish VUZ students dropped by 13 percent over an eleven-year span (1960/61-1970/71), while the fall during that decade was more than twice as great (28 percent) in the USSR as a whole. We may therefore deduce that the percentage of Jewish VUZ students in these SSRs in the overall Jewish VUZ student population rose in this period. The five republics for which we have data from 1960/61 and 1965/66 accounted for 7 percent of all Jewish VUZ students in the USSR in 1960/61 and 9 percent in 1965/66—a 29 percent rise. Three of these SSRs (Moldavia, Lithuania, and Uzbekistan) accounted for 6 percent of all the Jewish VUZ students nationwide in 1960/61 and 9 percent in 1970/71—a 50 percent increase. These facts lead us to conclude that the extent of restriction placed on the Jews was not equal in each of these SSRs and that it was affected by local conditions prevailing in each of them as well.

The decline in the proportion of Jews in nationwide VUZ enrollment is influenced by three major factors: the aging of the Jewish population, social and national group pressure in the VUZs, and emigration.

The aging of the Jewish population tends to reduce the size of the youth stratum, the prime pool of *tekhnikum* and VUZ candidates. Official figures from the 1970 census show 88,000 Jews in the 20-29 age bracket in the RSFSR. Schmelz estimates that 121,000 Jews aged 19 to 28 dwelled in that republic in 1959.[62] About 65,000 of them studied in *tekhnikums* or VUZs in the early 1960s, or about 54 percent of all Jews in the 19-28 age bracket (see tables 5J and 5M).

Had this percentage remained stable, the absolute number of Jewish students in *tekhnikums* and VUZs in the RSFSR would have fallen; moreover, pressure was simultaneously applied to broaden the VUZ representation of various national groups and social strata (such as laborers and villagers) in which the proportion of Jews was not high. This pressure struck first of all at the weak link in Soviet society—the Jews—who historically enjoyed especially high representation in institutions of higher education. The government, being pragmatic, responded to these pressures and even added its own restrictions, such as closing certain departments to Jews. It may be said, however, that the roots of the difficulties that Jews encountered in their attempts to gain admittance to institutions of higher education are far deeper than one or another government decision or order. These difficulties stem rather from social and national group tensions in which VUZ representation is one of the focal points of friction. It therefore appears that the Jews' difficulties stem in essence not from government instructions, if such instructions in fact exist, but rather from a collision of interests in the higher education sector in which the Jews came out the worse. It would also appear, however, that deliberate government action against manifestations of anti-Jewish discrimination would successfully blunt the phenomenon. If this hypothesis is correct, we may expect even more energetic action to push Jews out of higher education institutions as a growing number of candidates demand admittance, as the aging process within the Jewish community becomes more acute, as distrust of Jews grows stronger, and as emigration continues.

TABLE 5A

PERSONS WITH SEVEN OR MORE YEARS OF SCHOOLING PER THOUSAND JEWS, BY SEX, FOR SELECTED REPUBLICS, 1939, 1959

	SEX AND YEAR					
	TOTAL		MALE		FEMALE	
REPUBLIC	1939	1959	1939	1959	1939	1959
RSFSR	462	690	461	695	463	686
Ukraine	280	582 [a]	275	578 [a]	285	585 [a]
Belorussia	205	513 [b]	194	495 [b]	217	529 [b]
Moldavia [c]	–	438	–	425	–	449
Azerbaidzhan	293	478	305	485	294	472
Latvia [c]	–	597	–	575	–	616
Lithuania [c]	–	464	–	441	–	484
Estonia [c]	–	690	–	678	–	700

Source: Calculated according to *Itogi, 1959,* Table 57 of the relevant volumes.

(a) According to the 1959 census, in those districts of the Ukraine which were part of the Soviet Union in January 1939 there were for each thousand Jews 591 with seven or more years of schooling (among males, 589, and among females, 592). Thus, it appears that the proportion with the indicated level of education, was **higher** in these districts than in those annexed in 1939.

(b) According to the 1959 census, in those districts of Belorussia which were part of the Soviet Union in January 1939, there were for each thousand Jews 510 with the indicated level of schooling (among males, 492, and among females, 524). Thus, it appears that the proportion with the indicated level of schooling was **lower** in these districts than in those annexed in 1939.

(c) A large part of the territory of the Moldavian SSR and all of Latvia, Lithuania and Estonia were annexed to the Soviet Union after the 1939 census was taken.

TABLE 5B

PERSONS WITH SEVEN OR MORE YEARS OF SCHOOLING IN THE JEWISH POPULATION, BY SEX, FOR SELECTED REPUBLICS, 1959

	SEX					
	TOTAL		MALE		FEMALE	
REPUBLIC	FREQUENCY (1,000'S)	PER THOUSAND	FREQUENCY (1,000'S)	PER THOUSAND	FREQUENCY (1,000'S)	PER THOUSAND
Total (8 republics)	**1,268**	**613**	**575**	**612**	**693**	**614**
RSFSR	604	690	280	695	324	686
Ukraine	489	582	216	578	273	585
Belorussia	77	513	34	494	43	529
Moldavia	42	438	19	425	23	449
Azerbaidzhan	19	478	9	485	10	472
Latvia	22	597	10	575	12	616
Lithuania	11	464	5	441	6	484
Estonia	4	690	2	678	2	700

Source: Calculated according to *Itogi, 1959,* Tables 53 and 57 of the relevant volumes.

128

PERSONS WITH SEVEN OR MORE YEARS OF SCHOOLING PER THOUSAND AGE TEN AND OVER IN THE JEWISH POPULATION, FOR SELECTED REPUBLICS, 1959, 1970

REPUBLIC	YEAR		RATIO
	1959	1970	$\frac{1970}{1959}$
RSFSR	764	824	1.08
Ukraine	652	747	1.15
Belorussia	606	710	1.17
Moldavia	520	660	1.27
Latvia	687	773	1.13

Source: *Itogi, 1970,* vol. 4, Tables 39–41, 47, 48.

TABLE 5D

PERSONS WITH SEVEN OR MORE YEARS OF SCHOOLING PER THOUSAND AGE TEN AND OVER IN THE JEWISH POPULATION, BY SEX AND RURAL / URBAN RESIDENCE, FOR SELECTED REPUBLICS, 1959, 1970

REPUBLIC AND YEAR	RURAL / URBAN RESIDENCE AND SEX					
	URBAN			RURAL		
	TOTAL	MALE	FEMALE	TOTAL	MALE	FEMALE
RSFSR						
1959	768	782	757	691	694	689
1970	825	843	811	730	751	705
Ukraine						
1959	657	667	649	528	541	517
1970	750	768	735	575	590	557
Belorussia						
1959	603	595	609	673	651	695
1970	711	715	707	683	684	679
Moldavia						
1959	520	513	524	546	560	530
1970	661	676	648	589	606	571
Latvia						
1959	687	671	700	710	714	703
1970	775	778	771	741	741	743

Sources as for Table 5C.

TABLE 5E

DISTRIBUTION OF THE JEWISH POPULATION WITH SEVEN OR MORE YEARS OF SCHOOLING, BY EDUCATIONAL LEVEL, FOR SELECTED REPUBLICS, 1959

REPUBLIC	EDUCATION					
	TOTAL	VUZ	VUZ INCOMPLETE	SECONDARY VOCATIONAL	SECONDARY	INCOMPLETE SECONDARY
Total (5 republics)	1,233,516	341,883	77,169	203,488	295,867	315,109
RSFSR	603,961	211,084	45,056	94,882	136,737	116,202
Ukraine	489,061	105,784	24,746	86,270	125,249	147,012
Belorussia	76,992	13,851	4,065	13,974	17,154	27,948
Moldavia	41,657	6,649	1,841	5,690	10,335	17,142
Latvia	21,845	4,515	1,461	2,672	6,392	6,805

Calculated according to *Itogi, 1959,*Table 57 in the relevant volumes, and Itogi, 1970, vol.4, Tables 39–41, 47,48.

TABLE 5F

PERSONS WITH SEVEN OR MORE YEARS OF SCHOOLING PER THOUSAND IN THE JEWISH POPULATION, BY LEVEL OF EDUCATION, FOR SELECTED REPUBLICS, 1959

REPUBLIC	EDUCATION					
	TOTAL	VUZ	VUZ INCOMPLETE	SECONDARY VOCATIONAL	SECONDARY	INCOMPLETE SECONDARY
Mean (5 Republics)	618	171	39	102	148	158
RSFSR	690	241	52	108	156	133
Ukraine	582	126	29	103	149	175
Belorussia	513	93	27	93	114	186
Moldavia	438	70	19	60	109	180
Latvia	597	123	40	73	175	186

Calculated from Table 5E.

DISTRIBUTION (PER THOUSAND) OF THE JEWISH POPULATION AGE TEN AND OVER, BY LEVEL OF EDUCATION, FOR SELECTED REPUBLICS, 1959, 1970

EDUCATION	RSFSR			UKRAINE			BELORUSSIA			MOLDAVIA			LATVIA		
	1959	1970	RATIO 1970/1959	1959	1970	RATIO 1970/1959	1959	1970	RATIO 1970/1959	1959	1970	RATIO 1970/1959	1959	1970	RATIO 1970/1959
VUZ	267	344	1.29	143	197	1.38	109	164	1.51	83	126	1.52	142	209	1.47
VUZ incomplete	57	55	0.97	33	37	1.12	32	37	1.16	33	34	1.03	46	72	1.57
Secondary vocational	120	135	1.13	114	150	1.32	110	142	1.29	71	112	1.58	84	119	1.42
Secondary	173	172	0.99	170	215	1.27	135	179	1.33	129	198	1.54	201	214	1.07
Incomplete secondary	147	118	0.80	197	151	0.77	220	188	0.86	214	190	0.89	214	159	0.74
Primary	152	116	0.76	205	158	0.77	235	190	0.81	293	227	0.78	214	163	0.76
Less than Primary	84	60	0.71	138	92	0.67	159	100	0.63	177	113	0.64	99	64	0.65

REPUBLIC AND YEAR

Source: *Itogi, 1970*, vol. 4, Tables 39–41, 47, 48.

TABLE 5H

TOTAL AND JEWISH *TEKHNIKUM* STUDENTS, 1961/62 – 1976/77 (SELECTED YEARS)[a]

| YEAR | TOTAL | JEWISH | | | | | PER 1,000 |
| | | NUMBER | % OF TOTAL | CHANGE | | | VUZ STUDENTS |
				AMOUNT	%		
1961/62	2,369,745	44,116	1.9	–	–		561
1962/63	2,667,700	47,200	1.8	+3,084	+6.99		595
1963/64	2,982,800	51,300	1.7	+4,100	+8.69		621
1965/66	3,659,300	52,000	1.4	+700	+1.36		550
1966/67	3,993,900	51,600	1.3	−400	−0.77		485
1967/68	4,166,600	46,700	1.1	−4,900	−9.50		425
1968/69	4,261,500	43,100	1.0	−3,600	−7.71		385
1969/70	4,301,700	41,000	1.0	−2,100	−4.87		372
1970/71	4,388,000	40,000	0.9	−1,000	−2.44		378
1972/73	4,437,900	37,100	0.8	−2,900	−7.25		419
1974/75	4,477,800	35,500	0.8	−1,600	−4.31		466
1976/77	4,622,800	33,300	0.7	−2,200	−6.20		498

Sources: *Srednee spetsial'noe obrazovanie v SSSR* (Moscow, 1962), p.72; *Narodnoe khoziaistvo SSSR 1922–1972 gg.* (Moscow, 1972), p.446; *Narodnoe khoziaistvo SSSR za 60 let* (Moscow, 1977), p.588; *Narodnoe khoziaistvo SSSR v 1963g* (Moscow, 1964), p.579, ibid, 1965, p.701; ibid, 1968, p.694; ibid 1969, p.690; ibid, 1970, p.651; ibid 1972, p.651; *Strana sovetov za 50 let* (Moscow, 1967), p.281; *Narodnoe obrazovanie, nauka i kul'tura v SSSR* (Moscow, 1977), p. 208.

(a) Start of academic year.

TABLE 5I

JEWISH AND TOTAL *TEKHNIKUM* STUDENTS, BY REPUBLIC, 1961/62[a]

| REPUBLIC | TOTAL | JEWISH STUDENTS | | |
		NUMBER	% OF TOTAL	% OF ALL JEWISH TEKHNIKUM STUDENTS	NUMBER PER 1,000 JEWS LISTED IN 1959 CENSUS
Total	2,369,745	44,116	1.9	100.0	19.5
RSFSR	1,453,462	19,237	1.3	43.6	22.0
Ukraine	454,809	15,737	3.5	35.7	18.7
Belorussia	73,036	3,220	4.4	7.3	21.5
Moldavia	20,125	1,710	8.5	3.9	18.0
Uzbekistan	62,670	1,379	2.2	3.1	14.6
Georgia	28,471	271	1.0	0.6	5.3
Azerbaidzhan	30,965	402	1.3	0.9	10.0
Latvia	27,887	676	2.4	1.5	18.5
Kazakhstan	97,584	553	0.6	1.3	19.7
Lithuania	37,775	389	1.0	0.9	15.8
Tadzhikistan	13,543	230	1.7	0.5	18.5
Kirgizia	19,216	172	0.9	0.4	20.0
Estonia	18,532	57	0.3	0.1	10.5
Turkmenia	13,865	70	0.5	0.2	17.2
Armenia	17,805	13	0.1	0.0	12.7

Source: *Srednee Spetsial'noe obrazovanie v SSSR* (Moscow, 1962), pp. 74–88.

(a) Start of academic year.

TABLE 5J

TOTAL AND JEWISH *TEKHNIKUM* STUDENTS IN THE RSFSR, FOR SELECTED YEARS, 1956/57–1976/77

YEAR	TOTAL	JEWISH		CHANGE		% OF ALL SOVIET JEWISH TEKHNIKUM STUDENTS	PER 1,000 VUZ STUDENTS		
		NUMBER	% OF TOTAL	NUMBER	%		JEWISH	RUSSIAN	OTHER
1956/57	1,243,624	21,490	1.7	–	–	–	417	1,040	779
1958/59	1,154,600	21,100	1.8	-390	-1.8	–	413	886	716
1960/61	1,260,300	18,500	1.5	-2,600	-12.3	–	397	880	713
1961/62	1,453,462	19,237	1.3	+737	+4.0	43.6	–	–	–
1962/63	1,641,200	19,600	1.2	+363	+1.9	41.5	411	945	723
1963/64	1,843,300	20,100	1.1	+500	+2.6	39.2	410	967	716
1976/77	2,732,300	13,400	0.5	-6,700	-33.3	40.2	380	952	921

Sources: *Kul'turnoe stroitel'stvo RSFSR*, (Moscow, 1958), p. 381; *Narodnoe khoziaistvo RSFSR v 1968 godu*, (Moscow, 1965), p. 495; *Narodnoe khoziaist za 60 let*, (1977), p. 312; *Srednee spetsial'noe obrazovanie v SSSR*, (Moscow, 1962), p. 74.

TABLE 5K

JEWISH AND TOTAL VUZ STUDENTS, FOR SELECTED YEARS, 1956/57–1978/79[a]

		JEWISH			
			% OF	CHANGE	
YEAR	TOTAL	NUMBER	TOTAL	AMOUNT	%
1956/57	2,001,000	84,600 [b]	4.2	–	–
1957/58	2,099,100	83,300 [b]	4.0	−1,300	−1.5
1958/59	2,178,900	79,000 [b]	3.6	−4,300	−5.2
1959/60	2,267,000	80,900 [b]	3.6	+1,900	+2.4
1960/61	2,395,545	77,177	3.2	−3,723	−4.6
1961/62	2,639,900	78,700 [b]	3.0	+1,523	+2.0
1962/63	2,943,700	79,300	2.7	+600	+0.8
1963/64	3,260,700	82,600	2.5	+3,300	+4.2
1965/66	3,860,500	94,600	2.5	+12,000	+14.5
1966/67	4,123,200	106,300	2.6	+11,700	+12.4
1967/68	4,310,900	110,000	2.6	+3,700	+3.5
1968/69	4,469,700	111,900	2.5	+1,900	+1.7
1969/70	4,549,600	110,100	2.4	−1,800	−1.6
1970/71	4,580,600	105,800	2.3	−4,300	−3.9
1972/73	4,630,200	88,500	1.9	−17,300	−16.3
1974/75	4,751,100	76,200	1.6	−12,300	−13.9
1976/77	4.950,200	66,900	1.4	−9,300	−12.2
1978/79	5,109,200	59,600 [c]	1.2	−7,300	−10.9

Sources: *Narodnoe khoziaistvo SSSR v 1963g*, p. 579; ibid., 1965, p. 701; ibid., 1967, p. 803; ibid., 1968, p. 694; ibid, 1969, p. 690; ibid., 1970, p. 651; ibid., 1972, p. 651; ibid., 1922–72, p. 446; *Strana sovetov za 50 let*, (1967), p. 281; *Narodnoe obrazovanie nauka i kul'tura v SSSR* (1977), p. 282; *Narodnoe khoziaistvo SSSR za 60 let* (1977), p. 288.

(a) Start of academic year.

(b) Estimates. For method of calculation, see Halevy, 1974, p. 38.

(c) Calculated according to I. Kapeliush, "Vegn eynike statistishe ongabn fun der folkstseylung fun 1979," *Sovetish heymland*, No. 12 (1980), p. 138.

TABLE 5L

JEWISH AND TOTAL VUZ STUDENTS, BY REPUBLIC, 1960/61

REPUBLIC	TOTAL	JEWISH		
		NUMBER	% OF TOTAL	NUMBER PER 1,000 JEWS LISTED IN 1959 CENSUS
TOTAL	**2,395,545**	**77,177**	**3.2**	**34**
RSFSR	1,496,097	46,555	3.1	53
Ukraine	417,748	18,673	4.5	22
Belorussia	59,296	3,020	5.1	20
Moldavia	19,217	1,225	6.4	13
Uzbekistan	101,271	2,902	2.9	31
Georgia	56,322	910	1.6	18
Azerbaidzhan	36,017	906	2.5	23
Latvia	21,568	800	3.7	22
Kazakhstan	77,135	837	1.1	30
Lithuania	26,713	413	1.6	17
Tadzhikistan	19,959	391	2.0	32
Kirgizia	17,379	263	1.5	31
Estonia	13,507	126	0.9	23
Turkmenia	13,151	104	0.8	26
Armenia	20,165	52	0.3	51

Source: *Vysshee obrazovanie v SSSR* (Moscow, 1961), pp. 85, 128–157.

136

TABLE 5M

VUZ STUDENTS IN THE RSFSR, BY NATIONALITY, FOR SELECTED YEARS, 1956/57–1976/77

YEAR	TOTAL	JEWISH		% DISTRIBUTION BY NATIONALITY			
		NUMBER	% OF TOTAL IN USSR	JEWISH	RUSSIAN	UKRAINIAN	OTHER
1956/57	1,266,729	51,561	61.0	4.07	83.26	4.56	8.11
1958/59	1,365,700	51,100	64.7	3.74	82.65	4.63	8.98
1960/61	1,496,700	46,555	60.3	3.11	83.00	4.53	9.36
1962/63	1,827,000	47,600	60.0	2.61	82.59	4.51	10.29
1963/64	2,013,600	49,000	59.3	2.43	82.38	4.58	10.61
1976/77	2,905,700	35,300	52.8	1.22	83.16	3.40	12.22

Sources: *Kul'turnoe stroitel'stvo RSFSR* (Moscow, 1958), p. 381; *Narodnoe khoziaistvo RSFSR v 1963 godu* (Moscow, 1965), p. 495; *Narodnoe khoziaistvo za 60 let* (Moscow, 1977), p. 312.

TABLE 5N

VUZ STUDENTS IN THE UKRAINE, BY NATIONALITY, FOR SELECTED YEARS, 1960/61–1961/62

	FREQUENCIES		% DISTRIBUTION BY NATIONALITY				
YEAR	TOTAL	JEWISH	JEWISH	UKRAINIAN	RUSSIAN	BELORUSSIAN	OTHER
1960/61	417,748	18,673	4.47	62.47	30.03	1.05	1.98
1961/62	460,600	18,000	3.91	62.74	30.18	0.98	2.19

The 1960/61 data according to *Vysshee obrazovanie v SSSR* (Moscow, 1961), pp. 130, 131. The 1961/62 data were derived from Naulko, who presents the total number of Jewish, Russian, Ukrainian and Belorussian students enrolled in either a VUZ or *tekhnikum*. For each of these nationalities we have eliminated the *tekhnikum* students, and thus arrived at the national structure of the VUZ student body of the republic. (V. Naulko, *Etnichnyi sklad naseleniia Ukrainskoi RSR* [Kiev, 1965]. p.103; *Srednee spetsial'noe obrazovanie v SSSR* [Moscow, 1962], p.75).

6   SOCIAL STRATIFICATION
AND ECONOMIC ACTIVITY

Published tabulations of the 1970 census divide the population of the Soviet Union into three strata on the basis of breadwinners' workplaces and their function in the economy. Dependent family members are classified as belonging to the social stratum of breadwinners; pensioners, military personnel, and scholarship beneficiaries are assigned to the social group to which they belonged before their retirement, enlistment, or commencement of studies.[1] One social stratum, called laborers, encompasses "people employed mainly at physical work."[2] A second stratum is labeled white-collar workers (*sluzhashchie*), a heterogeneous group that encompasses all wage earners not included in the laborers category. The third group, more homogeneous than the former, is that of *kolkhoz* members, of whom most work in agriculture. Social stratum affiliation is therefore determined by source of income.

Those employed in the national economy are

laborers and white-collar workers in factories, government and cooperative or public institutions and organizations, and *kolkhozes*; members of producers' or disabled citizens' cooperatives; *kolkhoz* members employed in the public *kolkhoz* sector or the private (auxiliary) sector (*podsobnoe khoziaistvo*); family members of laborers and white-collar workers employed in the [agricultural] auxiliary sector; peasants with legally-recognized private holdings; private artisans and the like. Students and military personnel are not considered to be employed in the national economy.[3]

We may therefore infer that the Soviet definition of "employed in the national economy" includes all working citizens in the public and private sectors, excluding standing army personnel. This definition apparently excludes only students who do not work; working students in evening or correspondence programs are included among the employed. Because the terms *employed in the national economy, members of the work force, working, employed,* and *self-supporting* (the economically active) are equivalent, I have used them as synonyms.

Available data on the social stratification and composition of the work force among Jews, though fragmentary, may nonetheless contribute to a better understanding of Jewish society in the Soviet Union. The data published thus far fall into four categories:

1. Distribution of the Jews of Lithuania by social strata.
2. Percentage of Jews with at least an incomplete secondary education in the Jewish work force in several SSRs according to the 1959 and 1970 censuses. Findings of the latter census also provide distribution of this group by educational level.
3. Absolute numbers of those with higher (VUZ) or secondary vocational (*tekhnikum*) education among working Jews.
4. A few details about Jews in certain occupations.

SOCIAL STRATIFICATION OF LITHUANIAN JEWRY (1970)

In the 1970 census, about 25 percent of those polled (every fourth dwelling unit) were asked about social stratum affiliation; the findings were then applied to the entire population. The published summaries therefore include population distribution by social stratum but not a cross-classification by nationality. Exceptions are data about the distribution of national groups in Lithuania by social stratum, found in an article by the deputy-director of the Lithuanian Bureau of Statistics (table 6.1). To examine these data, we should study the proportion of Jews in each stratum and compare it with the overall urban population (table 6.2).

While the Jews accounted for 0.8 percent of the population of Lithuania in 1970, they accounted for 0.6 percent of the laborers and 2.2 percent of the white-collar workers. Jews, 1.5 percent of Lithuania's urban population, provided 1 percent of its urban laborers and 2.6 percent of its white-collar workers. Within the stratum called laborers as well, however, differences apparently exist between the Jews and the general population as to branches of the economy in which they are employed. The differences are almost certainly larger even in the white-collar stratum, in which secretaries, bookkeepers, and the like are grouped with engineers, university professors, and others. The distribution into social groups, designed more to obfuscate than to clarify social structure, may therefore teach less about Soviet reality

TABLE 6.1

SOCIAL STRATA DISTRIBUTION OF NATIONALITIES IN LITHUANIA, 1970
(PERCENTAGE)

| | | | STRATUM | | |
NATIONALITY	TOTAL	LABORERS	WHITE COLLAR WORKERS	KOLKHOZ MEMBERS	OTHER
Jewish	100.0	44.5	55.3	0.1	0.1
Lithuanian	100.0	52.1	17.8	29.8	0.3
Russian	100.0	58.2	36.5	5.2	0.1
Polish	100.0	70.1	8.3	21.3	0.3

Source: P. Adlis, "Izmeniniia v sotsial'nom sostave naseleniia sovetskoi Litvy," *Kommunist* (Vil'nius) No. 10 (1974), p. 33.

TABLE 6.2

SOCIAL STRATA OF THE TOTAL, URBAN, AND JEWISH POPULATIONS: LITHUANIA, 1970

| | | | STRATUM | | | | | |
| | LABOURERS | | WHITE COLLAR WORKERS | | KOLKHOZ MEMBERS | | OTHER | |
POPULATION	NUMBER	%	NUMBER	%	NUMBER	%	NUMBER	%
Total	1,684,664	54.0	605,643	19.4	816,822	26.2	11,812	0.4
Urban	1,021,170	65.6	496,228	31.9	36,466	2.3	3,867	0.2
Jewish	10,486	44.5	13,031	55.3	24	0.1	23	0.1

Sources: See Table 6.1 and *Itogi, 1970,* vol. 4, Table 2; vol. 5, Table 2.

than can an examination of distribution by educational level in the Soviet work force.

DISTRIBUTION OF THE ECONOMICALLY ACTIVE BY EDUCATIONAL LEVEL

Data from the 1959 census on the proportion of those with at least seven years of schooling among all self-supporting Jews in eight SSRs relate to 91.2 percent of all those who declared themselves Jews (see table 6A). Despite some differences among the SSRs in the percentage of self-supporting citizens with seven years of schooling or more, in the eight SSRs

Appendix tables 6A-6G appear at the end of this chapter.

for which 1959 census data were published, there were 828 individuals with seven or more years of education per 1,000 self-supporting Jews. In that year the percentage of employed Jews with at least seven years of schooling surpassed that of the employed urban population of any other national group, exceeding that of the Georgians by 7 percent, the Latvians by 26 percent, and the Russians by 47 percent.[4]

The five SSRs for which data from the 1959 and 1970 censuses were published pertaining to education of employed Jews were home to 88.1 percent of Soviet Jews in the 1959 census and 86.8 percent in that of 1970. The weighted proportion of working Jews with at least seven years of schooling in these SSRs was 831 per 1,000 in 1959 and 916 in 1970, meaning that the proportion of those with at least seven years of education among self-supporting Jews in these SSRs rose by 10 percent during the 1960s. This stratum's rate of development, however, was slower than that of other national groups of urban population. Consequently the gap between self-supporting Jews with at least seven years of schooling and the urban population of other national groups narrowed. The gap between Jews and urban Georgians stood at 3 percent in 1970 as opposed to 7 percent in 1959; for the Armenians, 19 percent in 1970 as opposed to 32 percent in 1959; and for the Russians, 23 percent in 1970 as opposed to 47 percent in 1959.[5] The narrowing of this gap between self-supporting Jews and members of other national groups was apparently influenced by three factors:

1. The number of self-supporting Jews with at least seven years of education had approached a maximal percentage as early as 1959.
2. A higher percentage of Jews than of members of other national groups, by completing seven years of schooling and continuing to study, were not included in the working population.
3. The Compulsory Incomplete Secondary Education Law, implemented in 1959, raised the percentage of those with at least seven years of schooling in the entire working population, while a great majority of Jewish youth had reached this educational level even before incomplete secondary education became compulsory.

Although the gap between the percentage of self-supporting Jews with at least seven years of schooling and that of the working population of other national groups narrowed, the percentage of working Jews with that level of education still remained higher than that of any other national group. In the five SSRs for which data were published, there were 84 working Jews with less than incomplete secondary education (seven years of schooling) per 1,000 working Jews in 1970, as opposed to 111 urban Georgians, 224 Ukrainians, and 253 Russians. By the same measure, the educational level of economically active Jewish women was higher than that of Jewish men in each of the republics for which data have been published.

Education is extremely important in determining employment in the Soviet Union, but in this case, the distribution of those employed with at least seven years of schooling on the one hand and those with less than incomplete secondary education on the other is still not adequate for obtaining a good picture of the social profile of the working population. Those with primary education often hold positions similar or even identical to those held by workers with incomplete secondary education (laborers, work foremen, and so on). This phenomenon is not widespread, however, in the case of those with higher or secondary vocational education. Unlike Western practice, the Soviet state, which plans higher and secondary vocational education, is committed to hiring VUZ and *tekhnikum* graduates according to profession and training. It therefore appears that the distribution of self-supporting Soviet citizens by educational level is one of the important indicators by which we may determine the social stratification of the Soviet Jewish community; herein too lies the great importance of the 1970 census data on distribution of employed Jews by seven educational levels. The percentage of VUZ-educated self-supporting Jews was 2.5 times higher in the RSFSR than in Moldavia, 1.9 times higher there than in Belorussia, 1.7 times higher than in the Ukraine and 1.6 times higher there than in Latvia. The highest proportion of *tekhnikum*-trained self-supporting Jews, by contrast, was found in the Ukraine, while the highest percentage of those with incomplete secondary education or less occurred in Moldavia. The percentage of those with seven years of schooling or less among the self-supporting Jews in Moldavia was 2.2 times greater than that in the RSFSR, 1.7 times than in the Ukraine, 1.4 times greater than in Latvia and 1.3 times greater than in Belorussia (see table 6B). Any estimate of the distribution of self-supporting Jews by educational level must take these differences into account.

If we weight the data in the five SSRs, apply the data relating to distribution of working Jews in Latvia to the Jewish community in Lithuania and Estonia, and apply data pertaining to Moldavia to the Jewish population of the other SSRs, we may arrive at an estimate of the distribution by educational level of self-supporting Jews in the entire Soviet Union (table 6.3). This estimate indicates that one-third of self-supporting Jews in 1970 had a VUZ education and that about another fourth (those with incomplete higher or *tekhnikum* education) belonged to the subacademic professional stratum. More than 56 percent of the self-supporting Jews in the Soviet Union therefore appear to have constituted a defined professional work force, with 44 percent lacking professions obtained through regular study frameworks—a factor of importance in determining the social profile of the Soviet Jewish community. Furthermore, the percentage of the VUZ educated among economically active Jews was 3.7 times greater than their share in the urban work force, and the percentage of those with incomplete higher or secondary vocational

TABLE 6.3

LEVELS OF SCHOOLING AMONG THE ECONOMICALLY ACTIVE JEWISH AND TOTAL URBAN POPULATIONS, 1970
(PER THOUSAND ECONOMICALLY ACTIVE PERSONS)

	EDUCATIONAL LEVEL							
POPULATION	VUZ	VUZ INCOMPLETE	SECONDARY VOCATIONAL	SECONDARY	INCOMPLETE SECONDARY	PRIMARY	LESS THAN PRIMARY	MEAN YEARS OF STUDY [a]
(1) Jews (est.)	334	40	188	196	145	74	23	11.1
(2) Urban	90	16	131	192	319	192	60	8.1
Ratio: (1) to (2)	3.7	2.5	1.4	1.0	0.5	0.4	0.4	1.4

(a) The calculation was made according to the following assumptions: VUZ education = 15 years of study; incomplete VUZ education = 13; secondary vocational training = 12; secondary school = 10; incomplete secondary school = 7; primary school = 4; less than primary = 2.

education was 1.6 times greater among the Jews than the average for all the urban employed. The average educational level (years of schooling) for self-supporting Jews was 1.4 times higher than that for the total urban work force. Among working Jews, however, differences occur among the SSRs in terms of education.

Using the average education (years of schooling) of self-supporting Jews in the RSFSR as an index level of 100, the corresponding figure for the Ukraine is 92, for Latvia, 89; for Belorussia, 88; and for Moldavia, 80. Because a certain correlation exists between wage earnings and educational level, especially among the Jews—to whom the party apparatus, security services, and advancement in the army are closed—there is reason to assume that the differences in employed Jews' educational levels in the various SSRs reflect differences in income as well.[6] We may therefore say that the Jews of the RSFSR enjoy not only the many possibilities that the metropolises (Moscow, Leningrad) afford them but a higher average income level than that of Jews in other SSRs.

The educational-level distribution of self-supporting Jewish men as opposed to women can also be calculated by the method used earlier in estimating the distribution of the general self-supporting Jewish population by educational level (table 6.4). The average education of working Jewish women is almost idential to that of Jewish men, a consequence of the low percentage of working Jewish women with seven years of schooling or less (263 men per 1,000 and 218 women). It is reasonable to assume that women at low educational and therefore low income levels tend less to work outside the home than educated women would. The stratum of those with secondary or higher education is larger among employed Jewish women (782 per 1,000) than men (737), but the percentage of VUZ educated is higher among men (343 per 1,000) than women (323). The data on those with VUZ or *tekhnikum* training prove that women accounted for close to half of all employed Jews in these educational strata in the 1960s.

A question arises as to the percentage of those in the work force among all Soviet Jews. Since census conclusions do not pinpoint the Jews directly, we must resort to an indirect technique and avail ourselves of current statistical data. At the end of 1969 there were about 178,000 employed Jews with *tekhnikum* education[7] and close to 349,000 with VUZ education[8] in the Soviet Union—a total of close to 527,000 employed Soviet Jews with higher or secondary vocational education. The estimate of working Jews' distribution by educational level (census of January 1970) indicated 522 VUZ- or *tekhnikum*-educated individuals per 1,000 self-supporting Jews. We may therefore assert that there were about 1,010,000 self-supporting Jews in the Soviet Union (47 percent of the population) at the beginning of 1970. Hence the percentage of Jewish employed was almost identical to that of the general Soviet population but lower than that of the urban population, for 47.7 percent of all Soviet Union residents were employed in

TABLE 6.4

LEVELS OF SCHOOLING AMONG THE ECONOMICALLY ACTIVE JEWISH POPULATION, BY SEX, 1970
(PER THOUSAND ECONOMICALLY ACTIVE PERSONS)

POPULATION	EDUCATIONAL LEVEL							
	VUZ	VUZ INCOMPLETE	SECONDARY VOCATIONAL	SECONDARY	INCOMPLETE SECONDARY	PRIMARY	LESS THAN PRIMARY	MEAN YEARS OF STUDY
(1) Male	343	43	173	178	148	89	26	11.0
(2) Female	323	38	205	216	141	56	21	11.2
Ratio: (1) to (2)	1.06	1.13	0.84	0.82	1.05	1.59	1.24	0.98

early 1970 as opposed to 52.1 percent of the city dwellers.[9] The high urban employment rate is a result of migration from rural to urban areas, where the proportion of workers is especially high. We would not appear to err in asserting that the Soviet Jews' employment rate exceeds that of Israeli Jews: 34.2 percent of Israel's Jewish residents were employed in 1971.[10] The main reason for the 12.8 percent discrepancy between Israeli and Soviet Jewish employment rates appears to be attributable to the labor of women, more widespread in the Soviet Union than in the Israeli Jewish community.

If we were forced to resort to indirect means to arrive at approximations of the distribution of working Jews by educational level, as reflected in the 1970 census, absolute figures are available in current statistical publications for those with VUZ or *tekhnikum* education. These data also enable us to examine the dynamic in these strata of employed individuals during the 1960s and 1970s.

THE *TEKHNIKUM*-TRAINED EMPLOYED

Those with secondary vocational (*tekhnikum*) education play an important role in the Soviet economy, and their numbers are progressively growing. In eighteen years (December 1957-November 1975), the number of self-supporting individuals at this educational level rose by 232 percent, exceeding 13 million in 1975. The data on the Jewish *tekhnikum*-trained employed indicate the percentage of Jews in the Soviet subacademic intelligentsia (table 6.5).

During those eighteen years, the number of self-supporting *tekhnikum*-trained Jews rose by 67 percent, while their proportion in the entire employed population in this educational bracket dropped by 48.2 percent. Unlike the working Jewish population, where we found about 500 *tekhnikum* trained for every 1,000 with VUZ education, the general Soviet population displays a ratio of 1,500 employed with *tekhnikum* education for every 1,000 who had VUZ education.

The average annual rate of growth in the number of Jewish *tekhnikum*-trained employed showed a constant decline during the eighteen years under discussion, as table 6.6 shows.

The 1960s witnessed an obvious downward trend in the rate of increase in the number of self-supporting *tekhnikum*-trained Jews, which actually became negative during the first half of the 1970s. Two major factors underlie this phenomenon:

1. The gap between the number of *tekhnikum* trained who left the Soviet work cycle (due to death, pension, illness, and, in the 1970s, emigration) and the number who joined it progressively narrowed in the 1960s. In the 1970s those leaving the cycle outnumbered those who joined it.

2. Jewish youth preferred VUZ to *tekhnikum* education.

TABLE 6.5

NUMBER OF ECONOMICALLY ACTIVE PERSONS WITH SECONDARY VOCATIONAL
SCHOOLING FOR TOTAL AND JEWISH POPULATIONS, 1957–1975

DATE	TOTAL	JEWISH		
		FREQUENCY	% OF TOTAL	PER 1,000 ECONOMICALLY ACTIVE WITH VUZ EDUCATION
1 XII 57	4,016,100	108,000	2.7	414
1 XII 60	5,238,500	136,400	2.6	469
1 XII 61	5,609,100	143,200 (a)	2.6	–
1 XII 62	5,906,100	146,800 (b)	2.5	473
15 XI 64	6,702,100	159,700 (c)	2.4	495
15 XI 66	7,696,800	169,300 (d)	2.2	517
16 XI 70	9,988,100	181,800	1.8	510
14 XI 75	13,319,300	180,700	1.4	469

Sources: *Strana sovetov za 50 let* (Moscow, 1967), pp. 233–234; *Trud v SSSR* (Moscow, 1968), p. 296;
Srednee spetsial'noe obrazovanie v SSSR (Moscow, 1962), p. 43; *Narodnoe khoziaistvo
SSSR v 1963g.*, p. 493; ibid., 1964 , p. 567; *Narodnoe obrazovanie, nauka i kul'tura v SSSR*
(Moscow, 1971), p. 240; ibid., 1977, p. 296.

(a) Including 78,100 women, who constituted 2.2% of all economically active women in the straum , and
54.6% of the Jewish part of the stratum.(*Srednee*, p. 43)

(b) Including 79,900 women, who constituted 2.2% of all economically active women in the stratum, and
54.4% of the Jewish part of the stratum. (*Nar. khoz.*, 1963, p. 493).

(c) Including 87,100 women, who constituted 2.1% of all economically active women in the stratum, and
54.5% of the Jewish part of the stratum. (ibid, 1964, p. 567).

(d) Including 92,300 women, who constituted 1.9% of all economically active women in the stratum, and
54.5% of the Jewish part of the stratum; (*Trud*, p. 296).

TABLE 6.6

MEAN ANNUAL RATE OF GROWTH OF ECONOMICALLY ACTIVE JEWS
WITH SECONDARY VOCATIONAL TRAINING

	1957–1960	1961–1962	1963–1964	1965–1966	1967–1970	1971–1975
Growth Rate (%)	8.8	3.8	4.4	3.0	1.9	−0.1

The distribution of the *tekhnikum*-trained Jewish employed, on the
whole, did not match the Jewish community's geographic distribution
(table 6.7). In the six SSRs (the RSFSR, the Ukraine, Belorussia,
Kazakhstan, Estonia, and Turkmenia) in which close to 84 percent of Soviet
Jews lived according to the 1959 census, the percentage of self-supporting
Jews at the *tekhnikum* educational level surpassed the average for Soviet
Jews. The data I have succeeded in collecting for six SSRs (see table 6C)

indicate that in most of them during the 1960s, a distinct upward trend emerged in the numbers of employed *tekhnikum*-trained self-supporting Jews and a downward trend in their proportion among all those employed at that educational level. The partial data published on this topic from the RSFSR relate to *oblast's* with a small Jewish population and do not allow us to draw conclusions concerning the total Jewish population of this republic.[11]

Concerning the Jews of the Ukraine in this regard, the only information to have been published, to the best of my knowledge, relates to the city of Kiev. Since Kiev was home to 18 percent of the Ukraine's Jews according to the 1959 census and close to 20 percent according to the 1970 census, we should analyze even this solitary datum. On December 1, 1962, there were in Kiev 9,599 employed Jews who had undergone *tekhnikum* training—16 percent of the total of those employed at that educational level.[12] At the end of 1962, therefore, there were 63 employed with *tekhnikum* education for every 1,000 individuals registered in the 1959 census as Jews.

TABLE 6.7

ECONOMICALLY ACTIVE JEWS WITH SECONDARY VOCATIONAL SCHOOLING, BY REPUBLIC

	ECONOMICALLY ACTIVE (1.XII.61)			JEWISH POPULATION (15.I.59)	
REPUBLIC	FREQUENCY	% OF TOTAL	PERCENTAGE DISTRIBUTION	PERCENTAGE DISTRIBUTION	ECONOMICALLY ACTIVE WITH VOCATIONAL EDUCATION PER 1,000 POPULATION
Total	143,146	2.6	100.0	100.0	63
RSFSR	58,294	1.7	40.7	38.6	67
Ukraine	54,521	5.2	38.1	37.0	65
Belorussia	10,318	5.7	7.2	6.6	69
Moldavia	4,730	9.0	3.3	4.2	50
Uzbekistan	4,926	3.5	3.4	4.2	52
Georgia	1,106	1.2	0.8	2.3	21
Azerbaidzhan	1,890	2.3	1.3	1.8	47
Latvia	1,953	3.0	1.4	1.6	53
Kazakhstan	2,327	1.0	1.6	1.2	83
Lithuania	1,149	2.0	0.8	1.1	47
Tadzhikistan	684	1.9	0.5	0.5	55
Kirgizia	489	1.1	0.3	0.4	57
Estonia	439	1.1	0.3	0.2	81
Turkemenia	266	0.8	0.2	0.2	65
Armenia	54	0.2	0.1	0.1	53

Source: *Srednee spetsial'noe obrazovanie v SSSR* (Moscow, 1962), pp. 44–45.

The Belorussian SSR offers published data for 1957-1973 concerning self-supporting Jews with *tekhnikum* education (see table 6C). The 1957-1961 period witnessed an increase in the number and percentage of Jews among all *tekhnikum*-trained employed. In the 1960s, however, the percentage of Jews in this category began to drop despite a constant increase in their number. For every 1,000 individuals registered as Jews on January 15, 1959, there were 58 in the work force with *tekhnikum* education on December 1 of that year and 96 in 1970. Hence the proportion of working Jews with *tekhnikum* education exceeded the national average by 12 percent (58 as opposed to 52) in 1959, and by 16 percent (96 as opposed to 83) in 1970.

Kazakhstan, if not all its *oblast's*, displayed both a numerical and a proportional increase in the category of *tekhnikum*-trained working Jews until the mid-1960s (see table 6C).[13] The Khrushchev regime pursued a policy of transferring professionals to this SSR, and the percentage of *tekhnikum*-trained employed Jews rose as a result. There were about 1,900 Jews in this category in Kazakhstan in November 1959—or 68 at that educational level per 1,000 individuals registered as Jews in the 1959 census (January 15). After Khrushchev was deposed in 1964, Jews apparently began to leave Kazakhstan, explaining the reduction in the number of self-supporting Jews with *tekhnikum* education. We may therefore say that the relatively high percentage of *tekhnikum*-trained working Jews in Kazakhstan was a consequence not of development within the local Jewish community but rather of a deliberate infusion of such personnel as a matter of policy.

Of all *tekhnikum*-trained self-supporting Jews in Moldavia, a majority lived in Kishinev. On December 1, 1962, 2,349 Jews at this educational level worked in that city, accounting for 19 percent of all the *tekhnikum* trained.[14] Hence there appear to have been 55 workers with *tekhnikum* education in Kishinev at the end of 1962 per 1,000 Jews registered in the 1959 census.

In Azerbaidzhan, where 1.8 percent of Soviet Jews dwelled according to the 1959 census and 1.9 percent in the 1970 census, an upward trend in the number and percentage of self-supporting Jews with *tekhnikum* education became noticeable in the first half of the 1960s. At the end of 1959 we find in Azerbaidzhan 25 self-supporting Jews at that educational level per 1,000 individuals registered as Jews in the 1959 census. Of these, a great majority lived in Baku, capital of the SSR.[15]

Lithuania, unlike Azerbaidzhan, displays no uniform trend of changes in the number of *tekhnikum*-trained Jewish workers. In the latter half of the 1950s, a downward trend was clearly evident in this SSR in both number and percentage of employed Jews in this educational bracket (table 6C). In the 1960s, however, their number grew steadily even as their share in the overall *tekhnikum*-educated work force was declining. We find an average annual decrease of 4.9 percent in the number of Jewish employed at this educational level between 1957 and 1960 and an average annual increase of 7.5 percent between 1961 and 1970. We may therefore estimate that for every 1,000 individuals registered as Jews in the 1959 census, there were 38 workers with *tekhnikum* education in Lithuania; there were 62 at the time of the 1970 census. Application of the same method of calculation to Tadzhikistan enables us to assert that there were 37 *tekhnikum* trained employed per 1,000 Jews in 1959, of whom a great majority lived in Dushanbe, the capital.[16] Both their number and proportion grew in that SSR during the 1960s. In Kirgizia their absolute numbers grew, while their percentage among all workers in the *tekhnikum*-educated bracket remained unchanged.[17]

The lowest percentage of self-supporting Jews at the *tekhnikum* education level occurred in Georgia—only 10 per 1,000 Jews in early 1959. In the early 1960s, an upward trend in both number and percentage was observed there (set table 6C). This, however, apparently slowed in the the the decade's latter half, as data from the Abkhaz ASSR, part of the Georgian SSR, also hint.[18]

We cannot even estimate the vocational distribution of the self-supporting *tekhnikum*-trained Jews, for the only data published on this matter relate to Kazakhstan, where approximately 1.5 percent of the employed Jews at this educational level live. Data presented in table 6.8 lead us to believe that technicians and medical personnel accounted for more than two-thirds of all Jewish workers with *tekhnikum* education. By contrast, the sphere of culture, in which the Jews played a prominent role in the 1920s and 1930s, absorbed only about 10 percent of the employed Jews in this educational bracket. There is reason to assume that this outline characterizes a majority of *tekhnikum*-trained employed Jews in a general sense.

TABLE 6.8

ECONOMICALLY ACTIVE JEWS IN KAZAKHSTAN WITH SECONDARY VOCATIONAL
SCHOOLING BY OCCUPATION, DECEMBER 1959

OCCUPATION	FREQUENCY	% OF ALL EMPLOYED IN OCCUPATION	% OF ECONOMICALLY ACTIVE JEWS IN INDICATED STRATUM
Total	1,893	1.0	100.0
Technicians	685	1.2	36.2
Agronomists, zoo-technicians, veterinarians, forestry technicians	33	0.2	1.7
Medical and dental technicians	615	1.4	32.5
Teachers and cultural workers	199	0.4	10.5
Others	361	1.4	19.1

Source: *Kazakhstan za 40 let* (Alma-Ata, 1969), pp. 304–305.

SELF-SUPPORTING VUZ-EDUCATED JEWS

Although those with VUZ education are customarily referred to as intelligentsia, the term is not unequivocal.[19] I therefore prefer *professionals,* which indicates those with a defined formal education. The professional public as well, however, is not of a single character. A factory engineer does not share the status and social prestige of a Doctor of Sciences serving in a scientific institution. I have therefore tried, as far as the data allow, to examine differentiation within the professional stratum as well.

Professionals Employed in the Soviet economy

Weighted calculation of data from the census indicates that for each self-supporting Jewish resident with secondary vocational (*tekhnikum*) education at the beginning of 1970, there were close to two employed Jews with higher (VUZ) education, with the professionals constituting about one-third of all economically active Jews. From late 1957 through late 1977, the number of working Soviet professionals rose by 376 percent, while the number of VUZ-educated Jewish employed increased by only about 49 percent (graph 6A). Therefore the percentage of Jews in the total VUZ-educated employed decreased during those twenty years by 60.2 percent (table 6.9). It is true that the number of VUZ-educated employed Jews increased steadily between 1957 and 1977, but the average annual growth exhibits a downward trend.

In the twenty years under discussion, the average annual growth in the number of employed VUZ-educated Jews dropped by 86.8 percent with the low annual average growth evinced in 1965-1966 especially worthy of note (table 6.10). This circumstance stems from a downturn in the number of Jewish students in VUZs in the early 1960s.[20] Because the 1970s witnessed a noticeable drop in the number of Jewish students in VUZs, we may reasonably estimate that for the end of that decade and in the early 1980s, the average annual increase in the number of VUZ-educated Jewish workers will have dropped significantly and may even reach a negative growth rate (that is, a drop in absolute numbers of working Jews in this educational bracket). Indeed, in 1976-1977, average annual growth was already down to 0.5 percent per year.

Using the annual average increase of VUZ-educated working Jews in the 1957-1959 and 1966-1970 periods as a basis, we may estimate the number of employed Jews at this educational level at the end of 1958 and 1969 with a rather high degree of precision. There were approximately 269,000 VUZ-educated Jewish employed in December 1958 and about 349,000 at the end of 1969. It therefore appears that there were 119 professionals employed per 1,000 individuals registered as Jews in January 1959 and 162 in 1970. Between the two censuses, therefore, the proportion of the professionals employed in the Jewish population grew by 36 percent.

ECONOMICALLY ACTIVE JEWS WITH SECONDARY-VOCATIONAL AND HIGHER EDUCATION, 1957–1977

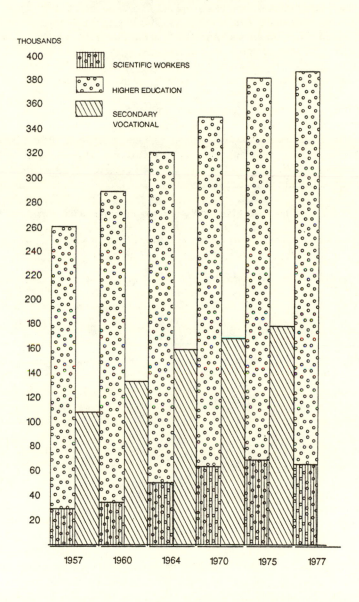

THOUSANDS

SCIENTIFIC WORKERS

HIGHER EDUCATION

SECONDARY VOCATIONAL

400
380
360
340
320
300
280
260
240
220
200
180
160
140
120
100
80
60
40
20

1957   1960   1964   1970   1975   1977

TABLE 6.9

PROFESSIONALS IN THE SOVIET ECONOMY: TOTAL AND JEWISH POPULATIONS,
1957–1977

| DATE | TOTAL | JEWISH | |
		FREQUENCY	PERCENTAGE
1 XII 1957	2,805,500	260,900	9.3
1 XII 1959 [a]	3,236,000	277,000	8.6
1 XII 1960	3,545,200	290,700 [b]	8.2
1 XII 1962	4,049,700	310,600 [c]	7.7
15 XI 1964	4,547,600	322,700 [d]	7.1
15 XI 1966	5,226,900	327,800 [e]	6.3
16 XI 1970	6,852,600	356,800	5.2
XI 1973 [a]	8,384,000	375,000	4.5
14 XI 1975	9,477,000	385,000	4.1
XI 1977 [a]	10,537,000	389,000	3.7

Sources: *Trud*, 1968, p. 277; *Vysshee obrazovanie v SSSR* (Moscow, 1961), p. 67; *Narodnoe khoziaistvo*, 1963, p. 493; ibid., 1964, p. 567; *Narodnoe obrazovanie, nauka i kul'tura* (Moscow, 1971), p. 240; ibid., 1977, p. 296.

(a) Calculated from: *Sovetishe yidn: faktn un tsifern* (Moscow, 1980), p. 11; I. Kapeliush, *Sovetish heymland*, No. 12 (1980), p. 138; *Narodnoe khoziaistvo SSSR v 1959g.*, (Moscow, 1960), p. 602; ibid., 1973, p. 592; ibid., 1977, p. 392.

(b) Including 141,800 women, who constituted 7.7% of all economically-active women professionals (*Vysshee obrazovanie*, p. 67).

(c) Including 151,800 women, who constituted 7.3% of all economically-active women professionals (*Narodnoe khoziaistvo*, 1963, p.493).

(d) Including 156,300 women, who constituted 6.5% of all economically-active women professionals (*Narodnoe khoziaistvo*, 1964, p. 567).

(e) Including 157,199 women, who constituted 5.8% of all economically-active women professionals (*Trud*, p. 277).

TABLE 6.10

MEAN ANNUAL RATE OF GROWTH
OF ECONOMICALLY ACTIVE JEWISH PROFESSIONALS

	1957–60	1961–62	1963–64	1965–66	1967–70	1971–75	1976–77
Growth rate (%)	3.8	3.4	2.0	0.8	2.2	1.6	0.5

Women accounted for an important share of the VUZ-educated Jewish employed, as the data in table 6.11 indicate. It appears that women accounted for 48.5 percent of all VUZ-educated working Jews between 1960 and 1966. The employed Soviet Jewish professional public may be said to be evenly balanced in its gender distribution.

TABLE 6.11

PERCENTAGE DISTRIBUTION BY SEX OF ECONOMICALLY ACTIVE JEWISH PROFESSIONALS, 1960–1966

1960		1962		1964		1966	
MEN	WOMEN	MEN	WOMEN	MEN	WOMEN	MEN	WOMEN
51.2	48.8	51.1	48.9	51.6	48.4	52.0	48.0

To examine future developmental changes in the Jewish professionals' stratum, however, it is proper to examine the numerical ratio of professionals employed in the Soviet economy and VUZ students, the reservoir for this stratum (table 6.12). These data indicate that the ratio of the VUZ-educated employed and the academic reserve (the students) was 2.2-2.6 times higher in the general population than among the Jews in the second half of the 1950s and in the 1960s, 2.8 times greater in the first half of the 1970s, and 3.2 times in the second half of the decade. This fact will undoubtedly lead to a significant drop in the percentage of Jewish VUZ-educated employed among all professionals employed from the end of the 1970s and into the 1980s. Moreover, due to discrimination and national group pressures, the pace at which Jews join the stratum of working

TABLE 6.12

NUMBER OF VUZ STUDENTS PER THOUSAND ECONOMICALLY ACTIVE PROFESSIONALS, FOR TOTAL AND JEWISH POPULATIONS, 1957–1977

YEAR	TOTAL	JEWISH
1957	748	319
1960	676	266
1962	727	255
1966	789	324
1970	669	297
1975	512	186
1977	477	163

professionals—and most of those joining are young—is slower than that for this stratum as a whole. Therefore VUZ-educated employed Jews are on an average older than all those employed at that educational level. Because of the same circumstance, the percentage of VUZ-educated Jewish pensioners is higher than that of the general public of those similarly educated.

This assumption may be verified by examining the ratio of the numbers of the VUZ educated to the number of employed professionals. Members of the former category who do not appear in current statistics as employed fall into three main groups:

1. Professionals in miltary service. It may be estimated that the proportion of Jewish professionals in the standing army does not exceed their proportion in the general body of workers at that educational level. On the contrary, it is more reasonable to assume that Jewish presence among army professionals is even lower than the national average. Therefore the absence of data on this sector does not significantly affect the calculation of the ratio between VUZ-educated Jewish and general employed and unemployed.

2. Working-age people unemployed for health, family situation, or other reasons. It is not at all probable that Jewish representation in this group exceeds that of the general professional populace. Hence, this group does not upset the ratio we seek to examine.

3. Pensioners. If there is a gap between Jews and the rest of the Soviet population in matters pertaining to the percentage employed in the VUZ-educated stratum, it must be attributed in the main to differences in the size of this group.

As estimated calculation based on data from the January 1959 census indicates close to 363,000 VUZ-educated Jews in the USSR, while about 269,000 academically trained Jews were employed in the Soviet economy at the end of 1958. The 1959 census indicated 3,778,000 VUZ-educated individuals in the USSR, of whom 3,052,000 were employed in the national economy at the end of the preceding year. Hence, 81 percent of all VUZ-educated—and only 74 percent of the Jews—were employed in early 1959. If we assume an equal percentage of Jews and non-Jews among professionals not listed in current Soviet statistics as employed in the national economy for reasons of standing army service, illness, family reasons, and the like and if we assume that the bulk of the difference was in the size of the retired groups, it will become clear that although Jews accounted for 8.6 percent of employed professionals in 1959, their proportion among academically trained pensioners was at least 13 percent.

Because of a proportional drop in the Jewish student community on the one hand and the fact that employed Jewish professionals were older than the average on the other, the percentage of Jews among academically trained workers indeed dropped steadily—from 8.6 percent in 1959 to 3.7 percent in 1977. Given the slow entry of young Jews into the employed professional stratum on the one hand and the progressively growing departure of Jews from that stratum on the other, the absolute numbers of employed Jewish professionals in the Soviet Union may also be expected to diminish in the future.

The nationwide changes in the Jewish working professional stratum—those that have occurred thus far and those expected in the future—are not reflected to the same extent in the various SSRs due to significant differences among the Jews of the respective SSRs in this sphere. Table 6.13 indicates two differences among the SSRs: differences in the percentage of Jews in the overall stratum of employed professionals and variation in the proportion of the VUZ-trained employed in the Jewish population.

Examining the percentage of Jews among all VUZ-educated self-supporting persons, we may divide the SSRs into two blocs: those in which the percentage of Jewish professionals employed among all VUZ-educated economically active persons is equal to or lower than the national average and those where Jewish representation exceeds that average. In eleven SSRs

TABLE 6.13

ECONOMICALLY ACTIVE JEWISH PROFESSIONALS, BY REPUBLIC

REPUBLIC	ECONOMICALLY ACTIVE PROFESSIONALS (1.XII.1960)			JEWISH POPULATION (15.I.1959)	
	NUMBER	% OF ALL ECON. ACTIVE PROFES.	PERCENTAGE DISTRIBUTION	PERCENTAGE DISTRIBUTION	ACTIVE PROFESSIONALS PER 1,000 POPULATION
Total	290,707	8.2	100.0	100.0	128
RSFSR	160,732	7.7	55.3	38.6	184
Ukraine	83,689	12.2	28.8	37.0	100
Belorussia	12,632	11.5	4.3	6.6	84
Moldavia	6,206	18.7	2.1	4.2	65
Uzbekistan	8,161	7.5	2.8	4.2	87
Georgia	1,818	1.7	0.6	2.3	35
Azerbaidzhan	4,110	5.6	1.4	1.8	102
Latvia	3,611	8.9	1.3	1.6	99
Kazakhstan	4,148	3.3	1.4	1.2	148
Lithuania	1,800	4.8	0.6	1.1	73
Tadzhikistan	1,169	5.0	0.4	0.5	94
Kirgizia	1,073	3.6	0.4	0.4	125
Estonia	868	3.6	0.3	0.2	160
Turkmenia	486	2.2	0.2	0.2	119
Armenia	204	0.5	0.1	0.1	199

Source: *Vysshee obrazovanie v SSSR*, (Moscow, 1961), pp. 70–71.

in which close to 64 percent of all VUZ-educated employed Jews were found in late 1960 and where about 51 percent of Soviet Jews dwelled in early 1959, the Jews constituted only 6.9 percent of all academically trained employed, while they accounted for 12.2 percent of all academically trained employed in four SSRs (the Ukraine, Belorussia, Moldavia, and Latvia). These differences stem not from the high percentage of VUZ-educated employed Jews in those SSRs but primarily from the relatively small numerical dimensions of the overall VUZ-educated stratum there.

Examining the percentage of the VUZ-educated employed in the national economy in the overall Jewish community allows us to divide Soviet Jewry into four blocs (table 6.14). Changes occurred in this distribution in the 1960s, for the shifts in absolute and relative numbers of the academically trained Jewish work force were not uniform in all the SSRs. The partial data that have been published will indicate this (see table 6C).

TABLE 6.14

CATEGORIES OF UNION REPUBLICS BY PERCENTAGES OF EMPLOYED PROFESSIONALS
IN THE JEWISH POPULATION

% OF ECONOMICALLY ACTIVE PROFESSIONALS IN JEWISH POPULATION	REPUBLIC	% OF SOVIET JEWRY
0–5	Georgia	2.3
6–10	Ukraine, Belorussia, Moldavia, Uzbekistan, Latvia, Lithuania, Tadzhikistan	55.2
11–15	Azerbaidzhan, Kazakhstan, Kirgizia, Turkmenia	3.6
16+	RSFSR, Estonia, Armenia	38.9

The sparse information collected from a number of RSFSR communities indicates an upward trend during the 1960s in the number of academically trained Jewish employed and a downward trend in their proportion out of all self-supporting persons at this educational level.[21]

Since no direct data, as well as I can ascertain, have been published on Jewish professionals employed in the Ukrainian SSR, I am forced to use an indirect technique. From the distribution of working professionals in this SSR in December 1960, it becomes clear that Ukrainians and Russians accounted for 84.55 percent and other nationalities 15.45 percent. Of those other nationalities, 80.14 percent were Jews.[22] I have assumed that the percentage of Jews in the category of other nationalities was at least equal to the 1960 level in preceding years and came to no more in ensuing years than it had been that year. Under this assumption I have calculated the size of the academically trained Jewish work force in 1957, 1962, and 1964, years for which data have been cited on the overall number of the academically trained employed in the national economy and the percentage of Ukrainians and Russians among them.[23] By this way of calculating, it becomes clear that there were about 78,000 working Jewish professionals in the Ukraine at the end of 1957, approximately 91,800 in 1962, and at least 97,600 in 1964. During those seven years (1957-1964) the number of academically trained Jews in the work force of the Ukraine grew by 25 percent, while their proportion of all employed at that educational level dropped by 24 percent (from 14.6 percent in 1957 to 11.1 percent in 1964). More than one-fifth of the VUZ-educated working Jews dwelled in Kiev: 19,815 employed Jewish professionals at the end of 1962, or 21.2 percent of the total employed in that educational bracket.[24] For every 1,000 individuals registered in Kiev as Jews in the 1959 census, there were 129 employed VUZ-educated Jews in that city in 1962.

Over a thirteen-year period (1957-1970) the Jewish academically trained work force grew by close to 73 percent in Belorussia and by more than 83 percent in Lithuania. During the same interval, however, the proportion of employed VUZ-educated Jews dropped by 38.3 percent in Belorussia and by 33.9 percent in Lithuania (see table 6C). Between 1957 and 1970, the average annual increase in the number of employed VUZ-trained Jews was 5.6 percent in Belorussia and 6.4 percent in Lithuania. It therefore appears that the average annual increase in Jewish VUZ-educated employed was higher in these two SSRs by a factor of 2.3-2.7 than in the USSR as a whole (2.4 percent as opposed to 5.6 percent and 6.4 percent). Calculating the average annual rise, it appears that there were about 11,300 working Jewish professionals in Belorussia and close to 1,700 in Lithuania in December 1958. The average annual increase in the numbers of working Jewish professionals was 4.1 percent in Belorussia and 6.1 percent in Lithuania between 1966 and 1970. It seems that at the end of 1969, there were 17,800 self-supporting VUZ-educated Jews in Belorussia and 2,800 in Lithuania. Hence, for every 1,000 individuals registered as Jews in the 1959 census, there were 75 VUZ-educated employed in Belorussia and 65 in Lithuania. For every 1,000 Jews in the 1970 census, there were close to 120 VUZ-educated workers in each SSR. It therefore becomes clear that between the censuses, the percentage of employed professionals in the Jewish population grew by about 60 percent in Belorussia and by about 85 percent in Lithuania. The discrepancies between the two SSRs may be explained primarily against a background of the changes that took place in the Jewish student public, While Belorussia displayed a clear downward trend in the percentage of Jewish students, the Lithuanian SSR evinced not only a numerical but also a proportional increase. It may also be that there was a migration of VUZ-educated Jews to Lithuania from other SSRs during the 1960s.

Only a few data have been published on VUZ-educated employed Jews in Moldavia. A total of 2,686 Jewish women with higher education were employed in that SSR at the end of 1959, meaning that per 1,000 females registered in the 1959 census as Jews, there were only 5 academically trained employed at the time.[25] This percentage is quite low, as we see when we compare these data with the concurrent situation in Kirgizia, where 468 VUZ-educated Jewish women, or 10 per 1,000 Jewish females, were employed at the end of 1959.[26] A large majority of the academically trained Jewish employed in Moldavia apparently worked in the capital of Kishinev. In December 1962, this city was the workplace of 3,938 VUZ-educated Jews, and Jews constituted 7 percent of all professionals there.[27] It therefore appears that for every 1,000 individuals registered as Jews in the 1959 census, there were 92 employed professionals in late 1962. Consequently it may be said that the proportion of the VUZ-educated employed is relatively small in the Jewish community of Moldavia as a whole, while their proportion in the capital exceeds the SSR-wide average by far.

The sparse data on the distribution of employed academically trained Jews indicate that a weighty proportion of them are concentrated in SSR capitals, where the percentage of academically trained Jews in the work force is higher than that of Jews in the SSR in general.[28] The 1960s displayed minor changes in the distribution of VUZ-educated employed Jews in the various SSRs. In five SSRs, Belorussia, Georgia, Kazakhstan, Lithuania, and Tadzhikistan, where the total of VUZ-educated Jews amounted to 7.5 percent of the nationwide number at the end of 1960, their proportion rose to 8.1 percent by the end of 1966. A similar tendency may be discerned in the Ukraine as well, where the academically trained accounted for 29.9 percent of nationwide VUZ-educated Jews employed in 1957 and 30.3 percent in 1964. A certain upward trend therefore appears to exist in the percentage of VUZ-educated working Jews in those SSRs in which their proportion was low; a disparity, however, still exists between the percentage of the VUZ-educated employed in the Jewish community of the RSFSR and the other SSRs.

The social profile of the Soviet Jewish community is influenced not only by the size of its academically trained stratum but by the internal distribution of that stratum as well, differentiated in terms of social status, professions, and standard of living. In the absence of detailed data concerning this internal distribution, however, we are forced to base the analysis on division into two groups: scientific workers and "other academically trained employed."

The data in table 6.15 indicate that the percentage of scientific workers

TABLE 6.15

ECONOMICALLY ACTIVE PROFESSIONALS BY TYPE OF EMPLOYMENT:
JEWISH AND TOTAL POPULATIONS, 1960–1975

| | JEWISH POPULATION | | SCIENTIFIC WORKERS PER 1,000 PROFESSIONALS | | |
YEAR	SCIENTIFIC WORKERS	OTHER PROFESSIONALS	JEWISH POPULATION	TOTAL POPULATION	RATIO OF JEWISH TO TOTAL RATE
1960	33,500	257,200	115	100	1.15
1964	50,900	271,800	158	135	1.17
1966	56,000	271,800	171	136	1.26
1970	64,400	292,400	181	135	1.34
1975	69.400	315,600	180	129	1.40

among all VUZ-educated Jews employed rose during the 1960s but stopped rising in the 1970s. The gap between the percentage of scientific workers among all professionals employed in the USSR and their proportion among academically trained self-supporting Jews has progressively widened. In the mid-1970s, scientific workers therefore accounted for about one-fifth of all academically trained employed Jews.

Scientific Workers

The stratum of scientific workers, numbering more than 1.2 million individuals as of 1975, is highly differentiated internally in terms of educational level, function (all academic disciplines, including the social sciences, the humanities, and the arts), and social prestige. One's place in this social group is determined by two unrelated criteria: academic rank and degree and place of employment.[29] According to the former, the scientific workers' stratum is reserved for "members (both regular and associate) of all academies of science, all holders of the academic degrees of *Doktor nauk* and *Kandidat,* along with those with the titles of professor, *dotsent, asistent,* senior researcher and junior researcher, irrespective of place and nature of their work."[30] It would therefore appear that someone who had reached a position that awards the rank of professor, *dotsent,* or similar title, and who has gone over to administrative or other kinds of work— essentially leaving the field of research or instruction in a VUZ—will continue to belong to the scientific workers' stratum. Furthermore, the "scientific worker" designation includes "persons involved in research in scientific institutions or in teaching in VUZs, whether or not they possess scientific degrees or ranks."[31]

In terms of ranks, too, there are large discrepancies among scientific workers. The category includes bearers of the rank of *asistent,* junior research workers, professors, and members of the academies of science. In educational terms, the category takes in university graduates alongside holders of the degree of *Doktor nauk*, the highest academic degree in the Soviet Union. Clearly we must not view all scientific workers as scientists if we consider as "scientists" people with formal training for independent research. We may therefore view only those scientific workers who have degrees (*Kandidat* or *Doktor*) as scientists.

The percentage of scientists (at the level of *Kandidat* or *Doktor*) out of all scientific workers fell during the 1950s and 1960s, with a moderate upward trend discernible during the 1970s. Scientists accounted for 33.1 percent of all scientific workers in 1950, 30.8 percent in 1960, 26.7 percent in 1970, 29.3 percent in 1975, and 30.8 percent in 1977.[32] These aspects should be examined in discussion of Jewish scientific workers as well.

During a thirty-year period (1947-1977), the number of scientific workers in the USSR grew by a factor of 8.8, while the Jewish contingent grew by a factor of approximately 2.6 (see table 6D). Therefore Jewish representation in the scientific workers' stratum dropped proportionately during this period by 70.6 percent (from 18.0 percent in 1947 to 5.3 percent in 1977). With regard to the growth in numbers of Jewish scientific workers, we may subdivide the period as follows: 1947-1955, 1956-1975, and 1977 onward. In the first interval, the number of Jewish scientific workers dropped by 6 percent over eight years, and their numbers steadily increased in the second interval. In two years of the third interval, their number dropped by 1.4 percent.

The decrease noted between 1947 and 1955 is a result of the anticosmopolitan campaign of Stalin's last years (1948-1953), during which many Jews were dismissed from their jobs. The year 1955 thus marked a nadir in the numbers of Jewish scientific workers.

The twenty years from 1955 to 1975 witnessed a 182 percent increase in the number of Jewish scientific workers and a 546 percent rise in the overall numerical strength of the scientific workers' stratum. If we use 1955 as a baseline year, the average annual growth in the number of scientific workers was 9.1 percent for the Jews and 27.3 percent overall. Hence among the Jews, the increase was only a third of the overall annual average growth rate. If we examine average annual growth on the basis of the first and middle years of each decade, however, we shall discover a clear trend of deceleration in the average annual growth rate of the Jewish scientific workers.

The data in table 6.16 indicate that the gap between the annual average growth rate of the Jewish scientific workers and the national average widened most significantly in the first half of the 1970s. Because it is impossible to attribute decisive significance to the aging of the Jewish population in the case of scientific workers, whose numbers are not great, it can be reasonably assumed that the slow growth of Jewish representation in this stratum essentially stems from a toughening of the limitations that bar

TABLE 6.16

MEAN ANNUAL GROWTH RATES OF THE SCIENTIFIC WORKERS STRATUM:
TOTAL AND JEWISH POPULATIONS, 1956–1977
(PERCENTAGES)

POPULATION	PERIOD			
	1956–60	1961–65	1966–70	1971–77
Total	11.6	17.5	7.9	5.4
Jewish	7.2	11.5	4.3	0.9
Jewish as % of total	62.1	65.7	54.4	16.7

Jews from the stratum of scientific workers. Emigration, too, had some effect. Emigration notwithstanding, however, the absolute number of Jewish scientific workers grew in the first half of the 1970s. In contrast, there was a decline in both absolute and relative terms in the percentage of Jews among scientific workers in the latter half of the 1970s.

Between 1955 and 1975, the proportion of Jews in the scientific workers' stratum fell by 48.2 percent (from 11.0 percent in 1955 to 5.7 percent in 1975), and the rate of this decline has generally been accelerating. If in the second half of the 1950s (1955-1960) their representation dropped by 11.8 percent (from 11.0 percent in 1955 to 9.7 percent in 1960), it plunged by 17.4 percent in the first half of the 1970s (6.9 percent in 1970, 5.7 percent in 1975). There are grounds to assume that this phenomenon will prove to have persisted with greater force in the latter half of the 1970s and 1980s, as figures from 1977 seem to show.

The Jews were the second-largest national group in the scientific workers' stratum in 1959. Only the Russians (199,997 scientific workers) surpassed them; after the Jews, at a small interval, came the Ukrainians (30,255 as opposed to 30,633 Jews), with the Belorussians (7,278) at a considerable distance. In 1975, by contrast, the Jews fell to third place in national group representation in the scientific workers' stratum, with the Ukrainians surpassing them at a ratio of almost two to one (134,243 versus 69,374).[33] Nevertheless, the Jews evinced a higher percentage of scientific workers than any other Soviet national group.

The overall percentage of scientific workers in the Soviet population increased between the two censuses from 15 scientific workers per 10,000 individuals in 1959 to 38 in 1970, a 253 percent increase. The urban population accounted for 31 scientific workers per 10,000 individuals in 1959 and 68 in 1970, a 219 percent increase. This rise, however, was not distributed equally among the national groups. Of the fifteen national groups examined, only four (Russians, Ukrainians, Kazakhs, Uzbeks) marked an increase in percentage of scientific workers in the urban population that exceeded the nationwide average, while for the others, the Jews among them, the growth rate did not reach the national average. The greatest increase in percentage of scientific workers among city dwellers between 1959 and 1970 took place among the Russians and Ukrainians (see table 6E), both politically potent national groups. The decline in percentage of Jewish scientific workers should be attributed essentially to the rapid growth in the number of Russians and Ukrainians in this stratum. We may therefore infer that the national composition of the scientific workers' stratum is not free of national group pressure and that the Jews, as the weak link in the Soviet national group system, emerged for the worse and were forced to use not only their professional skills but also various devices to penetrate this social stratum. Because many Jews are highly motivated to engage in one form of research or another and inasmuch as the scientific workers' stratum is broad and covers the length and breadth of the Soviet Union, the Jews were able to arrange matters successfully to their own satisfaction; their absolute numbers in this stratum continued to rise until the mid-1970s but began to decrease in the second half of the decade.

Because the scientific workers' stratum draws its members primarily from VUZ graduates, we should examine the ratio of scientific workers and students. For every scientific worker in the USSR, there were 7.7 VUZ students in 1958 and 4.9 in 1970; corresponding figures for the Jews were 2.7 in 1958 and 1.6 in 1970. Thus the changes that occurred in the numerical ratio of students and scientific workers were almost identical for the overall Soviet population (7.7:4.9 = 1.6) and for the Jews (2.7:1.6 = 1.7). In the light of the declining numbers of Jewish students, however, this ratio may change significantly. For every scientific worker in 1977, there was approximately only one Jewish student in the 1976/77 academic year against a nationwide average of 3.9. As a result, during the second half of the 1970s, we can see the first signs of not only a relative but an absolute decline in the number of Jewish scientific workers, though there are no grounds to assume that this will take place at a uniform pace in all the SSRs.

In SSRs where the overall number of scientific workers was small and the number of Jewish scientific workers was also miniscule, their numbers grew faster than in the USSR as a whole during the 1960s. Between 1960 and 1971, the number of Jewish scientific workers in the USSR grew by 99.2 percent while it grew by 109.8 percent in Lithuania and by 153.3 percent in Moldavia in the same period. In Uzbekistan, by contrast, the number of Jewish scientific workers rose at a rate lower than the national average (96.4 percent). These SSRs, however, are home to a very small proportion of Jewish scientific workers. In six SSRs (Uzbekistan, Georgia, Lithuania, Moldavia, Kazakhstan, and Armenia) in which 13 percent of Soviet Jews dwelled in 1959, only 6 percent of Jewish scientific workers were found in 1960; in four SSRs (Moldavia, Uzbekistan, Georgia, and Lithuania), which accounted for 13 percent of the Soviet Jewish population in 1970, only 4.7

percent of the Jewish scientific workers were found in 1971 (see table 6F). Moscow, by contrast, was home to 17 percent of Soviet Jews according to the 1970 census, while 38.9 percent of all Jewish scientific workers in the USSR were found there in the same year.[34] In 1970 there were 25,023 Jewish scientific workers in Moscow, 10.7 percent of all such workers in the city. Jewish representation in Moscow's scientific workers stratum therefore exceeded the national average by 55.1 percent (10.7 percent as opposed to 6.9 percent). Because more than 31 percent of the Jews of the RSFSR lived in the city of Moscow according to the 1970 census, there are grounds to assume that their age composition approximates that of all Jews of the RSFSR and is no lower in any event. Inasmuch as scientific workers are by and large university graduates, the youngest are 22 years old (a high school graduate, aged 17, awaits five years' VUZ study). Retirement age in the Soviet Union is 55 for women and 60 for men. The 22-59 age bracket, according to the 1970 census, accounted for about 55.9 percent of all Jews of the RSFSR. If we apply this breakdown to the Jews of Moscow, there were close to 140,000 Jews in the 22-59 age bracket in that city in 1970. We may therefore estimate that every sixth Jew in this age group in Moscow in 1970 was a scientific worker. This fact determines the sociological profile of Moscow's Jewish community, one greatly different from Jewish communities elsewhere in the Soviert Union. This situation also exerts influence on demographic phenomena pertaining to the Jews of Moscow and sets them apart from other Soviet Jewish communities.

Scientific workers, more than any other stratum in Soviet society, have access to Western publications, and most know (more or less) a Western language. This makes for a more stimulating social and intellectual situation, especially if we take into account the Russian historical tradition of the intelligentsia as the self-consciously leading social group, bearing a moral responsibility for societal change. It is therefore no wonder that the relatively high proportion of scientific workers in the Jewish population influences the shaping of this community's self-image.

The cream of the crop among scientific workers are scientists who are thought of as independent researchers and who hold scientific degrees of *Kandidat* or *Doktor nauk*. Among Jews, 41.3 percent of scientific workers were scientists in 1973; the 1977 figure was 44.0 percent (table 6.17). This increase derived partly from the small growth in the number of scientific workers, as well as from growth in the number of scientists. However, the increase in Jewish scientists did not equal the national average (7.7 percent as against 24.0 percent). This accounts for the Jews' relative decline of 13.6 percent in this field. Over 90 percent of all scientists (90.6 percent in 1973 and 90.9 percent in 1977) held the degree of *Kandidat* and close to 10 percent that of *Doktor* (9.4 percent and 9.1 percent, respectively). Among Jewish scientists, about 85 percent held the degree of *Kandidat* (85.0 percent in 1973 and 85.4 percent in 1977) and 15 percent that of *Doktor*. In this

TABLE 6.17

TOTAL AND JEWISH SCIENTISTS, 1973, 1977

| YEAR | TOTAL | JEWS | | TOTAL | JEWS | | TOTAL | JEWS | |
		NUMBER	PERCENTAGE		NUMBER	PERCENTAGE		NUMBER	PERCENTAGE
				KANDIDAT			**DOKTOR NAUK**		
1973	318,067	27,957	8.8	288,261	23,775	8.3	29,806	4,182	14.0
1977	394,400	30,100	7.6	358,400	25,700	7.2	36,000	4,400	12.2

Sources: *Vestnik statistiki*, No. 4 (1974), p. 94; I. Kapeliush, *Sovetish heymland*, No. 12 (1980), p. 139; *Narodnoe khoziaistvo SSSR v 1977g.* (Moscow, 1978), p. 94.

three-year period, the share of Jewish *Kandidats* fell by 13.3 percent and of *Doktors* by 14.3 percent despite their increase in absolute numbers. The increase was partially the result of the increased number of Jewish VUZ students in the 1960s. Given the decline in the number of Jewish students in the 1970s, however, we may observe a decline in absolute as well as in relative terms with regard to Jewish scientists in the near future. But until the mid-1970s, Jewish representation rose in direct proportion to educational level. (In the 1976/77 academic year 1.4 percent of all VUZ students were Jews; in late 1977 they accounted for 5.3 percent of scientific workers, 7.2 percent of the *Kandidats,* and 12.0 percent of the *Doktor nauk.*)

Within this subgroup (scientists), the Jews were the third largest national group at the end of 1973 (following the Russians and Ukrainains), with the fourth-ranking national group (the Georgians) 3.5 times smaller than the Jews. Among workers holding the degree of *Doktor*, however, the Jews were the second largest national group, trailing only the Russians. About twice as many Jews held this degree as did Ukrainians.[35]

Because *aspirantura* is the main route to attaining the degree of *Kandidat,* we should examine the ratio of scientists holding this degree and *aspirants.* For every 100 working *Kandidats* in the USSR at the end of 1973, there were 34 *aspirants.* This ratio, however, was not identical for all national groups. For every 100 employed with the degree of *Kandidat,* there were 35 Russian *aspirants,* 37 Ukrainian *aspirants,* and 15 Jewish *aspirants.* It therefore appears that the percentage of Jews among scientists bearing the degree of *Kandidat,* which apparently began to drop as early as the 1960s as data from Uzbekistan hint (see table 6G), continued to fall even more rapidly during the 1970s. Developments in this sphere, however, will be determined primarily in places where Jewish scientists live in large numbers, such as Moscow, and not in areas where their number is extremely small.[36]

In 1970 there were 8,967 Jewish scientists in Moscow—13.6 percent of all scientists there. Of these, 82.6 percent held the degree of *Kandidat* and 17.4 percent of *Doktor nauk.* Jews accounted for 12.8 percent of scientists in Moscow who held the degree of *Kandidat* and 19.3 percent of the *Doktor.*[37] Hence almost every fifth *Doktor nauk* in Moscow in 1970 was Jewish. Of Jewish scientists in 1973, 32 percent worked in Moscow in 1970. If we bear in mind that Leningrad and other RSFSR cities are also research and science centers, we will be able to say that the great majority of Jewish scientists in the Soviet Union are concentrated in the RSFSR.

"Other Academically Trained Employed"

It is impossible to apply the general professional distribution of VUZ-trained employed in the Soviet Union to the Jews specifically. For one, the

Jews exhibit a tendency to concentrate in a limited number of professions; for another, certain fields such as diplomacy, the army, security services, and the like are almost closed to them. We must therefore settle for citing bits of information on this subject that may hint at the general trend but will not enable us to reach even a conjectural estimate.

A breakdown of working VUZ-educated Jews on a basis of profession was published pertaining only to Kazakhstan, where fewer than 1.5 per cent of all working Jews at that educational level dwelled in 1959 (table 6.18).

TABLE 6.18

ECONOMICALLY ACTIVE JEWISH PROFESSIONALS IN KAZAKHSTAN,
BY OCCUPATION, DECEMBER 1959

| | JEWS | | PERCENTAGE DISTRIBUTION | |
OCCUPATION	NUMBER	% OF ALL PERSONS IN OCCUPATION	JEWS	TOTAL
Total	4,042	3.6	100.0	100.0
Engineers	1,425	5.2	35.3	24.1
Agronomists, veterinarians, and foresters	93	0.8	2.3	10.0
Physicians	1,023	8.2	25.3	11.0
Teachers, librarians and cultural workers	925	1.8	22.9	44.8
Others	576	5.0	14.2	10.1

Source: *Kazakhstan za 40 let* (Alma-ata, 1969), pp.304–305.

A large majority of academically trained Jewish workers for whom no profession is specified are apparently scientific workers (see table 6F). The data also indicate that in the sphere of cultural activity, a field in which Jews were highly active in the past, the percentage of Jews is very low. This assumption finds support in partial data pertaining to Belorussia. Although Jews accounted for close to 8 percent of all VUZ-educated employed in Belorussia in 1970 (see table 6C), they accounted for only 3.1 percent (66 out of 2,163) of Belorussian high school principals, 5.4 percent (20 out of 368) of principals of schools for working youth, and 3.8 percent (21 out of 548) of supervisory personnel in the education departments of the cities and *raions*.[38] It is hard to suppose that these partial data, indicating similar trends in Kazakhstan and Belorussia, are coincidental. It would rather appear that this state of affairs stems from a combination of government objectives and the Jewish professionals' own aspirations. The regime, which doubts the Jews' reliability, tries to reduce their representation in culturally and educationally active positions, while the Jews, aware that this sector of professional employment, more than any other, is subject to the influence of Soviet political developments, prefer to pursue careers in the exact and applied sciences such as engineering and medicine, where they enjoy greater security. Indeed the Kazakhstan data confirm that Jews are more highly represented in the engineering profession than in the overall professional field. Particularly evident is the high percentage of physicians among VUZ-educated Jews—almost twice as high as their proportion among all the VUZ trained in Kazakhstan.

A number of Soviet publications have reported that 14.7 percent of all physicians in the Soviet Union in 1964 were Jewish.[39] There were 532,100 physicians that year and therefore about 78,200 practicing Jewish physicians.[40] Physicians thus accounted for 24 percent of all VUZ-educated Jews, compared with a figure of close to 12 percent of all VUZ-educated employed.[41] It emerges, therefore, that the proportion of physicians among all VUZ-trained working Jews in Kazakhstan in 1959 approximated the national average for 1964.

If we consider physicians and scientific workers together (78,200 physicians, 50,900 scientific workers), it will become clear that 40 percent of all working VUZ-educated Jews in 1964 were employed in these two fields, against 25 percent of all VUZ-educated employed in the Soviet Union that year.

Inasmuch as a majority of Soviet writers (authors, critics, and journalists)—primarily those of the young and middle generations—are academically educated, the Jewish members of this group should be discussed in this context.[42] All officially recognized writers in the Soviet Union are organized in the Writers' Union. The former encompasses authors and poets along with literary critics and scholars of literature and folklore.[43] Some Writers' Union members, therefore, would also appear to be scientific workers. The Journalists' Union comprises all journalists in newspapers, journals, radio, and television.[44] Some members of this union, too, probably belong to the stratum of scientific workers. Although overlapping therefore occurs between scientific workers and members of these unions, we should relate to the latter group as a distinct unit.

The Soviet Writers' Union numbered 4,801 members in 1959 and 6,587 at the beginning of 1967.[45] On the basis of average annual increase, the Soviet Writers' Union had a membership of about 5,900 at the beginning of 1964. In the Journalists' Union, founded in 1959, there were more than 38,000 journalists in early 1964.[46] Taken together, the two unions therefore comprised about 44,000 members at the beginning of 1964. In that year, Jews accounted for 8.5 percent of all writers and journalists in the Soviet Union—about 3,700 individuals, or close to 1 percent of all working VUZ-educated Jews.[47] In 1964, members of the Writers' and Journalists' unions accounted for approximately 0.97 percent of all VUZ-trained employed in the Soviet economy. This means that the percentage of writers, translators, literary researchers, and journalists out of all VUZ-educated workers was

nearly identical among the Jews and in the entire Soviet Union. Hence
Jewish representation in the Writers' and Journalists' unions only slightly
exceeded that of all professionals employed in the Soviet Union. In the
second half of the 1960s and in the 1970s, the percentage of Jews in this
group declined. In 1978 they represented 6.5 percent of the total, down
from 8.5 percent in 1964, or a decrease of 23.5 percent.[48] The picture,
however, is not uniform in all SSRs, as the data pertaining to Belorussia
hint. In 1970, 7.9 percent of all VUZ-educated employed were Jewish, while
Jews accounted for 12 percent in the "creative unions" (*tvorcheskie
organizatsii*) of Belorussia, as table 6.19 instructs.

TABLE 6.19

JEWISH AND TOTAL MEMBERSHIP OF "CREATIVE UNIONS"
IN BELORUSSIA, 1970

NAME OF UNION	TOTAL	JEWISH	
		NUMBER	% OF TOTAL
Total	1,154	140	12.1
Writers	287	22	7.7
Painters and sculptors	390	47	12.1
Architects	328	41	12.5
Cinematographers	109	20	18.4
Composers (music)	40	10	25.0

Source: *Struktura sovetskoi intelligentsii* (Minsk, 1970), p.105.

The relatively small Jewish representation in cultural activity, especially
that which requires direct contact with the public (administration of
educational frameworks, mass media and the ideological apparatus), is an
indication that the authorities were trying to restrict Jewish participation in
these spheres as much as possible, leading them to concentrate in the
sciences, medicine, and related fields of research. As we have seen,
however, progress in these fields became harder as well during the 1970s.

Analysis of the data on economically active Jews in the Soviet Union
proves that the percentage of Jewish professionals rose significantly during
the 1960s and that the proportion of the Jews in the stratum of VUZ-
educated Soviet workers was rather large. The average age of the
academically educated employed Jews, however, was far higher than the
overall average age in this stratum, and in view of the drop in relative
numbers—and, in the 1970s, in absolute numbers as well—of Jewish
students, it appears that the Jews' weight in this stratum will progressively
fall. A drop in absolute numbers began to occur when the number of those

leaving the work cycle exceeded the number of those joining it. There is a general awareness of this situation among Soviet Jews, although few have dealt with the actual published data, and this has aroused widespread fear and anxiety among college-educated Soviet Jews, particularly among scientists in the 1970s. They perceived that their children's chance of attaining their professional level and status were much smaller than they had been previously. The parents' desire to ensure that their children's social status would at least equal their own thus became a significant factor in the emigration movement, especially among the educated and professional elite.[49]

A significant percentage of the Jewish academically trained employed is concentrated in research institutes and VUZs, with a particularly high percentage among Soviet scientists. The concentration of many Jewish professionals in the scientific workers stratum apparently stems from two main factors: the historical tendency of Jews to make disproportionate use of advanced educational opportunities and the fact that the road to advancement was still open to Jews in the sphere of research—in the main, apparently, in the sciences—more than in the fields of political or public activity, where Jews face highly limited opportunities for advancement. More recently, however, there has been a definite trend toward increasingly greater limitations upon Jews in this field as well, especially apparent with regard to young people embarking on careers. Part of this younger group sees its future advancement taking place outside the USSR, prompting them to seek permission to emigrate.

TABLE 6A

PROPORTIONS OF ECONOMICALLY ACTIVE JEWS WITH SEVEN OR MORE YEARS
OF SCHOOLING, BY SEX, FOR SELECTED REPUBLICS, 1959, 1970
(PER 1,000 PERSONS)

| | | | SEX | | | |
| | TOTAL | | MALE | | FEMALE | |
REPUBLIC	1959	1970	1959	1970	1959	1970
RSFSR	872	934	852	927	898	943
Ukraine	814	915	770	894	871	937
Belorussia	783	898	726	868	852	928
Moldavia	673	813	604	782	787	850
Azerbaidzhan	752	–	731	–	779	–
Latvia	823	881	779	865	884	898
Lithuania	703	–	642	–	795	–
Estonia	892	–	873	–	918	–

Sources: *Itogi, 1959,* Table 57 of the relevant volumes; *Itogi, 1970,* vol. 4, Tables 56, 58–60, 66, 67.

TABLE 6B

PROPORTIONAL DISTRIBUTION OF ECONOMICALLY ACTIVE JEWS, BY EDUCATION AND SEX, FOR SELECTED REPUBLICS, 1970 (PER 1,000 PERSONS)

REPUBLIC AND SEX	EDUCATION							MEAN SCHOOLING (a)
	VUZ	VUZ INCOMPLETE	SECONDARY VOCATIONAL	SECONDARY	INCOMPLETE SECONDARY	PRIMARY	LESS THAN PRIMARY	
RSFSR								
Total	468	41	173	139	113	50	16	12.0
Male	486	45	163	123	110	57	16	12.1
Female	447	37	185	159	115	40	17	12.0
Ukraine								
Total	283	39	214	236	143	64	21	11.0
Male	286	42	200	218	148	81	25	10.8
Female	279	36	230	255	137	45	18	11.1
Belorussia								
Total	248	35	210	208	197	84	18	10.5
Male	256	37	189	186	200	110	22	10.3
Female	240	34	231	230	193	57	15	10.7
Moldavia								
Total	184	38	161	233	197	143	44	9.6
Male	181	38	138	217	208	167	51	9.3
Female	186	39	188	252	185	114	36	9.9
Latvia								
Total	285	66	159	211	160	96	23	10.7
Male	295	68	148	190	164	109	26	10.6
Female	273	63	172	235	155	82	20	10.8

Sources: *Itogi, 1970*, vol. 4, Tables 58–60, 66, 67.

(a) See note (a) to the Table 6.3 for the method of assignment of number of years of schooling to each level of educational attainment.

TABLE 6C

ECONOMICALLY ACTIVE JEWS WITH SECONDARY VOCATIONAL AND VUZ SCHOOLING: FREQUENCIES AND PERCENTAGE OF TOTAL FOR SELECTED REPUBLICS

REPUBLIC AND YEAR [a]	SECONDARY VOCATIONAL		VUZ	
	FREQUENCY	% OF TOTAL	FREQUENCY	% OF TOTAL
Belorussia				
1957	7,044	5.4	10,713	12.8
1959	8,700	5.7	11,900	11.8
1960	9.400	5.7	12,632	11.5
1961	10,300	5.7	13,400	11.3
1966	12,581	4.9	15,906	9.3
1970	14,207	4.2	18,515	7.9
1973	15,075	3.6	20,855	7.0
Georgia				
1959	700	0.9	1,800	1.8
1960	–	–	1,800	1.7
1961	1,106	1.2	2,000	1.8
1962	1,200	1.3	–	–
1966	1,000	0.8	2,300	1.6
Azerbaidzhan				
1959	1,300	1.8	3.700	5.5
1960	–	–	4,100	5.6
1961	1,900	2.3	–	–
1962	1,900	2.2	4,200	5.3
1964	2,200	2.2	4,200	4.7
Kazakhstan				
1957	406	1.5	–	–
1959	1,893	1.0	4,000	3.5
1960	2,000	0.9	4,200	3.4
1961	2,300	1.0	4,500	3.2
1964	3,300	1.1	4,900	2.7
1966	2,100	0.6	4,600	2.2
1968	2,000	0.5	4,500	2.1
Lithuania				
1957	1,016	2.6	1,628	5.9
1959	859	1.8	1,736	5.8
1960	867	1.6	1,800	4.8
1961	1,149	2.0	1,965	4.8
1962	1,238	2.0	2,086	4.7
1964	1,676	2.3	2,548	5.1
1966	1,329	1.5	2,402	4.1
1968	1,454	1.4	2,521	3.6
1970	1,515	1.2	2,983	3.9

173

(Table 6C continued)

REPUBLIC AND YEAR [a]	SECONDARY VOCATIONAL		VUZ	
	FREQUENCY	% OF TOTAL	FREQUENCY	% OF TOTAL
Tadzhikistan				
1957	406	1.5	999	5.6
1959	514	1.7	1,114	5.2
1960	592	1.8	1,169	5.0
1961	684	1.9	–	–
1962	659	1.7	1,307	4.5
1964	784	1.8	1,338	4.2
1966	867	1.8	1,408	3.6
Armenia				
1960	–	–	204	0.5
1964	–	–	203	0.4
1966	–	–	205	0.3
1968	–	–	242	0.3

Sources: *Narodnoe khoziaistvo BSSR* (Minsk, 1963), p. 315; ibid., 1971, p. 132; ibid., 1972, p. 158; *Sovetskaia Gruziia za 40 let* (Tbilisi, 1961), p. 140; *Narodnoe khoziaistvo Gruzinskoi SSR v 1961 godu,* p. 413; ibid., 1962, p. 288; *Sovetskaia Gruziia k 50–letiiu velikoi oktiabr'skoi revoliutsii* (Tbilisi, 1967), p. 211; *Dostizheniia sovetskogo Azerbaidzhana za 40 let v tsifrakh* (Baku, 1960), p. 181; *Azerbaidzhan v tsifrakh* (Baku, 1964), p. 174; *Narodnoe khoziaistvo Azerbaidzhanskoi SSR v 1963 godu,* p. 190; ibid., 1964 , p. 153; *Kazakhstan za 40 let* (Alma-Ata, 1969), pp. 304–305, *Narodnoe khoziaistvo Kazakhstana* (Alma-Ata, 1968), p. 258; *Narodnoe khoziaistvo Kazakhstana v 1968 godu,* p. 243; *Narodnoe khoziaistvo Litovskoi SSR v 1965 godu,* p. 190; Ekonomika i kul'tura Litovkoi SSR v 1967 godu, pp. 220–221; ibid., 1970, p. 278; ibid., 1972, p. 363; *Narodnoe khoziaistvo Tadzhikskoi SSR v 1964 godu,* p. 168; *Tadzhikistan za gody sovetskoi vlasti* (Dushanbe, 1967), p. 139; *Narodnoe khoziaistvo Armianskoi SSR v 1964 godu,* p. 190; ibid., 1967, p. 160; ibid,. 1968, p. 154; *Srednee spetsial'noe obtrazovanie v SSSR,* p. 45; *Vysshee obrazovanie v SSSR,* pp. 70–71.

(a) The data relate to November of each year.

TABLE 6D

TOTAL AND JEWISH SCIENTIFIC WORKERS, 1947–1977

YEAR [a]	TOTAL	JEWISH		
		NUMBER	PERCENTAGE	PER 1,000 VUZ STUDENTS
1947	145,600	26,186 [b]	18.0	–
1950	162,508	25,125	15.5	–
1955	223,893	24,620	11.0	–
1958	284,038	28,966	10.2	367
1959	310,022	30,633	9.9	379
1960	354,158	33,529	9.5	434
1961	404,126	36,173	9.0	460
1963	565,958	48,012	8.5	581
1964	611,964	50,915	8.3	–
1965	664,584	53,067	8.0	561
1966	712,419	56,070	7.9	528
1967	770,013	58,952	7.7	536
1968	822,910	61,131	7.4	546
1969	883,420	63,661	7.2	578
1970	927,709	64,392	6.9	609
1971	1,002,930	66,793	6.7	–
1973	1,108,268	67,698	6.1	–
1975	1,223,428	69,374	5.7	970 [c]
1977	1,279,600	68,400 [b]	5.3	1,081 [c]

Sources: *Narodnoe khoziaistvo SSSR v 1959 godu,* p. 757; ibid., 1961, p. 701; ibid., 1962, p. 584; ibid., 1964, p. 701; ibid., 1965, p. 771; ibid., 1968, p. 697; ibid., 1969, p. 696; ibid., 1970, p. 658; ibid., 1977, p. 93; *Narodnoe obrazovanie, nauka i kul'tura v SSSR* (Moscow, 1971), p. 270; ibid., 1977, pp. 309–310; I. Tsameriian, "Velikaia oktiabr'skaia sotsialisticheskaia revoliutsiia i korennoe izmenenie natsional'nykh otnoshenii v SSSR," *Voprosy filosofii,* No. 5 (1957), p. 57; Vestnik statistiki, No. 4 (1974), p. 92; I. Kapeliush, *Sovetish heymland,* No. 12 (1980), p. 139.

(a) All data relate to end of year.

(b) Calculated estimate.

(c) Calculated on the basis of the mean number of Jewish VUZ students for the academic years 1974/75 – 1976/77 and 1976/77 – 1978/79.

TABLE 6E

**NUMBER OF SCIENTIFIC WORKERS PER 10,000 PERSONS
IN THE TOTAL AND URBAN POPULATIONS, BY NATIONALITY, 1959, 1970 [a]**

NATIONALITY	1959		1970	
	TOTAL POPULATION	URBAN POPULATION	TOTAL POPULATION	URBAN POPULATION
Total USSR	15	31	38	68
Jewish	135	142	299	306
Buriat	12	73	38	153
Georgian	27	75	57	129
Kirgiz	6	51	13	90
Armenian	26	46	57	88
Estonian	19	41	47	85
Latvian	17	36	42	79
Azerbaidzhanian	15	43	30	75
Russian	10	30	47	70
Lithuanian	11	31	31	66
Kazakh	6	24	15	56
Uzbek	5	24	13	53
Ukrainian	8	21	25	51
Peoples of Dagestan	5	24	13	49
Belorussian	7	22	21	48

Sources: *Narodnoe khoziaistvo SSSR v 1959 godu,* p. 757; *Norodnoe khoziaistvo SSSR, 1922–1972gg.,* p. 105; *Itogi, 1959,* General volume, Table 53; *Itogi, 1970,* vol. 4, Tables 1, 4.

(a) The table is organized in descending order of the proportions of scientific workers in the 1970 urban population. Data on nationalities with less than a thousand scientific workers in 1970 are not presented.

TABLE 6F

JEWISH SCIENTIFIC WORKERS IN SELECTED REPUBLICS

REPUBLIC AND YEAR	FREQUENCY	% OF TOTAL
Belorussia		
1969	1,457	7.8
Uzbekistan		
1960	857	8.3
1963	1,255	8.4
1966	1,348	7.5
1967	1,391	7.0
1968	1,488	6.7
1969	1,611	6.7
1970	1,664	6.5
1971	1,683	6.4
Moldavia		
1960	259	13.0
1965	408	10.9
1967	616	10.8
1971	656	11.0
Georgia		
1960	177	1.9
1966	325	2.3
1970	447	2.2
1971	446	2.2
Azerbaidzhan		
1963	663	6.5
Kazakhstan		
1960	523	5.4
1961	527	4.8
1963	713	4.5
1966	828	4.6
Lithuania		
1960	163	4.9
1967	282	4.3
1968	278	3.9
1969	291	3.8
1970	322	3.9
1971	342	3.8
Armenia		
1960	31	0.7
1965	41	0.5
1966	52	0.6
1967	63	0.7
1968	72	0.7

Sources: *Struktura sovetskoi intelligentsii* (Minsk, 1970), p. 81; *Narodnoe khoziaistvo Uzbekskoi SSR za 50 let*, p. 225; *Narodnoe khoziaistvo Uzbekskoi SSR v 1967 godu*, p. 277; ibid., 1968, p. 299; ibid., 1969, p. 275; ibid., 1970, p. 270; ibid., 1971, p. 303; Narodnoe khoziaistro Uzbekskoi SSR za 50 let (Tashkent, 1964), p. 225; *Narodnoe khoziaistvo Moldavskoi SSR v 1972 godu*, p. 20; *Sovetskaia Gruziia k 50–letiiu velikoi oktaibr'skoi revoliutsii* (Tbilisi, 1967), p. 240; *Gruzinskaia SSR v tsifrakh v 1971 godu*, p. 181; *Azerbaidzhan v tsifrakh* (Baku, 1964), p. 212; *Narodnoe khoziaistvo Kazakhstana v 1968 godu*, p. 344; *Ekonomika i kul'tura Litovskoi SSR v 1969 godu*, p. 426; ibid., 1970, p. 370; ibid., 1971, p. 370; *Narodnoe khoziaistvo Armianskoi SSR v 1967 godu*, p. 214; ibid., 1968, p. 208.

TABLE 6G

JEWISH AND TOTAL SCIENTISTS IN UZBEKISTAN, 1960–1971

| YEAR | | JEWS | | | KANDIDAT | | | DOKTOR NAUK | |
| | | | | | JEWS | | | JEWS | |
	TOTAL	NUMBER	PERCENTAGE	TOTAL	NUMBER	PERCENTAGE	TOTAL	NUMBER	PERCENTAGE
1960	2,664	307	11.5	2,442	275	11.3	222	32	14.4
1963	3,352	355	10.6	3,082	319	10.4	270	36	13.3
1966	4,723	431	9.1	4,376	385	8.8	347	46	13.3
1968	5,980	494	8.3	5,578	451	8.1	402	43	10.7
1969	6,718	536	8.0	6,278	495	7.9	440	41	9.3
1970	7,401	574	7.8	6,907	524	7.6	494	50	10.1
1971	8,229	601	7.3	7,661	551	7.2	568	50	8.8

Sources: *Sovetskii Uzbekistan za 40 let* (Tashkent, 1964), p. 326, *Narodnoe khoziaistvo Uzbekskoi SSR v 1967 godu*, p. 225; ibid, 1968, p. 299; ibid, 1969, p. 275; ibid, 1970, p. 270; ibid, 1971, p. 303.

7 LANGUAGE AND NATIONALITY

In the Soviet Union, language has come to be accepted as one of the chief indicators of nationality. In each population census, the respondent was asked, in addition to nationality, which "language [he] considers to be his 'native tongue'" (*rodnoi iazyk*). This term, used as early as the first Russian census in 1897, is not precise and has been used with various definitions in the censuses conducted since then.[1] Etymologically the term is related to matters of ethnic origin (*rod*), but in every day speech it refers to the language used in childhood.[2]

Analyzing the data of the first Russian census (1897), however, B. Brutskus commented that "groups often emerge among the Jews . . . which, under the influence of school or environment, have been weaned from use of the language they had acquired in childhood."[3] The discrepancy between the language used by Jews in childhood and that employed in day-to-day life widened after the revolution as a result of internal migration and a greater measure of integration into the surrounding culture and society. The use of Jewish languages as languages of instruction declined in the later 1930s; the percentage of those who declared a Jewish language as their native tongue dropped as a consequence. In the 1926 census 72.6 percent of all Soviet Jews declared a Jewish language as their native tongue; this figure dropped to 41 percent in the 1939 census.[4] The annihilation of most *shtetl*-raised Jews during the Holocaust and the complete liquidation of Jewish cultural activity in the late 1940s caused the number of Jews who used or knew a Jewish tongue to decrease further. Declaration of a Jewish native tongue thus began to acquire an increasingly subjective-psychological significance; at the same time, it became a deliberate means of expressing Jewish nationality. As such, it does not necessarily relate even to a respondent's command of that language, let alone daily use of it. Since many peoples in the Soviet Union have been putting the Russian language to broader use, a discrepancy between declaration of a national native tongue and use or command of that language has emerged not only among the Jews but among other peoples as well. Several Soviet scholars therefore emphasize that a census declaration concerning a certain language as a respondent's native tongue does not necessarily indicate that it is his or her spoken tongue but rather that he or she feels a proximity and psychological connection to it.[5] Some census respondents' declarations of native tongue—or, at times, of knowledge of an additional language—may stem chiefly from their psychological or conceptual identification with a certain culture, though they themselves have no command of the language. This phenomenon is apparently especially commonplace among Soviet Jews, particularly when the language in question is Jewish. We may therefore divide those who declare a Jewish language as native tongue into those who use a Jewish language fully or partially in day-to-day life and those who never resort to such a language at all and for whom it may not even have been a language of their childhood.

A clue to the existence of census respondents who declared a Jewish language as their native tongue while never using it may be found in data from a project, "The National Reawakening of Soviet Jews," conducted at the Hebrew University.[6] A total of 447 Zionist activists who had reached Israel till the end of 1975, plus a random sample of 2,080 Jews who had arrived in Vienna during the second half of that year, were interviewed for the study. Only twenty (4.5 percent) of the 447 Zionist activists and 89 (4.3 percent) of the 2,080 interviewees in the latter group testified that the language spoken in their families was a Jewish one. The Zionist activists were also asked about the language they had declared as native tongue in the Soviet population censuses of 1959 and 1970. We may therefore compare the actual speakers of a Jewish language to their own census declarations (table 7.1).

Among the Zionist activists the data indicate a discrepancy of 35.3 percent between declaration of a Jewish language as native tongue in the 1959 census and the actual situation. This discrepancy widened considerably in the 1970 census, reaching 55.2 percent. This group, however, for which declaration of a Jewish language as native tongue was considered a demonstrative expression of Jewish nationality, does not represent all of Soviet Jewry.[7] The exact percentage of Soviet Jews who declared a Jewish language as their native tongue though they do not use it is uncertain. Still, the study of émigré Jews tends to bear out the hypothesis that census respondents' declaration of a Jewish language as native tongue should be treated not necessarily as proof of their command of that language alone but as expression of Jewish identity as well.

The 1959 and 1970 census summaries and the few published details from the 1979 census include data on respondents "whose native tongue is identical to the language of their respective peoples"; the last two censuses also report on respondents "who have fluent command of an additional tongue which is one of the languages of the Soviet peoples." These formulations may raise a number of problems pertaining to Jewish languages.

The language recognized by the Soviet authorities as the national language of the Jews is Yiddish, known in Russian as *evreiskii* ("Jewish"). The overwhelming majority of Jews in Russia indeed once spoke this language, but there are other languages spoken by Jews as Jewish languages. A small group of Central Asian Jews, known for centuries as Bukharian Jews, speaks a Jewish dialect of Tadzhik, in which it developed a written literature and even a periodical press. In the eastern Caucasus there are groups of mountain Jews who speak a Jewish form of Tat. Both dialects were written in the Hebrew alphabet and include many Hebrew and Aramaic elements. In the western Trans-Caucasus area, the Georgian Jews have not developed a special Jewish dialect and use Georgian as their language, possibly with certain vocabulary components of its own, as some have claimed.

In these areas (Central Asia, eastern Caucasus, and western Trans-Caucasus), there are also Jewish inhabitants whose forebears migrated there from the Pale Settlement, beginning in the early nineteenth century. Most of these Jews at one time spoke Yiddish.

In Russian, Yiddish (*evreiskii*) is terminologically identical to the nationality of its speakers (*evrei*). This is not the case for the other Jewish languages and non-European Jewish communities. Hence when I refer to declarations of a Jewish language (or languages) as a native or a second language, I shall include only respondents who, in the terminology of the censuses, speak a language identical to that of their people.

In the 1959 census, 21.5 percent of all Soviet Jews (487,786 individuals) declared a Jewish language as their native tongue, 76.4 percent (1,733,183) Russian, and 2.1 percent (46,845) other tongues. In the 1970 census, the percentage of respondents declaring a Jewish language as their native tongue fell to 17.7 percent (381,078); those declaring Russian increased by 1.9 percent (1,682,798), and those declaring other languages rose to 4.0 percent. In the most recent census 14.2 percent (257,813) declared a Jewish language as native tongue, 83.3 percent (1,508,246) Russian, and 2.5 percent (44,817) other. During the twenty-year period, the percentage of respondents who declared a Jewish language as their native tongue decreased by 34 percent (from 21.5 to 14.2 percent).

Since respondents in the 1959 census were allowed to declare only one language (their "native tongue"), there were no few Jews who indeed understood a Jewish language, even to the point of literacy, but preferred to declare Russian or another language as their native tongue either because they did not use the Jewish language for day-to-day purposes or for some other reason.[8] Respondents in the censuses of 1970 and 1979, by contrast, were entitled to declare a command of an additional language among those used by the Soviet peoples as well. Hence when speaking of respondents' command of and/or personal connection with a certain language, we should take into account not only those who declared it as their native tongue but also those who cited it as their second language. In the 1970 census, 17.7 percent of all Soviet Jews declared a Jewish language their native tongue; another 7.8 percent, however, reported a Jewish language as their second tongue. In this census, then, 25.5 percent of all Soviet Jews declared knowledge of or personal connection with a Jewish language.

In the most recent census, 5.4 percent of the respondents reported a Jewish language as their second tongue. Between the 1970 and 1979 censuses, then, the proportion of those declaring a Jewish language as either their native tongue or a second language appears to have decreased by 23.1 percent (from 25.5 to 19.6 percent). The fall registered during the 1970s in the percentage of respondents who declared a command of or subjective affinity with a Jewish language originates in two major factors. First, the knowledge and use of Jewish languages is more common among older than among younger population strata. As the elder generation dies off, the number of Yiddish speakers diminishes. Second, some of the young and middle-aged respondents who declared a Jewish language as native tongue or second language as an expression of their national identity in the 1970 census, though they neither actually knew nor used that language, left the Soviet Union during that decade. This notwithstanding, 354,711 Jews declared knowledge of or subjective affinity with a Jewish language in the last census.

The 450,000-plus Jews (an average of the last two censuses, the precise figure being 451,718) who declared a Jewish language as their native tongue or a second language have been offered ninety new Yiddish books and smaller publications in the period from 1959-1981 (see table 7E). By annual average, then, only 0.1 publication has been published during the period under discussion for every 10,000 Jews who had declared Yiddish as either native tongue or second language.

As table 7.2 demonstrates, the number of publications in Yiddish, proportionate to the number of census respondents declaring this language as their native tongue or having a cultural affiliation to it is among the lowest in the Soviet Union—roughly fifty times smaller in relative terms than for the Karakalpaks and about twenty times smaller than for the Poles. The discriminatory treatment of Jewish languages becomes especially

Appendix tables 7A-7E appear at the end of this chapter.

TABLE 7.1

ZIONIST ACTIVISTS INTERVIEWED IN ISRAEL,
BY LANGUAGE SPOKEN WITHIN THE FAMILY AND BY CENSUS DECLARATIONS

	LANGUAGE SPOKEN IN FAMILY (PERCENTAGE)	CENSUS DECLARATIONS			
		1959		1970	
		FREQUENCY	PERCENTAGE	FREQUENCY	PERCENTAGE
Total	100.0	447	100.0	447	100.0
Jewish language	4.5	178	39.8	267	59.7
Russian	94.8	204	45.6	140	31.3
Other	0.7	4	0.9	2	0.5
Not stated	–	61	13.7	38	8.5

See text.

TABLE 7.2

MEAN ANNUAL NUMBER OF PUBLICATIONS IN INDICATED LANGUAGE
PER 10,000 DECLARING KNOWLEDGE OF THAT LANGUAGE
AS EITHER NATIVE OR SECOND TONGUE [a]
(1959–1968, 1970–1974, 1978–1981)

LANGUAGE	PUBLICATIONS	LANGUAGE	PUBLICATIONS	LANGUAGE	PUBLICATIONS
Karakalpakian	4.8	Kumyk	1.8	Kabardin	1.4
Hungarian	4.1	Buriat	1.8	Dargin	1.3
Uigur	3.9	Polish	1.7	Lezgin	1.1
Tuvin	3.8	Osetin	1.6	Avar	0.9
Iakutian	3.4	Karachaev	1.5	Korean	0.9
Kalmyk	2.4	Ingush	1.4	Jewish	0.1

Sources: *Pechat' SSSR v 1959 godu,* Table 10; ibid., 1960, Table 10; ibid., 1961, Tables 4, 35; ibid., 1962, Tables 3, 36; ibid., 1963, Tables 3, 37; ibid., 1964, Tables 4, 46; ibid., 1965, Table 6; ibid., 1966, Table 6; ibid., 1967, Table 6; ibid., 1968, Table 6; ibid., 1970, Table 6; ibid., 1971, Table 6; ibid., 1972, Table 6; ibid., 1973, Table 6; ibid., 1974, Table 9; ibid., 1978, Table 9; ibid., 1981, Table 10.

(a) The basis for calculation was the mean for the last two censuses (1970, 1979).

conspicuous if we consider that the educated reading public is disproportionately greater among Jews than among the other people represented in table 7.2 and that they are a book-loving public. Even by the Soviet criteria customarily applied to other languages and peoples, then, the Jews appear to fall beneath the accepted standard in terms of quantity of publications in their languages.

The proportion of declarations of a Jewish language as native tongue in the two censuses (1959, 1970) was about 10 percent higher among the rural Jewish population than it was in the urban sector (table 7.3). But since only

TABLE 7.3

PERCENTAGE DISTRIBUTION OF THE URBAN AND RURAL JEWISH POPULATION
BY NATIVE LANGUAGE, 1959, 1970

	YEAR AND LANGUAGE					
	1959			1970		
LOCALITY	JEWISH	RUSSIAN	OTHER	JEWISH	RUSSIAN	OTHER
Urban	21.0	77.3	1.7	17.5	78.6	3.9
Rural	31.1	58.3	10.6	29.6	59.7	10.7

Sources: *Itogi, 1959,* General volume, Table 53; *Itogi, 1970,* vol. 4, Table 4.

a miniscule proportion of Soviet Jewry is rural, their declaration of native tongue makes no substantive contribution to the overall picture.

Differences between the sexes in declaration of native tongue are also worthy of attention: 1.3 percent more Jewish females than Jewish males declared a Jewish language as their native tongue in the 1959 census, a discrepancy that widened to 1.5 percent in the 1970 census. Furthermore, 24.1 percent of the males declared a Jewish language as either their native tongue or their second language in the 1970 census, while 26.6 percent of the females did so.[9]

We have reason to assume that the differences between males and females in declaration of Jewish language originate in two major factors. First, women's average age exceeds that of the men; since the percentage of those who declare Jewish language either as native tongue or as second language is relatively higher in the higher age brackets, the percentage of females who so declare exceeds that of the males. Second, proportionately fewer women than men work outside the home; women consequently might find it slightly more consistent with their life-style to declare a Jewish language as their native tongue than the men, who use Russian on the job.

Along with the decrease in the percentage of Jews stating that the Jewish language was their native tongue came a concomitant increase in the percentage of those declaring Russian their native language. From the data in table 7.4, we observe that the rate of linguistic acculturation among Soviet Jews was very high during the second half of the 1920s and during the 1930s compared with more recent periods. Over the course of twelve years (1926-1939), the percentage declaring Russian as their native tongue grew by a factor of 2.1. This was a result of large-scale urbanization and industrialization on the one hand and of the limits placed on cultural and educational activity in Yiddish on the other. A large part of the Yiddish-speaking population perished in the Holocaust. Among the remainder, processes of linguistic acculturation proceeded apace, albeit at a slower rate, given the fact that by the 1930s the majority of Soviet Jews had already been linguistically Russified.

TABLE 7.4

PERCENTAGE OF THE JEWISH POPULATION DECLARING RUSSIAN
AS THEIR NATIVE TONGUE IN SOVIET CENSUSES

1926	1939	1959	1970	1979
26.0	54.6	76.4	78.3	83.3

Sources: T. Semenov, "Evreiskoe naselenie SSSR po polu, vozrastu, rodnomu
iazyku i gramotnosti," *Evrei v SSSR* (Moscow, 1929), p. 67; A. Isupov,
Natsional'nyi sostav naseleniia SSSR (Moscow, 1964), p. 34; and
Table 7A below.

During the twenty-year span fromn 1959 to 1979, the proportion of Jews
who declared Russian as their native tongue increased by 9 percent. The rate
of increase, however, varied between the 1960s and 1970s. The annual
average increase in the percentage of those declaring Russian as their native
tongue during the 1960s, a mere 0.23 percent, tripled in the 1970s to an
annual average of 0.71 percent. The reasons for this acceleration are similar
to those noted for the diminishing percentages of Jews who report a Jewish
language as their own.

In addition to those who had declared Russian as their native tongue,
16.3 percent (350,172 individuals) of all Soviet Jews declared it their second
language in 1970, as did 13.7 percent (248,833) in 1979. At the beginning of
the 1970s, then, 94.6 percent of the Jews declared Russian as either their
native or second language. The corresponding 1979 figure is 97 percent.

The linguistic acculturation of the Jews was primarily oriented toward the
predominant Soviet language. Other Soviet languages were adopted only to
a marginal extent according to the results of the Soviet censuses (table 7.5).
In addition to those Jews for whom another Soviet language—apart from
Jewish and Russian—was the native tongue, in 1970 an additional 21.0
percent (452,594 persons) declared such a tongue as their second language;
in 1979 there were 22.2 percent of Soviet Jews (402,051 persons) in this
category.

Command of a second language in general decreased among Soviet Jews
between the 1970 and 1979 census from 45.1 percent (969,332 persons) to
41.3 percent (747,782). This was in contrast to the overall trend in Soviet

TABLE 7.5

PERCENTAGE OF THE JEWISH POPULATION DECLARING LANGUAGES
OTHER THAN RUSSIAN AND JEWISH AS THEIR NATIVE TONGUE
IN SOVIET CENSUSES

1926	1939	1959	1970	1979
0.9	4.4	2.1	4.0	2.5

Sources: As for Table 7.4.

society, where an increase in knowledge of a second language took place in the 1970s—from 22 percent of the census respondents (1970) to 28 percent (1979). Jews' bilingualism therefore is not exceptional.

Among the sixty-four nationality groups examined in this regard, incidence of knowledge of a second language (as stated in census findings) was higher than the Jews' in forty-two cases. In 1970, these nationality groups constituted almost 15 percent of the Soviet population, and the extent to which they professed a fluent command of a second Soviet language was 65.5 percent.

Some of the peoples whose collective bilingualism exceeded the Jews' were populous groups, such as the Belorussians (more than 9 million persons in 1970, 56.3 percent bilingual) and the Tatars (close to 6 million, 67.8 bilingual). Others were small in numbers, with Soviet populations of only several tens of thousands (for example, Slovaks, Shorts, and Abazins). Several peoples who displayed a smaller percentage of bilingual individuals than the Jews in 1970, such as the Ukrainians (42.3 percent), the Uzbeks (17.8 percent), and the Kazakhs (43.6 percent), registered significantly higher percentages during the 1970s, as reflected in the 1979 census (Ukrainians, 57.0 percent; Uzbeks, 52.1 percent; Kazakhs, 54.4 percent).[10]

The fact that 22.7 percent (close to 55 million people) among the non-Russian nationalities stated in 1970 that Russian was either their native tongue or their second language, as did 29.6 percent (close to 77.5 million non-Russians) in 1979, has important implications. These people continue to identify with their nationality groups despite the fact that they have partially or completely lost facility with their ethnic language, to say nothing of its use as a medium of cultural creativity. This is the background for the ongoing development of ethnic literatures in Russian. Even Soviet critics have been compelled at times to recognize authors writing in Russian as ethnic writers. Thus, Jewish literary and scholarly activity in Russian, once an exception to the norms of Soviet cultural policy, need not be considered out of the ordinary, in linguistic terms, today.

The breakdown according to age group with regard to those declaring a Jewish native language is a matter of particular interest, but data are available only for the RSFSR (table 7.6). The percentage of those declaring a Jewish language as native tongue is higher in the youngest (0-15) and the oldest (50 and above) age brackets than in the intermediate brackets. Of those aged 0-15, 13.8 percent, and of those at least 50 years of age 15.0 percent, declared a Jewish language as native tongue, while only 8.1 percent in the 16-49 bracket did so. Although the figures seem to show that the percentage of census respondents who either speak or aurally comprehend a Jewish language is higher among children than among the middle-aged (16-49), that probably is not so. The explanation for the relatively high 0-15 representation has to be sought in the manner in which the census was conducted. Children's native tongues were declared by parents, while those in the 16-49 category answered this question themselves.[11] The latter

TABLE 7.6

DISTRIBUTION OF THE JEWISH POPULATION OF THE RSFSR
BY NATIVE LANGUAGE, FOR AGE GROUPS, 1970
(PERCENTAGE)

AGE	JEWISH	RUSSIAN	OTHER
0–10	14.6	84.9	0.5
11–15	12.5	87.1	0.4
16–19	9.9	89.3	0.8
20–29	8.1	91.2	0.7
30–39	7.4	92.3	0.3
40–49	8.3	91.3	0.4
50–59	10.6	89.0	0.4
60+	17.7	82.1	0.2

Source: *Itogi, 1970,* vol. 4, Table 33.

preferred to declare Russian as native tongue. Examination of declarations concerning knowledge of a second language yields fundamentally the same picture.

Of the 26.3 percent of all Jews in the RSFSR (212,069 individuals) who declared knowledge of a second language in 1970, 9.5 percent identified this language as a Jewish one, 10.7 percent mentioned Russian, and 6.1 percent cited other languages (table 7.7). If we add the respondents who declared a Jewish second language to those who declared a Jewish language as native

TABLE 7.7

PERCENTAGE DISTRIBUTION OF JEWS IN THE RSFSR WHO DECLARE A SECOND
LANGUAGE, BY AGE GROUP, 1970

AGE	JEWISH (NATIVE OR 2ND TONGUE)	SECOND LANGUAGE			
		TOTAL	JEWISH	RUSSIAN	OTHER
0–10	15.0	10.9	0.4	10.4	0.1
11–15	13.3	13.0	0.8	11.9	0.3
16–19	11.9	17.5	2.0	9.8	5.7
20–29	11.4	17.9	3.3	7.8	6.8
30–39	11.7	17.3	4.3	6.8	6.2
40–49	16.1	22.8	7.8	7.6	7.4
50–59	24.3	32.3	13.7	9.9	8.7
60+	36.1	40.2	18.4	16.3	5.5

Source: As for Table 7.6.

tongue, we shall see that 21.3 percent of the Jews in RSFSR affirmed their affiliation with a Jewish language in the 1970 census as opposed to only 14.9 percent who did so in the 1979 census. Respondents who by declaration had command of or a subjective affinity for a Jewish language in 1970 were not equally distributed in all age groups: 14.3 percent of the 0-15 bracket declared a special relationship with a Jewish language (as native tongue or second language), as did 31.6 percent of the 50 and over category. In the intermediate 16-49 group, by contrast, only 13.5 percent did so. It therefore appears that the percentage of respondents in the RSFSR who declared an actual or professed connection with a Jewish language, whether as native tongue or as second language, was lower in the 16-49 age bracket, with the 20-29 subgroup lowest of all (11.4 percent). This lowest category consists of Jewish RSFSR residents born between 1941 and 1950, a category with a high proportion of students. Another noteworthy detail is the fact that 29 percent of the Jews who petitioned the Soviet authorities and Western agencies between 1968 and 1970 for help in leaving the Soviet Union for Israel belonged to the 21-30 bracket.[12] Moreover, 21 percent of the Zionist activists questioned in the study, "The National Reawakening of Soviet Jews," were born after 1945. If the declaration of affinity for a Jewish language (as native tongue or second language) indeed serves as a certain indicator of Jewish identity, the 20-29 age bracket may be more polarized than other groups, with this polarization expressed in national activity and assimilationist tendencies. In the absence of corresponding data from other republics, however, unequivocal conclusions on this topic are hard to draw. We shall therefore explore regional differences regarding declaration of language.

With respect to declaration of Jewish native tongue in the 1959 census, we can divide Soviet Jewry among three categories of union republics: a) those in which the percentage of respondents who declared a Jewish language as native tongue fell below the national average; b) republics in which their percentage exceeded the national average but by less than twice that average; and c) republics in which Jews declared a Jewish language as their native tongue at a rate at least twice the national average.

It appears that 34.1 percent of all Soviet Jews who declared a Jewish language as their native tongue dwelled in five republics (Group c), which, according to the 1959 census, were home to only 13.3 percent of all Soviet Jews (table 7.8). The Jewish population in these republics was special in two respects: the Jewish communities of two of them (Uzbekistan and Georgia) contained a mix of Ashkenazi and non-Ashkenazi Jews, and the remaining three (Moldavia, Latvia, and Lithuania) had been annexed to the Soviet Union during World War II. These factors almost certainly influenced the high proportion of Jews who declared a Jewish language as native tongue in the 1959 census.

Between the censuses of 1959 and 1970, the proportion of those declaring

TABLE 7.8

SOVIET REPUBLICS BY PROPORTION OF THEIR JEWISH POPULATION
DECLARING A JEWISH NATIVE LANGUAGE, 1959

GROUP	REPUBLIC	NUMBER	PERCENTAGE
a	RSFSR, Ukraine, Armenia	259,872	15.1
b	Belorussia, Azerbaidzhan, Kazakhstan, Tadzhikistan, Kirgizia, Estonia, Turkmenia	61,550	24.7
c	Uzbekistan, Moldavia, Georgia, Latvia, Lithuania	166,364	55.0

a Jewish language as native tongue decreased nationwide by 17.7 percent (21.5 percent in the 1959 census, 17.7 percent in that of 1970), but the decrease was not uniform in the three categories of republics. Group a registered a decline of 17.9 percent (15.1 percent in 1959, 12.4 percent in 1970), Group b a 6.9 percent decrease (24.7 percent in 1959, 23.0 percent in 1970), and Group c a plunge of 27.3 percent (55.0 percent in 1959, 40.0 percent in 1970). It appears that the most conspicuous decrease in the percentage of those declaring a Jewish language as native tongue occurred in the Jewish communities in which the percentage of those so declaring in the 1959 census had been extremely high. If we analyze the 1970 census by the standards of measurement used in table 7.8, we shall see that several union republics switched groups.

TABLE 7.9

SOVIET REPUBLICS BY PROPORTION OF THEIR JEWISH POPULATION
DECLARING A JEWISH NATIVE LANGUAGE, 1970

GROUP	REPUBLIC	NUMBER	PERCENTAGE
a	RSFSR, Ukraine	197,161	12.4
b	Belorussia, Georgia, Kazakhstan, Tadzhikistan, Kirgizia, Estonia, Turkmenia, Armenia	52,901	20.1
c	Uzbekistan, Moldavia, Azerbaidzhan, Latvia, Lithuania	131,016	43.3

Comparison of tables 7.8 and 7.9 yields several observations. In the Armenian SSR, in which the percentage of 1959 census respondents who declared a Jewish native tongue failed to reach the national average, this percentage exceeded the national average in the 1970 census. In Azerbaidzhan, where the percentage of respondents declaring a Jewish native tongue exceeded the national average in the 1959 census but by a factor less than two, their percentage exceeded the national average by that much and more in the 1970 poll. In Georgia, by contrast, the percentage of individuals declaring a Jewish language as their native tongue decreased significantly between the two censuses.

In the Armenian SSR, the percentage of those declaring a Jewish language as their native tongue rose, from 7.0 percent in the 1959 census to 21.2 percent in that of 1970. The numbers, however, are extremely small (72 individuals in 1959, 222 in 1970); the change may have stemmed from the migration of several hundred Jews to Armenia (table 7B).

In Azerbaidzhan, 14,146 Jews (35.2 percent of the total) declared a Jewish native tongue in the 1959 census, as compared with 17,067 (41.3 percent) in 1970—an additional 2,921 Jews compared with the 1959 census (see tables 7A and 7B). There is reason to suppose that the increase in the numbers and percentages of those declaring a Jewish native tongue originated in growth of the population of mountain Jews, of whom a majority declared the Judeo-Tat dialect their native tongue in both censuses.

The most conspicuous intercensus difference in this regard surfaced in Georgia, where 72.3 percent (37,270) of all Jews declared a Jewish language as their native tongue in the 1959 census and 23.1 percent (12,809) in that of 1970 (see tables 7A and 7B). Examination of the data, however, reveals that the major differences between the two censuses involve terminology. The 37,270 Jews in Georgia who were recorded in 1959 census summaries as having native tongues identical to their nationality were structured as follows: 35,322 speakers of Georgian, 56 Judeo-Tat, 18 Judeo-Tadzhik, 14 Crimean-Tatar, and only 1,860 individuals declared the Jewish (evreiskii) language as their native tongue.[13] At the same time, published summaries of the 1959 census indicated that 1,423 Jews (2.7 percent) had declared the language of the republic, Georgian, as their native tongue.[14] Because there is no Judeo-Georgian language, the 1959 census summaries are somewhat unclear. Thus, 35,322 Jews who had declared Georgian as their native tongue were recorded as having a native tongue identical to their nationality (a Jewish one). Another 1,423 who had similarly declared Georgian as their native tongue were recorded (for unexplained reasons) as speaking the language of the republic. This terminological confusion was apparently rectified in summaries of the 1970 census. Here, only those respondents who explicitly declared the "Jewish" (evreiskii) language were enumerated among those with a native tongue identical to nationality, whereas anyone who reported Georgian as their native tongue was counted among those with a native tongue identical to the language of the republic. If we wish to compare the 1959 and 1970 censuses data with regard to the native tongue of the Jews in Georgia, we must unify the data with regard to Georgian and the Jewish languages. In the 1959 census, 38,693 Jews declared a Jewish language or language of the republic as native tongue; in the 1970 census,

44,841 did so. It appears that 75.0 percent of all Jews in Georgia in the 1959 census and 80.9 percent in the 1970 census declared a Jewish language or Georgian (the language of Georgia's Jews) as their native tongue. By implication, not only was there no decrease; in fact, there was an evident increase between the two censuses in the proportion of Jews in Georgia who declared a Jewish and/or Georgian native tongue. The major change is that most Jews who declared Georgian as their native tongue in the 1959 census were recorded in census summaries as having a native tongue that matched their nationality, while 1970 census summaries listed them among those whose native tongue was the language of the republic. To create a common standard for comparing 1959 and 1970 census findings with regard to declaration of Jewish native tongue in Georgia, we should subtract the 35,322 Jews who were recorded as having native tongues identical to their nationality—though this tongue was Georgian—from the earlier census findings. Viewed thus, 3.8 percent of the Jewish population in Georgia (1,948 individuals) declared a Jewish (*evreiskii*) language as their native tongue in the 1959 census, and 23.1 percent (12,809) did so in the 1970 census.

When comparing data concerning declaration of Jewish native tongue nationwide as well, we should similarly subtract these 35,322 Georgian Jews whose native tongue was considered identical to their nationality (though that language is Georgian) from the inclusive number of those recorded in 1959 census findings as having a Jewish native tongue. Hence, according to 1970 census measurement standards, only 20.9 percent of all Soviet Jews declared a Jewish native tongue in the 1959 census compared with the 17.7 percent who did so in the 1970 census. The resulting decrease is only 3.2 percent rather than the 3.8 percent that appeared at first glance.

Distribution of the 1979 census findings by declaration of native tongue, using the measurement standards invoked for the previous censuses, clearly indicates that the relative decline in declaration of Jewish language was larger in several union republics than in others.

Tables 7.9 and 7.10 make it clear that the Jewish communities in Belorussia, Azerbaidzhan, Latvia, and Georgia switched positions between 1970 and 1979 with regard to the percentage of those declaring a Jewish native tongue. In three of these republics (Belorussia, Azerbaidzhan, and Latvia), the 1979 percentage compared to that of 1970 decreased at a faster rate than the national average, while the Jews of Georgia registered an increase. While the nationwide average of census respondents who declared a Jewish language as native tongue dropped by 19.8 percent, corresponding declines in Azerbaidzhan, Belorussia, and Latvia came to 32.9 percent, 37.1, and 39.0 percent, respectively. The reasons for these results, however, appear to have been different in each of the three republics. In Azerbaidzhan the conspicuous decrease in the percentage of declaration of Jewish language as native tongue stemmed mainly from an increase in the

TABLE 7.10

SOVIET REPUBLICS BY PROPORTION OF THEIR JEWISH POPULATION
DECLARING A JEWISH NATIVE LANGUAGE, 1979

GROUP	REPUBLIC	NUMBER	PERCENTAGE
a	RSFSR, Ukraine, Belorussia	142,522	9.7
b	Azerbaidzhan, Latvia, Tadzhikistan, Estonia, unspecified (Kazakhstan, Kirgizia, Turkmenia, Armenia)	28,697	24.4
c	Uzbekistan, Moldavia, Georgia, Lithuania	86,594	38.8

recording of Azerbaidzhani as the Jews' language (2.3 percent in 1970, 12.3 percent in 1979). There is reason to ascribe this phenomenon in essence to a change in recording the language of Azerbaidzhan's mountain Jews, who use the Judeo-Tat language. Most Jews who declared Tat as their native tongue were recorded in the 1970 census as having a native tongue identical to their nationality, whereas this language was apparently classified in the most recent census as a language identical to that of the republic. The decrease in Belorussia occurred under the influence of accelerated linguistic assimilation and a broadened influence of Russian. In Latvia, by contrast, massive emigration was one of the decisive factors behind the conspicuous drop in the percentage of declarations of Jewish language as native tongue in 1979 compared to 1970. In Georgia, similarly a major center of emigration during the 1970s, the percentage of respondents who declared a Jewish language as their native tongue grew between the two censuses (23.1 percent in 1970, 33.1 percent in 1979). We therefore have reason to assume that 1979 census practice reverted at least in part to the 1959 standard: that Jews of Georgia who declared Georgian as their native tongue were registered as having a native tongue identical to nationality (a Jewish language). Thus local conditions in each republic were at work in determining the decrease in percentage of those declaring a Jewish language as native tongue, in addition to the general factors applying throughout the Soviet Union.

The data with regard to declaration of Jewish native tongues, however, fail to reflect the full extent of knowledge of these languages and/or the attitude to them. We should therefore examine respondents' declarations of a Jewish language as second tongue as well.

Table 7.11 indicates that the rate of declaration of Jewish language as native and second language decreased during the 1970s in seven republics (the RSFSR, the Ukraine, Moldavia, Azerbaidzhan, Latvia, Lithuania, and Estonia) at a pace in excess of the Soviet Union average. In three republics (Uzbekistan, Georgia, and Tadzhikistan), the percentage of those declaring a

TABLE 7.11

PERSONS DECLARING A JEWISH NATIVE OR SECOND LANGUAGE,
BY REPUBLIC, 1970, 1979

REPUBLIC	1970		1979	
	NUMBER	PERCENTAGE	NUMBER	PERCENTAGE
Total	547,644	25.5	354,711	19.6
RSFSR	171,837	21.3	104,662	14.9
Ukraine	157,467	20.3	89,093	14.1
Belorussia	41,908	28.3	32,082	23.7
Uzbekistan	43,517	42.3	49,252	49.3
Moldavia	51,140	52.2	31,321	39.1
Georgia	13,357	24.1	9,758	34.5
Azerbaidzhan	19,201	46.5	10,834	30.5
Latvia	18.120	49.4	9,117	32.2
Lithuania	14,852	63.0	6,320	43.0
Tadzhikistan	3,196	21.9	3,242	22.1
Estonia	1,312	24.8	871	17.5
Kazakhstan	7,632 ⎫	27.6 ⎫		
Kirgizia	2,574 ⎬ 11,737	33.5 ⎬ 29.4	8,159	23.9
Turkmenia	1,280 ⎪	36.6 ⎪		
Armenia	251 ⎭	24.0 ⎭		

Sources: *Itogi, 1970,* vol. 4, Tables 5, 7, 9, 11, 13, 15, 17, 19–22, 24, 26–27, 29; *Vestnik statistiki,* No. 7
(1980), pp. 41, 43; No. 8, pp. 64, 69; No. 9, p. 61; No. 10, pp. 69–72; No. 11, pp. 63–64.

special relationship with a Jewish language (native tongue or second
language) increased between 1970 and 1979; these republics, however, are
home to a very small proportion of Soviet Jewry, and their impact on the
overall picture is accordingly marginal.

A higher percentage declared a Jewish language as their native tongue or
second language in the RSFSR than in the Ukraine in the two censuses. The
Jews' distribution by the *oblast*'s and autonomous republics of the RSFSR
as found in the most recent census was not published, but the distribution
reported from the 1970 census appears valid for the late 1970s as well.
According to the 1970 census, then, the percentage of those declaring a
Jewish language as their native or second language was lower than the
republic-wide average in twenty-six *oblast*'s, *krais*, and autonomous
republics of the RSFSR and higher than this average in the other twenty (see
table 7C). Although 73.1 percent of the Jews of the RSFSR resided in the
twenty-six *oblasts'*, only 57 percent of those who declared a Jewish
language as their native tongue or second language lived there. These
oblasts', krais, and autonomous republics produced an average of Jewish-

language declaration of only 16.6 percent. Although only 22.5 percent of the Jews of the RSFSR dwelled in the other twenty *oblasts', krais*, and autonomous republics for which details were provided in summaries of the 1970 census findings, these represented 39 percent of all declarations of Jewish language in the RSFSR. Those declaring a Jewish language in these areas accounted for 36.9 percent of the Jewish population there. Detailed examination of the data from the twenty *oblast's, krais,* and autonomous republics where the percentage of declarations of Jewish language exceeded the RSFSR average enables us to advance two major explanations for the phenomenon. First, three autonomous republics (Dagestan, Kabardino-Balkar, and Checheno-Ingush) and the *krai* of Stavropol' are home to mountain Jews, of whom an especially high percentage declare a Jewish language. The average percentage of declaration of Jewish language in these areas was 73 percent (28,422 of 38,912 Jews). Second, five *oblast's* (Kuibyshev, Cheliabinsk, Saratov, Orenburg, and Gor'ki) served during World War II as centers for Jewish refugees, of whom some settled there permanently. These Jews apparently tend more strongly to declare a Jewish language either as their native or second language. Indeed, the percentage of those so declaring in these *oblast's* was 26.1 percent (18,310 of 70,077 Jews).

Turning to the Ukraine, 1970 census data provide the distribution of the Jewish population by native and second language in 23 *oblast's*; 1979 census data do so for only nine *oblast's*. The 1970 data may be divided as follows: fourteen *oblast's* in which the percentage of declaration of Jewish language was lower than the republic-wide average and nine *oblast's* where this percentage exceeded the average.

As of the 1970 census, 75.6 percent of all Ukrainian Jews, who accounted for 57 percent of those who declared a Jewish language as their native tongue or second language, resided in the fourteen *oblast's* of the first category, yielding an average rate of declaration of Jewish language of only 15.4 percent.

The remaining nine *oblast's*, though home to only 24.0 percent of the Ukraine's Jews in 1970, accounted for 42.1 percent of the declarations of Jewish language as native or second language. Here the rate of such declaration reached an average of 35.5 percent, more than twice that of the *oblast*'s in the first category. Geography may explain the discrepancies, if only in part: all the *oblast's* in which the percentage of declarations of Jewish language exceeded the Ukrainian average are in the southwestern section of the Ukraine. Parts of several of them had been annexed by the Soviet Union during World War II, the result being a relatively high percentage of Jews who either speak or know Yiddish. Furthermore, the proportion of Jews who resided in towns or intermediate-sized cities exceeds the republic-wide average in these *oblast's*, apparently an additional factor of influence on the relatively high proportion of declarations of Jewish language as either their native or second language.

The few available 1979 census data indicate that *oblast's* in the Ukraine where declaration of Jewish language exceeded the republic-wide average in 1970 continued to display this trend at the end of the 1970s as well (table 7.12). We therefore have reason to assume the existence of this phenomenon in the *oblast's* for which no data from the last census have appeared and to surmise that the factors influencing these differences in 1970 were apparently at work in 1979 as well.

Of the six *oblast's* of the Belorussian SSR, figures from the most recent census, unlike the 1970 poll, have been published only for three. The 1970 census reported an average of 23.5 percent of declaration of Jewish language (as native or second tongue) in three *oblast's* (Brest, Grodno, and Minsk) and 31.8 percent in the remaining three (Vitebsk, Gomel', and Mogilev) (see table 7C). In the latter *oblast's*, the proportion of census respondents who declared a Jewish language in the 1979 census was 29.2 percent as opposed to only 16.5 percent in the former *oblast*'s, as reflected in table 7.13.

TABLE 7.12

DISTRIBUTION OF CENSUS RESPONDENTS WHO DECLARED A JEWISH LANGUAGE
AS NATIVE OR SECOND TONGUE IN THE UKRAINE, BY OBLAST', 1970, 1979

OBLAST'	1970		1979	
	NUMBER	PERCENTAGE	NUMBER	PERCENTAGE
Total	157,467	20.3	89,093	14.1
Zhitomir	11,067	31.0	7,267	25.1
Vinnitsa	13,883	32.9	8,407	24.8
Crimea	4,513	17.7	2,845	12.6
Odessa	21,797	18.6	11,600	12.6
Nikolaev	2,649	14.7	1,776	11.7
Donetsk	4,876	12.2	3,237	9.1
Dnepropetrovsk	8,266	11.9	5,333	8.7
Zaporozh'e	2,285	11.3	1,489	8.4
Khar'kov	9,075	11.9	5,150	8.0
Unspecified	79,056	23.8	41,989	16.0

Sources: *Itogi, 1970*, vol. 4, Table 8; *Vestnik statistiki,* No. 8 (1980), pp. 64–68.

Although no details from the last census with regard to declarations of Jewish language (as native or second language) in the major Soviet cities have appeared in print, examination of the 1970 census data proves that declaration of Jewish language in ten cities failed to reach the average for their respective republics and exceeded republic-wide averages only in six

TABLE 7.13

DISTRIBUTION OF CENSUS RESPONDENTS WHO DECLARED A JEWISH LANGUAGE
AS NATIVE OR SECOND TONGUE IN BELORUSSIA, BY OBLAST', 1970, 1979

	1970		1979	
OBLAST'	NUMBER	PERCENTAGE	NUMBER	PERCENTAGE
Total	41,908	28.3	32,082	23.7
Gomel'	13,034	30.8	12,211	31.8
Mogilev	9,264	36.0	6,942	30.0
Vitebsk	4,915	28.3	3,201	21.2
Unspecified	14,695	23.5	9,728	16.5

Sources: *Itogi, 1970,* vol. 4, Table 9; *Vestnik statistiki,* No. 8 (1980), pp. 69–70.

(Tbilisi, Riga, Alma-Ata, Frunze, and Tallin). In four of the latter (Riga, Alma-Ata, Frunze, and Tallin), the difference in percentage between the city and its respective republic was miniscule, ranging from 0.1 percent in Alma-Ata to 1.5 percent in Tallin. The situation was different in Tbilisi, where 42.5 percent of the Jews declared a Jewish language as either their native tongue or second language against a republic-wide average of 24.1 percent. This difference (18.4 percent) is explained by the fact that Tbilisi is home to many of Georgia's Ashkenazi Jews who declared a Jewish language; these were included among the census respondents whose language was identical to nationality. By contrast, the Georgian Jews, who almost certainly declared Georgian as either their native or second language, dwelled in other parts of Georgia and were almost certainly included among those whose declared language was identical to that of the republic. As a rule, then, we may say that Jews in metropolitan cities declared a Jewish language as their native or second language in the 1970 census at a rate lower than the republic-wide average, though the large cities served as important centers of the Jewish national movement. This fact may be a further indication of polarization among the Jews in the cities, to an extent more acute than that of Jews in smaller communities. While the cities are active centers of the Jewish national movement, they are also sites of accelerated processes of assimilation, of which nondeclaration of a Jewish language as native or second language is only one form of expression.

Analysis of the 1970 and 1979 census data proves that close to one-fourth of the Soviet Jewish community expressed an affinity for a Jewish language in the former census and about one-fifth in the latter, despite the virtual absence of any substantial Jewish cultural activity in the Soviet Union for almost two generations. This relationship with Jewish language, at least in its declared manifestation, is almost certainly influenced by the fact that declaration of a Jewish language, under Soviet conditions, is one way of expressing nationality. For this reason, even people who do not know a Jewish language, let alone use one, declare it as their native tongue or second language. There is also reason to believe that the historic continuity of Jews in the Soviet Union, unlike Jewish communities in lands of immigration overseas, militates in favor of maintaining relationships with an age-old cultural inheritance.

PERCENTAGE DISTRIBUTION OF THE JEWISH POPULATION
BY DECLARED NATIVE LANGUAGE, BY REPUBLIC, 1959, 1970, 1979

LANGUAGE AND YEAR

REPUBLIC	JEWISH			RUSSIAN			LANGUAGE OF REPUBLIC			OTHER		
	1959	1970	1979	1959	1970	1979	1959	1970	1979	1959	1970	1979
Total	21.5	17.7	14.2	76.4	78.3	83.3	1.6	2.9	–	0.5	1.1	2.5 (a)
RSFSR	13.4	11.8	10.0	86.1	87.8	89.5	–	–	–	0.5	0.4	0.5
Ukraine	16.9	13.2	9.0	79.9	84.2	88.9	2.8	2.3	2.0	0.4	0.3	0.1
Belorussia	21.9	17.8	11.2	76.1	80.1	86.7	1.9	2.0	2.1	0.1	0.1	0.0
Uzbekistan	49.7	37.6	44.7	48.5	46.0	52.9	0.3	0.3	0.2	1.5	16.1	2.2
Moldavia	50.0	44.7	33.2	48.6	54.5	66.1	1.0	0.6	0.5	0.4	0.2	0.2
Georgia	72.3	23.1	33.1	24.2	18.7	31.0	2.7	57.8	35.4	0.8	0.4	0.5
Azerbaidzhan	35.2	41.3	27.7	60.8	56.2	59.3	1.8	2.3	12.3	2.2	0.2	0.7
Latvia	48.0	46.2	28.2	50.0	52.2	70.0	1.5	1.2	1.4	0.5	0.4	0.4
Lithuania	69.0	61.9	41.0	28.0	35.0	54.4	2.6	2.8	4.2	0.4	0.3	0.4
Tadzhikistan	23.2	20.0	19.8	47.3	37.3	44.8	29.0	42.3	35.1	0.5	0.4	0.3
Estonia	24.8	21.5	15.1	67.2	70.0	76.4	7.2	7.7	8.1	0.8	0.8	0.4
Kazakhstan	23.1	22.8 }		73.4	74.9 }		–	–	–	3.5	2.3 }	
Kirgizia	30.3	26.7 }	21.1	68.6	69.4 }	76.6	0.1	–	–	1.0	3.9 }	2.3 (a)
Turkmenia	28.8	30.2 }		68.3	65.9 }		0.1	0.1	–	2.8	3.8 }	
Armenia	7.0	21.2		89.4	76.4		3.0	1.2	–	0.6	1.2	

Sources: *Itogi, 1959*, Table 53; *Itogi, 1970*, vol. 4, Tables 5, 7, 9, 11, 13, 15, 17, 19–22, 24, 26, 27, 29; *Vestnik statistiki*, No. 7, (1980), pp. 41, 43; No. 8, pp. 64, 69; No. 9, p. 61; No. 10, pp. 69–72; No. 11, pp. 63–64.

(a) Including languages of the republics.

**DISTRIBUTION OF THE JEWISH POPULATION BY DECLARED NATIVE LANGUAGE,
BY REPUBLIC, 1959, 1970, 1979**

REPUBLIC	LANGUAGE			
	JEWISH	RUSSIAN	LANGUAGE OF REPUBLIC	OTHER
Total				
1959	487,786	1,733,183	34,783	12,062
1970	381,078	1,682,798	62,436	24,395
1979	257,813	1,508,246	44,817	
RSFSR				
1959	117,559	753,686	–	4,062
1970	94,971	709,502	–	3,442
1979	70,204	627,371	–	3,076
Ukraine				
1959	142,241	671,443	23,410	3,217
1970	102,190	654,620	17,936	2,380
1979	57,179	563,511	12,437	1,027
Belorussia				
1959	32,913	114,225	2,815	131
1970	26,391	118,608	2,911	101
1979	15,139	117,408	2,818	85
Uzbekistan				
1959	46,944	45,722	239	1,439
1970	38,621	47,308	332	16,594
1979	44,677	52,836	212	2,183
Moldavia				
1959	47,584	46,230	926	367
1970	43,795	53,476	578	223
1979	26,533	52,996	426	172
Georgia				
1959	37,270	12,496	1,423	393
1970	12,809	10,359	32,032	182
1979	9,362	8,777	10,020	139
Azerbaidzhan				
1959	14,146	24,451	728	879
1970	17,067	23,187	936	98
1979	9,841	21,046	4,365	245
Latvia				
1959	17,541	18,302	564	185
1970	16,946	19,166	435	133
1979	8,006	19,825	395	105

199

(Table 7B continued)

	LANGUAGE			
REPUBLIC	JEWISH	RUSSIAN	LANGUAGE OF REPUBLIC	OTHER
Lithuania				
1959	17,025	6,912	640	95
1970	14,587	8,237	667	73
1979	6,022	7,990	619	66
Tadzhikistan				
1959	2,879	5,867	3,601	68
1970	2,914	5,457	6,184	60
1979	2,905	6,564	5,155	43
Estonia				
1959	1,350	3,651	392	43
1970	1,139	3,699	408	42
1979	749	3,795	402	20
Kazakhstan [a]				
1959	6,475	20,589	5	979
1970	6,322	20,744	1	622
Kirgizia [a]				
1959	2,613	5,908	5	84
1970	2,048	5,332	–	300
Turkmenia [a]				
1959	1,174	2,786	4	114
1970	1,056	2,302	3	133
Armenia [a]				
1959	72	915	31	6
1970	222	801	13	12

Sources   As for Table 7A.

(a) Data from the 1979 census were not published.

PERSONS DECLARING JEWISH NATIVE AND SECOND LANGUAGE, BY OBLAST,
KRAI, AND AUTONOMOUS REPUBLIC, 1959, 1970

| | NATIVE LANGUAGE | | | | SECOND LANGUAGE | |
| | 1959 | | 1970 | | 1970 | |
AREA	FREQUENCY	PERCENTAGE	FREQUENCY	PERCENTAGE	FREQUENCY	PERCENTAGE
R S F S R	**117,559**	**13.4**	**94,971**	**11.8**	**76,866**	**9.5**
Northwest region						
Oblast' (or ASSR)						
Kaliningrad	315	7.0	354	7.8	343	7.6
Leningrad (a)	15,118	8.7	8,974	5.3	16,998	10.1
Murmansk	114	3.8	134	5.0	141	5.3
Pskov	640	21.2	363	15.6	330	14.1
Karelian ASSR	–	–	111	7.0	63	4.0
Komi ASSR	–	–	186	10.1	126	6.9
Central region						
Oblast'						
Briansk	2,431	17.7	1,477	12.9	1,520	13.3
Ivanovo	–	–	201	11.4	131	7.4
Kalinin	–	–	317	9.2	360	10.4
Kaluga	–	–	201	8.8	215	9.4
Moscow (a)	28,902	9.6	22,940	8.0	27,569	9.6
Smolensk	–	–	601	11.3	688	12.9
Tula	–	–	453	9.3	325	6.7
Iaroslavl'	–	–	195	6.6	286	9.6
Volga-Viatka region						
Gor'ki oblast'	2,953	16.2	2,325	13.8	2,273	13.5
Central Black Earth region						
Voronezh oblast'	771	11.5	455	7.1	505	7.9
Kursk oblast'	–	–	734	15.8	585	12.6
Volga region						
Oblast' (of ASSR)						
Astrakhan'	–	–	562	16.2	390	11.3
Volgograd	–	–	500	9.9	426	8.5
Kuibyshev	3,240	16.1	2,472	13.2	2,418	12.9
Saratov	1,997	14.5	1,565	13.1	1,381	11.5
Tatar ASSR	2,387	23.0	2,043	21.5	1,130	11.9
North Caucasus region						
Krasnodar krai	–	–	1,019	13.2	599	7.8
Stavropol' krai	–	–	946	15.4	618	10.1
Rostov oblast'	1,395	6.7	1,045	5.8	1,513	8.3
Dagestan ASSR	18,190	84.9	19,212	86.7	219	1.0
Kabardino-Balkar ASSR	1,850	52.4	4,400	78.9	132	2.4
Severo-Osetin ASSR	515	24.7	595	29.1	134	6.6
Checheno-Ingush ASSR	2,094	40.1	2,548	50.5	347	6.9

AREA	NATIVE LANGUAGE				SECOND LANGUAGE	
	1959		1970		1970	
	FREQUENCY	PERCENTAGE	FREQUENCY	PERCENTAGE	FREQUENCY	PERCENTAGE
Ural region						
Oblast' (or ASSR)						
Orenburg	1,776	20.4	1,204	17.5	827	12.0
Perm'	–	–	1,102	13.6	842	10.4
Sverdlovsk	2,787	10.7	2,107	9.9	2,202	10.4
Cheliabinsk	2,865	15.1	2,181	13.9	1,664	10.6
Bashkir ASSR	1,362	18.2	1,055	15.8	680	10.2
West Siberian region						
Oblast'						
Kemerovo	–	–	531	10.6	353	7.0
Novosibirsk	1,084	8.7	829	7.0	658	5.6
Omsk	933	9.9	731	9.1	529	6.6
Tomsk	–	–	260	10.9	186	7.8
East Siberian region						
Krasnoiarsk krai	–	–	500	9.4	314	5.9
Irkutsk oblast'	883	8.6	570	7.1	577	7.2
Chita oblast'	–	–	96	5.5	102	5.9
Buriat ASSR	211	7.8	140	6.7	119	5.7
Far East region						
Primorskii krai	–	–	204	5.3	197	5.1
Khabarovsk krai	1,262	14.9	835	11.2	892	12.0
Jewish Autonomous						
oblast'	5,597	39.2	1,970	17.2	1,669	14.8
Magadan oblast'	–	–	93	5.7	108	6.6
Not specified	15,887	11.9	3,635	10.2	3,182	8.9
UKRAINE	**142,241**	**16.9**	**102,190**	**13.2**	**55,277**	**7.1**
Donets-Dneper region						
Oblast'						
Dnepropetrovsk	5,394	7.4	3,631	5.2	4,635	6.7
Donetsk	2,787	6.6	1,997	5.0	2,879	7.2
Zaporozh'e	1,212	5.8	1,162	5.7	1,123	5.6
Voroshilovgrad	1,124	8.1	894	7.1	1,011	8.1
Poltava	1,567	12.8	1,120	10.4	819	7.6
Sumy	809	12.9	444	9.4	412	8.7
Khar'kov	6,503	7.7	3,686	4.8	5,389	7.1
Southwest region						
Oblast'						
Vinnitsa	18,927	37.7	11,347	26.9	2,536	6.0
Zhitomir	12,230	29.1	8,772	24.6	2,295	6.4
Zakarpat'e	5,954	48.9	5,866	54.0	42	0.4
Ivano-Frankovsk	–	–	957	26.7	132	3.7
Kiev [a]	24,548	14.6	15,123	9.2	12,280	7.5
Kirovograd	1,406	14.8	903	11.7	586	7.6
L'vov	5,040	16.8	4,287	15.5	1,597	5.8
Rovno	–	–	444	17.6	114	4.5

AREA	NATIVE LANGUAGE				SECOND LANGUAGE	
	1959		1970		1970	
	FREQUENCY	PERCENTAGE	FREQUENCY	PERCENTAGE	FREQUENCY	PERCENTAGE
Khmel'nitskii	4,976	26.1	4,060	25.2	843	5.2
Cherkassy	3,003	22.9	2,101	19.7	780	7.3
Chernigov	2,247	17.9	1,362	13.2	662	6.4
Chernovtsy	21,042	49.9	18,369	49.0	1,775	4.7
Southern region						
Oblast'						
Crimea	2,801	10.6	2,324	9.1	2,189	8.6
Nikolaev	2,009	9.9	1,426	7.9	1,223	6.8
Odessa	15,316	12.6	10,763	9.2	11,034	9.4
Kherson	977	9.4	745	7.4	835	8.3
Not specified	2,369	24.7	407	15.3	86	3.2
BELORUSSIA	**32,913**	**21.9**	**26,391**	**17.8**	**15,517**	**10.5**
Oblast'						
Brest	1,180	19.6	806	16.1	403	8.0
Vitebsk	4,056	21.4	3,006	17.3	1,909	11.0
Gomel'	11,555	25.7	9,595	22.7	3,439	8.1
Grodno	756	20.2	481	15.0	161	5.0
Minsk [a]	7,732	16.1	7,355	13.5	5,489	10.1
Mogilev	7,634	26.8	5,148	20.0	4,116	16.0
UZBEKISTAN	**46,944**	**49.7**	**38,621**	**37.6**	**4,896**	**4.8**
Oblast'						
Andizhan	2,965	53.0	2,891	65.7	154	3.5
Bukhara	5,171	80.5	1,832	21.8	53	0.6
Kashkadar'ia	–	–	1,848	75.4	17	0.7
Samarkand	10,491	72.4	4,581	28.7	294	1.8
Surkhandar'ia	2,360	76.7	–	–	–	–
Tashkent [a]	20,306	36.5	19,383	32.7	4,007	6.8
Fergana	5,577	64.2	6,362	69.2	300	3.3
Not specified	74	18.3	1,724	56.6	71	2.3
GEORGIA	**37,270**	**72.3**	**12,809**	**23.1**	**548**	**1.0**
Tbilisi (city) [b]	9.374	53.8	7,934	40.5	380	1.9
Raions attached						
to Republic	23,907	87.0	1,223	4.3	35	0.1
administration						
Abkhaz ASSR	1,772	53.2	2,978	68.1	113	2.6
Adzhar ASSR	548	33.9	652	42.2	16	1.0
Iugo-Ostin						
Autonomous oblast'	1,669	96.9	22	1.5	4	0.3
AZERBAIDZHAN	**14,146**	**35.2**	**17,067**	**41.3**	**2,134**	**5.2**
Baku city and						
attached localities	5,776	19.8	7,993	26.9	1,864	6.3
Raions attached to						
Republic administration	8,353	76.6	9,066	78.7	269	2.3
Not specified	17	17.7	8	15.7	1	2.0

AREA	NATIVE LANGUAGE				SECOND LANGUAGE	
	1959		1970		1970	
	FREQUENCY	PERCENTAGE	FREQUENCY	PERCENTAGE	FREQUENCY	PERCENTAGE
KAZAKHSTAN	**6,475**	**23.1**	**6,322**	**22.8**	**1,310**	**4.7**
Oblast' (or city)						
Dzhambul	251	24.7	–	–	–	–
Kzyl-Orda	459	41.7	440	40.4	29	2.7
Chimkent	1,093	33.4	1,406	42.5	103	3.1
Alma-Ata (city)	1,925	22.9	1,987	21.6	559	6.1
Karaganda	1,099	22.0	913	18.1	177	3.5
Not specified	1,648	17.9	1,576	17.4	442	4.9
TADZHIKISTAN	**2,879**	**23.2**	**2,914**	**20.0**	**282**	**1.9**
Dushanbe (city)	1,811	20.8	1,841	16.1	215	1.9
Raions attached to Republic administration	1,065	29.0	–	–	–	–
Leninabad oblast'	–	–	769	34.2	43	1.9
Not specified	3	13.6	304	32.3	24	2.6
KIRGIZIA	**2,613**	**30.3**	**2,048**	**26.7**	**526**	**6.9**
Frunze (city)	1,821	31.2	1,558	26.1	462	7.8
Raions attached to Republic administration	212	19.6	–	–	–	–
Not specified	580	34.4	490	28.5	64	3.7
TURKMENIA	**1,174**	**28.8**	**1,056**	**30.2**	**224**	**6.4**
Ashkhabad (city)	163	12.8	212	17.0	86	6.9
Chardzhou oblast'	–	–	331	41.4	50	6.3
Not specified	1,011	36.1	513	35.4	88	6.1

Sources: *Itogi, 1959,* Table 54; *Itogi, 1970.* vol 4, Tables 6, 8, 10, 12, 14, 16, 18, 23, 25, 28.

(a) Including the metropolitan region.

(b) Including the urban locality of Abchala and villages under the jurisdiction of the city.

TABLE 7D

**PERSONS DECLARING A JEWISH NATIVE OR SECOND LANGUAGE
IN SIXTEEN MAJOR CITIES, 1959, 1970**

| CITY | NATIVE LANGUAGE | | | | SECOND LANGUAGE | |
| | 1959 | | 1970 | | 1970 | |
	FREQUENCY	PERCENTAGE	FREQUENCY	PERCENTAGE	FREQUENCY	PERCENTAGE
Moscow	20,331	8.5	19,071	7.6	23,657	9.4
Leningrad	14,439	8.6	8,454	5.2	16,409	10.1
Kiev	19,910	13.0	12,216	8.0	11,648	7.7
Minsk	5,716	14.7	5,286	11.2	4,955	10.5
Tashkent	18,492	36.7	18.095	32.5	3,799	6.8
Kishinev	18,500	43.1	19,944	40.0	4,017	8.1
Tbilisi	9,328	53.9	7,934	40.5	380	1.9
Baku [a]	5,776	19.8	7,993	26.9	1,864	6.3
Riga	14,526	48.0	14,415	47.1	970	3.2
Alma-Ata	1,925	22.9	1,987	21.6	559	6.1
Vil'nius	11,326	69.3	10,133	61.5	181	1.1
Kaunas	2,614	54,6	–	–	–	–
Dushanbe	1,811	20.8	1,841	16.1	215	1.9
Frunze	1,821	31.2	1,558	26.1	462	7.8
Tallin	947	25.5	865	23.0	125	3.3
Ashkhabad	163	12.8	212	17.0	86	6.9

Sources: As for Table 7C

(a) Including dependent localities.

TABLE 7E

BOOKS AND PAMPHLETS PUBLISHED IN YIDDISH AND TRANSLATIONS FROM THAT LANGUAGE 1959–1981 (a)

| YEAR | YIDDISH | | | TRANSLATIONS TO: | | | | | |
| | | | | RUSSIAN | | | OTHER LANGUAGES | | |
	NUMBER	MEAN PAGES	MEAN COPIES	FREQUENCY	MEAN PAGES	MEAN COPIES	FREQUENCY	MEAN PAGES	MEAN COPIES
Total	90	331	9,300	–	–	–	–	–	–
1959	2	431	30,000	17	241	88,300	11	157	16,900
1960	2	269	16,500	17	262	267,000	7	104	12,900
1961	2	460	20,000	18	330	48,900	12	105	6,800
1962	*	*	*	20	232	122,500	12	187	8,600
1963	*	*	*	21	125	154,300	7	221	12,700
1964	1	486	15,000	18	110	259,900	3	199	8,700
1965	6	258	13,000	14	160	80,000	5	234	13,700
1966	4	263	8,100	12	148	105,400	9	214	12,200
1967	4	410	6,400	6	146	274,500	6	229	5,900
1968	2	314	5,100	20	206	236,800	7	295	8,300
1969	10	386	4,600	22	128	370,200	6	80	8,800
1970	4	327	2,700	11	143	374,600	5	156	5,400
1971	3	306	1,600	9	288	161,800	*	*	
1972	3	399	2,800	6	158	246,800	4	101	4,100
1973	5	315	2,000	12	297	76,400	3	323	31,700
1974	4	400	1,400	9	252	255,000	2	186	69,000
1975	7	254	1,600	–	–	–	–	–	–
1976	7	261	1,400	–	–	–	–	–	–
1977	6	222	9,500	–	–	–	–	–	–
1978	8	–	2,200	–	–	–	–	–	–
1980	6	300	1,600	–	–	–	–	–	–
1981	4	232	1,400	11	66	211,800	2	188	16,800

Sources: Prepared according to: *Sovetish heymland*, No. 1 (1966) pp. 149–156; ibid, No. 1 (1970) pp. 177–193; *Behinot*, No. 1 (1970) pp. 177–193; ibid, No. 11 (1970), pp. 202–206; ibid, No. 2–3 (1972), pp. 187–192; ibid, No. 5 (1974) pp. 174–200; ibid, No. 7 (1976), pp. 167–205; *Ezhegodnik knigi SSSR, 1975*, vol. I; ibid, 1977, vol. I; ibid, 1980, vol. I; ibid, 1981, vol. I; *Pechat' SSSR v 1978 godu* (Moscow, 1979), Table 9; ibid, 1981, Tables 10, 11.

(a) For 1979 and for those entries marked (–) we have been unable to obtain the relevant data. An asterisk (*) represents years for which there were no publications.

8 JEWS IN THE COMMUNIST PARTY AND THE SOVIETS

THE COMMUNIST PARTY

The Communist party is the dominant political organization in the Soviet Union, with all its members supposedly participating in governance. Although policy is in fact determined by a small group, party members are given a feeling of active participation in rule, supervising—by means of cells in workplaces, executive authorities, and public organizations—the execution of policy, serving as agents of sorts in guidance and direction, and acting as spokesmen for Marxist-Leninist doctrine as enunciated in the latest leadership decisions.[1] Perhaps most important are the facts that party membership is an inviolable prerequisite for public activity and that it facilitates advancement in employment and education.

Policy guidelines for admitting new members stipulate on the one hand that party members be the "best and most progressive" people in Soviet society and on the other hand that the party give preference to "those who labor beside the machine, and *kolkhoz* members." It is therefore natural that constant tension reigns between the elitist principle of the "best and most progressive" and the class principle of "laborers and *kolkhoz* members"; the leadership tries consciously to balance the dichotomy as needs indicate. Political considerations, then, exert no small influence on the way the proportionate representation of certain social or national groups in the party, even in excess of their weight in the national population, is determined.[2] The tasks of adjusting and balancing the number of party members, for which an optimum figure is determined from time to time, are carried out in two ways. One is purges, or campaigns aimed at reducing the number of members of certain strata or national groups in party ranks; the second is preference in admission of new members and candidates who belong to certain strata or national groups.

General policy concerning the profile of party membership is evident in the Jews' case as well; however, two contradictory policy lines may counterbalance one another. Thus, for example, a policy aimed at faithfully reflecting national population makeup in party membership—a policy that leads to reduction in Jewish representation in the party—may be offset by the objective of raising the percentage of professionals in the party ranks because the proportion of Jews is high in this stratum. Hence general policy concerning the composition of party membership does not always find direct and evident quantitative expression where the Jews are concerned.

Full data on the national group composition of Communist party members and candidates have thus far been released only concerning 1922, August 1927, and January 1976.[3]

With the end of the civil war and a subsequent purge of the party ranks, a census of Communist party members and candidates was taken in 1922.[4] At the time, 19,562 Jews were counted—5.2 percent of all Communists.[5] Between then and 1927, a policy of expanding party ranks was pursued. Indeed, party membership grew by approximately 130 percent during that period. Another census of members and candidates was held on August 1, 1927, reporting 1,144,053 Communists, of whom 49,511 (4.3 percent) were Jewish. We should note here that Jews accounted for 4.9 percent of full party members but only 3.2 percent of candidates.[6] These data lead to the conclusion that Jews were admitted to the Communist party at a rate slower than that of the entire USSR population between 1922 and 1927. Because as the party census (August 1, 1927) was conducted shortly after the population census (December 17, 1926) and because a great deal of information was released for each, we may calculate precisely the proportion of party members among Jews in the various regions of the Soviet Union.

The data in table 8.1 indicate that the percentage of Communists in the Jewish community in 1927 varied greatly from area to area. In the Jews' historical areas of residence (Belorussia and the Ukraine), 1.3 percent of all Jews were Communists, whereas in the other areas of the USSR, chiefly those to which Jews were migrating, 3.7 percent were Communists. These discrepancies almost certainly narrowed somewhat in the late 1920s and the 1930s, but there is reason to assume that they remained in force on the eve of World War II as well. It is therefore doubtful that we can accept Rigby's estimate: "In 1940, 13.4 percent of all communists in the Ukraine were Jews. If the incidence of party membership among Jews in other areas of the USSR was the same as in the Ukraine, this would mean that Jews

TABLE 8.1

JEWS IN THE COMMUNIST PARTY, BY REGION, 1927

REGION	FREQUENCY	PERCENTAGE	COMMUNISTS PER 10,000 JEWS
Total	49,511	4.3	190
RSFSR	17,837	2.3	315
Moscow	8,054	8.5	614
Leningrad	2,991	3.6	354
Ukraine	20,306	12.1	129
Belorussia	6,012	23.8	149
Remainder of USSR	5,356	3.0	1.019

Calculated according to: *Statisticheskie materialy po evreiskoi demografii i ekonomike,* No. 4 (1929), p. 28, and *Evreii v SSSR* (Moscow, 1929), pp. 38, 51.

constituted 4.9 percent of the CPSU in 1940."[7] There are grounds to assume that the proportion of Communists among Jews outside the Ukraine in 1940, as in 1927, was larger than that in the Ukraine; the percentage of Jews in the Communist party on the eve on the Soviet-German war was therefore higher than Rigby's assessment. There is some indication that the proportion of Communists among the Jews rose in World War II period even as the percentage of Jews among all party members dropped. Party membership in the Jewish communities of regions not conquered by the Nazis was high. The proportion of Communists was also almost certainly large among Jews evacuated from Nazi-occupied areas, and many more Jews joined the party during the war. To this we should add that during World War II and particularly in the forty years after, an increasing number of Jews joined the VUZ-educated stratum, in which the percentage of party members is high.[8] All these factors raised the percentage of Communists among the Jews.[9]

The January 1976 data on party membership inform us that of the 15,638,891 party members and candidates,[10] 294,774, or 1.9 percent, were Jewish.[11] The Jews were therefore the sixth largest national group in the Communist party, following the Russians, Ukrainians, Belorussians, Uzbeks, and Tatars. The percentage of Jews in the Communist party exceeds that of the Jews in the overall urban population, a fact that should apparently be credited to the traditionally high proportion of Jews in the party, their relatively high average educational and professional level, and their relatively elderly age structure.

To arrive at an estimate of the proportion of Communists in the entire Jewish population, one must take two factors into account: emigration and the negative rate of natural increase. In the six years between the 1970 national census and January 1976, more than 114,300 Jews left the Soviet Union (see table 2E). If the drop in Jewish population in those years was equal to the average annual decline in the intercensus period, then the Jewish population fell by about 112,000 during that time. We may therefore estimate that there were close to 1,532 Communists for every 10,000 Jews in early 1976. Ranked in order after this high figure, the Georgians had approximately 800, the Russians close to 740, and the Armenians about 600. Accordingly, the percentage of Communists among the Jews at the beginning of 1976 surpassed that of any other Soviet national group. The percentage of Jews in the party almost certainly varied from republic to republic, but as best as I could ascertain, data have thus far been published on Jewish party membership in six union republics (Belorussia, Uzbekistan, Moldavia, Georgia, Lithuania, and Azerbaidzhan), which, according to findings of the censuses, were home to 20 percent of the Soviet Union's Jews in 1959, 22 percent in 1970, and 21 percent in 1979.

In Azerbaidzhan there were 3,560 Jewish members and candidates in the Communist party on January 1, 1979. These constituted 1.1 percent of the total for that SSR, or twice the proportionate share of the Jews in the republic's population (0.6 percent) as reported in the 1979 census. For every 10,000 Jews, there were 1,003 Communists, while in the Azerbaidzhan population as a whole, there were only 521 per 10,000.[12]

On January 1, 1962, there were 16,000 Jewish Communists in Belorussia, 6.4 percent of all party members and candidates.[13] If the drop in Jewish population in Belorussia between 1959 and 1962 was equal to that which took place in the intercensus period, there were 1,070 Communists for every 10,000 Jews in the beginning of 1962.

The data on the percentage of Jewish Communists in these two SSRs demonstrate the disparities among the SSRs but do not enable us to understand the dynamics involved in the admittance of Jews to the party. Change over time, however, can be examined in the data released thus far pertaining to Uzbekistan, Moldavia, Lithuania, and Georgia.

The proportion of Jews in the Communist party (members and membership candidates) of Uzbekistan in the twenty-eight years between the 1937 purge and 1964 may be deduced from data published in the 1960s (table 8.2). The data from Uzbekistan may be divided into three periods: (1) up to the Soviet-German war; (2) 1942-1946; and (3) from 1946 onward.

In the five years between 1937 and 1941, the proportion of Jews among the Communists was 2.6 times larger than their populational weight in that SSR but smaller than their share of the urban population. According to the 1939 census, the Jews accounted for 3.1 percent of the urban population of Uzbekistan, but their average party representation (members and membership candidates) was only 2.1 percent during those years.[14] The fact that the percentage of Jews in the Communist party rose perceptibly in early 1939 while no significant numerical increase took place is explained by the

TABLE 8.2

JEWS IN THE COMMUNIST PARTY OF UZBEKISTAN, 1937–1964

YEAR (a)	FREQUENCY	PERCENTAGE	YEAR	FREQUENCY	PERCENTAGE
1937	524	1.8	1951	4,626	3.4
1938 (b)	495	1.6	1952	4,676	3.4
1939	595	3.6	1953	4,691	3.3
1940	1,078	1.7	1954	4,637	3.3
1941	1,252	1.7	1955	4,774	3.3
1942	6,822	8.8	1956	4,862	3.2
1943	9,235	12.0	1957	5,069	3.1
1944	9,282	11.5	1958	5,239	3.0
1945	6,825	8.3	1959	5,422	2.9
1946	5,060	5.2	1960	5,582	2.8
1947	4,763	3.9	1961	5,884	2.6
1948	5,125	3.8	1962	6,147	2.5
1949	4,036	3.0	1963 (c)	6,380	2.4
1950	4,504	3.4	1964	6,659	2.3

Source: *Kommunisticheskaia partiia Uzbekistana v tsifrakh* (Tashkent, 1964), Tables 81, 88, 96, 103, 110, 117, 124, 131, 138, 145, 152, 159, 166, 173, 180, 187, 194, 201, 208, 215, 222, 229, 236, 243, 250, 257, 264, 271.

(a) The data relate to the first of January, unless otherwise indicated.

(b) The data for this year relate to July.

(c) The data relate to 10 December 1962, but are treated as if they relate to 1 January 1963.

purges of the late 1930s. As a consequence of this purge, the number of Communists in Uzbekistan dropped by 45.4 percent (from 30,233 in January 1938 to 16,498 in January 1939).[15] The Jews, however, were almost untouched by this campaign, and their absolute numbers in Uzbekistan actually rose. The purges were followed by an accelerated party recruiting drive; as it proceeded, Jewish representation in the party returned to its previous level. At the beginning of 1939, there were 117 Jewish Communists in Uzbekistan for every 10,000 Jews.[16] There is reason to assume that a large majority of Jewish Communists in Uzbekistan were Ashkenazi Jews who had reached this SSR in the course of their work.

Between 1942 and 1946, the Uzbek SSR served as a haven for masses of refugees, many Jews among them, a fact reflected in both the numbers and percentage of Jewish Communists. With the end of World War II, a repatriation process was set in motion under which Jewish Communists returned to their previous areas of residence. In 1947 a stabilization in the percentage of Jews in the Communist party began to set in. The general trend in this period was one of slow growth in the number of Jewish Communists and constant decline in their percentage of all party members and candidates. We should certainly note that this trend, which lasted into the first half of the 1960s, was discernible even during the last years of Stalin's rule.

In early 1959, 2.9 percent of the Communists in Uzbekistan were Jewish, a proportion more than twice as high as their demographic weight but less than their share of the urban population (3.3 percent). In that year, there were 575 Communists for every 10,000 Jews—about 1.5 times more than in Georgia.

During the twenty-six years from 1945 to 1970, Jewish party members and candidates in Georgia doubled in number, although their percentage share among all Communists in that republic remained almost the same (table 8.3). In 1959, for every 10,000 Jews in Georgia, there were 357 Communists. This figure may be compared to 347 for Russians in Georgia and 574 for Georgians. In 1970, Communists amounted to 384 per 10,000 Jews; Russians had grown to 406 and Georgians to 706 per 10,000. Most of the Jewish Communists lived in the capital, Tbilisi, where 574 out of every 10,000 Jews were party members or candidates in 1959 and 620 in 1970. In Moldavia, the proportion of Communists in the Jewish population was almost similar to the figures for Tbilisi and Uzbekistan (table 8.4). The data illustrate three phenomena:

1. The number of Jewish Communists was constantly rising, which means that the new party members and candidates in the five years under discussion not only replaced those who had died but even led to a rise of 1,199 individuals (26.9 percent) in the absolute numbers of Jewish Communists in Moldavia.

2. The percentage of Communists in the Jewish community of Moldavia displayed an upward trend during those years.

3. There was a highly evident downward trend in the percentage of Jews among all Communists in Moldavia.[17]

These trends were discernible in Uzbekistan in the first half of the 1960s and are confirmed by published data on the national group distribution of Communists in Lithuania.

The Jewish population of Lithuania (including Vilna and its surroundings, not part of interwar independent Lithuania) has been estimated at close to 240,000—about 8 percent of the population—on the eve of the Soviet-German war.[18] The Communist party was very small, numbering only 2,486 individuals (1,968 members, 518 candidates) on January 1, 1941, of whom 412 (355 members, 57 candidates) were Jewish—16.6 percent of all Communists.[19] Hence at the beginning of 1941 there were about 17 Communists for every 10,000 Jews. Even if the percentage of Jews in the Communist party of Lithuania surpassed their share in the overall population, the estimates cited by a number of

TABLE 8.3

JEWS IN THE COMMUNIST PARTY OF GEORGIA, 1945–1970

YEAR	NUMBER	PERCENTAGE	YEAR	NUMBER	PERCENTAGE
1945	1,081	1.2	1959	1,841	0.9
1947	1,437	0.9	1960	1,830	0.9
1948	1,511	0.9	1961	1,905	0.9
1949	1,468	0.9	1962	1,934	0.8
1950	1,429	0.9	1963	1,977	0.9
1951	1,436	0.9	1964	2,052	0.9
1952	1,491	0.9	1965	2,076	0.8
1953	1,482	0.9	1966	2,047	0.8
1954	1,576	0.9	1967	2,090	0.8
1955	1,638	0.9	1968	2,116	0.8
1956	1,734	1.0	1969	2,150	0.8
1957	1,790	0.9	1970	2,128	0.8
1958	1,807	0.9			

Source: *Kommunisticheskaia partiia Gruzii v tsifrakh,* 1921–1970 (Tbilisi, 1971), Tables 203, 224, 234, 244, 254, 264, 274, 284, 295, 305, 315, 325, 335, 345, 356, 366, 375, 384, 393, 402, 411, 420, 429, 438, 447.

TABLE 8.4

JEWS IN THE COMMUNIST PARTY OF MOLDAVIA, 1963–1967

DATE	FREQUENCY	PERCENTAGE	PARTY MEMBERS PER 10,000 POP.
Jan. 1963	4,463	6.4	464
Dec. 1963	4,742	6.3	492
Jan. 1966	5,553	5.9	573
Oct. 1967	5,662	5.7	581

Sources: *Kommunist Moldavii,* No. 9 (1963), p. 37; *Ocherki istorii kommunisticheskoi partii Moldavii* (Kishinev, 1964), p. 488; D. Ursul, *Razvitie obshchestvennykh otnoshenii v sovetskoi Moldavii* (Kishinev, 1967), p. 355; *Ocherki istorii kommunisticheskoi partii Moldavii* (Kishinev, 1968), p. 468.

Lithuanian émigrés in the West to the effect that Jews account for 75 percent of Communist party membership in Lithuania on the eve of the Soviet-German war are highly exaggerated.[20]

The figures pertaining to Jewish Communists in Lithuania in the thirty-three years between 1945 and 1977 may be divided into three periods: 1945-1953, 1954-1971, and 1972-1977.

The rapid growth in the absolute number of Jewish Communists in

Lithuania between 1945 and 1947 almost certainly stemmed from the postwar repatriation process through which many Jews returned to that SSR (table 8.5). In the last years of Stalin's rule as well, however, the absolute number of Jewish Communists in Lithuania grew constantly. The data indicate that the number of Jewish Communists in Lithuania rose by 780 individuals between 1947 and January 1953, in addition to those who had died during that interval. At the same time, their relative strength dropped by 27.8 percent.

TABLE 8.5

JEWS IN THE COMMUNIST PARTY OF LITHUANIA, 1945–1953

YEAR	FREQUENCY	PERCENTAGE	YEAR	FREQUENCY	PERCENTAGE
1945	238	6.7	1950	1,921	6.9
1946	644	8.0	1951	1,956	6.5
1947	1,275	7.9	1952	2,003	5.8
1948	1,691	7.6	1953	2,055	5.7
1949	1,871	7.6			

Sources: *Lietuvos komunistu partija skaiciais, 1918–1975* (Vil'nius, 1976), pp. 120–121.

Immediately preceding and following Stalin's death, it appears that no new members and candidates were admitted to the Communist party in Lithuania and that some Communists were perhaps even expelled from party ranks; the number of Communists in Lithuania therefore dropped from 36,178 in January 1953 to 34,544 in January 1954. The Jewish Communists similarly decreased, from 2,055 in January 1953 to 1,941 in January 1954. From that year until 1971, however, the absolute number of Jewish Communists in Lithuania grew steadily (table 8.6).

The percentage of Communists in the Lithuanian Jewish community increased by 34.5 percent in the eleven-year intercensus period (841 Communists per 10,000 Jews in 1959 and 1,131 in 1970). During the eighteen years reflected in table 8.6, however, the proportion of Jews among party members and candidates dropped by 60.7 percent. Nevertheless, the typifying trend for the entire period under discussion is constant growth in the absolute numbers of Jewish Communists. In these eighteen years (1954–1971), their absolute number grew by 743; thus more than 750 Jews joined the Communist party in Lithuania during that period. In the last six years, by contrast, the absolute number of Jews in the Communist party in Lithuania dropped; the main factor behind this, by all appearances, was emigration (table 8.7).

In those six years the Jewish proportion in the Lithuanian Communist

TABLE 8.6

JEWS IN THE COMMUNIST PARTY OF LITHUANIA, 1954–1971

YEAR	FREQUENCY	PERCENTAGE	PARTY MEMBERS PER 10,000 POP.
1954	1,941	5.6	–
1955	2,010	5.7	–
1956	2,112	5.5	–
1957	2,075	4.9	–
1958	2,038	4.5	–
1959	2,074	4.2	841
1960	2,088	3.8	850
1961	2,180	3.6	891
1962	2,280	3.4	935
1963	2,362	3.3	973
1964	2,408	3.1	996
1965	2,497	2.9	1,037
1966	2,578	2.7	1,075
1967	2,577	2.6	1,079
1968	2,640	2.5	1,109
1969	2,670	2.4	1,127
1970	2,664	2.3	1,131
1971	2,684	2.2	–

Source: As for Table 8.5, pp. 121–123.

TABLE 8.7

JEWS IN THE COMMUNIST PARTY OF LITHUANIA, 1972–1977

YEAR	FREQUENCY	PERCENTAGE	YEAR	FREQUENCY	PERCENTAGE
1972	2,577	2.0	1975	2,257	1.6
1973	2,432	1.9	1976	2,236	1.5
1974	2,317	1.7	1977	2,232	1.5

Sources: As for Table 8.5, p. 123 and *Kommunisticheskaia partiia Litvy v tsifrakh 1918–1977* (Vil'nius, 1977), pp. 129, 274.

party dropped by 25 percent in relative terms and by 13.4 percent, or 345 individuals, in absolute terms. Here we should note that more than 9,600 Jews from Lithuania left the USSR between January 1970 (when the census was held) and the beginning of 1977. The necessary conclusion is that the percentage of Communists among Lithuanian Jews who left the Soviet

Union was far smaller than their proportion in the Jewish community in that SSR, a circumstance that caused the percentage of Communists among Lithuanian Jews to rise. Thus the Jewish population of Lithuania in January 1977 stood at 14,000-15,000 and there were therefore between 1,488 and 1,594 Jewish Communists for every 10,000 Jews in the population. In contrast, the rate per 10,000 in 1970 was only 1,131. We may therefore expect that as long as the Soviet Jewish emigration movement continues—a movement in which the percentage of Communist party members is almost certainly small—and as long as the number of Jews in the USSR continues to drop, the percentage of Jewish Communists among all party members nationwide will progressively fall even as their proportion in the Jewish community steadily grows.

JEWS IN THE SOVIETS

We may divide the soviets (councils) in the Soviet Union into two types: (1) the Supreme Soviet along with the soviets in the fifteen union republics and the autonomous republics, which are elected legislative bodies but are in fact political showpieces and no more; and (2) soviets of the various *krais, oblast's, raions,* cities, and villages, which are in effect municipal councils.

The Supreme Soviet and Soviets of the Republics

The Supreme Soviet and the union republics' and autonomous republics' soviets are representative institutions of miniscule political importance. Although they virtually rubber-stamp all proposals prepared in advance by the leadership, they do have the capacity of granting their members personal prestige and may also convey a sense that the different nationalities have a share in the government.[21] Although the criteria by which candidates for these bodies—who are always elected unopposed—are determined are unclear, there are grounds to assume that their respective national group affiliation is one of the factors taken into account at the time of selection. The various national groups' representation in the parliamentary institutions of the Soviet Union may therefore serve to a certain extent as an indicator—which should be seen in relation to other indicators—of the regime's attitude to particular national groups.

The quadrennially elected Supreme Soviet of the USSR is bicameral, consisting of a Soviet of the Union and a Soviet of Nationalities. The Soviet of Nationalities gives a fixed representation for all union republics, autonomous republics, national *oblast's*, or *raions,* regardless of the number of qualified voters in each. The Soviet of the Union, by contrast, is elected by all citizens of the Soviet Union.[22] In the five Supreme Soviet elections held in 1950 and between 1958 and 1970, the percentage of Jews in this body fluctuated between one-third to one-half their share of the population, as opposed to the elections of December 17, 1937, in which the percentage of the Jews elected to the Supreme Soviet was 2.3 times larger than their percentage in the population (table 8.8).[23] The miniscule rise in the number of Jews in the 1970 elections stemmed from the fact that two of the five delegates elected to the Soviet of Nationalities from the Jewish autonomous *oblast'* (Birobidzhan) were Jewish, as opposed to one Jewish delegate between 1958 and 1966.

Each union republic and autonomous republic has its own supreme soviet, for which elections are held every four years. Although a rise in the absolute and relative numbers of Jews in the union republics' soviets took place after the Khrushchev era, Jewish representation in these institutions fell short of their share in the population throughout the entire period under discussion (table 8.9). Jewish representation in the SSR soviets in 1959 amounted to about one-fourth their share of the population, which was 1.1 percent according to the census held that year. In 1971, their representation in the supreme parliamentary bodies of the union republics was about one-third.

Although the underrepresentation of Jews in union republic soviets is influenced by a general policy that sets out to limit the number of Jews in representative institutions, it also appears to bear the imprint of the regional policy pursued in each republic (see table 8.10). The decline in the number of Jews elected to union republic soviets is particularly evident in the RSFSR and the Ukraine, which account for two-thirds of Soviet Jewry. Elections to the RSFSR soviet in June 1938 brought in 30 Jewish candidates (4.1 percent of the total). In 1947 there were seven Jewish delegates; in 1951, five, and in 1959 only one.[24] In 1938, the Jewish representation in the RSFSR soviet was 4.6 times greater than the Jews' share in the total population there (4.1 percent as opposed to 0.9 percent, according to January 1939 figures). At the end of the 1950s, the relationship was the reverse: the Jews' share in the soviet was six times smaller than their share in the population.

While the Jews were overrepresented in the RSFSR soviet of 1938, they were already underrepresented at that time in the Ukraine soviet. In June 1938, only two Jewish candidates were elected, comprising 0.7 percent of the house, although Jews accounted for 4.9 percent of the population; they were underrepresented by a factor of 7.[25] They continued to be underrepresented over the following two decades, and in 1959 the level of underrepresentation reached a factor of 9 relative to their share in the population.

In Belorussia on the eve of World War II, there were twenty-one Jewish delegates to the republic soviet, roughly proportional to the Jewish share in the population (7.7 percent of the soviet delegates as compared to a 6.7 percent share in the population). In the elections of 1947, however, only seven Jews were returned, and at the end of the 1950s, only two Jews were

TABLE 8.8

TOTAL AND JEWISH DELEGATES ELECTED TO THE SUPREME SOVIET BY CONSTITUENT SOVIET, 1950–1970

| | SUPREME SOVIET | | | SOVIET OF NATIONALITIES | | | UNION SOVIET | | |
| | | JEWISH | | | JEWISH | | | JEWISH | |
YEAR	TOTAL	NUMBER	PERCENTAGE	TOTAL	NUMBER	PERCENTAGE	TOTAL	NUMBER	PERCENTAGE
1950	1,316	6(a)	0.46	–	–	–	–	–	–
1958	1,384	5(a)	0.36	646	3(a)	0.46	738	2(a)	0.27
1962	1,443	5	0.35	652	3	0.46	791	2	0.25
1966	1,517	5	0.33	750	3	0.40	767	2	0.26
1970	1,517	6	0.40	750	4	0.53	767	2	0.26

Sources: *Izvestiia*, March 15, 1950, March 19, 1958; *Deputaty verkhovnogo soveta SSSR* (Moscow, 1962), pp. 82, 142, 233, 445, 481; ibid, 1966, pp. 149, 466, 479, 507; ibid, 1970, pp. 10, 100, 140, 340, 464, 475; *Verkhovnyi sovet SSSR vos'mogo sozyva* (Moscow, 1970), p. 33.

(a) Determined according to family names of the delegates.

TABLE 8.9

TOTAL AND JEWISH DELEGATES ELECTED TO THE SOVIETS
OF THE UNION REPUBLICS, 1959–1971

YEAR	TOTAL	JEWISH	
		NUMBER	PERCENTAGE
1959	5,312	14	0.26
1963	5,761	13	0.23
1967	5,830	19	0.33
1971	5,879	19	0.32

Sources: *Sostav deputatov verkhovnykh sovetov soiuznykh, avtonomnykh respublik i mestnykh sovetov deputatov trudiashchikhsia, 1959 g.* (Moscow, 1959), pp. 12–13; *Itogi vyborov i sostav deputatov verkhovnykh sovetov soiuznykh, avtonomnykh respublik i mestnykh sovetov deputatov trudiashchikhsia, 1963g.* (Moscow, 1963), pp. 28–29, *Itogi vyborov i sostav deputatov verkhovnykh sovetov soiuznykh i avtonomnykh respublik, 1967g.* (Moscow, 1967), pp. 17–18; ibid., 1971, pp. 18–20.

TABLE 8.10

JEWISH DELEGATES ELECTED TO UNION REPUBLIC SOVIETS, 1959

REPUBLIC	NUMBER OF JEWS	PERCENTAGE OF TOTAL	PERCENTAGE OF JEWS IN TOTAL POPULATION
RSFSR	1	0.12	0.7
Ukraine	1	0.22	2.0
Belorussia	2	0.49	1.9
Uzbekistan	2	0.45	1.2
Moldavia	–	–	3.3
Georgia	–	–	1.3
Azerbaidzhan	1	0.31	1.1
Latvia	–	–	1.7
Kazakhstan	2	0.44	0.3
Lithuania	3	1.44	0.9
Tadzhikstan	1	0.33	0.6
Kirgizia	–	–	0.4
Estonia	–	–	0.5
Turkmenia	1	0.36	0.3
Armenia	–	–	0.1

Sources: *Sostav deputatov verkhovnykh sovetov soiuznykh, avtonomnykh respublik i mestnykh sovetov deputatov trudiashchikhsia, 1959g.* (Moscow, 1959), pp. 12–13.

selected—a share four times smaller than the proportion of Jews in the population.[26]

In the Uzbek SSR, where a great many Jewish refugees were living at the time, the republic soviet of 1947 included eight Jewish delegates,[27] a number that dropped to one in 1951[28] and rose again to two in 1959—proportionally 2.5 times smaller than the Jews' percent share in the population.

In the Moldavian SSR, the Jewish share in the general population is higher than in any other republic, yet not a single Jew was in the republic soviet at the end of the 1950s. At the end of the 1970s, there were two Jews in the soviet, or 0.5 percent of the delegates, which was equivalent to one-fourth of the percentage of Jews (2.0 percent in 1979) in the general population.[29]

Only in three SSRs (Kazakhstan, Lithuania, and Turkmenia) did the percentage of Jews in the soviets in 1959 slightly exceed their share of the population. Anti-Jewish discrimination in these institutions becomes evident if we examine the profile of the soviets. Close to 42 percent of the delegates belonged to the VUZ educated, a stratum in which Jews are especially well represented; more than 70 percent of the delegates were Communist party members, and here too the Jews' share is relatively large.[30]

Jewish representation in autonomous republic soviets increased significantly in 1963 in comparison with the 1959 elections, but a downward trend became apparent after the Six-Day War (June 1967) and was expressed in the elections of June 1971. In the 1967 elections, held in March, this trend was not yet visible (table 8.11).

Local Soviets

Local soviets are municipal councils that select executive committees. Local soviet elections are held every two years; nine such elections took place between 1959 and 1975 (table 8.12).

The Jews were underrepresented on the local soviets throughout the entire period under discussion—by factors of 2.5 in 1959 and 3.2 in 1971 in comparison with their weight in the population. Because underrepresentation in local soviets is an expression of policy, it would appear that fluctuations in the percentage of Jews in these soviets indicate changes in this policy. In the last years of Khrushchev's rule, this policy, designed to restrict the numbers of Jews in representative institutions, took on palpable form; this was reflected in the 1963 local soviet elections, when the number of Jews elected, in comparison with the 1961 elections, fell by 103 individuals and their proportionate share of all delegates fell by 9.5 percent. The post-Khrushchev Soviet leadership sought at first to raise Jewish representation in the soviets; an increase in their absolute number (634 individuals) and proportionate strength (5.3 percent) took place in the 1965

TABLE 8.11

TOTAL AND JEWISH DELEGATES ELECTED TO THE SOVIETS
OF THE AUTONOMOUS REPUBLICS, 1959–1971

YEAR	TOTAL	JEWISH	
		NUMBER	PERCENTAGE
1959	2,506	4	0.16
1963	2,842	11	0.39
1967	2,925	11	0.38
1971	2,994	9	0.30

Sources: As for Table 8.9.

TABLE 8.12

TOTAL AND JEWISH DELEGATES ELECTED TO LOCAL SOVIETS, 1959–1975

YEAR	TOTAL	JEWISH	
		NUMBER	PERCENTAGE
1959	1,801,663	7,724	0.42
1961	1,822,049	7,593	0.42
1963	1,958,565	7,490	0.38
1965	2,022,427	8,124	0.40
1967	2,045,419	7,881	0.39
1969	2,071,333	6,619	0.32
1971	2,166,004	6,030	0.28
1975	2,210,932	4,519	0.20

Sources: *Sostav deputatov verkhovnykh sovetov soiuznykh, avtonomnykh respublik i mestnykh
sovetov deputatov trudiashchikhsia, 1959g.* pp. 70–85; *Itogi vyborov i sostav deputatov mestnykh sovetov deputatov trudiashchikhsia, 1961g.* pp. 73–89; ibid., 1963, pp. 28–29; ibid., 1967, pp.
22–25; ibid., 1969, pp. 26–31; ibid., 1971, pp. 22–27; ibid., 1975, pp. 24–31; *Sostav deputatov
mestnykh sovetov deputatov trudiashchikhsia, 1965g.* pp. 22–25.

elections. After the Six-Day War, and particularly in the face of the Jewish
national movement in the Soviet Union, a clear policy line was adopted in
which Jewish representation in local soviets was reduced with increasing
severity. The number of Jews in local soviets dropped by 3,362 individuals,
and their proportionate share by 48.7 percent, between 1967 and 1975.

To examine this underrepresentation to determine whether it is peculiar
to the Jews or typical of general national group policy in the Soviet Union,
we shall examine the situation of twenty-four national groups: the fifteen
that have their own union republics, five national minorities with
homelands located in the Communist bloc (Bulgarians, Hungarians, Poles,
Czechs, and Rumanians), and four national minorities with national states
outside the Eastern Bloc (Jews, Germans, Greeks, and Finns) (table 8.13).

TABLE 8.13

THE REPRESENTATION OF NATIONALITIES ON LOCAL SOVIETS, 1959, 1971

| | DELEGATES PER 10,000 POPULATION | | % OF ALL DELEGATES | |
NATIONALITY	1959	1971	1959	1971
Lithuanian	124	97	1.7	1.2
Latvian	122	136	1.0	0.9
Georgian	118	118	1.8	1.8
Estonian	113	107	0.6	0.5
Kazakh	108	106	2.2	2.6
Turkmen	108	103	0.6	0.7
Kirgiz	105	108	0.6	0.7
Azerbaidzhani	102	101	1.7	2.0
Ukrainian	100	121	20.7	22.8
Belorussian	95	77	4.2	3.8
Moldavian	92	98	1.1	1.2
Armenian	84	88	1.3	1.4
Uzbek	81	77	2.7	3.3
Takzhik	80	77	0.6	0.8
Russian	78	77	49.5	46.3
Czech	81	86	–	–
Hungarian	73	103	0.1	0.1
Bulgarian	72	99	0.1	0.2
Romanian	61	107	–	0.1
Polish	29	69	0.2	0.4
Finnish	44	66	–	–
Jewish	33	28	0.4	0.3
Greek	20	77	–	0.1
German	13	71	0.1	0.6

Sources: *Sostav deputatov verkhovnykh sovetov soiuznykh, avtonomnykh-respublik i mestnykh sovetov deputatov trudiashchikhsia, 1959g.,* pp. 70–85; *Itogi vyborov i sostav deputatov mestnykh sovetov deputatov trudiashchikhsia, 1971g.,* pp. 22–27.

There were 86 local soviet delegates for every 10,000 residents in 1959 and 90 in 1971. For every 10,000 members of national groups with union republics, there were 101 delegates to the local soviets in 1959 and 99 in 1971. Members of national groups with union republics accounted for 90.3 percent of all local soviet delegates in 1959 and 90 percent in 1971. During the 1960s, then, those peoples lacking their own union republics displayed a trend of increased representation in local soviets. Indeed the number of local soviet delegates (for every 10,000 individuals) belonging to national minorities with national and historical homelands outside the boundaries of the Soviet Union, whether inside or outside the Eastern Bloc, also rose significantly in this general framework. The only exception to this rule—for whom the number of local soviet delegates for every 10,000 individuals not only failed to rise but actually fell during the 1960s—were the Jews. It therefore appears that the drop in percentage of Jews in local soviets is not a consequence of a uniform policy applied to all the national minorities that lack their own union republic but is a special policy applied to the Jewish minority alone.

Local soviet candidates are determined in meetings of party functionaries held in workplaces, public organizations, and the like.[31] Although these functionaries are aware of party policy and strive to make their selection of candidates for the soviets conform to it, they are almost certainly influenced by local conditions and the extent of popular anti-Semitism in each SSR as well. Accordingly, we should examine Jewish representation in the local soviets of the various republics of the USSR (table 8.14).

TABLE 8.14

TOTAL AND JEWISH DELEGATES ELECTED TO LOCAL SOVIETS
BY REPUBLIC, 1959, 1961

	1959			1961		
		JEWISH			JEWISH	
REPUBLIC	TOTAL	NUMBER	PERCENTAGE	TOTAL	NUMBER	PERCENTAGE
Total	1,801,663	7,624	0.42	1,822,049	7,593	0.42
RSFSR	972,004	3,471	0.36	971,437	3,522	0.36
Ukraine	381,477	1,966	0.52	392,033	1,991	0.51
Belorussia	77,944	853	1.09	78,090	759	0.97
Uzbekistan	58,826	261	0.44	62,777	215	0.34
Moldavia	26,518	210	0.79	27,102	227	0.84
Georgia	40,429	62	0.15	41,149	50	0.12
Azerbaidzhan	33,120	100	0.30	33,832	143	0.42
Latvia	20,876	88	0.42	20,976	73	0.35
Kazakhstan	81,186	337	0.42	84,146	358	0.43
Lithuania	33,174	74	0.22	32,844	85	0.26
Tadzhikistan	14,880	50	0.34	15,539	51	0.33
Kirgizia	17,493	83	0.48	17,721	57	0.32
Estonia	11,731	27	0.23	11,769	16	0.14
Turkmenia	14,123	38	0.27	14,508	46	0.32
Armenia	17,882	4	0.02	18,126	–	–

Sources: *Sostav deputatov verkhovnykh sovetov soiuznykh, avtonomnykh respublik i mestnykh sovetov deputatov, 1959g.,* pp. 70–85; *Itogi vyborov i sostav deputatov mestnykh sovetov deputatov, 1961g.,* pp. 73–89.

In three SSRs (Kazakhstan, Kirigizia, and Turkmenia) in which the percentage of Jews in the overall population is extremely small, the proportion of Jews in local soviets in 1959 surpassed their weight in the population. In four SSRs (RSFSR, Belorussia, Tadzhikistan, and Estonia), their percentage in local soviets was about half their proportion in the population, and in Uzbekistan it was three times smaller. The percentage of Jews in local soviets was approximately four times smaller than their share in the population in five SSRs (Ukraine, Moldavia,[32] Azerbaidzhan,[33] Latvia, and Lithuania), five times smaller in Armenia, and nine times smaller in Georgia. It would appear that in addition to general policy, local factors influence Jewish representation in local soviets in each SSR.

We do not have data concerning changes that have taken place in Jewish representation on local soviets in the various SSRs in the 1960s and the 1970s, but the data pertaining to the RSFSR—where close to 38 percent of Soviet Jews dwelled according to the 1970 census and 39 percent according to the 1979 census, and where more than 46 percent of all Jewish local soviet delegates nationwide were found in 1961—may be indicative of the trends in the other SSRs as well (table 8.15).

TABLE 8.15

TOTAL AND JEWISH DELEGATES TO LOCAL SOVIETS IN THE RSFSR
AND IN THE OTHER UNION REPUBLICS, 1959–1975

| | RSFSR | | | OTHER UNION REPUBLICS | | |
| | | JEWISH | | | JEWISH | |
YEAR	TOTAL	NUMBER	%	TOTAL	NUMBER	%
1959	972,004	3,471	0.36	829,659	4,253	0.51
1961	971,437	3,552	0.37	850,612	4,041	0.48
1969	1,092,900	3,550	0.33	978,433	3,069	0.31
1971	1,092,750	3,127	0.29	1,073,254	2,903	0.27
1973	1,102,759	2,694	0.24	–	–	–
1975	1,109,369	2,408	0.22	1,101,563	2,111	0.19

Sources: As for Table 8.14, and *Itogi vyborov i sostav deputatov mestnykh sovetov deputatov RSFSR, 1969g.,* pp. 26–31; ibid., 1971, pp. 22–23; ibid., 1973, pp. 22–25; ibid., 1975, pp. 22–25.

Both the absolute and relative numbers of Jews in the local soviets of the RSFSR increased between 1959 and 1969, as opposed to a decrease in these numbers in the rest of the USSR. There were 40 local soviet delegates for every 10,000 Jews in the RSFSR in 1959, as opposed to only 30 in the rest of the USSR. In 1969 there were 44 local soviet delegates in the RSFSR for every 10,000 individuals registered as Jews in the 1970 census, while their number in the rest of the Soviet Union dropped to 23.

The local soviets exist in the USSR in six forms:

1. The soviet of an *oblast'* (*oblsovet*) or *krai* (*kraisovet*) is the representative council of a large administrative district, which is divided into subunits (*raiony*).

2. Each *raion* council (*raisovet*) fulfills functions analogous to those of the *oblast'* and *krai* soviet but is subordinate to it.

3. Every city has a municipal council (*gorsovet*) responsible for municipal services.

4. Large cities are divided into smaller *raiony*, of which each has its own soviet whose task is to administer municipal services within its own jurisdiction.

5. Soviets in smaller towns (*poselok*) are similar in function to the *gorsovet* but have narrower authority.

6. Rural soviets (*sel'sovet*) deal with municipal services for a village or group of villages.

Table 8.16 illustrates the Jewish representation in each category of local soviets.

In the *krai* and *oblsovets* (in which delegates enjoy a relatively large measure of prestige) and in the *raisovets,* the representation of Jews was approximately three times smaller than their populational strength. Because the Jews are primarily an urban populace, however, it is worth examining their representation in soviets of communities of the urban type, *gorsovety, raisovety* in cities, and soviets of *poselki* separately (table 8.17).

The data indicate that the Jews' representation in soviets of communities of the urban type between 1959 and 1975 was about half their proportion in the overall urban population. Since the percentages of the VUZ educated and of party members are high in urban soviets and because these are strata in which the Jews are more highly represented than any other national group in the Soviet Union, the conclusion is that: blatant discrimination is practiced against the Jews in the matter of the local soviets. We may therefore conclude that a policy of anti-Jewish discrimination exists in the Soviet Union—not only in the ranks of national leadership but also in representative bodies at every level.

In *samizdat* writings and in material published in the West by Jewish emigrants, the complaint has been raised about Jewish underrepresentation in official organs, but these generally refer to senior echelons of the state and the Communist party. To the best of my knowledge, there have never been complaints to the effect that Soviet Jews encounter obstacles in becoming members of the party, and the data indeed indicate that the policy toward entrance to the party is different from the policy on Jewish representation in the soviets.[34] One can only speculate as to why this should be the case. Perhaps it is because party membership, particularly for the rank and file, is perceived in the Soviet Union as quite natural and normal and is not a matter of particular note. The soviets, however, are in a different category. Every soviet delegate, even in the local bodies, receives press coverage before the elections; he must appear at public election meetings and the like. He is therefore an object of media attention and a recipient of public notice. The prominence of Jews in such positions would be likely to arouse dissatisfaction, and the authorities are presumably

TABLE 8.16

JEWISH DELEGATES TO LOCAL SOVIETS BY TYPE OF SOVIET, 1959–1975

TYPE OF SOVIET

	OBLAST AND KRAI		RAION		CITY		BOROUGH (RAION)		URBAN AREA		VILLAGE	
	NUMBER	%	NUMBER	%	NUMBER	%	NUMBER	%	NUMBER	%	NUMBER	%
1959	71	0.37	989	0.54	2,390	1.30	1,043	1.53	1,037	0.85	2,094	0.17
1961	89	0.46	924	0.52	2,468	1.25	1,069	1.62	1,201	0.78	1,842	0.15
1965	155	0.58	975	0.47	2,862	1.24	1,344	1.64	1,254	0.70	1,534	0.12
1967	161	0.63	845	0.38	2,887	1.21	1,470	1.70	1,089	0.59	1,429	0.11
1969	148	0.55	666	0.29	2,452	1.00	1,260	1.38	1,188	0.62	905	0.07
1971	131	0.47	572	0.25	2,154	0.85	1,127	1.18	872	0.43	1,174	0.09
1975	90	0.30	436	0.19	1,561	0.59	937	0.78	667	0.32	828	0.06

Sources: As for Table 8.12.

TABLE 8.17

JEWISH DELEGATES TO ALL TYPES OF URBAN SOVIETS, 1959–1975

YEAR	NUMBER	PERCENTAGE	YEAR	NUMBER	PERCENTAGE
1959	4,470	1.20	1969	4,900	0.93
1961	4,738	1.13	1971	4,153	0.75
1965	5,460	1.23	1975	3,165	0.53
1967	5,446	1.07			

Sources: As for Table 8.12.

interested in reducing their numbers for this reason, despite their representative social profile. It would seem, then, that the factor of public exposure is the key criterion in determining the stance of the authorities regarding Jewish entry into the party ranks as against Jewish representation in local soviets, to say nothing of the Supreme Soviet.

9   CONCLUSION

Each Jewish community's social characteristics are shaped by its sociodemographic structure and the organizational frameworks that lend substance to its national (ethnic) and religious existence. In the Soviet Union, unlike noncommunist countries, the Jews have no legitimate organizational structures in which to express their collective existence. In the absence of such structures, sociodemographic attributes play a greater role in defining the group to both insiders and outsiders. Social and demographic factors, and phenomena affected by the interrelation of the two, substitute for more explicit collective markers.

On the demographic level, it is noteworthy that the Jewish national minority is the only wholly urban Soviet ethnic group. This is the culmination of a process that, though having originated in previous centuries, emerged chiefly in the World War II period. The great majority of rural Jews in the Nazi-occupied areas were annihilated during the Soviet-German war. In areas free of Nazi occupation, too, the migration of Jews from rural to urban areas proceeded apace. The handful of Soviet Jews still classified as part of the rural population did not engage in agriculture; some considered their residence in a rural area a temporary phase that would end at the conclusion of their service in that area. Therefore the distribution of Soviet Jewry between urban and rural areas is similar to that of Jewish communities elsewhere in the Diaspora and dissimilar to that of the surrounding population, of which almost half is still rural.

Because Soviet Jewry had become so overwhelmingly urban, the Jews' role in the ongoing migration from village to city has been negligible. Moreover, the Holocaust, which claimed the lives of millions of Soviet Jews, reduced the Soviet Jewish population and contributed to their diminished proportion in the urban population as a whole, as the following data on the percentage of Jews in the urban population indicate:

Year	1926	1939	1959	1970	1979
Percentage	8.2	4.7	2.2	1.5	1.1

Given the intensified urbanization process of recent years on the one hand and a dwindling Jewish population as the result of biological factors, assimilation, and emigration on the other, we may reasonably assume that this process has intensified during the 1980s. Soviet Jewry shares this phenomenon with the Jewish communities in most Western countries. Although the process is slightly blunted in some other countries (the United States in particular) by a positive migration balance, it has accelerated in the Soviet Union as the result of emigration.

Because a great majority of European Jews had become an urban element by the previous century and because the large city affords broader entrepreneurial opportunities and facilitates social mobility, most of today's Jewish communities are situated in metropolitan areas. These factors have left their imprint on Soviet Jewry as well. The metropolitanization of this community has accelerated due to the Holocaust, in which a large proportion of *shtetl* Jews perished while the survivors relocated to large cities instead of returning to their previous areas of residence. If we define any community with a population exceeding 1 million as a metropolis, we see that about 25 percent of all Soviet Jews dwelled in cities of this type in 1959 and close to 37 percent in 1970. There is reason to assume that about half of all Soviet Jews in the mid-1980s dwell in metropolises. In this respect, too, the Jews of the USSR bear greater resemblance to the Jewish communities of other countries than to other Soviet nationality groups or to the overall Soviet population. While close to 60 percent of Soviet Jews lived in cities (communities with populations between half a million and a million) and metropolises (1 million or over) by the early 1970s, only about 20 percent of all Soviet citizens resided in such places at the time. There is reason to believe that the disparity has progressively widened during the 1970s and 1980s.

Several Soviet cities and metropolises are home to large concentrations of Jews. For example, four metropolises with Jewish populations in excess of

100,000 in the early 1970s accounted for almost 34 percent of all Soviet Jews; another approximately 12 percent of Soviet Jewry resided in four cities with Jewish populations between 50,000 and 100,000; twenty-seven cities with Jewish populations between 10,000 and 50,000 accounted for another approximately 28 percent. Accordingly, only 26 percent of all Soviet Jews appear to have dwelled in communities with Jewish populations of less than 10,000.

The fact that large communities of Jews developed in certain cities, where they often apparently concentrated in certain districts, would tend to heighten their self-conscious common identity. This group consciousness, however, lacks a concrete outlet in organizational frameworks. There is therefore a tension between the objective and subjective realities of Jewish life in the Soviet Union. In this sense, Soviet Jewry is quite unlike most Diaspora Jewish communities. Although virtually identical to its non-Soviet counterparts in demographic structure, Soviet Jewry has no legitimate way of giving organizational form to its physical existence as a community or of filling such forms with religio-cultural content. One response to this dilemma has been emigration.

About 12 percent of all Soviet Jews left the Soviet Union between the early 1970s and the end of 1985. Of these, close to 60 percent settled in Israel, which they viewed as the most appropriate place for the expression of their collective existence. About 40 percent opted for other countries, either because they considered these destinations similarly appropriate settings for articulation of their ethnic-religious aspirations or under an assumption that these countries offer broader opportunities for professional and material advancement.

The Jews' historical heritage, which includes a pronounced appreciation for education, and the high priority East European Jewish parents accorded their children's studies contributed to making the average formal education of a Soviet Jew even prior to World War II more extensive than that of the urban Soviet population as a whole. In early 1939, the proportion of Jews with more than seven years of schooling (incomplete secondary education or beyond) was almost twice (a factor of 1.8) that of the overall urban population.

The regions in which the Jews' average educational level was lower than that of the Soviet Jewish population as a whole were those that fell under Nazi occupation. The prime victims of the Holocaust were Jews of small towns and elderly Jews—population strata whose levels of education were lower than that of the Soviet Jewish population as a whole. In the wake of the Holocaust, therefore, the average education level of Soviet Jews rose in relation to the prewar situation.

Postwar Soviet development on the one hand, and Soviet policy toward the Jews on the other, turned education into one of the most conspicuous social characteristics of Soviet Jewry. In twenty years—1939-1959—the number of academically educated Soviet citizens more than doubled. The Jews took part in this rapid growth both because of their traditional attitude toward study and because of the discrimination they suffered in other areas of life. For at least two generations, the chances of a Jew's advancement in politics, diplomacy, the army, and similar fields—in which progress is not necessarily related to formal education—have been slim. For the Jews, then, education has become almost the only path by which prestige and enhanced social status might be achieved. Jews devote the best of their energy and talent and mobilize all of their social connections in overcoming a range of obstacles placed in the path of their educational advancement. Because Jews are more highly motivated than other national groups in the pursuit of education, they have achieved a certain success, though not without compromises. Because, for example, pressure for admission in Soviet higher education institutes is heavier for day study programs than for evening and correspondence study, the percentage of Jews in the latter programs is higher. The same phenomenon occurs in selection of fields of study; Jews must choose a profession chiefly on the basis of the chance of admission to a particular department rather than on personal ambitions with regard to a particular field. Since the Soviet educational system is extremely broad and diverse, however, the Jews succeeded until the late 1970s in climbing the educational ladder despite the hurdles and difficulties placed in their way and have become the best educated of all Soviet nationalities. Indeed, by the late 1950s about half (49.1 percent) the Soviet Jews over 10 years of age had secondary or postsecondary education; in the early 1970s more than 61 percent had some postsecondary education. The proportion of Jews with secondary or postsecondary education was almost 3.5 times greater than that of the general urban population at the end of the 1950s, and almost 2.5 times greater in the early 1970s.

This disparity widened as educational level rose. In 1959 the proportion of Jews with secondary or vocational secondary education was 1.5 times that of the general urban population. Higher education (complete and incomplete) was 4 times more prevalent among the Jews than among city dwellers as a whole. More than one-fifth (22.1 percent) of Soviet Jews over the age of 10 had received an academic education. The academization of the Jewish community persisted through the 1960s; at the beginning of the 1970s, more than one-fourth (28.4 percent) of all Soviet Jews over the age of 10 had an academic education. Because this rate includes both the elderly Jewish population (in which the academically trained are proportionately fewer) and children who could not yet have acquired academic education, the incidence of academic education among Jewish young adults and the middle aged may be said to approach half the population. Data on students indicate that the academization of Soviet Jewry has persisted into the 1970s as well, though its pace decelerated. This process is no longer restricted to the Jews of certain republics with traditionally high proportions of Jewish professionals; it now extends to republics in which the proportion of academically trained Jews had been relatively low in the past. Moreover, the emigration of Jews during the first half of the 1970s actually accelerated the academization of Soviet Jewry because a large majority of Jewish emigrants belonged to ethnic groups of lower proportional incidence of professionals and came from areas (the Baltic region and Moldavia) where the percentage of professionals, Jews included, was not among the highest. Therefore Soviet Jewry, like most other Jewish communities, has undergone rapid academization. Here again Soviet Jewry bears closer resemblance to the Jewish communities of the developed countries than to the surrounding population.

The academization process in the Soviet context has had an even greater impact on the social stratification and professional structure of the Jews there than comparable processes have had on Western Jewish communities. This is due to both the structure of higher education in the Soviet Union and to the nature of its social and political regime. In most Western countries, primarily the United States (home to the largest Jewish community), higher education consists of three degrees, of which the first confers no profession and amounts essentially to a final stage of general education. In the Soviet Union, by contrast, higher education is built on two degrees, the first of which confers a profession. Furthermore, most Western institutions of higher education are private and have no obligation to guarantee most graduates employment in their respective professions. In the Soviet Union, however, all institutions of higher education are state owned. Because the economy is government planned, the state must guarantee employment to most graduates of these institutes in the professions they have acquired. In most Western countries, a substantial proportion of the academically trained, especially holders of bachelor's degrees, are not employed in their professions. In the Soviet Union, by contrast, a great majority of the academically trained work in the fields they have studied or at least fill positions that call for academic training. Although this situation occasionally leads to the hidden unemployment of professionals and the creation of positions of dubious efficiency and not necessarily requiring professionals, the subjective feeling of the employed and society's regard for them is not diminished thereby. Many Jews, knowingly or not, consider this regard compensation of sorts for the sense of degradation that often stems from others' attitudes toward their national origin.

Indeed the respective occupational distributions of the Jewish employed and the urban population as a whole diverge widely. While approximately four-fifths (76.3 percent) of all urban wage earners in the Soviet Union in the early 1970s had no formal professional training, less than half (41.2 percent) of all Jewish wage-earners belong to this category. About one-fifth (18.8 percent) of the Jewish employed had preacademic education (such as technicians, civil engineers, dental therapists, and nonacademically trained teachers), as opposed to slightly over one-tenth (13.1 percent) of all wage earners. The inference to be drawn is that the proportion of Jewish wage earners with preacademic education was almost 1.5 times greater than that of all urban wage earners. This disparity was especially broad with regard to wage earners with academic education. Although the academically educated (complete and incomplete) accounted for almost four-tenths (37.4 percent) of all Jewish wage earners in 1970, their proportion among all urban wage earners was only one-tenth (10.6 percent). The percentage of those with higher education, then, was 3.5 times greater among the Jewish employed than among all urban wage earners; their numbers in the mid-1970s approached about 400,000.

The distribution of employed Jewish professionals by profession is influenced by Jewish historical heritage and Soviet policy toward the Jews, at least during the past two generations. The proportion of Jews in the legal and medical professions has been traditionally high in most Diaspora Jewish communities. Most employed in the Soviet legal profession, however, belong to the security service apparatus or to the institutions and courts affiliated with those services in some way; the number of attorneys, by contrast, is limited. Due to Soviet policy toward the Jews, at least since World War II, the employment of Jews in these institutions has been restricted, and the proportion of legal practitioners among the Jewish professional employed is apparently not great. The picture in medicine is different. In the mid-1960s, nearly one-fourth of academically educated Jewish wage earners, as against only about 15 percent of all professional employed, were physicians. The percentage of Jews with preacademic education employed in the paramedical professions (dental therapists, medics, and the like) similarly appears to have been high. Therefore the phenomenon of high proportional Jewish representation in the medical field, well known in many Diaspora communities, holds true, perhaps emphatically so, in the Soviet Union.

Unlike in many Western countries, and the United States in particular, doctors in the Soviet Union do not enjoy a higher-than-average income and high status. The official salary and unofficial income of a skilled worker or warehouse manager, for example, are sometimes higher than that of a doctor. It would seem that the choice of this profession by so many Jews, including a high percentage of women, has more to do with the relatively open professional opportunities in the field and certain historical predilections than with practical considerations.

Research and instruction in higher education institutions is another field in which the share of Jews in most communities of the developed world has been relatively large in recent generations. Professionals employed in the field in the Soviet Union are known as scientific workers. At the beginning of the 1970s, about one-fifth (18 percent) of all academically educated Jewish wage earners, as opposed to only about one-tenth of all Soviet citizens at this educational level, were scientific workers. While Jews accounted for 5.2 percent of all wage earners with higher education, their share of scientific workers was 6.1 percent. This figure climbed at the higher end of the professional scale. If the Jews accounted for 6.1 percent of all scientific workers, they were 8.3 percent of all wage earners who possessed the *Kandidat* degree (parallel to a Western Ph.D.) and 14 percent of holders of the degree of *Doktor nauk*, the highest degree of science in the Soviet Union. Certain indicators allow us to infer that the professional distribution of Jewish scientific workers is different from that of all wage earners in this group. The Jews apparently concentrate on the exact sciences, biology, and medicine and less in the humanities and social sciences. This is both a direct and an indirect consequence of soviet policy.

In the exact sciences, in which the government has sought the greatest possible development, the potential of Jewish talent was hard to forgo; Jews therefore found advancement relatively easier to achieve than in the humanities and social sciences. Research and instruction in the latter fields are considered integral parts of the ideological front; here Jews are considered untrustworthy. Accordingly, Jews who seek to advance in these fields face more obstacles than their counterparts in the exact sciences. Changes in Soviet policy, too, have greater effect on professionals in the social sciences and humanities; the Jews, having learned the lessons of Stalin's last years and recent times as well, prefer not to commit their professional careers to these sensitive spheres. As a consequence of these factors, the percentage of Jewish scientific workers in the humanities and social sciences—especially the young and the middle aged—is lower than that of the overall Soviet scientific worker population. Research and instruction in institutes of higher education, together with medicine and engineering, are the major fields of employment for most Jews with higher or preacademic education.

Therefore despite attempts made in the Soviet Union in the 1920s and 1930s to restructure the Jewish community's social composition by integrating the Jews into agriculture, manual labor, and industry—and the military, the security services, and the like—the social structure of Soviet Jewry continues to resemble Jewish communities in developed countries more than the social structure of the surrounding population.

The mutual influence of the basic demographic and social facts that characterize the Soviet Jewish community leaves its mark on a range of sociodemographic phenomena. Of these, one of the most conspicuous is the fact—well known in the Soviet Union—that the larger is a city, the lower is the fertility rate of its population. Because most Soviet Jews live in metropolises and cities, the fertility of Soviet Jewish women is low. Furthermore, fertility occurs in inverse relation to women's level of education: the more highly educated a woman is, the fewer children she bears. Because the percentage of professionals and persons with postsecondary education is higher in the Jewish community than in any other and since about half the persons at this level are women, the factors underlying the diminishing fertility of Jewish women are so powerful that, certain regional differences notwithstanding, the fertility rate of Jewish women ranks at among the lowest levels in the Soviet Union.

Metropolises and cities, as administrative centers and foci of research, are highly involved in national group affairs, including a high percentage of nationally exogenous marriages. Intermarriage is especially common among the educated and the professionals. Compounding this tendency is the conscious or unconscious wish of some Jews to free themselves, or at least their offspring, of the stigma of being Jewish. No legitimate Jewish activity capable of counteracting these trends exists. Intermarriage has consequently become highly common in the Soviet Jewish community. During the 1960s and through the mid-1970s there were 40 to 50 mixed marriages for every 100 marriages involving at least one Jewish partner. The resulting proportion resembles that of several Jewish communities in Europe and apparently exceeds that of U.S. Jewry. But although some of the offspring of intermarriage in Europe and, even more, in the United States consider themselves Jews and even receive some Jewish education, a great majority of offspring of mixed marriages in the Soviet Union are registered as non-Jews and are almost certainly raised as such.

The combination of low fertility rates and mixed marriages with offspring who are registered as non-Jews and who apparently consider themselves non-Jews has upset the age equilibrium of the Jewish population. The result is an aging process which has led to negative natural increase—in other words, a decreasing number of Jews in the Soviet Union, a phenomenon well known in other Diaspora communities. The average annual rate of decrease was about 0.5 percent in the 1960s and approached 1 percent in the 1970s; there is reason to assume that it will exceed 1.5 percent during the 1980s, even without taking emigration into account. The future size of the Soviet Jewish community, however, will be determined not only by birth and intermarriage rates but by Soviet policy toward the Jews and the Jews' own resolve to continue existing as Jews. As Soviet government policy brings intensified discrimination to bear against the offspring of mixed marriages, the number of people who view themselves as Jews either willingly or for lack of choice will increase. The greater is the distrust and hostility that surrounding society reserves for the Jews, the more the rate of intermarriage involving Jews will fall. Indeed, recent accounts, though unsubstantiated, testify to a lower intermarriage rate in the Jewish community during the 1980s than during the 1960s and the 1970s.

The fact that many Jews concentrate in large cities and professional strata has contributed to a widening polarization within the Jewish community on the question of attitude to the Jewish national group. The metropolis accelerates the processes of assimilation, which affect the professional strata with particular force. At the same time, however, these strata are receptive to information reaching the Soviet Union from outside. This applies in particular to the professional intelligentsia, in which the percentage of persons who command a language in addition to Russian is relatively high. Moreover, scientific worker circles, toward whom the regime has displayed a certain if highly limited measure of tolerance—particularly those in the natural sciences—are foci of social and ideological ferment. These circles try to anchor their activity in Soviet law and the Soviet Union's international commitments. In this sense, the fact that much of Soviet Jewry resides in large cities and evinces a high percentage of professionals is a factor conducive to national activity. Every action taken by Jews resounds beyond Soviet borders and is bounced back by the Western mass media. Some members of the Jewish professional intelligentsia (we do not know how many) are increasingly concerned that the possibilities of social advancement through education are shrinking due to growing pressure for increased representation of parallel strata of other national groups. Career-related anxiety on the young generation's part has become one of the motives for emigration. Since career opportunities seem more promising in the United States than in Israel, such concern perhaps accounts in part for the high percentage of Jewish emigrants who prefer the United States to Israel as their destination.

Notwithstanding emigration, which reflects rejection of the Communist viewpoint, a relatively large number of Jews remain in the Communist party for ideological reasons, inertia, or opportunistic motives. Because the party does most of its recruiting in the large cities and because party membership is an important factor in the advancement of an individual's career, proportionately more party members are urban than rural. The leadership is also interested in fostering a relatively high percentage of professionals in the party ranks; it therefore stresses the recruitment of members from this group. Thus it is natural that the Jews' percentage in party membership exceeds their share of the population; moreover, the percentage of Communists among the Jews in areas not overrun by the Nazis exceeded that in areas affected by the Holocaust. It is therefore no surprise that the percentage of Jews affiliated with the party (as members or candidates) exceeded that of any other Soviet national group, approaching 15 percent in the mid-1970s. But while Jews accounted for about 2 percent of party members and candidates, more than twice their share of the population, Jewish representation in local and regional soviets (the representative bodies of government) came to only one-fourth to one-third of their proportion in the population, a fact that demonstrates anti-Jewish discrimination in politics (which intensified in the late 1970s and in the 1980s to encompass higher education as well) with greater clarity.

In summation, we may say that the sociodemographic profile of Soviet

Jewry resembles that of Jewish communities in other developed countries more than it does the other national groups in the Soviet Union. This Jewish community, like others throughout the Diaspora, is undergoing a process of population decrease due to a combination of biological factors and assimilation, most conspicuously expressed in intermarriage and loss of the offspring of mixed marriages. In the Soviet Jewish community, perhaps more than any other Jewish group, the polarization between assimilation trends of numerous and diverse forms and deepening national identity is progressively widening.

NOTES

CHAPTER 1

1. 5,215,805 Jews were enumerated in the 1897 census. See Y. Lestschinsky, *Dos idishe folk in tsifern* (Berlin, 1922), p. 29. Between then and World War I, the average annual rate of increase was 1.5 to 1.6 percent, or about 80,000 persons per year. During this period, the average annual emigration of Jews was of similar magnitude. Thus it is reasonable to conclude that the number of Jews in the Russian Empire at the outbreak of World War I was similar to that recorded in 1897.

2. In 1915, worldwide Jewish population was estimated at between 13,800,000 and 14,340,000 persons. Ibid., p. 14.

3. According to Lestschinsky's calculations, between 700,000 and 750,000 Jews emigrated from Eastern Europe to the United States alone during the nineteenth century. To these should be added the emigrants from Eastern Europe who settled in central and western Europe. The precise figures available for emigration from Russia to the United States indicate that 1,042,000 Jews arrived between 1900 and 1914. From 1840 to 1914, close to 280,000 Jews emigrated to Canada, Argentina, Brazil, and South Africa, among whom were a not-inconsiderable number of Russian Jews. Y. Lestschinsky, *Nedudei yisrael ba-dorot ha-aharonim* (Tel Aviv, 1965), pp. 141, 154-55, 161. I have therefore assumed that the number of Jewish immigrants to the United States from Eastern European countries other than Russia is balanced out by the number of Russian Jews who settled in Canada, Argentina, Brazil, South Africa, and Western Europe. I have determined the number of Jews to have exited Russia on this basis.

4. I have computed the average annual increase on the basis of the following estimates: (1) at the beginning of the nineteenth century, Russian Jewry numbered

from 1 million to 1.2 million. (2) In midcentury, the Jewish population of the Russian Empire amounted to approximately two million persons (Lestschinsky, *Dos idishe folk*, p. 30). (3) According to the 1897 census, there were in Russia at that time about 5,216,000 Jews, to which we add about 0.5 million who had emigrated from Russia during the second half of that century. According to my estimates, Russian Jewry, including its émigré community, amounted to approximately 7 million persons on the eve of the war. My calculations have not taken into account the natural increase of the émigré population in its new countries of residence.

5. At the beginning of the nineteenth century, the Jews amounted to 6 to 7 percent of the total population of the Pale of Settlement's twenty-five provinces (including Poland); this figure rose to 8 to 9 percent in midcentury and to about 12 percent in 1897. Ibid., p. 29.

6. L. Zinger, *Dos banayte folk: tsifern un faktn vegn di yidn in FSSR* (Moscow, 1941), p. 33, writes: "The Jewish population in the territory of the Soviet Union grew . . . by less than a hundred thousand persons relative to that of 1897." Y. Lestschinsky, *Ha-yehudim be-rusia ha-sovietit* (Tel Aviv, 1943), p. 56, estimates the 1897 Jewish population in the territory of the Soviet Union at 2,330,000.

7. According to L. Zinger's calculations, the Jewish population of the territories that later comprised the USSR (excluding Bukhara, Georgia, and Armenia) amounted to 2,504,000 in 1897. Since only urban population was counted in the 1923 census, Zinger added 188,000 Jews in the villages of Belorussia and 108,000 residing in villages of the Ukraine. On this basis, he concluded that the Soviet Jewish population, excluding Bukhara, Georgia, and Armenia, came to 2,454,000 in March 1923. L. Zinger, "Evreiskoe naselenie SSR—Diagrammy," *Materialy i issledovaniia statistiko-ekonomicheskoi komissii pri Ts. K. ORT* (1927), vypusk I, pp. 7-8. Another published study determined that the 1923 Jewish population of the Soviet Union was 2,431,000, and the decline between 1897 and 1923 was about 9 percent. L. Zinger and B. Engel, *Yidishe bafelkerung fun FSSR in tabeles un diagrames* (Moscow, 1930), table 7. Because the authors of the 1930 study did not demonstrate the specific system by which their calculation had been reached, I prefer to use the 1927 study.

8. There were 2,672,000 Jews in the Soviet Union in December 1926. About 100,000 of them resided in Bukhara, Georgia, and Armenia, areas not included in Zinger's calculations with regard to the 1923 census. It therefore appears that in the area for which data from the beginning of 1923 are available, there were about 2,572,000 Jews at the end of 1926, in contrast to 2,454,000 in 1923.

9. Zinger, *Dos banayte folk,* p. 35.

10. A. Nove and Y. Newth, "The Jewish Population: Demographic Trends and Occupational Patterns," in L. Kochan (ed.), *The Jews in Soviet Russia since 1917* (London, 1972), p. 143.

11. Y. Lestschinsky, *Tfutsot yisrael le-ahar ha-milhama* (Tel Aviv, 1948), p. 134. These data are estimates based on censuses held in the early 1930s and on calculation of rates of natural increase. It could well be that these estimates are slightly high since Jewish emigration during the decade was not taken into account.

12. B. Weinryb, "Poland," in P. Meyer, B. Weinryb, E. Duschinsky, and N. Sylvain, *The Jews in the Soviet Satellites* (Westport, Conn., 1971), p. 226.

13. World Jewish population on the eve of World War II has been estimated at 16 million. Lestschinsky, *Tfutsot yisrael,* p. 31.

14. R. Lewis, R. Rowland, and R. Clem, *Nationality and Population Change in Russia and USSR* (New York, 1976), p. 300.

15. With regard to the 1926 and 1939 censuses, I have included all of the Ukraine in the former Pale of Settlement, though certain parts of it were in fact outside the Pale.

16. Zinger, *Dos banayte folk,* p. 36.

17. *Evreiskaia entsiklopediia,* 11:539-40.

18. The *Shtetl* as a distinct, defined type of locality was eliminated in the Soviet Union in 1923-1924. The small towns were redefined—some as villages and others as urban localities. Soviet Jewish demographers who analyzed data from the 1926 census defined as a *Shtetl* any locality with a population under 10,000 and the majority of whose work force was engaged in occupations of an urban nature. I have used the same standard with regard to the 1926 census.

19. The computation is based on L. Zinger, "Chislennost' i geograficheskoe razmeshchenie evreiskogo naseleniia SSSR," in *Evrei v SSSR* (Moscow, 1930), pp. 40-41, 51; Y. Kantor, *Di yidishe bafelkerung in ukrayne* (Kiev, 1929), pp. 11-12.

20. Lestschinsky, *Dos idishe folk,* p. 70.

21. Y. Lestschinsky, *Ha-yehudim be-rusia ha-sovietit,* p. 143. The author does not explain how he reached this estimate; it appears overstated as I have indeed proved concerning the Jewish population of Moscow.

22. The entire population is considered as being within the framework of self-supporting Jews (they and their dependents).

23. B. Brutskus, *Professional'nyi sostav evreiskogo naseleniia Rossii* (Petersburg, 1908), p. 5.

24. Calculated according to ibid., pp. 10-14.

25. Of the total value of all commercial transactions, 28.8 percent was concentrated in the Pale of Settlement, where 75 percent of commercial turnover was in Jewish hands. *Evreiskaia entsiklopediia,* 13:654. Jews also engaged in commerce outside the Pale, and it may therefore be estimated that one-fourth of all commercial turnover at the end of the nineteenth century was in Jewish hands.

26. The 1897 and 1926 social distribution of self-supporting Jews is taken from Zinger, *Dos banayte folk,* pp. 8, 46.

27. S. Schwarz, *The Jews in the Soviet Union* (Syracuse, N.Y., 1951), p. 165.

28. Iu. Larin, *Evrei i antisemitizm v SSSR* (Moscow-Leningrad, 1929), p. 18.

29. Calculated according to Z. Mindlin, "Sotsial'nyi sostav i glavnye zaniatiia evreiskogo naseleniia SSSR," in *Evrei v SSSR* (Moscow, 1930), p. 18.

30. Zinger, *Dos banayte folk,* p. 46.

31. Larin, *Evrei i Antisemitizm,* p. 97.

32. Zinger, *Dos banayte folk,* p. 46.

33. Ibid., p. 46. The details presented from the 1926 census concerning the distribution of economically active Jews do not include 5.7 percent who received state pensions, students in institutions of higher learning who were supported by grants or scholarships, and the 1.6 percent active in the free professions.

34. In early 1939, there were about 25,000 Jewish families in *kolkhozes,* with 82 percent of these having settled in the Ukraine, Belorussia, or Crimea—areas conquered by the Germans. Only about 12 percent of the Jewish *Kolkhoz* families were found in Birobidzhan, with another 6 percent in Georgia and Central Asia. Zinger, *Dos banayte folk,* pp. 85-94.

35. In early 1939, there were some 364,000 self-supporting Jews defined in Soviet terminology as intelligentsia. Of these, 34.3 percent were bookkeepers; 25.6 percent engaged in teaching, culture, and art; 25.3 percent were technicians, dental technicians, and so on; 12.9 percent were engineers, doctors, agronomists and others; and 1.9 percent were researchers or teachers in institutions of higher education or research. Calculated from ibid., p. 106.

36. Ibid., p. 108.

37. Concerning the passport system in the USSR, see L. Boim, "Shitat ha-passportim be-vrit-ha-moaetzot ve-hashpa'atam al matzavam shel ha-yehudim,"*Shvut* (Tel Aviv, 1975), 3:7-16.

38. Although regulations stipulate that children be registered according to mother's nationality, the rules are not executed strictly, as the following statements relating to Khar'kov *oblast'* indicate: "A decisive majority of offspring of marriages between Jews, Poles, Armenians and others with Russians or Ukrainians are reported in *ZAGS* at the time of birth registration as being Ukrainian or Russian." M. Kurman and I. Lebedinskii, *Naselenie bol'shogo sotsialisticheskogo goroda* (Moscow, 1968), p. 128. These comments seem curious and demand further examination; they probably do not reflect reality in the Khar'kov *oblast'* and are meant only to explain the drop recorded in the number of Poles, Jews, and Armenians in the area.

39. The first internal passport is issued for a five-year period.

40. An unofficial ("*samizdat*") periodical issued by a group of Jewish activists in Riga in February 1970 stresses that "the administrative institutions . . . absolutely refuse to register offspring of mixed marriages as Jews; [these] arrived at their Jewish self-definition after having received their first passports." *Evreiskii samizdat* (Jerusalem, 1974), 1:1.

41. See I. Zinchenko, "O natsional'nom sostave i iazykakh naseleniia SSSR po dannym peripisi 1970 g.," *Vestnik statistiki* (March 1972):18-25.

42. V. Kozlov phrased this position thus: "In scientifically based ethnic statistics, especially those of the Soviet Union, preference in definition of national (ethnic) affiliation is given not to language but rather to the subjects' national (ethnic) consciousness. The response to the question of national affiliation . . . if it can be so expressed, is a synthesis of all the elements of which an ethnic group consists, which have blended within the subject's awareness; this [synthesis] serves to express a person's ethnic ties with other people, without which the very existence of a nation is inconceivable." V. Kozlov, *Dynamika chislennosti narodov* (Moscow, 1969), pp. 83-84.

43. Most of the demographic material published in the Soviet Union and elsewhere is registered in U. O. Schmelz, *Jewish Demography and Statistics: Bibliography for 1920-1970* (Jerusalem, 1976), pp. 90-199.

44. See Zinger, *Dos banayte folk.* This book was "authorized for print" on August 4, 1941. Another short work by the same author—L. Zinger, *Dos ufgerikhte folk* (Moscow, 1948)—is of clearly propagandistic nature and contains little useful material.

45. L. Zinger, *Sotsial'no-ekonomicheskie itogi razresheniia evreiskogo voprosa v SSSR* (Moscow, 1947).

46. See, for example, Y. Kantor, "Eynike bamerkungen un oysfirn tsu di farefntlekhte sakh-haklen fun folks-tseylung in ratnfarband dem 15tn yanuar 1959,"

Bleter far geshikhte (Warsaw, 1962-1963), 15:142-54; I. Kapeliush, "Yidn in sovetnfarband," *Sovetish heymland* (September 1974):174-77; I. Domal'skii, *Russkie evrei vchera i segodnia* (Tel Aviv, 1975), pp. 85-96.

47. At a conference of Soviet sociologists held in Sukhumi, Georgia, in 1967, the "guidelines concerning the state system of amassing statistical data [on social topics]" were proposed in a document stating that "[the science of] social statistics has been gradually sinking since about 1930. . . . Only material relating to economics has been published, while the statistics of ethics, of demographics, medicine and sanitation, of cultural activity, of politics—that is, almost all social statistics—have practically ceased to exist." A. Ezhov, assistant director of the Soviet Central Bureau of Statistics—who rejected the conclusion that social statistics had ceased to exist in the USSR—also admitted that data on these topics had not been made public, though they had been compiled. *Vsesoiuznoe soveshchanie statistikov, 22-26 aprelia 1968 g.* (Moscow, 1968), pp. 53-54.

48. "In the past three years," wrote D. Valentei in 1969, "more than 3,500 scientific articles, pamphlets and books dealing in these or other questions of population research have been published in our country." D. Valentei, "Nauka i demograficheskie protsessy," *Vestnik akademii nauk SSSR,* no. 3 (1969):71.

49. Concerning the development of sociology in the Soviet Union, see I. Zemtsov, *IKSI; The Moscow Institute of Applied Social Research* (Jerusalem, 1976).

50. Soviet law requires parents to report every birth within thirty days. When a child is born, parents fill out an eighteen-item form of which nine items relate to the newborn and nine to the parents. Mother's and father's nationalities are listed in response to the thirteenth question. Copies of this form are forwarded to statistical institutions for use in compiling current statistics; then they are returned to the ZAGS offices for filing. See V. Urlanis, *Rozhdaemost' i prodolzhitel'nost' zhizni v SSSR* (Moscow, 1963), p. 67.

51. Forms on which citizens report changes in residence are forwarded to the Central Bureau of Statistics and include the following information: age, nationality, destination, reason for change in residence, and children who have moved together with the applicant. A sample of 20 percent of these data is processed by the Soviet Central Bureau of Statistics and serves as a source for data concerning internal population migration. See P. Eglite, "Opyt izucheniia migratsii v Latviiskoi SSR," in *Statistika migratsii naseleniia* (Moscow, 1973), p. 238.

52. This fact was confirmed by P. Pod"iachikh, director of the 1959 and 1970 Soviet censuses: "With regard to indices, such as data on distribution of population according to nationality and native tongue, levels of education, family situation and a series of other important identifying signs—there is no possibility of obtaining them from calculations [derived from current statistics]. The only source for such data is the material which accumulates from censuses." P. Pod"iachikh, "Perepis' naseleniia 1959 goda—vazhneishaia zadacha statisticheskikh organov," *Vestnik statistiki* (February 1957): 19.

53. General Soviet censuses were held in 1920, 1926, and 1939. In addition, a census of urban population was conducted in 1923. A census was also held in 1937, but its results were never divulged. The only Soviet census that included a question on religion was that of 1937. Concerning Soviet censuses, see G. Pavlov, "Sovetskie perepisi naseleniia (1920-1959)," in *Sovetskaia statistika za polveka* (Moscow, 1972), pp. 9-34.

54. *Vsesoiuznaia perepis' naseleniia 1959 goda* (Moscow, 1958), pp. 28-29.

55. *Itogi vsesoiuznoi perepisi naseleniia 1959 goda* (Moscow, 1962-1963), 16 vols. Data from this census concerning the Jewish population appear in M. Altshuler (ed.), *The Jews in the Soviet Union—1959 Census* (Jerusalem, 1963).

56. Concerning the instructions for filling out the questionnaire, see B. Kolpakov, *Vsesoiuznaia perepis' naseleniia 1970 goda* (Moscow, 1969).

57. *Itogi vsesoiuznoi perepisi naseleniia 1970 goda* (Moscow, 1972-1973).

58. S. Bruk and V. Kozlov, "Voprosy o natsional'nosti i iazyke v predstoiashchei perepisi naseleniia," *Vestnik statistiki* (March 1968): 32-37.

59. *Vsesoiuznoe soveshchanie statistikov, 22-26 aprelia 1968 g.* (Moscow, 1969), pp. 205-10.

60. See *Instruktsiia o poriadke vsesoiuznoi perepisi naselenia 1970 goda i zapolnenii perepisnykh blankov* (Moscow, 1968). A photocopy of this internal booklet was placed at my disposal by Murray Feshbach (Washington), to whom I express my gratitude.

61. *Vsesoiuznoe soveshchanie statistikov,* pp. 578-86.

62. Ibid., p. 578.

63. The study was undertaken as commissioned by the Israel Ministry of Immigrant Absorption under the aegis of Yehudith Shuval and Yehuda Marcus and was carried out by the Israel Institute of Applied Social Research. I express my thanks to the researchers and directors of the Planning and Research Branch in the Ministry of Immigrant Absorption, Ephraim Ahiram, and Eli Leshem for having agreed to include questions concerning the Soviet census in this study.

64. Between January 1, 1970, and March 31, 1971, 1,239 Soviet emigrants reached Israel. The sample therefore includes more than one-third of the immigrants reaching Israel in the time frame under discussion.

65. Bruk and Kozlov, "Voprosy."

66. *Vsesoiuznoe soveshchanie statistikov,* p. 208.

67. Ibid., p. 208.

CHAPTER 2

1. M. Altshuler (ed.), *The Jews in the Soviet Union—1959 Census* (Jerusalem, 1963), table 1.

2. *Vestnik statistiki,* no. 7 (1980): 41.

3. Larisa Bogoraz contends in a *samizdat* "journal" that appeared in Moscow in 1972 that "there were some who tried to find a legal basis for considering themselves as Russians, or at least to declare their children as such." A. Ben-Arye (ed.), *Evreiskii samizdat* (Jerusalem, 1974), 4:41.

4. Research on "The National Reawakening of Soviet Jews" was conducted under the direction of Shmuel Ettinger, who kindly made available to me these data, for which I express my appreciation.

5. Izidor Liast, an emigration movement activist in the Soviet Union, noted that "when both parents are Jews, they declare [in the census] Jewish nationality, as a rule." Among some other nationality groups, though, there appears to be a tendency at times to state a different nationality. "But in the Jewish population, as our

observations show, such instances are quite rare." I. Akharon, "Issledovaniia demograficheskikh osobennostei evreiskogo naseleniia SSSR"; in J. Ingerman (ed.), *Evreiskii samizdat* (Jerusalem, 1978), 15:161. It is worth noting that Soviet demographer V. Kozlov, in discussing the national definition of children of mixed parentage, states that "though nationality is noted in the census on the basis of individuals' declarations, in most cases these declarations are determined to a large extent by what is written in the internal passport." V. Kozlov, *Natsional'nosti SSR* (Moscow, 1975), p. 231.

6. In areas populated largely by Muslim nationalities, the authorities apparently allow for flexibility in the registration of minors. This emerges from the following statement regarding Dagestan: "Children of mixed marriages are registered in the documents . . . generally *according to the father's nationality"* (my emphasis). *Sovremennaia kul'tura i byt narodov Dagestana* (Moscow, 1971), p. 187.

7. For further detail, see "National Definition of Offspring of Mixed Marriages," chapter 2.

8. See S. DellaPergola, *Jewish and Mixed Marriages in Milan, 1901-1968* (Jerusalem, 1972), p. 111-41.

9. *Statisticheskie materialy po evreiskoi demografii i ekonimike,* no 4 (1929): 21-22.

10. N. Borzykh, "Mezhnatsional'nye braki v SSSR v seredine 1930-kh godov," *Sovetskaia etnografiia,* no. 3 (1984): 101-12.

11. The analysis by J. Newth ("A Statistical Study of Intermarriage among Jews in Part of Vil'nius," *Bulletin on Soviet Jewish Affairs,* no. 1 [1968]:64-69) was based on the number of mixed marriages in the Novaia Vil'nia *raion* of Vil'nius, as in the following tabulation:

Years	Jewish Men with:		Jewish Women with:	
	Jewish Women	Non-Jewish Women	Jewish Men	Non-Jewish Men
1945-1949	71%	29%	76%	24%
1950-1954	52	58	68	32
1955-1958	77	23	92	8
1960-1964	65	35	93	7

These data would seem to indicate that the highest levels of mixed marriages occurred during the early 1950s. But it must be remembered that Newth worked not with numerical data but with a graph, which he proceeded to modify. Moreover, the number of Jewish marriages is probably very small, which itself leads to distortions. Newth based his analysis on an article by Gantskaia and Debets.

12. In questionnaires distributed among 500 couples getting married in the *ZAGS* Wedding Palace in Leningrad at the end of 1962 (where 85 percent of all marriages in the city took place that year among couples under 30 years of age), it was found that

17.5 percent of the couples had met at school and 27.2 percent in social settings (clubs, dance halls, theaters, and the like). A. Kharchev, *Brak i sem'ia v SSSR* (Moscow, 1964), pp. 178, 197. In a 1970 study of couples married that year in Kiev it was found that 50 percent of the men who were students had married students. *Vliianie sotsial'no-ekonomicheskikh faktorov na demograficheskie protsessy* (Kiev, 1972), p. 114.

13. At the time of the 1959 census, there were sixteen autonomous republics in the RSFSR. Seven of them included 52,779 Jewish residents; the remainder had negligible Jewish populations and are not included in the tabulations. Data on the Jewish population of nine autonomous republics were published for 1970, when their total number of Jewish residents amounted to 56,527.

14. During the 1960s, the percentage of mixed marriages out of all marriages involving at least one Jewish partner for various areas and periods, were as follows:

Switzerland	1961-1965	58.3 percent
	1966-1970	55.6 percent
Vienna	1961-1965	72.2 percent
	1966-1968	64.7 percent
Germany	1961-1965	81.3 percent
	1966-1969	74.0 percent
Indiana, United States	1960-1969	48.8 percent

DellaPergola, *Jewish and Mixed Marriages,* pp. 114, 122, 138.

15. O. Gantskaia and G. Debets, "O graficheskikh izobrazheniiakh rezul'tatov statisticheskogo obsledovaniia mezhnatsional'nykh brakov," *Sovetskaia etnografiia,* no. 3 (1966):109-118.

16. *Statisticheskii slovar'* (Moscow, 1965), p. 29.

17. M. Ptukha, *Vibrani pratsi* (Kyiv, 1971), pp. 183-250.

18. L. Chuiko, "O primenenii nekotorykh statisticheskikh metodov v issledovanii brakov," in *Problemy byta, braka i sem'i* (Vil'nius, 1970), pp. 34-36. Ptukha used the following formula in the derivation of the marriage indexes:

L: The number of males of a given subgroup who marry during a specified period (here, the number of Jewish males who marry during a year).

C: The number of females of the same subgroup who marry during the specified period.

A: The number of endogamous marriages contracted between *L* and *C*.

T: The total number of marriages in all subgroups contracted during the specified period.

According to Ptukha's formula, the probability that a male will marry a female of the subgroup being investigated is given by *C/T*, and the corresponding probability with regard to females is L/T. The probability of two members of the subgroup marrying each other in the absence of the influence of the factor under study—nationality—is given by $(CL)/T$. This (expected) value is compared with the actual value, A, and the difference between them makes it possible to fix the influence of the examined factor on the process of mate selection. If A is equal to the expression $(CL)/T$, nationality does not affect mate selection; when A is larger than $(CL)/T$, there exists a tendency toward endogamy, and when A is smaller, the tendency is toward exogamy. In order to find the relative values of endogamy or exogamy, Ptukha suggested the following indexes:

$$\text{For males, } S' = (AT - CL)/(L(T - C)).$$
$$\text{For Females, } S'' = (AT - CL)/(C(T - L)).$$

The index for both sexes together is the mean of S' and S''. The exogamy index for the two sexes together is $A + ((AT)/(CL) - 1)$.

19. Marriage indices among the chief nationalities of the various republics are as follows:

Armenians	+33.4	Estonians	+78.8
Ukrainians	+34.3	Georgians	+80.5
Belorussians	+39.0	Uzbeks	+86.2
Latvians	+61.6	Azerbaidzhanians	+98.8
Moldavians	+62.0	Turkmen	+90.7
Lithuanians	+68.2	Kazakhs	+93.6
Tadzhiks	+77.3	Kirgizians	+95.4

L. Chuiko, "Opyt analiza mezhnatsional'nykh brakov v SSSR," in *Razvitie naseleniia* (Moscow, 1974) pp. 47-54.

20. For further detail, see "Definition of Nationality in Soviet Statistics," chapter 1.

21. For information on this form, see G. Sergeeva and Ia. Smirnova, "K voprosu o natsional'nom samosoznananii gorodskoi molodezhi," *Sovetskaia etnografiia*, no. 4 (1971):87.

22. A. Terent'eva, "Opredelenie svoei natsional'noi prynadlezhnosti podrostkami v natsional'no-smeshannykh sem'iakh," *Sovetskaia etnografiia*, 3 (1969), pp. 20-30.

23. G. Sergeeva and Ia. Smirnova, "K voprosu o natsional'nom samosoznananii."

24. Ibid.; *Sovremennaia kul'tura*, p. 188.

25. See *Statisticheskii slovar'*, p. 527, for the meaning of the concept "family" in the population census. With regard to the meaning of the concept in recent population censuses in which all members of a given family are enumerated in a common questionnaire, it is useful to refer to the enumerators' instructions for 1970: "In instances where respondents experience difficulty in determining the structure of the family, it is necessary to start with the assumption that the family is

the total number of individuals who live together, characterized by family or other ties, and who maintain a common household budget." It is clear, therefore, that the concept of the family is not confined to a married couple and their children. Common residence is also not the sole determinant of family membership, as indicated by the following statement: "If the respondent is a member of a family who lives separately on a permanent basis, but maintains with them a common household budget or regular material connections, he is to be listed as a 'family member living separately,'" but in the absence of a common budget or regular material connections he is to be listed as an "individual." This is the source of the idea that common residence and family relationship are not in themselves sufficient to determine family membership, since it is also possible to be characterized by "other ties." *Instruktsiia o poriadke vsesoiuznoi perepisi naseleniia 1970 goda i zapolnenii perepisnykh blankov* (Moscow, 1968).

26. *Razvitie narodnogo khoziaistva Latviiskoi SSR* (Riga, 1962), p. 29.

27. My thanks to the Planning and Research Branch of the Israel Ministry of Immigrant Absorption, which provided these data.

28. From the sample, it appears that 73.7 percent of the households in Ukrainian cities and 94.2 percent of those in the countryside were uninational. V. Naulko, *Etnichnyi sklad naseleniia Ukrainskoi RSR* (Kyiv, 1965), p. 110.

29. For further information, see M. Altshuler, "Some Statistics on Mixed Marriages among Soviet Jews," *Bulletin on Soviet and East European Jewish Affairs,* no. 6 (1970): 30-32.

30. Data for 1959 on persons in the population of the USSR aged 0-19 are as follows (figures are in percentages):

Year of Birth	Age	Total Population	Urban	Rural
1955-1958	0-4	16.7	10.2	13.0
1950-1954	5-9	10.5	9.5	11.5
1945-1949	10-14	7.3	7.0	7.7
1940-1944	15-19	7.9	8.1	7.7

Itogi, 1970, vol. 2, table 3.

31. In 1950 the crude birthrate (number of births per 1,000 population) of the Soviet Union was 26.7; in 1960, it was 24.9; in 1965, 18.5; and in 1969, 17.0. The general fertility rate shows a similar trend (the general fertility rate is the annual number of births per 1,000 women of child-bearing age). It was 86.9 in 1950 and had declined to 68.5 by 1966-1967. S. Bruk, "Etnodemograficheskie protsessy v SSSR," *Sovetskaia etnografia,* no. 4 (1971): 14; Y. Berent, "Causes of Fertility Decline in Eastern Europe and Soviet Union," *Population Studies,* no. 1 (1970): 35-58.

32. V. Boldyrev, *Itogi perepisi naseleniia SSSR* (Moscow, 1974), pp. 9-11. Soviet studies have demonstrated the existence of considerable variations between different regions not only in the birthrate itself but also in the desired number of children. See V. Belova, *Chislo detei v sem'e* (Moscow, 1975), p. 95; P. Mazur, "Expectancy of Life and Birth in 36 Nationalities of the Soviet Union: 1958-1960," *Population Studies,* no. 2 (1969): 225-46.

33. V. Urlanis, *Rozhdaemost' i prodolzhitel'nost' zhizni v SSSR* (Moscow, 1963), p. 9.

34. R. Sifman, *Dinamika rozhdaemosti v SSSR* (Moscow, 1974), pp. 67-85.

35. G. Kisileva, "Faktory rozhdaemosti v krupnykh gorodakh," in *Rost gorodov i sistema rasseleniia* (Moscow, 1975), pp. 72-80; E. Zagorskaia, *Demograficheskie protsessy v Modlavskoi SSR* (Kishinev, 1971), p. 26.

36. "Moscow and Leningrad stand in last place from the birth rate point of view as well as in natural increase, among all cities with a population of over half a million. . . . In one Moscow *raion* . . . the average number of children among families surveyed was 1.04, while the average desired number was 1.6." D. Valentei, "Nauka i demograficheskie protsessy," *Vestnik akademii nauk SSSR,* no. 3 (1969): 63-64; cf. L. Darskii, "Izuchenie plodovitosti brakov," in *Voprosy demografii* (Moscow, 1970), p. 193.

37. See P. Zvidrin'sh, "Iz opyta provedeniia sotsial'no-demograficheskikh issledovanii v Latviiskoi SSR," *Vestnik statistiki,* no. 3 (1973): 28; A. Akhmedov, "Nekotorye rezul'taty obsledovaniia mnenii molodykh zhenshchin o chisle detei v sem'e," *Vestnik statistiki,* no. 8 (1974): 19; Sifman, Dinamika Rozhdaemosti, pp. 131-42; Belova, *Chislo detei,* p. 52; L. Akinfeeva, "Sotsial'no-demograficheskie obsledovaniia Odesskoi oblasti," in *Demograficheskaia situatsiia v SSSR* (Moscow, 1976), pp. 100-101.

38. P. Mazur, "Birth Control and Regional Differentials in the Soviet Union,"*Population Studies,* no. 3 (1968): 328.

39. This relationship is also manifested in the 1970 census, as shown here for number of children per 1,000 mothers, by her education:

Beyond secondary	1,436
Secondary	1,527
Incomplete secondary	1,741
Primary and less	1,856

Boldyrev, *Itogi perepisi,* p. 40

40. L. Davtian, "O zavisimosti mezhdu blagosostoianiem i rozhdaemost'iu," in *Problemy demograficheskoi statistiki* (Moscow, 1966), pp. 146-60; Akinfeeva, "Sotsial'no-demograficheskie obsledovaniia," pp. 98-99; *Vestnik statistiki,* no. 8 (1974): 20.

41. L. Darskii, "Tablitsy brachnosti zhenshchin SSSR," in *Uchenye zapiski po statistike* (Moscow, 1968), 14:78-106; R. Sifman, "Dinamika plodovitosti kogort zhenshchin v SSSR," in *Voprosy demografii* (Moscow, 1970), p. 157. In the 1960s, the average age at marriage rose somewhat throughout the population, as reflected in data from Belorussia. See S. Pol'skii, "Braki i razvody v BSSR," *Zdravokhranenie Belorussii,* no. 5 (1967): 57-59.

42. U. Schmelz, "'Al ba'ayot yesod be-demografia shel yehudei brit-ha-moatsot," *Behinot,* no. 5 (1974): 47.

43. M. Kurman and I. Lebedinskii, *Naselenie bol'shogo sotsialisticheskogo goroda* (Moscow, 1968), p. 128.

44. I. Mulladzhavov, *Narodonaselenie Uzbekskoi SSR* (Tashkent, 1973), p. 109.

45. Schmelz, "Al ba'ayot yesod", p. 47.

46. *Itogi, 1959,* table 57, in the relevant volumes.

47. *Itogi, 1970,* vol. 4, tables 39-41, 47, 48.

48. For an example of the method of calculation, I used in each 1,000 Jews in Belorussia, the number with seven or more years of schooling amounted to 513 (*Itogi 1959,* volume Belorussia, table 57). The total number of Jews in Belorussia amounted to 150,084 in 1959, which implies that there were 76,994 with the indicated level of schooling. In each 1,000 Jews aged 10 or more in 1959, the number with seven or more years of schooling amounted to 606 (*Itogi 1970,* volume 4, table 41). This implies that there were in Belorussia in 1959 127,051 Jews aged 10 or over and 23,033 children aged 0 to 10.

49. Kurman and Lebedinskii, *Naselenie bol'shogo sotsialisticheskogo goroda* p. 128.

50. In the period under discussion, some Jews did in fact leave the Soviet Union on non-Israeli visas to the United States and Western Europe within the framework of "unification of families," but their number was quite small.

51. The basis for this calculation was the average number of Jews in the Soviet Union between the censuses of 1959 and 1970.

52. The basis for this calculation was the average number of Jews in the Soviet Union between the censuses of 1970 and 1979.

CHAPTER 3

1. The definition of an *oblast', krai,* or autonomous republic as Asiatic or European is determined by the location of its major city.

2. Journalist Alexander Werth writes: "The drift of so many tens of thousands of Jews to the vast, scarcely explored expanses of Siberia is highly characteristic. . . . This migration of the Jews to Asiatic Russia is perhaps one of the most significant phenomena in recent years—and, both geographically and psychologically, the very opposite to Zionism, with its oppressive 'togetherness' and 'exclusiveness.'" A. Werth, *Russia: Hopes and Fears* (London, 1969), p. 257. The figures do not confirm this assertion; Novosibirsk appears to have been the only city in Asiatic RSFSR that enjoyed a positive migration balance of Jews during the 1960s.

3. See table 3C and I. Zinchenko, "Natsional'nyi sostav naseleniia SSSR," in *Vsesoiuznaia perepis' naseleniia 1979 goda* (Moscow, 1984), p. 156.

4. *Resheniia partii i pravitel'stva po khoziaistvennym voprosam* (Moscow, 1968), 4:51.

5. Ibid., p. 52.

6. Ibid., p. 121.

7. *Kommunisticheskaia partiia SSSR v rezoliutsiiakh* (Moscow, 1971), 7:61.

8. There were 1,679 cities in the USSR in 1959 and 1,935 in 1970. There were 2,940 urban settlements at the time of the 1959 census and 3,569 in 1970. A. Vostrikova, "Chislennost' i sostav naseleniia SSSR," *Vestnik statistiki,* no. 2 (1972): 31.

9. *Itogi vsesoiuznoi perepisi naseleniia 1970 goda* (Moscow, 1972), vol. 1, table 4.

10. Ibid.

11. The 1959 census reported 8,509 Jews in the rural population of Vinnitsa *oblast';* the 1970 census found only 3,464.

12. *Itogi vsesoiuznoi perepisi naseleniia 1959 goda,* Ukraine volume, table 3; *Itogi, 1970,* vol. 1, table 5.

13. The 1959 census reported 2,243 Jews in the rural settlements of Zhitomir *oblast'*; the 1970 census found only 575.

14. M. Altshuler, "Kavim le-dmuto ha-demografit shel ha-kibuts ha-yehudi be-vrit-ha-moatsot," *Gesher,* No. 2-3 (1966): 19.

15. The following data from the 1979 census have appeared in print thus far: (1) 18,733 Jews, as opposed to 22,149 recorded in the 1970 census, dwelled in the Dagestan autonomous republic; (2) 10,166 Jews dwelled in the Jewish autonomous *oblast'*, or 5.4 percent of the total population; (3) 30,450 Jews (0.5 percent of the population) dwelled in Moscow *oblast'* outside the city itself in 1979, as opposed to the 36,316 reported in the 1970 census; (4) 6,361 Jews dwelled in Khabarovsk *krai* (not included in the Jewish autonomous *oblast'*) against 7,461 in 1970. *Vestnik statistiki,* no. 7 (1980): 46, 50, 56, 60.

16. For data on emigration, see Ts. Alexander (Ts. Netser), "Mediniyut ha-aliya shel brit-ha-moatsot (1968-1978)," *Behinot,* nos. 8-9 (1977-1978): 47. In 1970-1979 11,750 Jews emigrated from Kiev, 14,860 from Chernovtsy, and 5,460 from L'vov.

17. J. Newth, "Jews in the Ukraine: A Statistical Analysis," *Bulletin on Soviet and East European Jewish Affairs,* no. 2 (1969): 16-19.

18. Calculations based on A. Susokolov and A. Novitskaia, "Etnicheskaia i sotsial'no-professional'naia gomogennost' brakov," *Sovetskaia etnografiia,* no. 6 (1981): 18.

19. Alexander, "Mediniyut ha-aliya," p. 47.

20. Y. Lestschinsky writes, without indicating a source or the basis for his calculations, that at the time of the 1939 census, there were 400,000 Jews in Moscow. Y. Lestschinsky, *Ha-yehudim be-rusia ha-sovietit* (Tel Aviv, 1943), p. 143. Doubt, however, must be expressed with regard to the accuracy of this figure.

M. Vydro, *Naselenie moskvy* (Moscow, 1976), p. 13, however, provides the following data on the total population of Moscow between 1926 and 1939:

Date	Population
December 1926	2,026,000
1933	3,663,000
1936	3,550,000
January 1939	4,137,000

These data indicate that between 1926 and 1933, Moscow's population grew at a rate of 11.5 percent per year. Between 1933 and 1936, the population declined at a rate of 1.0 percent per year, following the new passport laws. Between 1936 and January 1939, the number of residents increased by 8.3 percent per year. Between 1933 and 1939, the mean annual rate of growth was 2.2 percent. In December 1926, Jews comprised 6.5 percent of the residents of the city, or 131,700 persons, and in 1933, they comprised 6.6 percent, or 241,800 persons. Ibid., p. 30. Thus, between 1926 and 1933, the mean annual rate of growth of the Jewish population was 12 percent, compared with 11.5 percent for the population as a whole. Hence, it appears that the annual rate of growth of the Jewish population was 4.3 percent, higher than that of the population as a whole. It will be assumed, therefore, that between 1933 and 1939, the mean annual rate of increase of the Jewish population exceeded that of the total population by 5 percent, and amounts to 2.3 percent, or even to 3 percent, a year, in contrast to the 2.2 percent noted for the total. Even if the annual growth rate of the Jewish population amounted to 3 percent between 1933 and 1939, this would imply an increment of 44,000, and the Jewish population of the city would have amounted to about 286,0000 persons in January 1939, or 6.9 percent of the total.

21. For a description of the city's districts, see *Kyiv, Entsiklopedichnii dovidnyk* (Kyiv, 1981), pp. 155-56, 198-99, 206-8, 338-39, 401, 484-86, 514-15, 695-96.

CHAPTER 4

1. L. Zinger, *Dos banayte folk* (Moscow, 1941), p. 42; *Itogi vsesoiuznoi perepisi naseleniia 1959 goda* (Moscow, 1962), general volume, table 5.

2. Calculated according to *Itogi, 1959,* general volume, table 5.

3. It is difficult to accept the hypothesis of J. Litvak and M. Checinski, "Yehudei brit-ha-moatzot be-mifkad ha-ukhlusim mi-shnat 1970," *Shvut,* no. 4 (1976): 13, who state: "the Nazis spared neither men nor women [in the areas they controlled], while [in Soviet-controlled areas] the majority of men of military age apparently were conscripted, many of whom did not return, while a relatively large number of the women were evacuated to the rear, and not a few of them returned afterward to their previous places of residence." In the Soviet-German war, the proportion of Jewish soldiers among those who fell in battle was similar to their proportion in the population as a whole. If the hypothesis of Litvak and Checinski were correct, the imbalance between the sexes reported in the 1959 census would have to be greater in the Jewish than in the total population; the reverse is in fact the case. Study of the Holocaust in the pre-1939 territory of the Soviet Union is still in its infancy, although the article by W. Orbach, "The Destruction of the Jews in the Nazi-Occupied Territories of the USSR," *Soviet Jewish Affairs,* no. 2 (1976): 14-51, does present the distribution by sex of Jews aged 15 and over who were murdered by the Germans in Lepel and Smolensk. These data indicate that 804 women and 474 men were murdered.

4. Computed according to Zinger, *Dos banayte folk,* appendix 2.

5. *Itogi vsesoiuznoi perepisi naseleniia 1970 goda,* vol. 2, table 1.

6. Zinger, *Dos banayte folk,* appendix 2; *Itogi, 1959,* Uzbekistan volume, table 53.

7. *Narodnoe khoziaistvo i kul'turnoe stroitel'stvo Bashkirii* (Ufa, 1964), p. 19.

8. *Narodnoe khoziaistvo Tatarskoi ASSR* (Kazan', 1966), p. 7.

9. Computed according to *Permskaia oblast'* (Perm', 1959), p. 269; *Itogi, 1959,* RSFSR volume, table 5.

10. See *Statistika migratsii naseleniia* (Moscow, 1973); V. Perevedentsev, "Vzaimosviaz' migratsii naseleniia i etnicheskogo sblizheniia narodov v sovremennykh usloviiakh SSSR," in *Voprosy naseleniia i demograficheskoi statistiki* (Moscow, 1966), pp. 106-15; V. Perevedentsev, "Sovremennaia migratsiia naseleniia SSSR," in *Narodonaselenie i ekonomika* (Moscow, 1967), pp. 99-118; A. Maikov, "Osnovnye napravleniia migratsii i sovershenstvovanie territorial'nogo

pereraspredeleniia trudovykh resursov," in *Narodonaselenie* (Moscow, 1973), pp. 27-42; W. Pokszyszewski, "O etnograficzno-geograficznych aspektach migracji wewnetrznych w ZSSR," in *Problemy migracji wewnetrznych w Polsce i ZSSR* (Warsaw, 1978), pp. 218-25.

11. *Vestnik statistiki*, no. 2 (1973): pp. 87-88.

12. Ibid.

13. A. Kholmogorov, *Internatsional'nye cherty sovetskikh natsii* (Moscow, 1970), p. 48.

14. Computed according to V. Onikienko and V. Popovkin, *Kompleksnoe issledovanie migratsionnykh protsessov* (Moscow, 1973), p. 34; V. Naulko, *Razvitie mezhetnicheskikh sviazei na Ukraine* (Kiev, 1975), pp. 78-79.

15. Onikienko and Popovkin, *Kompleksnoe issledovanie*, pp. 32, 38-44.

CHAPTER 5

1. *Narodnoe obrazovanie v SSSR, sbornik dokumentov, 1917-1973 gg.* (Moscow, 1974), pp. 111-15, 120.

2. Ibid., pp. 49-61, 70, 167, 194-95. E. Efanasenko, "Nekotorye zadachi vseobshchego obucheniia detei," *Narodnoe obrazovanie*, no. 1 (1959): 14-20; E. Zhil'tsov, "Rol' srednikh uchebnykh zavedenii v povyshenii obshcheobrazovatel' nogo urovnia naseleniia," in *Obrazovatel'naia i sotsial'no professional'naia struktura naseleniia SSSR* (Moscow, 1975), pp. 12-23.

3. *Narodnoe obrazovanie* (1974): 218.

4. Ibid., p. 58.

5. *Srednee spetsial'noe obrazovanie v SSSR* (Moscow, 1962), pp. 3-10, 32.

6. *Vysshaia shkola v SSSR za 50 let* (Moscow, 1967), p. 165; *Vysshee obrazovanie v SSSR* (Moscow, 1961), p. 10.

7. On the distribution of institutions of higher learning within the various republics and on the mean number of students enrolled, see M. Altshuler, "Talmidim yehudiim be-hinukh ha-miktsoi ha-al-tikhoni ve-hagavoha be-vrit-ha-moatsot be-shnot ha-shishim," *Behinot*, no. 7 (1976): 22, and L. Novikov, "Die Nationalitätenproblematik der sowjetishen Hochschulen," *Osteuropa*, no. 12 (1981): pp. 1090-98.

8. *Vysshaia shkola*, pp. 204-6; *Vysshee obrazovanie v SSSR, statisticheskii sbornik* (Moscow, 1961), p. 17.

9. According to a decree of the Soviet Ministry of Education dated July 3, 1956, all institutions of higher education are required to teach three specified courses: Communist party history, political economy, and dialectical and historical materialism. The decree specifies that between 390 and 460 hours are to be devoted to these subjects. In the mid-1960s, between 20 and 27 percent of the total number of teaching hours in technical institutes and medical and agricultural schools were devoted to such subjects as political economy, history of the party, and historical materialism and scientific atheism. *Vysshaia shkola*, pp. 215-17; *Vysshee obrazovanie*, pp. 80-82.

10. The length of the course of studies at *tekhnikum* and at VUZ relates to full-time students who do not work while engaged in study.

11. *Narodnoe obrazovanie*, p. 61.

12. Persons with incomplete higher education include students enrolled at the date of the census and those who had studied at a VUZ in the past (without finishing) who have completed at least half the course of study for which they were enrolled. Enrolled and former students who have completed less than half the course of study are listed in terms of the schooling they had acquired before entering VUZ—for the most part secondary school or secondary vocational education. *Itogi vsesoiuznoi perepisi naseleniia 1970 goda,* 3:4.

13. L. Zinger, *Dos banayte folk* (Moscow, 1941), appendix 2.

14. According to the 1939 census, there were at that time in the Soviet Union 83 persons with seven or more years of schooling per 1,000 persons in the population as a whole, while in 1959 their number was 281 per 1,000. *Itogi, 1959,* table 57, general volume.

15. In the eight specified republics, there were in the urban Jewish population 616 persons with seven or more years of schooling per 1,000 and 543 in the rural population. Calculated from *Itogi, 1959,* tables 53, 57, of the relevant volumes.

16. There were for each 1,000 males in the urban Jewish population 615 who had attended school for seven or more years, and in the rural 548. For females, the corresponding figures were 617 and 538, respectively (calculated from the source cited in note 15).

17. Number of persons per 1,000 with seven or more years of schooling in the urban population for selected nationalities, 1959, are as follows:

Jews (total Jewish population in eight republics)	613
Russians	370
Ukrainians	404
Belorussians	405
Georgians	545
Azerbaidzhanis	312
Lithuanians	311
Latvians	432
Armenians	392

Itogi, 1959, general volume, table 57.

18. The proportion of Jews in the RSFSR with secondary vocational education was 1.8 times that of the Jewish population of Moldavia, 1.2 times that of Belorussia, and 1.1 times that of the Ukraine. See table 5F.

19. The proportion of Jews in the RSFSR with a secondary education was 1.4 times that of Moldavia and Belorussia and 1.1 times that of the Ukraine. See table 5F.

20. Calculated according to *Itogi, 1959,* table 57, in the relevant volumes, and *Itogi, 1970,* vol. 4, tables 39-41, 47, 48.

21. Calculated according to *Itogi, 1970,* vol. 4, tables 39-41, 47, 48.

22. In 1959 there were 23 persons with a VUZ education for every 1,000 persons

aged 10 or more in the Soviet Union; in 1970 there were 42. Corresponding figures for the urban population were 40 and 62, respectively. *Itogi,* 1970, vol. 3, table 3.

23. In 1959 there were 11 persons with an incomplete VUZ education for each 1,000 persons aged 10 or over in the Soviet Union; in 1970 there were 13. Corresponding figures for the urban population were 17 and 20. Ibid.

24. Ibid.

25. Number of *Tekhnikum* students per 1,000 VUZ students for selected nationalities, 1961-1976, are as follows:

Nationality	1961/62	1965/66	1970/71	1972/73	1974/75	1976/77
Russian	1,114	998	990	977	959	942
Lithuanian	1,278	1,166	1,133	1,114	1,098	1,039
Estonian	1,093	968	866	853	865	803
Latvian	1,183	981	904	891	903	888
Azerbaidzhani	907	785	669	655	701	731

Narodnoe khoziaistvo SSSR v 1961g. (Moscow, 1962), p. 700; *Narodnoe khoziaistvo SSSR v. 1965g.* (Moscow, 1966), p. 701; *Narodnoe obrazovanie, nauka i kul'tura v SSSR* (Moscow, 1971), p. 196; *Narodnoe khoziaistvo SSSR v 1972g.* (Moscow, 1972), p. 651; *Narodnoe obrazovanie, nauka i kul'tura v SSSR* (Moscow, 1977), pp. 208, 282; *Narodnoe khoziaistvo SSSR za 60 let* (Moscow, 1977), p. 588.

26. For exact tabulation, see Altshuler, "Talmidim yehudiim," pp. 43-45.

27. Ibid., pp. 46, 49.

28. Ibid., pp. 47, 48.

29. Ibid., p. 46.

30. Ibid., p. 47.

31. In 1965/66 there were 8 million students enrolled in the two highest grades of secondary school, and in 1976/77 there were close to 10 million. *Narodnoe obrazavanie SSSR za 60 let* (Moscow, 1977), p. 577.

32. Zhil'tsov, "Rol' srednikh uchebnykh zavedenii," p. 21.

33. Table 5K.

34. M. Sonin, "Otsenka urovnia i struktury obrazovaiia," in *Obrazovatel'naia i sotsial'no-professional'naia struktura naseleniia SSSR* (Moscow, 1975), pp. 3-11. In 1970 there were 1.8 students enrolled in VUZs (including day, evening and correspondence students) for each secondary school graduate; in 1975 there were 1.4 and in 1977 only 1.2. *Vestnik statistiki,* no. 7 (1978): 94-95.

35. M. Daniialov, "K voprosu o natsional'noi strukture spetsialistov s vysshim obrazovaniem," in *Sotsiologicheskii sbornik* (Makhachkala, 1970), pp. 103-16.

36. M. Mishin, *Obshchestvennyi progress* (Gor'ki, 1970), pp. 282-83.

37. Tabulations are not available for 1964/65, 1971/72, 1975/76, and 1977/78. All tabulations on students in institutions of higher learning include the three frameworks of courses of study (day, evening, and correspondence courses) unless otherwise specified.

38. See Altshuler, "Talmidim yehudiim," p. 52.

39. An official verification of a case of expulsion from an institute of higher learning as a consequence of requesting an exit visa was published in *Evreiskii samizdat* in 1970.

40. Calculated from *Itogi, 1959*, general volume, table 53; *Narodnoe obrazovanie* (1971): 196.

41. *Sovetskii soiuz*, no. 11 (1965): 10.

42. *Narodnoe obrazovanie* (1971): 278.

43. For the distribution of *aspirants* allocated to "other national groups," see Altshuler, "Talmidim yehudiim," p. 33.

44. Table 1 of Zvi Halevy's article and his explication are not sufficiently clear. There is a reference to students in programs leading to "advanced degrees" without any indication of what degrees are meant. In his explication, the author uses the term *students* and states that "the majority of the 'others' among the students in institutions of higher learning are Jews . . . the group of 'others' consists of at least 90 percent Jews, if not more." Since the group of others includes all people who lack a union republic, as shown by the tabulations, this statement is not precise. Z. Halevy, "Yehudim be-kerev studentim u-vaalei miktsoot hofshiim be-vrit-ha-moatsot ba-shanim 1947-1970," *Shvut*, no. 1 (1974): 36-38.

45. As the tabulations indicate, the distribution of Jewish VUZ students by republic is not the same in 1970/71 and 1960/61. Checinski's estimates with regard to this matter are not precise in any case M. Checinski, "Soviet Jews and Higher Education," *Soviet Jewish Affairs*, no. 2 (1973): 14.

46. Calculated from tables 3G and 5.11.

47. In 1965/66 there were 447 Jewish students in Omsk *oblast'*, comprising 1.21 percent of all VUZ students. Of these, 210 (47.0 percent) were day students, 124 (27.7 percent) evening students, and 113 (25.3 percent) studied by correspondence. The calculation of the Jewish population of the *oblast'* for this year is derived from the censuses of 1959 and 1970. *Narodnoe khoziaistvo Omskoi oblasti* (Omsk, 1967), p. 221.

48. In 1959/60 there were 118 Jewish students in this republic, comprising 2.1 percent of all VUZ students; in 1966/67 there were 132, or 1.0 percent of the total. *Checheno-Ingushskaia ASSR za 40 let* (Groznyi, 1960), p. 154; *Checheno-Ingushskaia ASSR za 50 let* (Groznyi, 1967), p. 147.

49. Dan Fischer, Moscow correspondent for the *Los Angeles Times*, described the extensive preparations in the city in advance of the entrance qualification procedure for university students in 1977. In that year, there were five to six candidates for every available place in higher education institutions in Moscow. *Maariv*, August 31, 1977.

50. See Z. Halevy, *Jewish University Students and Professionals in Tsarist and Soviet Russia* (Tel Aviv, 1976), pp. 209-11.

51. M. Hindus, *House without a Roof* (New York, 1961), p. 315.

52. On this topic see A. Nove, "La populazione ebraica nell'URSS," in *Gli ebrei nell'URSS* (Milano, 1966), pp. 49-75.

53. See Altshuler, Talmidim yehudiim," p. 52.

54. See also A. Nove and J. Newth, "The Jewish Population: Demographic Trends and Occupational Patterns," in L. Kochan (ed.), *The Jews in Soviet Russia Since 1917* (London, 1972), p. 146.

55. W. Korey, *The Soviet Cage* (New York, 1973), p. 59.

56. See Altshuler, "Talmidim yehudiim," pp. 54, 56.

57. Ibid., p. 54.

58. The number of VUZ students in the Soviet Union increased by 87 percent between 1960/61 and 1968/69, while in Kazakhstan the increase was 144 percent.

59. See Altshuler, "Talmidim yehudiim," p. 56.

60. Ibid., pp. 55-56.

61. Ibid., pp. 55-57.

62. See tables 2.25 and 2.26.

CHAPTER 6

1. *Itogi, 1970,* vol. 5, pp. 3, 4.

2. N. Fedorova, "Sotsialno-ekonomicheskii sostav naseleniia SSSR," in *Vsesoiuznaia perepis' naseleniia 1970 goda* (Moscow, 1976), p. 211.

3. *Narodnoe khoziaistvo SSSR v 1959 g.* (Moscow, 1960), pp. 843-44.

4. Persons with seven or more years of schooling per 1,000 economically active urbanites, 1959, are as follows:

Georgians	774
Latvians	658
Armenians	628
Kirgiz	607
Estonians	588
Ukrainians	575
Azerbaidzhanis	570
Russians	565
Belorussians	544
Kazakhs	516
Turkmen	511
Uzbeks	491
Lithuanians	430
Tadzhiks	428
Moldavians	353

Itogi, 1970, vol. 4, table 56.

5. Persons with seven or more years of schooling per 1,000 economically active urbanites, 1970, are as follows:

Georgians	889
Kirgiz	784
Ukrainians	776

Armenians	772
Russians	747
Belorussians	742
Latvians	742
Kazakhs	739
Azerbaidzhanis	731
Estonians	722
Uzbeks	693
Turkmen	684
Tadzhiks	641
Moldavians	635
Lithuanians	628

Itogi, 1970, vol. 4, table 56.

6. See A. Vinokur, *Average Net Monetary Income of Worker and Employee Families in the USSR from 1964 to 1973* (Jerusalem, 1976), pp. 49-52.

7. In November 1966, there were 169,300 employed Jews with secondary vocational training in the USSR; in November 1970, there were 181,800 (see table 6.5). The annual growth averaged 1.85 percent, and therefore the figure for November 1969 was 178,400.

8. In November 1966, there were 327,800 employed Jews with a VUZ education in the USSR and 356,800 at the end of 1970 (see table 6.9), an average annual increase of 2.21 percent. Hence, at the end of 1969, the figure stood at 348,900.

9. Calculated from *Itogi, 1970,* vol. 2, table 1; vol. 6, table 1.

10. Calculated from *Shnaton statisti leyisrael, 1972* (Jerusalem, 1973), pp. 21, 23.

11. Economically active Jews with secondary vocational education in the RSFSR by area, year, and percentage in total of this stratum in the area are as follows:

Area	Year	Economically Active Jews	Percentage of Total Stratum	Source
Irkutsk *oblast'*	1959	719	1.4	*Narodnoe khoziaistvo*
	1960	749	1.3	*Irkutskoi oblasti*
	1961	931	1.5	(Irkutsk, 1962), p. 200
Vologda *oblast'*	1966	107	0.2	*Narodnoe khoziaistvo Vologodskoi oblasti* (Vologda, 1967), p. 119
Penza *oblast'*	1966	264	0.6	*Penzenskaia oblast' za 50 let sovetskoi vlasti (Saratov,* 1967), p. 143;
	1970	241	0.4	*50 let v edinoi mnogonatsional'noi*

				sem'e naradov SSSR (Penza, 1972), p. 164
Smolensk *oblast'*	1970	476	1.0	*Narodnoe khoziaistvo Smolenskoi oblasti v 1970 godu* (Smolensk, 1972), p. 136
Chita *oblast'*	1957	110	0.6	*Narodnoe khoziaistvo*
	1961	118	0.5	*Chitinskoi oblasti*
	1964	104	0.4	(Irkutsk, 1965), p. 115
Chuvash ASSR	1957	66	0.4	*Chuvashiia za 40 let*
	1959	79	0.4	(Cheboksary, 1960), p. 140
	1960	97	0.4	*Sovetskaia Chuva-*
	1964	96	0.3	*shiia za 45 let* (Cheboksary, 1965), . 127
Checheno-Ingush ASSR	1959	155	1.1	*Chechino-Ingushskaia ASSR za 40 let* (Groznyi, 1960), p. 177
	1966	224	0.8	*Checheno-Ingushskaia ASSR za 50 let* (Groznyi, 1967), p. 117
Iakut ASSR	1966	147	0.5	*Iakutiia za 50 let* (Iakutsk, 1967), p. 109
Mordvin ASSR	1957	43	0.3	*Mordovskaia ASSR*
	1960	54	0.3	*za gody sovetskoi*
	1964	58	0.2	*vlasti* (Saransk, 1967),
	1966	48	0.2	p. 139
Altai *krai*	1966	301	0.4	*Altaiskii kpai za 50 let* (Barnaul, 1967), p. 76

12. *Narodne gospodarstvo mista Kyeva* (Kyiv, 1963), p. 99.

13. In the Karaganda *oblast'*, in which 4,999 Jews lived in 1959 and 5,040 in 1970, there were only 385 economically active Jews in the indicated stratum in 1961 and 389 in 1966. *Narodnoe khoziaistvo Karagandskoi oblasti* (Karaganda, 1967), p. 528.

14. *Kishinev* (Kishinev, 1963), p. 107.

15. In December 1959, there were in Baku 1,100 economically active Jews in the indicated stratum, who constituted 4.1 percent of the active persons in the stratum as a whole. At the end of 1966, this number amounted to 1,500, or 3.4 percent of the total. *Baku za 40 let v tsifrakh* (Baku, 1960), p. 51; *Baku v tsifrakh* (Baku, 1967), p. 62.

16. In 1957 there were in Dushanbe 246 economically active Jews in the indicated stratum (4.1 percent of the total); in 1960 there were 412 (4.5 percent) and in 1966 632 (4.1 percent). *Gorod Dushanbe k 50-letiiu velikoi oktiabr'skoi sotsialisticheskoi revoliutsii* (Dushanbe, 1967), p. 66.

17. In 1960 there were in Kirgizia 478 Jews in the indicated stratum, and in 1961

there were 489, or 1.1 percent of the total number of economically active persons in that stratum. *Narodnoe khoziaistvo Kirgizskoi ASSR v 1960 godu* (Frunze, 1960), p. 168; *Srednee spetsial'noe obrazovanie v SSSR* (Moscow, 1962), pp. 44-45.

18. Economically active persons in the indicated stratum in the Abkhaz ASSR, 1961-1970, for total and Jewish populations are as follows:

Year	Total	Jewish	Percentage
1961	8,056	74	0.9
1964	9,769	74	0.8
1965	11,573	126	1.1
1970	12,437	121	1.0

Narodnoe khoziaistvo Abkhazskoi ASSR (Tbilisi, 1967), p. 233; Ibid. (1973), p. 290.

19. According to the Soviet definition, "The intelligentsia is an intermediary social stratum in which are included persons occupied in intellectual work. The intelligentsia plays an important role in the development of society and its activities. Those associated with it are primarily occupied with the development of science, technology, art, education, etc." *Istoricheskaia entsiklopediia,* vol. 6, p. 111. The Soviets generally include in this stratum persons with higher or secondary vocational education along with writers, artists, and the like. On the term *Soviet intelligentsia* see also L. Churchward, *The Soviet Intelligentsia* (London, 1973), pp. 3-15.

20. See table 5K.

21. Economically active Jews with VUZ education in the RSFSR by area, year, and group size relative to total economically active stratum in area (sources as for note 11 and *Narodnoe khoziaistvo Tuvinskoi ASSR* [Kyzyl, 1967], p. 133; ibid., 1971, p. 222) are as follows:

Area	Year	Economically Active Jews	Percentage of total Stratum
Irkutsk *oblast'*	1959	1,195	4.1
	1960	1,296	4.2
	1961	1,508	4.4
Vologda *oblast'*	1966	178	0.9
Penza *oblast'*	1966	548	2.2
	1970	581	1.8
Smolensk *oblast'*	1970	796	3.4
Chita *oblast'*	1957	306	3.2
	1961	283	2.4
	1964	232	1.8
Chuvash ASSR	1957	148	1.5

	1959	164	1.4
	1960	164	1.3
	1964	197	1.3
Checheno-Ingush ASSR	1959	445	4.9
	1966	468	3.0
Iakut ASSR	1966	212	1.4
Mordvin ASSR	1957	108	1.2
	1960	153	1.4
	1964	149	1.1
	1966	132	0.8
Tuvin ASSR	1957	28	1.6
	1959	30	1.3
	1960	21	0.9
	1966	13	0.3
	1970	13	0.3
Altai *krai*	1966	630	1.7

22. *Vysshee obrazovanie v SSSR* (Moscow, 1961), p. 70.

23. *Ukrains'ka RSR v tsifrakh v 1964 rotsi* (Kyiv, 1965), p. 129.

24. *Narodne gospodarstvo mista Kyeva* (Kyiv, 1963), p. 99.

25. *Zhenshchiny Moldavii* (Kishinev, 1961), p. 39.

26. *Zhenshchiny v Kirgizskoi SSR* (Frunze, 1960), p. 54.

27. *Kishinev,* p. 107.

28. In 1957 there were 760 economically active Jewish professionals in Dushanbe, capital of Tadzhikistan, who constituted 10.4 percent of the economically active stratum in the city and 67 percent of all economically active Jewish professionals in the republic. In 1960 this number had increased to 832, which was now 9.8 percent and 71 percent, respectively, of the indicated base populations. In 1966 these values were 1,059; 7.2 percent, and 75 percent, respectively. *Gorod Dushanbe,* p. 66.

29. On March 20, 1937, the Soviet government decided to distinguish two academic degrees (*uchenye stepeni*) and three academic ranks. The two degrees, *Kandidat* and *Doktor nauk,* are conferred upon the completion of certain research tasks, and the academic ranks are determined according to employment. The first of these ranks is *asistent* in VUZs and junior researcher at research facilities. The second rank is that of *dotsent* in teaching institutions and senior researcher at research institutes. The third level is professor, applicable to those employed in both types of facility. The term *professor* does not connote a higher rank than *Doktor nauk.* A Soviet professor may not, in fact, be a *Doktor.* See *Narodnoe obrazovanie v SSSR* (Moscow, 1974), pp. 483-85.

30. *Narodnoe khoziaistvo SSSR v 1961 g.* (Moscow, 1962), p. 810. See also *The Scientific Intelligentsia in the USSR: Structure and Dynamics of Personnel* (Moscow, 1976), pp. 91-92.

31. *Narodnoe khoziaistvo SSSR v 1961 g.* (Moscow, 1962), p. 810. Laboratory assistants, technicians, and others who perform auxiliary tasks at teaching and research institutions are not counted as scientific workers. See *Statisticheskii slovar'* (Moscow, 1965), p. 333.

32. *Narodnoe khoziaistvo,* 1959, p. 75; *Narodnoe obrazovanie,* 1977, pp. 308-9.

33. *Vestnik statistiki,* no. 4 (1974): 92; *Narodnoe obrazovanie,* 1977, pp. 382, 308-9.

34. *Moskva v tsifrakh, 1966-1970 gg.* (Moscow, 1972), p. 140. The tabulations on scientific workers in Moscow are as of January 1, 1971, but those with regard to the nation as a whole and in the individual republics relate to the end of the year; for this reason the Moscow data are treated as if they relate to the end of 1970.

35. *Vestnik statistiki,* no. 4 (1974): 92.

36. For example, in 1963 there were in Azerbaidzhan 124 Jewish scientists (of whom 110 possessed the degree of *Kandidat* and 14 of *Doktor*), who comprised 4.6 percent of all scientists in the republic. *Azerbaidzhan v tsifrakh* (Baku, 1964), pp. 212-13. In Georgia there were in 1960 only 45 Jewish scientists (1.2 percent), and in 1966 there were 83, who comprised 1.7 percent of all scientists in the republic. *Sovetskaia Gruziia k 50-letiiu velikoi oktiabr'skoi sotsialisticheskoi revoliutsii* (Tbilisi, 1967), p. 240.

37. *Moskva v tsifrakh,* p. 140.

38. *Struktura sovetskoi intelligentsii* (Minsk, 1970), p. 97.

39. *Sovetskaia Moldaviia,* May 16, 1964.

40. *Narodnoe khoziaistvo SSSR v 1964 g.* (Moscow, 1965), p. 734.

41. In 1978 Jews constituted 3.4 percent of the Soviet Union's medical personnel. The total number of such personnel for that year was 3,600,800 (928,700 doctors and 2,672,100 workers with a secondary professional certificate). Thus, there were about 122,400 Jews in this sector. If the ratio among Jews of doctors to other medical workers was the same as among non-Jews, the number of Jewish doctors would have been 31,600. There is reason to suspect, however, that among Jews, the proportion of doctors exceeded the average for the country, making 31,600 a minimum figure. Calculated from I. Kapeliush, "Vegn eynike" p. 140, and *Narodnoe khoziaistvo SSSR v 1978 g.* (Moscow, 1979), p. 507.

42. Out of 5,687 members of the Writers' Union in February 1967, there were 4,116 (72 percent) who had completed a VUZ and another 1,167 (21 percent) with an incomplete higher education. Forty-four members of the Writers' Union wrote in Yiddish. *Chetvertyi s"ezd pisatelei SSSR* (Moscow, 1968), pp. 280-89. By 1972 the number of members of the Writers' Union had increased to 7,280, of whom 49 wrote in Yiddish. *Literaturnaia entsiklopediia,* vol. 7:112. At the initial appearance of the Yiddish periodical *Sovietish heymland* in 1961, there were 113 persons employed as writers or correspondents, and, according to a statement by the editor, there were 134 correspondents in 1967. A. Vergelis, "Sakh-haklen un oiszikhtn," *Sovietish heymland,* no. 8 (1976): 7, 8. It therefore appears that the majority of these writers are not members of the Writers' Union.

43. *Chetvertyi s"ezd pisatelei,* p. 254.

44. *Pervyi vsesoiuznyi s"ezd zhurnalistov* (Moscow, 1960), p. 284.

45. *Tretyi s"ezd pisatelei SSSR* (Moscow, 1959), p. 64; *Chetvertyi s"ezd pisatelei,* p. 289.

46. *Ezhegodnik bol'shoi sovetskoi entsiklopedii* (1964), p. 25.

47. *Sovetskaia Moldaviia,* May 16, 1964.

48. I. Kapeliush, "Vegn eynike," pp. 139-40.

49. See A. Voronel', "Sotsial'nye predposylki natsional'nogo prebuzhdeniia evreev," *Evreiskii samizdat* (Jerusalem, 1974), 4:3-18.

CHAPTER 7

1. In the first Soviet census (1920), "native tongue" was defined as "the language spoken within the family (and in multilanguage families, that of the mother)." In the 1926 census, this was defined as the "language which the respondent commands most fully or which he generally speaks." *Statisticheskii slovar'* (1965), p. 707.

2. See *Tolkovy slovar' russkogo iazyka* (Moscow, 1939), 3:1368-69, 1372.

3. B. Brutskus, *Statistika evreiskogo naseleniia* (Petersburg, 1909), p. 34.

4. Z. Lipset, "A Note on Yiddish as the Language of Soviet Jews in the Census of 1939," *The Jewish Journal of Sociology,* no. 1 (1970): 55-57.

5. G. Sariev formulated this approach in the following words: "Every other language [other than the native tongue] is differentiated from the native tongue by the fact that while it indeed may be a means of communication, it also acts as a means of acquaintance with other cultures, but if the social and psychological connotations associated with this language are not acceptable to the speaker, if they are foreign to his personal sense of being, it is clear that it cannot become his native tongue." G. Sariev, "K obshchestvenno-psikhologicheskoi sushchnosti poniatiia 'rodnoi iazyk'," *Izvestiia akademii nauk Azerbaidzhanskoi SSR,* no. 4 (1974): 102.

6. My thanks to S. Ettinger, who heads this project and has made these data available to me.

7. Zionist activists published shortly before the 1970 census a special proclamation calling on Soviet Jews to declare a Jewish language as their native tongue. This declaration was mentioned several times at the Leningrad trial (December 1970) as evidence of anti-Soviet activity. *Ma'ariv* (Tel Aviv), weekly supplement, July 23, 1971.

8. J. Kantor, "Eynike bamerkungen un oysfirn tsu di farefntlekhte sakh-haklen fun folks-tseylung in ratnfarband dem 15tn yanuar 1959," *Bleter far geshikhte* 15 (1962-1963): 142-54.

9. *Itogi, 1959,* general volume, table 53; *Itogi, 1970,* vol. 4, table 4.

10. See E. Lewis, *Multilingualism in the Soviet Union* (The Hague and Paris, 1972), pp. 44-48, 149; *Itogi, 1970,* vol. 4, table 4; *Vestnik statistiki,* no. 7 (1980): 41-43.

11. I. Zinchenko, "Natsional'nyi sostav i iazyki naseleniia," in *Vsosoiuznaia perepis' naseleniia 1970 goda* (Moscow, 1976), p. 195.

12. Sh. Redlich, "Ha-atsumot shel yehudei brit-ha-moatsot ke-bitui le-hitorerut leumit (1968-1970)," *Behinot,* no. 5 (1974): 24.

13. *Itogi, 1959,* Georgia volume, note to table 53.

14. Ibid., table 53.

CHAPTER 8

1. See T. Rigby, *Communist Party Membership in the USSR, 1917-1967* (Princeton, 1968), pp. 10-12.

2. Ibid., pp. 3-6; M. Fainsod, *How Russia Is Ruled* (Cambridge, Mass., 1963), p. 247.

3. Until the publication of these tabulations, T. Rigby, *Communist Party Membership,* p. 387, estimated that between 1.5 and 1.7 percent of party

membership was Jewish. J. Newth and Z. Katz, "Proportion of Jews in the Communist Party of the Soviet Union," *Bulletin on Soviet and East European Jewish Affairs,* no. 4 (1969): 37-38, assumed that in 1961 between 2 and 3 percent of the party membership was Jewish.

4. Rigby, *Communist Party Membership,* pp. 88-100.

5. *Statisticheskie materialy po evreiskoi demografii i ekonomike,* no. 4 (1929): 29.

6. Ibid.

7. Rigby, *Communist Party Membership,* p. 373.

8. At the beginning of 1959, 2.9 percent of the population aged 20 or more had a VUZ education; at the beginning of 1956, 11.2 percent of party members and candidates had that level of schooling and 13.7 percent at the beginning of 1962. With regard to secondary and incomplete higher education, the corresponding proportions were 12.7 percent and 25.8 percent, respectively. In 1964 about half of all Soviet scientists were party members. Ibid., pp. 407, 448.

9. For example, in the city of Sverdlovsk, a refugee center during World War II and in which many of these refugees appear to have settled afterward, the total number of party members and candidates increased by 295 percent between 1940 and 1965, while the number of Jews increased by 326 percent. In the city of Nizhnii Novgorod, the total number of Communists rose by 390 percent during this period, while the Jews' factor of increase was 13.5. Part of these increases was due to the growth of the local Jewish communities, but it is almost certain that rising membership rates contributed as well. S. Begiian, "Leninskii internatsional'nyi printsip postroeniia kommunisticheskoi partii v deistvii," in *Rastsvet i sblizhenie sotsialisticheskikh natsii v SSSR* (Ufa, 1971), pp. 197-98.

10. Admission to candidate membership is by a set procedure whose purpose is to filter out a portion of the applicants. The application for party membership must be accompanied by the recommendations of three current members, each of whom has seniority of at least three years. If the applicant turns out not to live up to the trust placed in him by the party, his sponsors are also liable to be disciplined. After the candidate receives the recommendation of the cell to which he belongs, his application is sent for approval to a higher party echelon. An applicant who has been accepted as a candidate member remains in this status for a year, during which time a wide variety of assignments are given him. Candidacy may be extended for a second year or terminated in failure. J. Hazard, *The Soviet System of Government* (Chicago, 1957), pp. 18-20.

11. *Partiinaia zhizn',* no. 10 (May 1976): 16.

12. *Kommunisticheskaia partiia Azerbaidzhana - boevoi otriad KPSS v tsifrakh, skhemakh i diagrammakh* (Baku, 1979), p. 61.

13. *Kommunist Belorussii,* no. 5 (May 1962): 57.

14. Jews comprised 0.8 percent of the population of the republic. Calculated according to L. Zinger, *Dos banayte folk: tsifern un faktn vegn di yidn in FSSR* (Moscow, 1941), appendix 2, and *Itogi, 1970,* vol. 2, table 1.

15. *Kommunisticheskaia partiia Uzbekistana v tsifrakh* (Tashkent, 1964), table 88.

16. Calculated according to Zinger, *Dos banayte folk,* appendix 2, and *Kom. partiia Uzbekistana,* table 96.

17. This trend is also strongly manifested in other places. For example, in Perm' *oblast'* the total number of party members increased by 32 percent between 1959 and 1965, while the number of Jewish members rose by only 8 percent. It is therefore clear that the proportion of party members who were Jewish declined. Begiian, "Leninskii international'nyi printsip," p. 197.

18. On the eve of the Soviet-German war, there were about 150,000 Jews in Lithuania (not including Vil'nius and environs), and additional 75,000 in the city of Vil'nius, and another 15,000 in the small towns in the neighborhood of this city, all of them annexed at the time. Jews comprised about 46 percent of the urban population of this republic. Y. Lestschinsky, *Tfutsot yisrael le-ahar ha-milhama* (Tel Aviv, 1948), p. 134; D. Levin, "Yerushalaim de'Lita," in *Galed* (Tel Aviv, 1976), 3:214; *Itogi, 1959*, general volume, table 5.

19. *Lietuvos Koministu Partija Skaiciais, 1918-1975* (Vil'nius, 1976), p. 55.

20. *Lietuviu Enciklopedija*, 15 (Boston, 1968), p. 361. My thanks to D. Levin for directing my attention to this book.

21. See B. Pinkus," "Ha-yehudim be-shilton ha-sovieti be-shanim 1939-1971," *Shvut*, no. 2 (1974): 15-35.

22. One delegate for each 300,000 persons is elected to the Soviet of the Union, and to the Soviet of Nationalities, twenty-five from each union republic, eleven from each autonomous republic, five from each autonomous *oblast'*, and one from each national *raion*. Fainsod, *How Russia Is Ruled*, p. 373; *Istoricheskaia entsiklopediia*, 3:377-88.

23. There were 47 Jewish delegates among a total of 1,143 (32 to the Union Soviet and 15 to the Soviet of nationalities), or 4.1 percent. According to the 1939 census, Jews comprised 1.8 percent of the population. *Vybory v verkhovnyi sovet SSSR i v verkhovnye sovety soiuznykh i avtonomnykh respublik* (Moscow, 1939), pp. 11-13; Zinger, *Dos banayte folk*, p. 35.

24. *Vybory* (1939), p. 16; *Eynikayt*, January 4, 7, 9, 28, February 18, 1947; *Pravda*, February 22, 1951.

25. *Vybory* (1939), p. 16; Zinger, *Dos banayte folk*, appendix 2.

26. *Vybory* (1939), p. 16; Zinger, *Dos banayte folk*, appendix 2; *Eynikayt*, January 8, 1947.

27. Zinger, *Dos banayte folk*, appendix 2.

28. *Pravda vostoka*, March 1, 1951.

29. I. Kalin, "Druzhba i bratstvo—moshchnyi faktor obshchestvennogo progressa," *Kommunist Moldavii*, no. 12 (1982): 25.

30. *Sostav deputatov verkhovnykh sovetov soiuznykh, avtonomnykh respublik i mestnykh sovetov deputatov trudiashchikhsia, 1959 g.* (Moscow, 1959), pp. 7, 9.

31. M. Mote, *Soviet Local and Republic Elections: A Description of the 1963 Elections in Leningrad Based on Official Documents, Press Accounts and Private Interviews* (Stanford, 1965), pp. 23-31.

32. In the 1967 elections, the number of Jews in local soviets in Moldavia increased to 257. Their percentage share in the total remained unchanged, however, at 0.8 percent. In 1981, the number of Jewish delegates in local soviets in this republic fell to 118. D. Ursal, *Razvitie obshchestvennykh otnoshenii v sovetskoi Moldavii* (Kishinev, 1967), p. 354; Kalin, "Druzhba i bratstvo," p. 25.

33. In the elections of 1967, 155 Jews were elected to local soviets in

Azerbaidzhan, representing 0.37 percent of the total number of delegates. *Itogi vyborov i sostav deputatov Azerbaidzhanskoi SSR, 1967 g.*, p. 33.

34. D. Harris, "Reasons for CPSU Membership: Insights from Interviews with Emigrants," *Soviet Jewish Affairs,* no. 1 (February 1986): 21-33.

SELECTED BIBLIOGRAPHY

This bibliography includes articles and books that are mainly devoted to the subject of Soviet Jewish demography. It does not include the large number of Soviet publications in which statistical data on Jews can also be found and which appear in the notes of this book.

Abrahamovitz, M. "Ha-yehudim be-mifkad ha-sovieti" (The Jews in the Soviet census). *Molad,* nos. 114-115 (1959): 320-29.

Akharon, I. "Issledovaniia demograficheskikh osobennostei evreiskogo naseleniia SSSR" (A study in the demographic particularities of the Jewish population in the USSR). *Evreiskii samizdat* 15 (1978): 158-76.

Alexander, Z. "Immigration to Israel from the USSR." *Israel Yearbook on Human Rights* 7 (1977): 268-335.

_____. "Mediniyut ha-aliya shel brit-ha-moatsot (1968-1978)" (The emigration Policy of the Soviet Union, 1968-1978). *Behinot,* nos. 8-9 (1977-1978): 7-51.

_____. "Jewish Emigration from the USSR in 1980." *Soviet Jewish Affairs,* no. 2 (1981): 3-21.

Altshuler, M. (ed.). *The Jews in the Soviet Union—1959 Census.* Jerusalem, 1963.

_____. "Kavim le-dmuto ha-demografit shel ha-kibuts ha-yehudi be-vrit-ha-moatsot" (An overview of the demographic physiognomy of the Soviet Jewish community). *Gesher,* nos. 2-3 (1966): 9-30.

_____. "Some Statistics on Mixed Marriages among Soviet Jews." *Bulletin on Soviet and East European Jewish Affairs,* no. 6 (1970): 30-32.

_____. "Ha-yehudim be-mifkad ha-ukhlusin ha-sovieti" (The Jews in the Soviet population census). *Behinot* nos. 2-3 (1972): 9-23.

_____. "The Jews in the Scientific Elite of the Soviet Union." *The Jewish Journal of Sociology,* no. 1 (1973): 45-55.

_____. "Talmidim yehudiim be-hinukh ha-miktsoi ha-al-tikhoni ve-hagavoha be-vrit-ha-moatsot be-shnot ha-shishim" (Jewish students in vocational and higher education in the USSR in the sixties). *Behinot,* no. 7 (1976): 20-57.

_____. "The Jews in the 1979 Soviet Census." *Soviet Jewish Affairs,* no. 3 (1980): 3-12.

_____. "Magamot demografiyot be-kerev yehudei brit-ha-moatsot be-shnot ha-shivim" (Demographic trends of Soviet Jewry in the seventies). *Shvut,* no. 8 (1981): 7-14.

Brutskus, B. *Professional'nyi sostav evreiskogo naseleniia Rosii* (The occupational profile of the Jewish population in Russia). Petersburg, 1908.

_____. *Statistika evreiskogo naseleniia* (Statistics of the Jewish population). Petersburg, 1909.

Checinski, M. "Soviet Jews and Higher Education." *Soviet Jewish Affairs,* no. 2 (1973): 3-16.

DellaPergola, S. *Jewish and Mixed Marriages in Milan, 1901-1968.* Jerusalem, 1972.

Domal'skii, I. *Russkie evrei vchera i segodnia* (Russian Jews in the past and present). Tel Aviv, 1975.

Engelman, U. "Intermarriage among Jews in Germany, USSR and Switzerland." *Jewish Social Studies,* no. 2 (1940): 157-78.

Florsheim, Y. "Le-dmuto ha-demografit shel ha-kibuts ha-yehudi be-vrit-ha-moatsot" (Demographic character of the Jewish community in the USSR). *Behinot,* no. 7 (1976): 58-63.

_____. "Demographic Significance of Jewish Emigration from the USSR." *Soviet Jewish Affairs,* no. 1 (1980): 5-22.

_____. "Mifkad ha-ukhlusin ke-makor le-mispar ha-yehudim be-vrit-ha-moatsot" (The 1979 Census figure for Russian Jewry). *Yahadut Zemanenu* 1 (1983): 343-47.

Halevy, Z. "Yehudim be-kerev studentim u-vaalei miktsoot hofshiim be-vrit-ha-moatsot ba-shanim 1947-1970 (Jews among Soviet students and professionals, 1947-1970). *Shvut,* no. 2 (1974): 36-47.

_____. *Jewish University Students and Professionals in Tsarist and Soviet Russia.* Tel Aviv, 1976.

Hirszovicz, L. "Soviet Jewry in the 1979 Census: Statistical Data." *Soviet Jewish Affairs,* no. 2 (1980): 59-63.

_____. "Further Data on the Jewish Population from the 1979 Soviet Census." *Soviet Jewish Affairs,* no. 2 (1981): 53-61.

Jacobs, E. "Jewish Representation in Local Soviets, 1959-1973." *Soviet Jewish Affairs,* no. 1 (1976): 18-26.

Kantor, J. *Di yidishe bafelkerung in Ukraine* (The Jewish population in the Ukraine). Kiev, 1929.

_____. "Eynike bamerkungen un oysfirn tsu di farefntlekhte sakh-haklen fun folks-tseylung in ratnfarband dem 15tn yanuar 1959" (Some observations on the published data from the 1959 Soviet census). *Bleter far geshikhte* 15 (1962-1963): 142-54.

Kapeliush, I. "Yidn in sovetnfarband" (Jews in the Soviet Union). *Sovetish heymland* (September 1974): 174-77.

_____."Vegn yeinike statistishe ongaban fun der folkstseylung fun 1979" (On some statistical data from the 1979 census). *Sovetish heymland* (December 1980): 136-42.

Larin, Iu. *Evrei i antisemitizm v SSSR* (Jews and anti-Semitism in the USSR). Moscow-Leningrad, 1929.

Lestschinsky, Y. *Dos yidishe folk in tsifern* (The Jewish people in numbers). Berlin, 1922.

_____. *Ha-yehudim be-rusia ha-sovietit* (The Jews in Soviet Russia). Tel Aviv, 1943.

_____. *Tfustsot Yisrael le-ahar ha-milhama* (The Jewish Diaspora after the war). Tel Aviv, 1948.

_____. *Nedudei Yisrael ba-dorot ha-aharonim* (Jewish wanderings in the last generations). Tel Aviv, 1965.

Lewis, R.; Rowland, R.; and Clem, R. *Nationality and Population Change in Russia and USSR.* New York, 1976.

Lipset, Z. "A Note on Yiddish as the Language of Soviet Jews in the Census of 1939." *The Jewish Journal of Sociology,* no. 1 (1970): 55-57.

Litvak, J. and Checinski, M. "Yehudei brit-ha-moatsot be-mifkad ha-ukhlusim mi-shnat 1970" (Soviet Jewry in the 1970 population census). *Shvut,* no. 4 (1976): 7-29.

Mindlin, Z. "Sotsial'nyi sostav i glavnye zaniatiia evreiskogo naseleniia SSSR" (Social composition and employment of the Jewish population in the USSR). *Evrei v SSSR.* Moscow, 1930.

Neuweld, M. "The Latest Soviet Census and the Jews." *Commentary* (May 1960): 426-29.

Newth, J. "A Statistical Study of Intermarriage among Jews in Part of Vil'nius." *Bulletin on Soviet Jewish Affairs,* no. 1 (1968): pp. 64-69.

_____. "Jews in the Ukraine: A Statistical Analysis." *Bulletin on Soviet and East European Jewish Affairs,* no. 2 (1969): 16-19.

Newth, J., and Katz, Z. "Proportion of Jews in the Communist Party of the Soviet Union." *Bulletin on Soviet and East European Jewish Affairs,* no. 4 (1969): 37-38.

Nove, A., and Newth, J. "The Jewish Population: Demographic Trends and Occupational Patterns." In *The Jews in Soviet Russia since 1917.* Edited by L. Kochan. London, 1972.

Redlich, Sh. "Ha-atsumot shel yehudei brit-ha-moatsot ke-bitui le-hitorerut leumit (1968-1970)" (Petitions of Soviet Jews as an expression of national revival, 1968-1970). *Behinot,* no. 5 (1974): 7-24.

Rukhadze, A. *Jews in the USSR.* Moscow, 1978.

Schmelz, U. "Al baayot yesod ba-demografia shel yehudei brit-ha-moatsot" (On basic problems in the demography of Soviet Jews). *Behinot,* no. 5 (1974): 42-54.

_____. *Jewish Demography and Statistics: Bibliography for 1920-1970.* Jerusalem, 1976.

Schwarz, S. *The Jews in the Soviet Union.* Syracuse, N.Y., 1951.

Sovetishe yidn: faktn un tsifern (Soviet Jews: Facts and figures). Moscow, 1980.

Voronel', A. "Sotsial'nye predposylki natsional'nogo prebuzhdeniia evreev" (Social roots of the national reawakening of Soviet Jews). *Evreiskii samizdat* 4 (1974): 3-18.

Zinger, L. *Evreiskoe naselenie SSSR: dvizhenie za vremia s 1897 po 1923 g.* (Jewish
    population in the USSR: Changes from 1897 to 1923). Moscow, 1927.
————. "Evreiskoe naselenie SSSR—diagrammy" (Jewish population in the
    USSR). *Materialy i issledovaniia statistiko-ekonomicheskoi komissii pri Ts.
    K. ORT,* no. 1 (1927): 1-10.
————. "Chislennost' i geograficheskoe razmeshchenie evreiskogo naseleniia
    SSSR" (The number and geographic distribution of the Jewish population in
    the USSR). *Evrei v SSSR.* Moscow, 1930.
————. *Dos banayte folk: tsifern un faktn vegn di yidn in FSSR* (The renewed
    people: Numbers and facts on the Jews in the USSR). Moscow, 1941.
————. *Dos ufgerikhte folk: di sotsial-ekonomishe ibergeshtaltung fun der yidisher
    bafelkerung in FSSR* (The restored people: The social and economic recon-
    struction of the Jewish population in the USSR). Moscow, 1948.
Zinger, L., and Engel, B., *Yidishe bafelkerung fun FSSR in tabeles un diagrames*
    (The Jewish population of the USSR in tables and diagrams). Moscow, 1930.

INDEX

About the Author

MORDECHAI ALTSHULER, of the Institute of Contemporary Jewry of the Hebrew University of Jerusalem, is a recognized authority on Soviet Jewry.